The Early Modern Englishwoman:
A Facsimile Library of Essential Works

Series III

Essential Works for the Study of
Early Modern Women: Part 1

Volume 1

Legal Treatises, 1

The Early Modern Englishwoman: A Facsimile Library of Essential Works

Series III

Essential Works for the Study of Early Modern Women: Part 1

Volume 1

Legal Treatises, 1

Selected and Introduced by
Lynne A. Greenberg

General Editors
Betty S. Travitsky and Anne Lake Prescott

Routledge
Taylor & Francis Group
LONDON AND NEW YORK

First published 2005 by Ashgate Publishing

Published 2016 by Routledge
4 Park Square, Milton Park, Abingdon, Oxon OX14 4RN
605 Third Avenue, New York, NY 10017

Routledge is an imprint of the Taylor & Francis Group, an informa business

British Library Cataloguing-in-Publication Data
Legal treatises
Vol. 1 – (The early modern Englishwoman : a facsimile library of essential works)
1.Women – Legal status, laws, etc. – England – Early works to 1800 2.Women – Legal status, laws, etc. – Wales – Early works to 1800
I.Greenberg, Lynne A.
346.4'2'0134

Library of Congress Cataloging-in-Publication Data
The early modern Englishwoman: Essential works for the study of early modern women / general editors, Betty S. Travitsky and Anne Lake Prescott.

See page vi for complete CIP Block

The woodcut reproduced on the title page and on the case is the emblem from page 178 of *A Collection of Emblemes* by George Wither, Book 3 1635. *STC* 25900c. Reproduced by permission of the Folger Shakespeare Library, Washington, DC.

ISBN 13: 978-0-7546-0609-3 (hbk)

CONTENTS

Library of Congress Cataloging-in-Publication Data
Legal treatises : essential works for the study of early modern women / edited by Lynne A. Greenberg.
p. cm. – (The early modern Englishwoman. Essential works, Series 3, Part 1)
Includes bibliographical references.
Contents: v. 1. The lawes resolutions of womens rights, or, The lawes provision for Woemen: a collection of such statues and customes as doe properly concerne women – v. 2. A treatise of feme coverts, or, The lady's law : containing all the law and statutes relating to women, under several heads. Hardships of the English laws : in relation to wives / [attributed to] Sara Kirkham Chapone – v. 3. Baron and feme : a treatise of law and equity concerning husbands and wives.
ISBN 0-7546-0609-0 (v.1 : hardback) – ISBN 0-7546-3017-X (v. 2 : hardback) – ISBN 0-7546-3113-3 (v. 3 hardback)
1. Women–legal status, laws, etc.–England. 2. Women's rights–England. I. Greenberg, Lynne A. II. Chapone, Sarah Kirkham, 1699–1764. Hardships of the English Laws. III. Lawes resolutions of womens rights. IV. Treatise of feme coverts, or, The Lady's Law V. Baron and feme. VI. Series

KD734.L44 2003
342.4208'78–dc22

2003060979

PREFACE
BY THE GENERAL EDITORS

Until very recently, scholars of the early modern period have assumed that there were no Judith Shakespeares in early modern England. Much of the energy of the current generation of scholars has been devoted to constructing a history of early modern England that takes into account what women actually wrote, what women actually read, and what women actually did. In so doing, contemporary scholars have revised the traditional representation of early modern women as constructed both in their time and in ours. The study of early modern women has thus become one of the most important – indeed perhaps the most important – means for the rewriting of early modern history.

The Early Modern Englishwoman: A Facsimile Library of Essential Works is one of the developments of this energetic reappraisal of the period. As the names on our advisory board and our list of editors testify, it has been the beneficiary of scholarship in the field, and we hope it will also be an essential part of that scholarship's continuing momentum.

The Early Modern Englishwoman is designed to make available a comprehensive and focused collection of writings in English from 1500 to 1750, both by women and for and about them. The three series of *Printed Writings* (1500–1640, 1641–1700, and 1701–1750) provide a comprehensive if not entirely complete collection of the separately published writings by women. In reprinting these writings we intend to remedy one of the major obstacles to the advancement of feminist criticism of the early modern period, namely the limited availability of the very texts upon which the field is based. The volumes in the facsimile library reproduce carefully chosen copies of these texts, incorporating significant variants (usually in appendices). Each text is preceded by a short introduction providing an overview of the life and work of a writer along with a survey of important scholarship. These works, we strongly believe, deserve a large readership – of historians, literary critics, feminist critics, and non-specialist readers.

The Early Modern Englishwoman also includes separate facsimile series of *Essential Works for the Study of Early Modern Women* and of *Manuscript Writings*. These facsimile series are complemented by *The Early Modern Englishwoman 1500–1750: Contemporary Editions*. Also under our general editorship, this series includes both old-spelling and modernized editions of works by and about women and gender in early modern England.

New York City
2005

INTRODUCTORY NOTE

Early modern Englishwomen legally stood, in the words of *The Lawes Resolutions of Womens Rights*, "strictly tyed to mens establishments, little or nothing excused by ignorance" (2). The texts reprinted here in *Legal Treatises* in The Early Modern Englishwoman: A Facsimile Library of Essential Works: Series III reconstruct the legal status of the early modern Englishwoman. They have been reprinted in the hope that we will not find ourselves in a position of ignorance vis-à-vis one of the "essential" frameworks governing her life. In order to provide this framework for the years 1600–1750, the first volume of "Legal Treatises" reproduces *The Lawes Resolutions of Womens Rights* (1632), the first known treatise devoted to the legal rights of women. The second volume reproduces a significant legal treatise concerning married women, *A Treatise of Feme Coverts: Or, The Lady's Law* (1st ed. 1732). Because "The Early Modern Englishwoman" series is devoted to the voices of women, the second volume also reproduces *Hardships of the English Laws. In Relation to Wives* (1735), the only known statement authored by a woman in the period that systematically analyzes and criticizes her legal position. The third volume reproduces the third edition of *Baron and Feme: A Treatise of Law and Equity, Concerning Husbands and Wives* (3rd ed., 1738). Together, these four texts provide an overview of the laws that directly concerned women's lives during the sixteenth and seventeenth centuries and detail the major changes to these laws that occurred during the century that separates the treatises.

The introduction to the laws of the period that follows here provides concise overviews of the general structure of the English legal system, the legal education of practitioners of the law, the kinds of legal literature produced in the period, and the legal position of early modern Englishwomen. This introduction is meant to facilitate a reading of the treatises by broadly defining many of the laws discussed in great detail in them. Introductions to each of the reproduced works are also provided, including information about each work's publication and authorship, intended audience, content and reception. The appended bibliography of important secondary scholarship devoted to the early modern Englishwoman's legal position should assist the reader in obtaining more specialized knowledge.

I would like here to express my gratitude to John H. Baker and Amy Louise Erickson for their extraordinary generosity in answering my several questions concerning early modern law. I am also indebted to the late Janice Thaddeus for providing me with access to her unpublished research and to Margaret Hunt for assisting me in my attribution of *Hardships of the English Laws*. My special thanks as well to Eric Avram for his support, Patrick Cullen for first giving me this opportunity and to the series editors Betty S. Travitsky and Anne Lake Prescott and editor Claire Annals of Ashgate for their careful attention to this project. I also acknowledge the tremendous efforts of the many research librarians and curators who assisted me in the research of these volumes, particularly Susan Harris at the Bodleian Library, Darren Lomas at The British Library and Alan Jutzi at The Henry E. Huntington Library.

The Structure of the Early Modern English Legal System

English law was not centralized in a single, uniform jurisdiction during the early modern period, but rather dispersed in a complex web of exclusive jurisdictions. Functioning independently of each other, these jurisdictions developed separate bodies of law, applied and overseen by their own distinct networks of courts. Only together did these several jurisdictions produce a workable legal system in England. The rules at times overlapped, for example in the regulation of property ownership; and the rights they protected and the remedies they provided at times conflicted with each other. Sir Edward Coke recognized sixteen such jurisdictions operative during the early modern period.[1] The following overview surveys the most important of these jurisdictions: the common law, equity, ecclesiastical law and local custom.[2]

Common Law

With its origins in the customs of the king's court, the common law emerged during the twelfth century as the reigning law of the realm.[3] The common law was that law deemed customary, or common, to all of England and comprised a constantly growing body of legal principles. By the early modern period, the common-law system was embodied in case law, i.e., the courts' reasonings, decisions and rulings in individual cases. These general principles were viewed as authoritative precedent throughout the realm. Judges, following these precedents in passing judgment in subsequent cases, commonly understood their function as applying these ancient principles to new fact patterns, rather than as making new law. Certain common-law principles, such as primogeniture and coverture, had far-reaching impact on the lives of women and will be discussed at greater length below.

The common law must be distinguished from parliamentary legislation or statutes passed by the Parliament. Statutory law was deemed superior to the common law, and the courts were bound to uphold statutes, even if they directly conflicted with common-law precedent. Parliament had absolute power to make new laws, set aside old laws and reverse the pronouncements of the common law.

Administration of the common law was centralized by the end of Charles II's reign in three main courts all located in Westminster: the Common Bench (or Court of Common Pleas); the Court of King's Bench; and the Exchequer of Pleas. The local administration of common-law justice throughout England was accomplished through the systems of "assizes" and "quarter sessions." The assizes provided for regular visits of the king's appointed commissioners to the various counties of England to hear criminal charges, conduct trials and make judgments in criminal cases. The system of quarter sessions provided for the hearing of criminal charges four times a year in each county in England by local "justices of the peace" (knights and gentry charged to keep the peace and empowered to punish offences).[4]

Equity

Equitable jurisdiction originally referred to the extraordinary authority of the "chancellor" (an officer of the state and minister of the Crown) to administer justice in individual cases. By the sixteenth century, this special authority became housed in specific courts of equity authorized to hear claims equitable in nature, including the Chancery, Court of Requests and the Exchequer and in the Palatinates of Lancaster, Chester and Durham. Individuals turned to the courts of equity when the common law had somehow failed to provide them with justice. As Lord Ellesmere explained in 1615, the rationale for equity jurisdiction was that

> men's actions are so diverse and infinite that it is impossible to make a general law which may aptly meet with every particular and not fail in some circumstances. The office of the chancellor is to correct men's consciences for frauds, breaches of trust, wrongs and oppressions of what nature soever they be, and to soften and mollify the extremity of the law.[5]

By the early modern period, the courts of equity had developed their own body of coherent principles and, like the common-law courts, treated judicial precedents as binding. Nevertheless, equity was generally regarded as more flexible than the common law, in large part because of the equity courts' procedures and special remedies. Equity judges were empowered to take account of the specific circumstances and facts of a given case and the particular resources, or lack thereof, available to the parties. The courts of equity were not permitted to award monetary damages to plaintiffs but did have a number of remedies unique to their jurisdiction, often of greater use to plaintiffs. For example, equity judges could grant "injunctions" (orders to stop an activity deemed unjust by the court); "stay" (halt) the bringing of an action at common law; order a defendant specifically to perform his contractual promise; and order the discovery of documents held by a third party. The flexibility, special procedures and remedies of the courts of equity were especially helpful to female litigants, who made up a significant number of suitors in these courts.[6]

Ecclesiastical Law

Ecclesiastical law in the early modern period derived from three sources: the canon law of the western church (the *Corpus juris Canonici*); the code of Roman law (the *Corpus juris civilis*); and ecclesiastical common law. Ecclesiastical jurisdiction was broad, encompassing a wide range of administrative, civil and disciplinary functions. Importantly, the administrative side of ecclesiastical jurisdiction regulated the laws of marriage formation and dissolution; "probate" matters (the process of proving deceased persons' wills and having them registered with the courts); and "intestate succession" (property inheritance in the absence of a will). The ecclesiastical courts had extensive jurisdiction in England to hear cases involving matrimonial disputes, broken marriage contracts, petitions for separations and annulments and disputed inheritances.

The ecclesiastical courts also had a significant disciplinary function. They were empowered to punish individuals for a wide range of moral and sexual offences, including drunkenness, fornication, bigamy, practicing midwifery, scolding, defamation, and religious offences (including heresy, apostasy, recusancy, absence from church and failure to receive communion).

Women appeared before the ecclesiastical courts in larger numbers than before any other jurisdiction in the early modern period. They found themselves called before these courts for moral and sexual infractions. Importantly, they took advantage of these courts to seek redress in matrimonial and inheritance disputes. So, too, large numbers of women appeared before the probate side of these courts to file and record wills.[7]

Custom

Unlike the common law, which represented the national custom of England, local custom represented only the traditional law of a given manor, borough or town. Manorial courts (or "court leets") and borough courts oversaw disputes involving local, civil customs; in addition, it should be noted that the common-law and equity courts had authority to enforce manorial customs. Well into the early modern period, manorial and borough courts handled debt issues and disputes relating to local customs of land inheritance.

Certain manorial customs still operative in the early modern period had an enormous impact on the lives of women. Some customs, such as "widow's bench" and the acceptance of "*femes sole* traders," as discussed below, provided women with more economic opportunity and freedom than common-law principles permitted. Yet, it must be emphasized that other local customs were more restrictive than the common law. Because many of the manorial rolls and borough records have not survived or have not been adequately studied, it is not possible at the present time to determine the full impact of customary law on the lives of women. One must assume that given the great variety of local customs on a wide range of issues of import to women, the locale in which a woman lived had a significant impact on her life.[8]

* * * * * *

During the course of the early modern period, the "balance of power"[9] among these competing legal systems shifted in favor of the common law. In the interests of uniformity, many conflicting ecclesiastical and manorial principles of significance to women were made to conform to common-law principles, often, as discussed below, to women's detriment.[10] These encroachments of common-law jurisdiction upon ecclesiastical, equitable and manorial jurisdiction were achieved through both statutory and judicial pronouncements. Cromwell's regime, in particular, lessened the power of ecclesiastical and equitable jurisdiction by abolishing certain ecclesiastical and equity courts (for example, the Court of Requests) and transferring jurisdiction to the common-law courts.[11]

Legal Education

Education in the common law took place in the western suburbs of London at the four Inns of Court and to a lesser degree in other Inns in the area. The exclusively male Inns were places of residence that provided accommodation, entertainment and, most importantly, formal education in the common law to the students. Training was standardized: after seven years attending "readings" (lectures) and performing "moots" (oral pleading exercises), the student would be certified as a barrister. One significant problem with the educational system in this period was its failure to provide a systematic and comprehensive overview of the common law. Students had to look outside their formal instruction for such an overview, often turning to the available legal literature as a resource.[12]

The education of advocates of ecclesiastical law occurred in the exclusively male universities of Oxford and Cambridge. After obtaining a doctorate of law, individuals could be admitted to practice law by the ecclesiastical authorities. Henry VIII abolished the study of canon law at the universities of Oxford and Cambridge, permitting only the study of civil law. Canon law was therefore learned only through self-education and practical experience.

Legal Literature

The history of English legal literature is intimately tied to the rise of the common law. Historians have characterized the sixteenth and seventeenth centuries as a period in which medieval law was transformed into modern law. In large part, this transformation was aided by the legal literature of this period, which became more systematized throughout the era.[13]

Because of the centrality of precedent to the formulation of English common law, literature that recorded judges' rulings became necessary as a means of educating apprentices and practitioners of the common law and of ensuring uniformity of decision-making. As judicial procedure became increasingly more standardized, literature that documented the proper methods for bringing actions in the common-law courts also became critical. By the early modern period, literature that accomplished these goals had become more available in the form of formularies; medieval yearbooks; reports of cases and abridgements; and legal treatises. Between 1600 and 1800, the number of legal texts published grew from 100 to 1,500 titles.

Formularies and Books of Precedent

In mastering the practice and procedures of the common-law courts, practitioners, lawyers and law clerks relied on texts that compiled sample precedents of "writs" (official statements in Latin of either the demand, or wrong, that commenced judicial actions), of pleadings before the courts and of entries in the court records. From the first quarter of the thirteenth century, writ formulae, or collections, became available, and, by the sixteenth century, books of "entries" (the pleadings that were entered on the "rolls", or records) were in great demand.

Books of precedent (also known as conveyancing manuals) contained models of various kinds of legal forms and were widely available by the end of the sixteenth century. The kinds of legal forms frequently provided in books of precedent include examples of valid wills, bonds, debts, contracts and property deeds and conveyances. These manuals served the practical function of providing legal practitioners with technically correct models on which to base actual legal documents. Thomas Phaer's *Newe Boke of Presidents* (1543) is one early example of this genre. Several others were published in the period, including Sir Orlando Bridgman's *Conveyances* (1689) and the anonymous *Precedents in Conveyancing* (1744). By the seventeenth century, simplified manuals also existed, such as the anonymous *The Country-Man's Counsellor: or, Everyman Made his Own Lawyer* (n.d.), providing basic models together with instructions on how to complete the forms.

Medieval Year-Books, Reports of Cases and Abridgements

The written records of the common-law courts set out the results of individual cases and became the most important source of precedents for future cases. But these records were formulaic and incomplete. They failed to record the factual evidence, lawyers' arguments or judges' reasonings underlying the cases' "holdings" (rulings). This missing information was critical to practitioners for a complete understanding of the rules of law and of pleading. Medieval year-books (circulated originally in manuscripts) and published reports of cases somewhat filled the gap. Year-books and reports of cases were written by members of the legal profession who attended court and took notes on specific cases. In the early modern period, several reports of cases were published, for example, Sir Edward Coke's *The Reports* (1610–16, 1658, 1659), providing reasoned expositions of select case holdings along with instructions to future lawyers.

Abridgements (also known as commonplace books) supplemented the reports. These texts divided legal principles into different headings, arranged them alphabetically, and explained them by reference to judicial holdings, parliamentary records and statutes. These abridgements methodized the common law by distilling the rules of law logically from the jumble of facts and ideas found in the chronologically organized reports of cases. Abridgements are precursors of modern digests and legal encyclopedias.

Legal Treatises

The earliest legal treatises date from the fourteenth century. Compiled from oral readings on statutory and common law at the Inns of Court, these manuscripts cannot be characterized as law books, per se. The first English legal treatise, as we understand the term today, was Sir Thomas Littleton's *New Tenures*, an introduction to the common law of real property, published in 1481. With the advent of printing came a proliferation of legal treatises on specific areas of the common law. The most important treatises of the seventeenth and eighteenth centuries were Sir Edward Coke's *Institutes of the Laws of England* (1628–44), Sir Matthew Hale's

History of the Pleas of the Crown (1736), and Sir William Blackstone's *Commentaries on the Laws of England* (1765–69).

Legal treatises, like abridgements, were intended to methodise the confused and disorderly morass of the common-law system. The best definition of the modern legal treatise (or text-book) is that of T. Plucknett:

> The characteristic of the modern English text-book … is its method. It begins with a definition of the subject matter, and proceeds by logical and systematic stages to cover the whole field. The result is to present the law in a strictly deductive framework, with the implication that in the beginning there were principles, and that in the end those principles were found to cover a large multitude of cases deducible from them.[14]

Such treatises are generally monographs, intended to focus on a discrete, substantive (as opposed to procedural) area of the law understood as unified and coherent. The arrangement of subject matter is logically divided and presents "a single branch of the law as a systematic body of definitions, principles, and distinctions".[15] The treatises frequently cite specific cases as authority for the announced legal principles and often provide several hypotheticals that apply these principles to other fact patterns.

The Legal Position of Early Modern Englishwomen

The following overview of the public and private legal position of early modern Englishwomen introduces the important principles, statutes, court holdings and customs explored in the treatises reprinted in these volumes. The public position of women at law refers to women's relationship to the public institutions responsible for enacting, maintaining, enforcing and punishing the transgression of the law. The private position of women at law refers to women's place in the private sphere of society as shaped by the laws of marriage formation and dissolution, contract, property and inheritance.

The Public Position of Women at Law

> Women… have nothing to do in constituting Lawes, or consenting to them, in interpreting of Lawes or in hearing them interpreted at lectures, leets or charges…[16]

Regardless of their age or marital status, early modern Englishwomen found themselves barred from all direct involvement in the public institutions central to the legal structure of England. Denied an active role in the exercise of political authority, women could not sit in Parliament or act as counselors or government officials. Women did have the right to petition Parliament, doing so with regularity throughout the early modern period and in great numbers during the civil war and Commonwealth.[17]

Women had little official role in the judicial process. They could bring suits and be sued in court, subject to the limitations imposed by common law on *femes covert* (as discussed below). They could also be required to give evidence to court officials and to act as witnesses in trials. Women could not, however, study the common law at the Inns of Court or the civil law at the universities, thus precluding them from serving as attorneys or judges. They also could not serve as jurors in court trials, except on "juries of matrons", empanelled to examine defendants' bodies for proof of pregnancy, virginity, physical evidence of witchcraft and the like and to testify in court as to their findings.[18] Under the common law, they were not permitted to serve as "compurgators" (oath-takers in court swearing to the reputation and character of a neighbor), although they were permitted to act as compurgators in the ecclesiastical courts. Women were not permitted, in most instances, to play an active role in the policing or enforcement of the criminal law at the local level. These disabilities persisted throughout the period in question, as no law reform ameliorated any of these basic impediments to women's legal status.

The most significant exception to women's exclusion from public participation in government occurred at the highest level of government, in their right of succession to the throne. Early in Mary I's reign, a parliamentary statute (1554) confirmed the "regal power" of a queen regnant, authorizing "that what or whensoever statute or law doth limit and appoint that the King of this realm may or shall… do anything as King … the same the Queen … may by the same authority and power likewise… do."[19]

Technically, women could serve certain limited, local functions in government and the church. Pearl Hogreve has documented a number of instances of women serving as "churchwardens" (legal representatives of the parishioners) and "overseers of the poor" (appointed by the courts to enforce compulsory financial relief of the poor) and a handful of examples of female "constables" (charged with seeking out and reporting on breaches of the peace) and "justices of the peace" (a commission of knights and gentry charged with keeping the peace and enquiring into, hearing and determining various criminal charges or offences).[20] Finally, there have been found scattered cases of women serving as "sheriffs" (responsible, among other things, for sitting on the bench of the assizes). Most female sheriffs obtained this office by right of inheritance, as did Anne Clifford, Countess of Dorset, Pembroke and Montgomery, who served as sheriff of Westmoreland from 1650–1675. Women could also hold wardships as ladies of the manor.

Women were excluded from the parliamentary franchise, although there are some examples of unmarried women voting in parliamentary elections prior to 1640.[21] In the early modern period, some women did participate in electoral activities at the constituency and local levels. Widows, heiresses and mothers of minor sons protecting their sons' political interests in constituencies could conduct political and electoral affairs. On the local level, women also routinely attended and voted in the parish vestry. By the eighteenth century, women could vote for and even hold the office of church sexton.

The definition of political action has received some revision by historians, its meaning broadened to encompass a wide range of activities impacting the public sphere: "dispensing patronage, influencing decisions and elections, petitioning, entertaining, haranguing, reporting seditious conduct, writing and disseminating ideas in printed form."[22] It is clear that women, particularly in the period from 1640 to the mid-eighteenth century, participated in such political action. So, too, women had at times great influence in the private sphere, thereby indirectly promoting public action through their relationships and kinship networks.[23] Generally, however, women's direct participation in government was limited.

The Private Position of Women at Law

As shown below, the author of *The Lawes Resolutions* delineates three important phases of a woman's life – maidenhood, wifehood and widowhood – each resulting in markedly different consequences to her private, legal status. This introduction, in recognition of the centrality of the act of marriage to a woman's legal position, will follow the same format and discuss each phase of her life separately.

Maidenhood

Before the age of majority, the parent or guardian retained a rigid control over minors, whether male or female, including the right of guardianship over their inherited estates. There were different ages of majority for different purposes, but generally the law set a lower age of majority for women than for men (twelve for women, fourteen for men), though in 1653 Parliament raised the legal age of women's consent to marry and to make a contract or will from twelve to fourteen.

The age of majority differed for men and women inheriting interests in land held in "military tenure" or "knight-service" (i.e., tenancy subject to several obligations, including mandatory aids, fines and monetary relief or payments to the lord or lady of the manor). If the tenant of inheritable land held in military tenure died leaving an heir under age (and, therefore, unable to perform his or her feudal obligations), then the heir became subject to "wardship". Under wardship, the lord or lady of the manor became the guardian of the ward, having custody both of the land and the body of the ward. Such custody entitled the lord to profits of the land during the heir's minority and even the right to select a suitable marriage partner for the ward. A ward who refused to consent to the marriage had to compensate the lord financially. A woman attained her freedom from wardship at the age of sixteen, while a man had to wait until he turned 21. Upon reaching the age of majority, the ward could finally take control of his or her land. The system of military tenure was not abolished until 1645.[24]

Upon reaching the age of majority, the *feme sole*, or single woman, gained most of the private legal rights held by men. The laws of succession permitted the *feme sole* to receive gifts or legacies of "personal property". (Personal property is defined as all forms of property, excluding real property, including money, clothing, furniture, household goods and debts.) The *feme sole* could also inherit "real property" (interests in land) under certain circumstances. The system of primogeniture dictated that in the absence of a will to the contrary, the eldest son inherited all of his deceased father's "freehold property" (land held for life or for uncertain duration, as opposed to land held in leasehold, for a set number of years). If there were no sons to inherit, then the daughter inherited such property. If there was more than one daughter, then all the daughters would inherit the freehold property equally. Manorial custom governed the succession of "copyhold property" (land held at the will of the lord of the manor and according to the manor's customs) in the absence of a will. Customs varied in the different boroughs of England – some boroughs followed the system of "primogeniture" (inheritance by the first-born son), some "female primogeniture" (inheritance by the first-born daughter in the absence of a son), some "ultimogeniture" (inheritance by the last-born child), some divided the land jointly among the sons and, in rare instances, some even allowed all of the children to inherit jointly.

These forced laws of succession could be avoided simply by the creation of a will permitting a parent to disinherit any or all of his or her children, unless the property at issue had been "entailed" (a specification that land must pass to a certain line of heirs) or was held in military tenure. The freedom to draft wills contrary to the forced laws of succession could lead to the avoidance of primogeniture in favor of a younger son, a daughter or even all of the daughters. Yet, such freedom could also lead to the disinheritance of daughters: in the face of only female, not male, children, a parent could will property to a brother or nephew, for example, in order to preserve the male line of property succession.

The rule of "reasonable parts" (or "thirds") governed the distribution of the deceased parent's personal property; it provided that children receive two-thirds of the property, if the parent died "intestate" (without a valid will) and, in certain northern boroughs, one-third of the property, if the parent died leaving a will prescribing less than the required two-thirds. The ecclesiastical courts had discretion to award even higher percentages and to divide the property between the children in any manner. A study of the records of the ecclesiastical courts reveals that before 1670, the courts were generous in their division of such property, often allocating even higher percentages than required by law to children and distributing the property equally amongst the children regardless of their sex.[25]

The *feme sole* could not only inherit and own real property in her own name but could also retain the same ancillary rights over such property as did men, including control over its disposal, maintenance, improvement and rental. The *feme sole* could also make a will, bequeathing property and gifts to third parties of her choosing. She stood vis-à-vis third parties in the same legal position as a man, fully capable of entering into binding contractual relationships with them. She could sue or be sued by third parties in her own name, and could plead in person. The legal system treated her as a fully capable and fully accountable subject with independent agency. The *feme sole* retained these rights as long as she remained a maid. Yet, her legal identity underwent radical alteration upon her marriage.

Legal pressures made it difficult for single women to support themselves, however. The Statute of Artificers, passed in 1563, provided that single men and women between the ages of 14 and 45 could be forced into service.[26] This statute, while theoretically gender neutral, was applied nearly exclusively to single women. Further, municipalities often overtly discouraged single women from establishing their own businesses or working autonomously by denying them licenses to trade independently or to set up alehouses,[27] though they were legally required to support themselves.

Concern with the *feme sole*'s ability to own and retain control over property in her own name led to the passage of several abduction statutes routinely passed throughout the medieval and early modern periods. These statutes punished the abduction (even with her consent) of a married or unmarried woman owning property either in goods or land or in wardship, by levelling severe monetary damages on the abductor. These damages were recoverable not by the woman, but by her husband, father or guardian, as the abductor's act was understood as the unlawful taking of the husband's or father's property. If the woman was an unmarried minor, then the abductor could also be imprisoned for two years. The more serious offence of forcibly abducting and marrying a woman of property (in either goods or land) or an heir apparent ("vulgarly called *stealing an heires*"[28]) was treated as a felony and therefore punishable by death. The offence of rape or ravishment, defined as the "the carnal knowledge of a woman forcibly and against her will",[29] was likewise treated as a felony.

> Now that I have brought up a Woman…me thinks she should long to be married.[30]

The legal treatises devote significant attention to the formation and dissolution of marriage, for the laws were complicated, if not inherently contradictory, and were undergoing significant change throughout the period. As previously discussed, ecclesiastical law governed marriage formation and its breakdown, and the ecclesiastical courts oversaw all suits involving marriage and divorce. From the twelfth century, canon law required evidence only of the mutual consent of the parties and did not require parental consent, physical consummation, set or prescribed words in the ceremony or even solemnization in church to uphold the legality of a marriage. Instead, canon law required that such consent be evidenced by *sponsalia per verba de praesenti* (spousals by words in the present tense). A couple could simply agree to take each other as husband and wife in the open air, with no witnesses, and the canon law would treat the couple as validly wed. *Sponsalia per verba de futuro* (spousals by words in the future tense, that is, promises to marry in the future) did not achieve legally valid marriages but only engagements that could be dissolved by the mutual consent of the parties. Such promises to marry in the future could immediately become legally binding by the subsequent recital of *sponsalia per verba de praesenti* or by physical consummation.

The system of spousals caused widespread irregularity in the formation of marriage and confusion and uncertainty over what words constituted present or future spousals. "Clandestine marriages" (secret marriages performed without witnesses) and "irregular marriages" (marriages that did not conform in some way to the Canons of 1604) were commonplace in the fifteenth and sixteenth centuries. Throughout the medieval and early modern periods, the English church attempted to impose more regularity upon marriage formation. The Canons of 1604 confirmed many of these efforts, requiring the publication of "banns" (public notice of the couple's intention to marry) three times before the marriage; the issuance of a marriage license evidencing the consent of the parents of a bride or groom under 21 years of age; and a public ceremony during certain prescribed seasons and hours at the church door of the diocese in which at least one of the parties lived. Ministers who performed marriage ceremonies not in accordance with such regulations faced severe penalties, as did the offending couples, who were often excommunicated for their misconduct.[31] So, too, the common law required proof of a church wedding in order to confer full property rights on married couples. Nevertheless, the Church of England continued to recognize, as valid, marriages that did not conform to the

1604 regulations. Thus, a prior clandestine or an irregular marriage would be upheld by the ecclesiastical courts over a subsequent solemnized marriage involving one of the same parties.

The Commonwealth further complicated the laws of marriage formation by radically reforming them. Parliament passed the "Act touching Marriages and the Registring hereof",[32] which took jurisdiction over marriage formation out of the church and into civil government. The Act required that couples be registered by the parish, prove parental consent for any party under twenty-one and submit to a civil service performed by the local justice of the peace. Upon the Restoration this statute became void, and the laws of marriage formation were returned to the ecclesiastical courts' jurisdiction. Yet the confusion and uncertainty over marriage formation continued unabated, not systematically addressed until the passing of Lord Hardwicke's "Act for the better preventing of clandestine Marriages" in 1753.[33]

Because canon law perceived marriage as an indissoluble bond, the Church of England did not permit couples to divorce, that is, to dissolve the marriage and thereafter be permitted to remarry. The ecclesiastical courts permitted couples to sue only for a *divorce a vinculo* (an annulment). Annulments were granted only if the marriage was deemed to have been null at the time of its creation by reason of one of the legally recognized impediments to its creation. Such impediments turned on either the couple's legal incapacity to marry or the lack of mutual consent to marry. The basic incapacities to marriage included "consanguinity" (a close relationship by blood between the parties); "affinity" (a relationship by marriage or carnal association); tender age (either one or both of the partners was below the age of majority); "precontract" (a previous marriage by one of the parties to a third party); permanent frigidity; or impotence. Lack of consent to marry turned on whether there had been some occurrence of fraud, duress, coercion, insanity or inadequate knowledge at the time of the marriage's formation. A *divorce a vinculo* left the partners free to remarry, barred the woman from her "dower" (see below), and left any children of the voided marriage bastards.

If no impediment existed, then a couple could not annul their marriage and could sue only for a *divorce a menso et thoro* (a legal separation from board and bed) with no right of either party to remarry during the lifetime of the other spouse. The ecclesiastical courts had complete discretion to decide whether to grant a *divorce a menso et thoro* and would do so only upon proof of the adultery or extreme cruelty of either spouse. The courts also had the authority (again at their discretion) to bestow "maintenance" (alimony) upon an innocent wife. A wife guilty of adultery, elopement or cruelty had no legal right to maintenance. In 1670, Parliament dissolved the marriage of Lord Roos and allowed him to remarry, establishing a precedent that, thereafter, permitted couples to separate and remarry upon such private acts of Parliament.[34]

One of the unintended ancillary effects of denying separating couples the right to remarry was the practice of bigamy. This problem was addressed by Parliament in the Bigamy Act of 1604 that made it a felony for previously married individuals to remarry unless the other partner had been absent for at least seven years, one of the parties had been under age at the time of the marriage's formation or the ecclesiastical courts had granted a *divorce a vinculo*.[35] In 1650, Parliament promulgated an even harsher immorality statute, the Act for "suppressing the detestable sins of Incest, Adultery and Fornication", that made adultery a capital offence. The statute defined adultery as sexual intercourse between a married woman and a man not her husband. Intercourse between a married man and an unmarried woman, however, was not deemed adultery for purposes of the Act.[36]

The problem of children born out of wedlock was addressed by statutes in 1597, 1610 and again in 1624. These statutes provided for the maintenance of bastard children and established severe punishments for the parents.[37] The 1624 statute criminalized only the mothers of illegitimate children, charging that they could be sent to the House of Correction for bearing children dependent upon the parish for support.[38] Because a ruling of bastardy led to the individual's disinheritance, the 1597 Act also endowed the ecclesiastical courts with expanded power to examine the circumstances of the child's birth to determine legitimacy. The crime of infanticide was also specifically addressed by statute in 1624. The "Act to prevent the Murthering of Bastard Children"[39] prosecuted any unmarried mother who concealed the birth of a child should the child die. The mother could prove her innocence only by establishing that the child had been stillborn.

The Legal Status of the Feme Covert

> When a small brooke or little river incorporateth with Rhodanus, Humber, or the Thames, the poore Rivolet loseth her name, it is carried and recarried with the new associate, it beareth no sway, it possesseth nothing during coverture. A woman as soone as she is married is called covert … that is, vailed, as it were, clouded and over-shadowed … she hath host her streame … her new selfe is her superior, her companion, her master.[40]

The moment a marriage became legally binding, the *feme sole* found herself radically transformed by the common-law doctrine known as "coverture" (or "unity of person"). Throughout the early modern period, coverture regarded the man and wife as *una caro* (one flesh) before the common law. The eighteenth-century legal commentator William Blackstone described the practical effects of coverture as follows:

> By marriage, the husband and wife are one person in law: that is, the very being or legal existence of the woman is suspended during the marriage, or at least is incorporated and consolidated into that of the husband: under whose wing, protection and *cover* she performs everything; and is therefore called in our law French a *feme covert*; is said to be *covert-baron*, or under the protection and influence of her husband, her *baron*, or lord; and her condition during her marriage is called her *coverture*.[41]

Placed in the same legal category under the common law as wards, lunatics, criminals and idiots, the *feme covert* lost nearly all of the private rights she had enjoyed as a *feme sole*.[42]

Having lost her independent agency, the *feme covert* could no longer enter into a legally binding contract or sue or be sued in a common-law court. The common law did permit a *feme covert* to order household necessities on credit, such as food, supplies and clothing from merchants, with the proviso that her husband had either given prior authority for or later ratified this act. The common law recognized this implied agency as an extension of the husband's duty to sustain his wife during marriage. But the separated husband had no further duty to maintain his wife. The only recourse for a separated *feme covert* was to sue her husband in the ecclesiastical courts for maintenance. Yet, as previously discussed, only innocent wives were eligible for maintenance; if the wife had eloped with another man or committed adultery, then the courts would not grant her maintenance. In the event of a couple's separation, a merchant gave the separated *feme covert* goods on credit at his own risk. In the important case of *Manby vs. Scott* (1663), printed in *A Treatise of Feme Coverts* and discussed at length in *Baron and Feme*, the court held that, having received notice of the husband's refusal to pay for necessities, the merchant could not recover payment.[43]

A *feme covert* could be named to fulfill the obligations of an executor (designated by the person making the will) or administrator (appointed by the court) to manage the property of a third party.[44] Acting in this capacity, a *feme covert* could sue or be sued. A *feme covert* could not otherwise sue or be sued in the common-law courts in her own right unless her husband was joined as a party to the action. Thus, if the *feme covert* suffered some harm, whether bodily or economic, then she could not bring an action to recover damages without obtaining her husband's consent and naming him as a party to the action. The husband was even entitled to file a separate cause of action in his own name against the defendant if the injury deprived him of his wife's "help or companionship". Any damages recovered against a third party automatically became the husband's property. Similarly, if the wife injured a third party, then the husband found himself personally liable for any damages sustained by the third party.

The economic consequences of coverture were grave. The *feme covert* could no longer accept grants, even from her husband, or legacies. Generally, she could not make a will without the express consent of her husband prior to their marriage.[45] She could no longer own property in her own name. All of her real and personal property became subject to the control of her husband. Title to real and copyhold property owned by the woman did not pass to the husband outright; however, the husband could take all rents and profits from such property and had exclusive control over its maintenance during his wife's lifetime. Because he could not permanently sell or otherwise dispose of such property, upon his death (in the event of such a transfer without his wife's consent) the widow could sue to recover ownership. If a husband and wife wanted to sell real property in the wife's name, then they had to obtain a "final concord" from the Common Pleas permitting them to do so. Concerned with a wife's potential coercion by her husband, the court took special care to determine whether such a conveyance indeed represented the wife's free will by insisting on separately examining her out of her husband's presence before granting the request. Upon the *feme covert*'s death (if there were surviving issue), the husband continued "in seisin" (in possession) for life in all of her real property by the doctrine known as "curtesy".

"Leasehold property", also referred to as "chattels real" (land held for a fixed term of years), became the husband's property outright during the marriage, freely disposable by the husband during his lifetime. Any personal property owned by a woman at the time of her marriage also became her husband's property outright, as did any personal property given to a wife after her marriage, if not explicitly reserved for her "sole and separate estate" (see below). If the *feme covert* managed to save a little of the money allotted to her for household use, then this money immediately became her husband's property. Even ownership of her "paraphernalia" (her clothing, jewelry, linens and plate) became her husband's property during his lifetime.

One significant exception to coverture occurred in some boroughs, such as London, where the courts treated married female merchants as *femes sole* for the purpose of conducting business. These "*femes sole* traders," as they were known, could enter into contracts, own property and sue or be sued in their own names. Very little is known, however, about the actual operation of *feme-sole* trader laws.

The leniency of the courts of equity, ecclesiastical courts and manorial courts tempered somewhat the more draconian consequences of common-law coverture, permitting *femes covert* to sue and be sued in their own names in a wide range of circumstances. One cannot over-emphasize the importance of this circumvention of the common-law's disablement of the *feme covert*, as recent scholarship has shown that women, even *femes covert*, had a considerable presence in the equity and ecclesiastical courts, "waging law" to define, create and protect their rights.[46] The courts of equity evaded the *feme covert*'s lack of standing to sue by permitting the naming of a *prochein amy* (next friend) of the *feme covert* to sue on her behalf. Also, the courts of equity had jurisdiction to entertain actions by women that would have gone unrecognized in the common-law courts and to provide for a range of equitable remedies, including injunctions, the staying of actions and document recovery, that were unavailable elsewhere. The ecclesiastical courts altogether disregarded the common-law disablement of the *feme covert*'s standing to sue, permitting a *feme covert* to sue and be sued even by her husband. Certain actions brought in the ecclesiastical courts, such as slander and defamation cases, were also dominated by the presence of women, who represented the majority of plaintiffs, defendants and witnesses.[47]

The *feme covert* had few legal remedies against acts done to her by her husband, however, since she was unable to sue him at common law in her own name. A husband had the legal right to impose "reasonable correction" on his wife, although she was permitted to have security of the peace brought against him in cases of extreme and life-threatening violence. While a wife was not usually permitted to testify against her husband in court, the court would lift this ban in cases of spousal abuse.[48]

The notion of the *feme covert* as covered by her husband was taken to its logical extreme in exempting the *feme covert* from criminal liability for acts done in her husband's presence or by his order. The law inferred that because she was so naturally dominated (or coerced) by her husband, she had no independent agency to refuse to act, even if unlawfully. The only exceptions to this principle were for particular felony crimes designated as "*male in se*", including treason, murder and running a brothel.

The law viewed any infraction of the *feme covert*'s legally imposed subordination to her husband as particularly egregious. Thus, a *feme covert*'s verbal assault upon her husband could amount to the cognizable crime of scolding, punishable in both the ecclesiastical and manorial courts.[49] A *feme covert* convicted of the murder of her spouse faced not a charge of murder and the punishment of hanging, as did a husband if he killed his wife, but the more aggravated felony of petty treason, punishable by burning at the stake.[50]

One area of the criminal law that progressively favored women in the seventeenth century was the extension of "benefit of clergy" to convicted female felons in 1624 for certain small felonies[51] and in 1691 for all crimes in which the benefit was available to men.[52] The pleading of benefit of clergy permitted a first-time convicted felon to avoid execution for specific felonies. Pregnant women convicted of a felony could also plead "benefit of the belly" (also known as "benefit of birth") to postpone the sentence until after the birth of the child.

> Women have no voice in Parliament, They make no Lawes, they consent to none, they abrogate none. All of them are understood either married or to be married and their desires… subject to their husband, I know no remedy though some women can shift it well enough.[53]

Recent scholarship has begun to address the extent to which the *feme covert* managed, in the words of the author of *The Lawes Resolutions*, to "shift it", or circumvent her common-law disablements. This scholarship explores the realities of living under a system of coverture, often concluding that the *feme covert* had far more economic and proprietary autonomy than the letter of the common law would seem to have permitted.[54] In particular, the early modern *feme covert* had opportunities for mitigating coverture's injunction against owning property by resort to a number of devices that developed in the mid- to late seventeenth century, for example separate maintenance agreements, marriage settlements and trusts.[55] The early treatise, *The Lawes Resolutions*, barely mentions these alternative property arrangements, for they were not common at the time of the treatise's publication. *A Treatise of Feme Coverts* and *Baron and Feme* devote considerable space to exploring these opportunities, even providing sample models of conveyancing documents used to effectuate these arrangements.

The separate maintenance agreement, a development of the late seventeenth century, provided for the voluntary payment by the husband of an agreed-upon sum to his wife (or to her trustees) during their legal separation, provided that she remained "chaste". The ecclesiastical courts could also order an innocent separated wife's maintenance or alimony. The courts of equity became the venue for enforcing such agreements, permitting a separated *feme covert* to sue or be sued by her husband as a *feme sole*. The courts of equity also developed the principle known as "equity of settlement" that routinely granted separated or divorced women a share of their husbands' estates commensurate with the portion they had brought into the marriage.

Originating at the end of the sixteenth century, marriage settlements were employed not only by the wealthiest of the population but also by ordinary people to preserve certain proprietary rights of the *feme covert*. Such settlements were arranged prior to the marriage, often by the father of the bride or by the woman herself before a second marriage. Only the courts of equity enforced such marriage settlements. One historian has found that 10 percent of marrying women entered into some form of settlement with their grooms prior to the marriage and has estimated that the actual proportion may well have been much higher.[56]

The settlement could take the form of a simple annuity (known as "pin money") that paid the *feme covert* a specified amount of cash annually to cover her out-of-pocket expenses and personal adornment.[57] Another simple arrangement employed by many ordinary women, and with the added advantage of being enforceable at common law, established the groom's promise to pay a bond of a specified amount to a relation of the bride for the bride's benefit at an agreed-upon date or to pay a certain amount to his wife upon her widowhood. The most common marriage settlements, employed regularly even by ordinary people, established the terms of a jointure (as discussed more fully below) to protect the wife in widowhood. Women marrying for the second time also employed marriage settlements to confirm the husband's promise to pay "portions" (dowries) to his wife's children by a previous marriage.

A marriage settlement could also establish the *feme covert*'s right to make a will once married, as any such consent made after the marriage would not be legally binding. Such an agreement could also stipulate that the husband had rights in only a portion of his wife's estate (in her possession at the time of her marriage) and that she had the right to dispose of the rest of her estate by her will. Any property that she attained subsequent to the marriage, however, would not be covered by such an agreement.

Another important type of marriage settlement that developed between 1640 and 1700 was the trust for a woman's "sole and separate estate". The trust became the most important means of creating a separate estate for the *feme covert* in the form of capital in real property. The courts of equity, particularly the Court of Chancery, were instrumental in enforcing this device. One effectuated such an arrangement by conveying legal title in land to trustees and their heirs in trust for the *feme covert*'s "sole and separate estate". The designated trustees oversaw the maintenance or conveyance of the property and the payment of its rents and profits to the wife. Married women's separate property could also be achieved through a bequest after the marriage. An individual could create a trust for the benefit of the *feme covert*, stipulating in the will that the heir, or trustee, would oversee the estate for her sole and separate use. Throughout the course of the seventeenth century, these trust arrangements became more complex and were utilized with greater frequency to protect the *feme covert* herself during her lifetime (and her heirs after her death) from the husband's curtesy right. Such arrangements could provide income for various family members over several generations.

Widowhood

> But alas, when she hath lost her husband, her head is cut off, her intellectual part is gone, the verie faculties of her soule are, I will not say, cleane taken

away, but they are all benummed, dimmed and dazled … Why mourne you so, you that be widowwes? Consider how long you have beene in subjection under the predominance of parents, of your husbands, now you be free in libertie… at your owne Lawe.[58]

The death of a husband propelled the *feme covert* back to the status of a *feme sole*, whereby she regained all of the private legal rights and liabilities lost upon her marriage. She frequently found herself in a new position of public responsibility, often named in her husband's will as the executrix of her husband's estate and guardian of her children during their minority. If a man died intestate, then the widow had the legal right to administer his estate. These new responsibilities thrust her into a more public legal position, requiring her to appear before the probate side of the ecclesiastical courts to present, prove and even contest wills and to exhibit inventories and file accounts detailing her actions a year later. She also found herself paying legacies and portions, collecting and discharging debts and litigating in the courts to enforce marriage settlements or to secure her inheritance.[59]

The laws of inheritance and succession provided the widow with certain carefully delineated rights to her deceased husband's personal and real property. The right known as "dower" entitled the widow to a life estate in one-third of all his freehold property held at any time during the marriage. Upon her death, the property passed to the heir named in the husband's will or as required by the entail. Considered the female equivalent of the husband's right of curtesy, dower provided the widow with a life interest not in all of her deceased spouse's property, as did curtesy, but only in one-third of such property. In order to enforce her right of dower, the widow had to bring an action in the common-law courts to compel the heir of the property to assign her the land. Dower rights were absolute, superseding any will of the husband that sought to limit or deprive his widow of this right. The widow could also recover any freehold property sold by the husband at any time during the marriage without her consent. Neither adulterous nor divorced women were permitted dower rights.

A pre-arranged settlement called a "jointure" could bar the widow's recovery of her dower rights. Medieval jointures entitled the widow to gain title to property held in joint tenancy of the husband and wife. Later jointures took the form of an annuity arising from a rent charge on specified lands. By the early sixteenth century, jointure had largely superseded dower as the common route of providing for widows. Jointures stayed in force either for the life of the widow or for the potentially more limited period of her widowhood. Experts generally considered jointure rights surer, as the land covered by jointure was specific. In 1536, the Parliament passed the Statute of Uses that effectively barred dower to widows who had agreed prior to the marriage to a jointure.[60] If a jointure was settled on a woman only after her marriage, then the widow could elect to take either the jointure or the dower. The Statute of Uses provided that jointure could limit dower only upon certain conditions, including, importantly, if the jointure gave the woman a "freehold estate" (an estate in land held for uncertain duration) at least as great as her dower right. Yet, a "theory of equitable jointure" developed which effectively evaded this requirement, permitting jointure rights to reside not simply in freehold property but even in personal property or "leasehold property" (land held for a set number of years), i.e. in property interests that were, as one historian has pointed out, often worth less over time.[61] The limitation of jointure to a woman's widowhood, rather than to her lifetime, also reduced the value of the jointure.

Local custom usually provided the widow with her right to "freebench", also known as "widow's bench", in place of dower. Freebench entitled the widow to the profits of a percentage of her deceased husband's "copyhold property" (land held at the will of the lord of the manor and according to the manor's customs). This percentage varied according to the custom of the manor from one-third to all of the deceased husband's copyhold property. Custom also determined whether such a right lasted for her lifetime, during her widowhood, or for an even shorter period, such as during the heir's minority.[62]

Upon her husband's death, the widow regained her rights in and title to most of the property she had brought into the marriage. She could recover any such previously owned freehold or copyhold property. Likewise, any of the *feme covert*'s "leasehold property" (land held for a fixed term of years) that remained intact at the time of her husband's death once again became the woman's property. She permanently lost title to her personal property after the marriage and so could not recover it upon her husband's death with the exception of her paraphernalia, which once again became her own. However, should a conflict arise between the widow and another legatee or a creditor, the law permitted her to recover only such paraphernalia deemed reasonable to her station. The rest of her jewelry and clothing would be granted to the legatee or sold to pay off the creditor.

With respect to the personal property of a deceased man, ecclesiastical law provided for fixed distributions. The "rule of reasonable parts" provided for the forced distribution of the deceased husband's personal property even in the face of a will to the contrary. If the husband and wife had issue at the time of the husband's death, then the widow received one-third of his personal property and the children received two-thirds of it. If they had no issue, then the wife received one-half of his personal property. This rule applied only in certain northern boroughs of England but not in the southern boroughs, where a man had complete freedom to dispose of his personal property by will. The administration of these rules fell to the ecclesiastical courts, which had discretion to give the widow an even greater percentage of the husband's personal property than the minimum percentage required by the rule of reasonable parts. One study of the ecclesiastical courts' administration of the rule of reasonable parts reveals that the courts acted generously, giving at least 63% of the personal property to widows with children.[63]

In 1670, however, Parliament passed the innocuously entitled "Act for the Better Settling of Intestates' Estates". This Act abolished the ecclesiastical courts' discretion to grant higher percentages than those spelled out by the rule of reasonable parts in the face of a will to the contrary.[64] Between 1692 and 1725, the rule of reasonable parts was abolished altogether by successive parliamentary legislation.

* * * * * *

The preceding overview has mapped out the contours of the most significant laws governing women's personal and property rights in early modern England. It has only hinted at the direct and indirect effects of these laws on women's lives, i.e. on how in fact, women actually fared individually and as a group under this legal system. Such an overview can present only an incomplete picture of the ways in which women directly ignored the strictures of coverture, for example, by owning property, managing money and forming contracts even in the face of law to the contrary, or how they indirectly evaded such law by resort to the ecclesiastical, manorial and equity courts and by reliance on jointures, marriage settlements, trusts and other equitable devices. The discrepancy between the laws and actual practice in the period suggests that women enjoyed greater privileges than the bare letter of the law provided. Yet, one must temper any such conclusion by an awareness that the jurisdictional, statutory and proprietary changes of the early modern period often left ordinary women in a weakened position with fewer venues for seeking redress and fewer customary practices or entitlements available to them.[65] More work must be accomplished by legal and social historians so as to reconstruct the lives of early modern Englishwomen in order to form more than speculative opinions as to whether their situation in fact worsened or improved over the course of the seventeenth century. Reprinting these early legal treatises, by providing easy access to the laws of the period, will offer assistance to scholars in their efforts.

The Lawes Resolutions of Womens Rights; Or, the Lawes Provision for Woemen. A Collection of Such Statutes and Customes, As Doe Properly Concerne Women

Publication and Authorship

The legal treatise *The Lawes Resolutions*, or "The Womans Lawyer", as its running headline and spine title read, was published anonymously in 1632. Thomas Edgar and Sir Egremont Thynne entered the work in the Stationers' 'Register' on 20 April 1632. The assignees of John More, Esquire printed the text for sale by the bookseller John Grove.

The title page fails to identify the original author of the work, and its authorship remains in question today. The epistle "To the Reader", signed by T.E., states that authorship of the text and the circumstances surrounding its composition are unknown. The "Preface to the Reader", signed by I.L., notes that "the Author's dead … [and the text] was long since collected" but provides no other information about the author. In the treatise, the author identifies himself as a married man, although he does not give the reader any other information about his background. Given the content and language of the treatise, its author was quite likely educated at the Inns of Court.

Authorship has sometimes been attributed to T.E., signatory of the epistle, although this conjectural attribution does not accord with T.E.'s own statement in the epistle that he merely revised the work. Early conjectures tentatively attributed the work to Sir John Doddridge, a distinguished judge of the King's Bench, legal writer and statesman.[66] Authorship has even been attributed to the other registrant of the work, Sir Aegremont Thynne, a serjeant at law (pleader in the Common Bench), antiquary and legal bibliophile,[67] and to the anonymous I.L., signatory of the Preface, about whom no biographical information has been found.[68]

The *STC* tentatively identifies T.E. as Thomas Edgar, who registered the book, although no extrinsic basis for making this identification seems to exist.[69] W.R. Prest found a Thomas Edgar admitted to membership of Gray's Inn in 1619 and has re-constructed pertinent biographical information about him in his article, "Law and Women's Rights in Early Modern England". He suggests that "[w]e cannot entirely exclude the possibility" that this Thomas Edgar could indeed have written the epistle and even the treatise itself.[70]

More information is known about the work's publisher. John More (or Moore), Esquire was a well-reputed publisher of legal texts during the period, having received the exclusive right from James I in 1618 to print all books of the English common law, statutes and abridgements for a period of forty years. It is not clear whether he was responsible for their publication, but he did provide a stock of type for the project. In 1629, he assigned his printing rights to Miles Fletcher and his partners, John Haviland and Robert Young, those responsible for the actual printing of *The Lawes Resolutions*.[71]

In the Epistle, T.E. emphasizes that he played a substantial role in the editing, correcting, amending, updating and revising of the anonymous manuscript. He also claims to have added many judicial opinions and case holdings to the work. It has been impossible to determine, however, which sections of the original manuscript were amended by T.E. or the extent of these revisions. It has also been impossible to date the original manuscript definitively. W.R. Prest, in an analysis of the treatise, has surmised that the author probably did not begin the treatise before the mid-1580's and may well have completed it early in James I's reign.[72]

Genre and Audience

Publication of *The Lawes Resolutions* represents a significant moment in the history of the Englishwoman. While the legal literature of the period provides some overview of the laws affecting women, *The Lawes Resolutions* is the first known text specifically devoted to recording methodically Englishwomen's legal rights, liabilities, immunities, advantages and interests as established by statutes and common-law rules and often contradictory case law.

The text is an early example of the legal treatise, sharing many attributes of later legal treatises, most importantly a synthesis of a discrete area of the common law and its systematic organization. The text, at 404 pages, represents a massive effort of consolidation, organizing the disparate and hitherto uncompiled aspects of the common law applicable to women into a logical framework. In the author's words: "things…are laid plaine together, and in some orderly connexion, which heretofore were smothered, or scattered in corners of an uncouth language" (403). The author acknowledges the difficulty of "mak[ing] a perfect method of the laws of England", yet describes his text as "an assay" at precisely this goal (2).

The text's methodology bears resemblance to that of other early modern legal treatises as well. It explicates complicated, often theoretical points of law and even obsolete legal principles by reciting common-law case holdings, judges' reasonings and statutes, and by providing lengthy historical discussions. The text's technical language, including its use of antiquated legalese and untranslated Latinate expressions, is also a familiar attribute of other legal treatises of the period.

Yet, the text is different from other early modern legal treatises in its stated goal of providing a "popular kind of instruction" (2) to its readers.

As Prest has noted, the work is one of the earliest legal treatises purporting to make the law accessible to the laity, rather than simply written for legal practitioners.[73] The treatise is not written in "law French", still the dominant language of the legal profession, but in English. The author also relies heavily on anecdotal examples ("because women learne faster by example then by precept" [156]) and frequently intersperses his discussions with narrative frames, personal asides, subjective opinions, editorializing advice and commentary. These stylistic features of the treatise suggest that the author was writing a text for a broader audience than the legal profession.

Frequently, the author's commentary, advice and addresses are directed at women, according with his explicit statement that he primarily intends the treatise for women: "they to whom my travels are chiefly addressed are women ... I have framed this worke...[to] enable you the better to understand the reasons and arguments of Law, and to conferre and enquire what the Law is" (403–4). He claims that his treatise is meant not "so much to satisfie the deep learned or searchers for subtillity, as woman kind" (2–3). Yet, the author's intended audience for the treatise is not only women, but also apprentices or "[s]tudents" of the law (2). As Prest has remarked, the treatise also caters to the male professionals of the Inns of Court. The treatise's nearly exclusive focus on the common law indicates that the intended audience of the treatise must certainly have included practicing common-law lawyers.[74]

The putative female readership of the treatise still remains in question. It is not clear how many women, if any, actually purchased or read the treatise. Nor, to the best of my knowledge, did women writers of the period quote the treatise, thereby providing direct evidence of a female readership. The frequently arcane material discussed and the use of Latinate and legal French expressions without translation or definition would have made the treatise difficult, if not inaccessible, to many women readers.[75] The nuances of the law of *feme covert* may well have been familiar to certain women, particularly propertied ones, and the treatise would have provided an invaluable resource for these women; but, nevertheless, the work would still have had greatest value to the legal profession, especially to those primarily responsible for overseeing women's rights.

Content

The system devised by the author to organize the laws affecting women traces a woman's life chronologically, dividing it into those stages that marked a change in her legal status. Beginning at a woman's birth, the first "Booke" (1–50) moves through the laws governing her minority status and wardship until her coming of age, with special attention given to her property rights. The second "Booke" (51–115) details the laws of marriage formation and dissolution, the financial aspects of marriage and the law of curtesy. The third "Booke" (116–229) concentrates on the laws of coverture, unremittingly explicating the loss of a *feme covert*'s property interests. Very little sympathetic editorializing accompanies this section, for it itemizes what property the *feme covert* lost upon her marriage. This section also explains the law of jointure. The fourth "Booke" (230–330) recounts the legal status of widows and describes in detail how a woman could attain her dower or jointure rights. The fifth "Booke" (331–404) addresses those aspects of the criminal law that affected women, in particular the appeals available to women, including how and where to bring such actions. This section also devotes a significant section to the past and contemporary laws of rape or ravishment (376–404). The author then ends rather abruptly with a brief section imploring his readership to look kindly upon his efforts.

The introductory sections to the first Booke set up an additional, non-legal frame for the treatise so as to explain the origin of the doctrine of coverture. Relying on Genesis, the author re-tells the story of the creation of man and woman. The author emphasizes that God created woman from man, "bone of his bones, flesh of his flesh", destined to become "one flesh" with her husband (4). This Scriptural justification for the law's subordination of women finds further justification in the author's account of the Fall. Eve, by helping to seduce Adam into eating the forbidden fruit, received a special punishment, "an especiall bane. In sorrow shalt thou bring forth thy children, thy desires shall bee subject to thy husband, and he shall rule over thee … The common law here shaketh hand with Divinitie …." (6) Yet, the author also defines his use of "woemen" in the treatise's title and, in so doing, re-casts a misogynist expression. He insists that the creation of woman "signifieth not the woe of Man as some affirme, but with Man: For in our hasty pronouncing wee turne the preposition with to woe, or wee, oftentimes, and so shee was ordained to bee with man as a helpe, a companion, because God saw it was not good that Man should bee alone" (4).

Several passages in the treatise evidence oscillations between patriarchal and more egalitarian views of women. For example, the author's introductory remarks to the Fourth Booke are fascinating for their embracing of the most orthodox statements on marital relations ("But alas, when she hath lost her husband, her head is cut off" [232]) and paradoxically radical statements ("Why mourne you so, you that be widowes … now you be free in libertie" [232]). The treatise, generally, is infused with sympathetic statements on women's unfair status ("But me thinkes here wanteth equality in the Law" [146]). The author also evinces a strong sense of women's vulnerability before the law and in their relationships with men ("But to what purpose is it for women to make vowes, when men have so many millions of wayes to make them break them? And when sweet words, faire promises, tempting, flattering, swearing, lying will not serve to beguile the poore soule: then with rough handling, violence, and plaine strength of armes …" [377]). He also emphasizes that his motive in writing the treatise is his sense of the "pitty and impiety … to hold from [women] such Customes, Lawes and Statutes, as are in a maner, proper, or principality belonging unto them" (2). Yet, the treatise fails to advocate or to encourage legal reform. Instead, the author in the final analysis instructs women to behave virtuously, to live a "modest and chast life at home" (146) and to look to God and the next life for comfort.

Reception

Resolutions must have provided an important resource to the legal profession, and legal commentators cited the treatise well into the eighteenth century.[76] *The Lawes Resolutions* remained in print for at least 25 years, although no new editions were issued. Quotations from the text are also nearly ubiquitous in recent articles discussing the legal status of the early modern Englishwoman. The most significant analysis of the treatise is Prest's "Law and Women's Rights", which investigates the authorship, subject matter and intended audience of the work in great detail. Prest's article provided an invaluable resource in the preparation of this introduction.

The treatise has been reprinted twice since its original publication, both times in facsimile as part of Garland Publishing's series, *Classics of English Legal History in the Modern Era* (1978), and Theatrum Orbis Terrarum's series, *The English Experience* (1979).

This facsimile of *The Lawes Resolutions* takes as its photographic copy text the very fine copy at The British Library. The following libraries likewise own copies: Bodleian Library, University of Oxford; Cambridge University Library; St. John's College Library, Oxford; Marsh's Library, Dublin; National Library of Scotland, Edinburgh; Folger Shakespeare Library; Edinburgh University Library; Henry E. Huntington Library; Harvard University Law Library; Columbia University Library; Newberry Library; Boston Public Library; Los Angeles County Law Library; Stanford University Law Library; Library of Congress; University of California Law Library; Yale University Library; New York University Law Library; University of Pennsylvania Library; and Chapin Library, Williams College.

A Treatise of Feme Coverts: Or, the Lady's Law Containing All the Laws and Statutes Relating to Women, Under Several Heads

Publication and Authorship

A Treatise of Feme Coverts was originally published in 1732 by E. and R. Nutt and R. Gosling for B. Lintot and sold by H. Lintot. In 1737, it was re-issued in a second edition with no substantive changes save the reversal of the order of the title, *A Treatise of Feme Coverts*, and the subtitle, *The Lady's Law*. The second edition was also printed by E. and R. Nutt and R. Gosling but for H. Lintot and sold by C. Corbett and E. Littleton.

The treatise appeared anonymously, and no attribution of authorship has been made. No autobiographical asides appear in the text that could provide information about the author's gender, age, marital status, education or class. Presumably, as in the case of *The Lawes Resolutions*, the treatise was written by a man.[77] The treatise's methodical approach and focus on the common law also suggest that the author graduated from the Inns of Court. The author's inclusion in the treatise of several sample legal deeds and conveyances also indicates that he likely practiced (or had at one point practiced) law.

One exciting aspect of the treatise's publication is that the first named printer, E. Nutt, was, in fact, a woman, Elizabeth Nutt, the widow of the printer and bookseller, Joseph Nutt.[78] She kept a pamphlet shop at the Royal Exchange and continued her deceased husband's substantial printing business. She went into partnership with Richard Nutt, whose familial relationship to Elizabeth Nutt is unknown. An eminent printer in his own right, Richard Nutt was responsible for printing the *Daily Post* from 1726–32 and the *London Evening Post* for several years.[79] Together, and with R. Gosling, a London printer, Elizabeth and Richard Nutt printed hundreds of legal texts, such as books of precedent, law dictionaries, abridgements, case reports, collections of statutes and treatises on a wide range of legal topics, including uses and trusts, tithes, forest and gaming laws, evidence, testaments and wills and tenures. Significantly, Elizabeth Nutt and Richard Nutt jointly published the second edition of *A Treatise of Feme Coverts*, the second edition of *Baron and Feme: A Treatise of the Common Law Concerning Husbands and Wives* and, with R. Gosling, the third edition of *Baron and Feme: A Treatise of Law and Equity Concerning Husbands and Wives* (reproduced in Volume 3). Elizabeth Nutt's involvement, then, in the printing of the two most significant eighteenth-century legal texts detailing the laws of women provides a wonderful example of the public role played by women in the legal history of England.

The eminence of the treatise's publisher suggests the authoritative nature of the treatise. Barnaby Bernard Lintot, father of Henry Lintot, was an important bookseller and publisher in London. George I appointed him one of only three printers of the Parliamentary votes, a capacity in which he served until 1727. He also published several important poems and plays, including those by Alexander Pope, Richard Steele, George Farquhar, John Gay and Thomas Parnell. His son, Henry, took over his father's business around 1730 and so would probably have been primarily responsible for the publication of *A Treatise of Feme Coverts*.[80]

Genre and Influence

The text, as its title explicitly states, falls squarely within the generic category of the legal treatise. It purports to provide, as does *The Lawes Resolutions*, a logically organized overview of "[a]ll the Laws and Statutes relating to Women" (t.p.) as set out in statutes and (predominantly) common-law cases. The format of the treatise is somewhat akin to that of the early modern abridgement. After announcing a particular legal principle, the treatise chronologically discusses relevant statutes and common-law cases that apply, expand or modify this principle. The discussion of these cases is often limited to a summary of their factual backgrounds and holdings without transitional commentary or explanation. Like *The Lawes Resolutions* and other early modern legal treatises, *A Treatise of Feme Coverts* frequently provides lengthy historical discussions of the development of a particular principle, at times laboring over obsolete nuances of the law.

The treatise prints the entire case report of the "remarkable" (200) decision of Justice Robert Hyde in the case of *Manby v. Scott* in the Court of Exchequer Chamber, a somewhat unusual inclusion in a legal treatise. Usually, legal treatises elucidated and quoted judges' decisions without printing them in their entirety. The inclusion of this decision indicates that the author of *A Treatise of Feme Coverts* thought the case seminal not only for the legal principle enunciated by the holding but also for the legal arguments and reasoning of Justice Hyde.

The treatise draws from books of precedent and conveyancing manuals of the period as well, reproducing a number of sample forms, deeds and conveyances. It is clear that the author added these sample forms to the treatise in order to supply legal practitioners with properly drafted models. The majority of these models are examples of marriage settlements that create married women's separate property. They illustrate effectuating a jointure, providing a sum of money in lieu of a jointure, establishing a trust for the separate use of the wife and portions for younger children and arranging for the wife to have her estate entirely at her disposition after marriage. The author also provides samples of two simpler arrangements: a bond on marriage to provide money to the widow and portions for the children and a bond in the event of a divorce. The treatise contains a number of more general sample legal documents as well: a marriage license, a petition for a writ and an order for the maintenance of a bastard child.

The treatise often directly quotes other legal commentators and judges to elucidate a legal principle. The author clearly relied extensively on *The Lawes Resolutions* for his organization, choice of subjects and discussions of cases. The treatise even opens by referring to and paraphrasing the earlier treatise: "an ancient Author has assur'd us, that all Women, in the Eyes of the Law, are either married or to be married; and their Desires are subject to their Husbands" (v). But the author is most directly indebted to the first two editions of *Baron and Feme* (discussed below). At times, his discussions of cases follow nearly word-for-word the discussions of the earlier treatise. Certain sections also follow the format and structure of *Baron and Feme* (see, for example, 31–5). It has even been suggested, by Amy Louise Erickson, that *A Treatise of Feme Coverts* was written as an "extended version"[81] of *Baron and Feme*, a reasonable conjecture given the similarities and printing history of the two treatises.

The tone of the treatises is also similar, more matter-of-fact than and without the sympathetic moralizing and narrative asides of *The Lawes Resolutions*. Unlike *Baron and Feme*, however, *A Treatise of Feme Coverts* provides anecdotal examples that seem designed not only to inform but also to entertain the reader. As the author mentions in his Preface, he has included "some Things of Entertainment, being writ long ago" (vi) as well as some antiquated laws and customs relating to women (vii). For example, the author recounts the unusual custom of requiring a widow with a bastard to forfeit her estate unless she rides into the Court of the Manor on a ram, reciting: "*Here I am/ Riding upon the Back of a black* Ram,*/ Like a Whore as I am;/ And for my* Crincum Crancum,*/ I have left my* Binkum Bankum;*/ And for my Tail's Game/ Have done this worldly Shame;/ Therefore pray, Mr.* Steward, *let me have/ my Land again*" (128). Anecdotal examples are employed sparingly, however, and the overall tone of the treatise is didactic and practical.

Audience

The author of *A Treatise of Feme Coverts* defines his readers as "all Practisers of the Law, and other curious Persons" (viii) and, like the author of *The Lawes Resolutions*, clearly intends his readership to include women. He emphasizes that he wants the treatise to provide a practical benefit to women: "The fair Sex are here inform'd, how to preserve their Lands, Goods, and most valuable Effects, from the Incroachments of any one; to defend themselves and their Reputations against all unlawful Attacks of Mankind, and to maintain Actions, and carry on Prosecutions in Cases of Violation of their Persons, to the Death of a daring Offender" (vii).

As in the case of *The Lawes Resolutions*, however, it has been impossible to prove definitively a female audience for the treatise; and it is likely that the treatise would in reality have been most useful as a reference for male practitioners of the law, to whom the sample deeds and conveyances and discussions of the fine points of case law would have been directed.

Content

The treatise, at 264 pages in length, like *The Lawes Resolutions* maps out the laws pertaining to every stage of a woman's life, beginning in her infancy and continuing through her marriage and widowhood, although its most detailed discussions pertain to the laws specific to the *feme covert*. The treatise is divided as follows: the first section begins with a discussion of unmarried females and their property rights (1–25); the second section (25–52) details the laws of marriage and the law of rape; the third section (52–77) delineates the proprietary consequences of marriage and the laws of dower and jointure; and the fourth section (78–109), though titled "Of the Privileges of Feme Coverts, and their Power, with Respect to their Husband, and all others", is largely a recitation of the losses accruing to women upon their marriages. The author insists, however, that "a Feme Covert is a Favourite of the Law" (81). This section also delineates the rights of the Queen of England and the Queen Dowager of England and details when the *feme covert* could bring legal action alone and when her husband had to be joined as a party to the action. This section, interestingly, sets out in great detail the law of slander, including a list of which words spoken against a woman were actionable. The fifth section (109–28) concerns the laws of the procreation of children and descent. A significant portion of this section focuses on the laws of bastardy and the maintenance of bastards, an area of law not included in *The Lawes Resolutions*. The sixth section (129–64) recites the laws of conveyances with respect to *femes covert* as well as recoveries, leases and wills made by and for husbands and wives. The final section of the treatise articulates the laws of divorce and details how to create separate maintenance contracts. The body of the treatise ends with the enunciation of the legal principle elucidated in *Manby v. Scott*. Immediately following this restatement appears the case report of *Manby v. Scott*. The final 64 pages of the treatise print sample precedents of deeds and conveyances.

Reception

The treatise was re-issued five years after its initial publication, suggesting that it was considered authoritative in the period. The treatise has been reprinted twice since its original publication and re-issue, both times in facsimile, as part of Garland Publishing's series, *Classics of English Legal History in the Modern Era* (1978), and Theatrum Orbis Terrarum's series, *The English Experience* (1979).

This facsimile of *A Treatise of Feme Coverts* takes as its photographic copy text the fine copy of the first edition (1732) at the Bodleian Library, University of Oxford. The following libraries likewise own copies of the original 1732 edition of the work: The British Library; Glasgow University Library; Thomas Plume's Library, Maldon, Essex; Mills Memorial Library, McMaster University, Hamilton, Ontario; Los Angeles County Law Library; Henry E. Huntington Library; University of California Law Library, Berkeley; Folger Shakespeare Library; Free Library of Philadelphia; U.S. Library of Congress; Library Company of Philadelphia; University of Michigan Law Library; Biddle Law Library, University of Pennsylvania; Harvard Law School Library; University of Cincinnati Law Library; Virginia Historical Society.

The Hardships of the English Laws. In Relation to Wives. With an Explanation of the Original Curse of Subjection Passed upon the Woman. In an Humble Address to the Legislature

Publication and Authorship

The anonymous *Hardships of the English Laws* was first published in 1735, simultaneously in London by W. Boyler for the printer and bookseller J. Roberts and in Dublin by and for George Faulkner.

The author identifies herself as a married woman, one whose husband, unlike the majority, "lets me be *alive*, and gives me leave to be *some* Body, and to tell other People what I think they are" (51). The tract does not provide any other pertinent biographical information about the author's age, class, education, marital status or work.

Authorship of the treatise can with some confidence be attributed to Sarah Chapone.[82] On December 14, 1741, Anna Hopkins wrote to George Ballard that for his project on the lives of women writers, Sarah Chapone would probably lend him her copy of Mary Astells' *A Serious Proposal to the Ladies*. Hopkins then added: "Tho' I knew that she was the Author of *Hardships of English Laws &c*: I did not mention it to you because I thought it was a Secret".[83] Added confirmation of this attribution comes from a note on the title page of the British Library copy, the one reprinted in this volume. It reads: "Said to be written by Mrs Cha[??]on of Glostershire wife to a clergyman yt [i.e. that] keeps a School". The following note written in the same handwriting as that used on the title page also appears on page 70, the last page of the text: "NB Mr Whittern told me ye lady had a very good husband & live'd happy only writ for ye good of her sex in general". It has not been possible to identify who wrote this note.

A writer, proto-feminist and educator, Sarah Kirkham Chapone – or Capon, as she spelled it – (1699–1764), was the daughter of a clergyman.[84] She married Reverend John Chapone, with whom she had five children. One of her sons, John, married the eminent writer, Hester Mulso. Sarah Chapone ran a school in Stanton and assisted George Ballard in his research on women writers. She seems to have been an active woman of letters, corresponding regularly with, amongst others, Ballard, John Wesley, Mary Delany and Samuel Richardson. Chapone addressed her only other published work, *Remarks* (1750), to the famous courtesan Teresia Constantia Phillips.

Genre

The work generically can be characterized, in Chapone's words, as an "address" to "his most sacred Majesty, and the Honourable Houses of Parliament" (4). In this address, Chapone sought "an Alteration or a Repeal of some Laws" (4) that applied to married women. Whether, in fact, Chapone actually intended her work to be read by the king and Parliament, or whether her address merely set up a fictitious audience, it is impossible to know. Nor has it been possible to determine whether Chapone's petition was actually read by the king or Parliament.

There was a well-established tradition of women petitioning Parliament in this period within which Chapone could consciously have been placing herself. Particularly during the civil-war period, women petitioned Parliament to reform a vast array of laws concerning religious, political, social and economic questions. Lois G. Schwoerer has identified 112 pamphlets and petitions to Parliament in the years 1640 to 1650 and approximately 700 petitions and tracts in the years 1640 to 1700 written by women.[85] Individual women also petitioned Parliament throughout the early modern period to redress specific matters of personal significance. These petitions often involve property entitlement and inheritance disputes.[86]

Chapone's address shares many of the attributes of these female-authored petitions, including their putative audience, organization and style. In particular, the petitions often begin with general arguments justifying the right of women to petition Parliament. Chapone opens her address in a similar vein, voicing many of the arguments used in Civil War petitions to support her claim. The petitions, like *Hardships*, also emulate the style and rhetoric of formal legal argument, using common-law precedent and citations to statutory law to prove their arguments. Nevertheless, the content of *Hardships* is unique. None of the other petitions written by women in the period constitutes an elaborated protest against the legal status of women or an elaborated demand for the reform of any laws responsible for women's inferior legal status.

Chapone's work also differs from traditional legal scholarship written by men in the period, for example *The Lawes Resolutions* and *A Treatise of Feme Coverts*, as it is not intended to provide an overview of the laws relating to women or to restate systematically specific points of law for the purposes of edification. Rather, it represents one woman's response to the laws of coverture, or, in her words, the "Law of Annihilation" (51).

Hardships bears some resemblance to other contemporaneous criticisms of married women's inferior position in society, particularly Margaret Cavendish's *The World's Olio* (1655) and *Orations of Divers Sorts Accomodated to Divers Places* (1688), Mary Astell's *Some Reflections on Marriage* (1700), Lady Mary Chudleigh's *The Female Advocate; Or, a Plea for the Just Liberty of the Tender Sex, and Particularly of Married Women. Being Reflections on a Late Rude and Disingenuous Discourse, Delivered By Mr. John Sprint, in a Sermon* (1700), the pseudonymous Sophia's *Woman Not Inferior to Man* (1739) and Mary More's *The Woman's Right* (circa 1670).[87] These works all share a vision of the married woman's lot as comparable to abject slavery. So, too, one of the central objects of *Hardships* is demonstrating "[t]hat the Estate of Wives is more disadvantagious than *Slavery* itself" (6). In particular, Mary More's *The Woman's Right*, written as advice to her unmarried daughter, shares with *Hardships* a sense of the pressing need for the *feme covert* to protect herself from the laws of coverture: "for the Laws of our Country … [give] A Man after marriage a greater Power of their Estate than ye Wife, unless ye Wife take care before hand to prevent it (which I advice thee to doe)".[88]

Like the above-cited works, *Hardships* also emphasizes the deleterious state of women's formal education as responsible in large part for women's complacency. Unlike these other early feminist tracts, however, Chapone provides more than just a general description of the lot of the married woman, for she analyses those specific laws that kept women in a position of such subordination. What is rare, then, about this text is its systematic objection to the laws relating to women. *Hardships* stands as a lone protest against not just a woman's generally subordinate status but also those specific legal constructions that conspired to keep her in this position.

Sources of the Text

Hardships offers proof that at least one early modern woman had a sophisticated knowledge of her legal status. Chapone displays familiarity with many common-law principles and with the formal style of legal argument, confidently criticizing judicial holdings and relying on precedents to make her claims. Her knowledge of the law extends well beyond the common law, for she relies on points of the civil law of community property, Levitical law and Portuguese law in order to bolster her arguments.

Chapone seems to have acquired her background in the law by reading both specialized legal and more general texts. She explains that she has written the petition after having read a number of recent court cases. She refers by name to one source for her knowledge of case law, William Salkeld's *Reports of Cases Adjudged in the Court of King's Bench* (1721, 1724) (16), and quotes at some length directly from Thomas Wood's legal treatise, *New Institute of the Imperial or Civil Law* (1709) (29). Yet her knowledge was not derived solely from legal texts. She admits to having learned of one of the cases from public prints, indicating the importance of popular sources, not just specialized legal treatises, to her education. Barbara Todd has shown that this case was originally reported in the *Old Bailey Session Papers* and mentioned in the *Gentleman's Magazine*,[89] suggesting two possible sources upon which Chapone could have relied.

Todd has conjectured that "the tone of the anonymous *A Treatise of Feme Coverts* (1732) and particularly the reprinting there of Justice Robert Hyde's opinion in *Manby v. Scott* may have aroused this author to respond".[90] Todd's connecting of these two works is, of course, of enormous interest, suggesting another explicit link between the works in this volume. Chapone does not quote the treatise or the case of *Manby v. Scott* directly; yet *Hardships* and Justice Hyde's discussion share the same concern with identifying the limits of the *feme covert*'s economic, social and legal independence. Furthermore, the similarity of the conclusions of *Hardships* and *Manby v. Scott* as to the scriptural origin of women's subordination to men also suggests that Chapone may have read the case itself, if not *A Treatise of Feme Coverts*.

Content

The structure of *Hardships* divides into three parts. The first section (3–6) asserts a woman's right to petition Parliament, relying on several arguments to justify her action. First, Chapone argues that a man, as a free-born subject, has the right to approach his Sovereign, represent his grievances, and seek redress therefrom. She then asserts: "We hope that this inestimable privilege is not wholly confined to the *Male* Line", because women are the most in need of protection, "being the least able to help ourselves, and most exposed to Oppression" (4). She situates women in the same category as men, as "English Subjects" (6), thereby directly challenging the law's derogation of married women's legal status.

The second part of *Hardships* (6–52) is devoted to proving three main grievances for which Chapone demanded redress: "I. That the Estate of Wives is more disadvantagous than *Slavery* itself. II. That Wives may be made prisoners for Life at the Discretion of their *Domestick Governors* … III. That Wives have no Property, neither in their *own Persons, Children* or *Fortunes*" (6–7). Her arguments derive primarily from biblical exegesis, political theory and comparative legal analysis. This section offers an alternative lens by which to read the three legal treatises in this series. Whereas they assert quite matter-of-factly that women lose all property rights upon marriage, *Hardships* provides harrowing examples of how this law actually functioned, allowing husbands to abuse physically and mentally, starve, confine and even murder their wives and squander their estates without penalty.[91] In Chapone's words: "My Design in these Representations is to shew the Scope and Tendency of the English Laws in Relation to Wives" (32).

She also anticipates and provides counter-arguments to eleven specific "objections" to her representations. Her counter-arguments have enormous value for the legal historian in reconstructing how women actually lived under a system of coverture. She takes on the argument that a woman could find judicial relief for being beaten by her husband. Yet, Chapone insists that, even if a woman could obtain this relief, which was not always possible, sending a husband to jail could potentially leave her in a worse condition, subject to his vengeance once home or a loss of his income while in jail. Another subject addressed by *Hardships* that, interestingly, has been the focus of much revisionist legal history is the trust agreement and the extent to which it served to protect women's property interests. Again, Chapone's remarks here serve as a cautionary tale. She acknowledges that a wife could put her property into trustees' control before marriage and so secure her use of it. Yet she reminds the reader that this could be accomplished only with the consent of her intended husband; otherwise the Court of Chancery would invalidate the trust. She insists that few actually made use of this precaution, so overswayed were they by confidence in their intended husbands (and by a lack of education). Even more discouraging, those that did make such a provision before marriage often revoked its power afterwards. Here she quotes "one of our present eminent Judges", who unfortunately remains nameless: "That he had hardly known an Instance, where the Wife had not been kissed or kicked out of any such previous Settlement" (34).

Chapone likewise re-evaluates the efficacy of jointures in providing ample financial security to widows, concluding that they, alone, do not (34–6). Also of interest, she denies the voluntary and consensual nature of marriage, emphasizing that "in many Instances Women are commanded and directed into it, by their Parents and Guardians, and in some other Circumstances 'tis their only Way of advancing themselves and settling in the World" (43). According to Chapone, then, arranged and forced marriages still persisted well into the eighteenth century.

The third part of *Hardships* (53–68) examines the reason for married women's inferior legal status. This section has enormous value as a reflection of and response to prevailing statements of the period that justified women's subordination by reference to their nature. Chapone grapples here with arguments derived from familiar seventeenth- and eighteenth-century debates on political science and philosophy. She first disclaims the argument made in William Wollaston's *The Religion of Nature Delineated* (1722) that men and women represent "exact Counter Parts to each other" (53) and because men are governed by greater reason than women, women must accordingly submit and allow men greater authority. Chapone surprisingly concludes that women in their present cultural condition, hindered by lack of education and opportunity, may "generally" lack greater reason, but that in a state of nature this would not be the case (54). She then turns to Thomas Hobbes's *Philosophical Rudiments concerning Government and Society* (1651), agreeing with him (albeit reluctantly) that, if a state of nature prevailed, women would have original dominion and authority over their children. Yet, believing that "we never were in a State of Nature, or can be so" (57), she looks elsewhere to find an explanation for women's subjection to men.

In an effort to comprehend women's subordinate status, Chapone turns for clarification to biblical authority, as did so many other political and legal theorists of the period. She relies specifically on both Genesis and Revelation and on the commentary of Patrick Delany's *Revelation Examined with Candour* (1733) to draw a distinction between prelapsarian and postlapsarian relations of the sexes. In sharp contrast to the author of *The Lawes Resolutions*, Chapone reasons that at their first creation equality of the sexes prevailed because human nature was "in a state of Perfection where Reason ruled and Perverseness had no Place, [thus] there seems to be no imaginable Reason why one Sex should be in Subjection to the other" (58). She then situates the "curse of female subjection" (59) after Eve's transgression as divine punishment for her sin. Only with the Second Coming would women once again enjoy "the Laws of Equality" (64). This orthodox conclusion, that woman's subordination is ultimately the will of God, divine punishment for her role in the Fall, places the work in a tradition of Christian thought, tempered only by Chapone's ultimate statement that the laws of England go far beyond God's decree and so require legal reform. While not seeking to place women on equal footing with men, she nevertheless advocates some bettering of women's legal position.

Reception

It is impossible to determine whether Chapone's work had any tangible effect on woman's legal status or perceptions of it. Certainly it did not lead to any law reform or even to parliamentary response. While the work was excerpted that same year in the May and June issue of *Gentleman's Magazine*[92] as a lead essay, indicating a non-trivial early reception, it did not inspire an answering pamphlet, tract or other response and did not get printed again until this century. Nor did it set the groundwork for further criticisms of women's relationship to property law. Indeed, it has been suggested that virtual silence followed in the wake of the text, and it would be nearly one hundred years later that a condemnation of the widow's legal status appeared in print.[93]

The most significant analysis of the work is Barbara J. Todd's article, "'To be some body': married women and *The Hardships of the English Laws*", an invaluable resource in the preparation of this introduction.

This facsimile of *The Hardships of the English Law in Relation to Wives* takes as its photographic copy text the fine copy of the original edition at The British Library. This copy text was chosen, as discussed more fully above, for its important annotations attributing the work to Sarah Chapone. The following libraries likewise own copies of the original edition: Trinity College Library; Cambridge University Library; Advocates Library, Edinburgh; Bodleian Library; Mills Library, McMaster University, Hamilton, Ontario; Folger Shakespeare Library; Lilly Library, Indiana University; University of Chicago Library; University of Minnesota Library; Boston Athenaeum Library; Harvard Law School Library; Historical Society of Pennsylvania; Library of Congress; and New York Public Library.

Baron and Feme; a treatise of law and equity, concerning husbands and wives

Publication and Authorship

In 1700, the assigns of Richard and Edward Atkyns, Esquires, for John Walthoe published *Baron and Feme; A Treatise of the Common Law Concerning Husbands and Wives*. In 1719, as noted earlier, E. Nutt and R. Gosling (assigns of E. Sayer), again for John Walthoe, re-issued it in a second edition, says the title page, "with large additions". In 1738 came a third edition, entitled *Baron and Feme; A Treatise of Law and Equity, Concerning Husbands and Wives*, reproduced here. The title page of this edition emphasizes that it "added many cases in law and equity, from the best books of reports." Again, E. Nutt and R. Gosling as well as R. Nutt printed the work, this time for T. Waller.

The treatise appeared anonymously, and no attribution of authorship has been found. Given the treatise's methodology, structure and content, one may fairly presume, as in the cases of *The Lawes Resolutions* and *A Treatise of Feme Coverts*, that the author was a man, and one who had received a formal legal education, presumably at the Inns of Court. The treatise's focus on both equitable and common-law principles and cases, and its comprehensive inclusion of sample pleadings, also suggest that the author practiced or had at one point practiced law.

The only biographical information about the author included in the treatise comes from the note entitled "To the Reader", printed only in the first and second editions. This note mentions that the author had previously written a work that "Methodized and Explained the Law concerning Infants" (A3), but fails to indicate either the title of this work or any further information about its publication. Considering its publication date, printing history, content and style, one can identify this work as the legal treatise entitled *The Infants Lawyer; Or, the Law (Ancient and Modern) Relating to Infants*, the only known work published in England a few years before *Baron and Feme* concerned primarily with infants. The assigns of R. and E. Atykins, Esquires, also printed this work; and, like *Baron and Feme*, it was reprinted twice, in 1712 by J. Nutt (Elizabeth Nutt's deceased husband) and in 1726 by E. Nutt and R. Gosling as the assigns of E. Sayer. Straightforward in tone, this treatise, like *Baron and Feme*, is organized topically, addresses not only common law but also equity cases and includes sample pleadings. Unfortunately, this work too was published anonymously without accompanying autobiographical information, and no attribution of authorship or further information about the author has been found.

As discussed in connection with *A Treatise of Feme Coverts*, Elizabeth and Richard Nutt were significant printers of legal works. So, too, John Walthoe, the publisher of the first edition, was a bookseller in London and well-known for printing and dealing in law books.[94] The publisher of the third edition, T. Waller, likewise specialized in the sale and publication of legal works, including a number of important law reports, legal treatises and abridgements. The reprinted text includes advertisements, before the title page and after the table at the end of the treatise, for many of the important legal works published and sold by Waller.

Genre and Audience

The first edition of *Baron and Feme* is the first known legal treatise that focuses exclusively on the laws concerning husbands and wives. As the author announces in the note "To the Reader", "I had some reason to conceive and hope that a Treatise of this nature (having been never hitherto designedly perused) might meet with an Entertainment agreeable" (A3). Like other legal treatises of the period, *Baron and Feme* provides, in the words of the note "To the Reader", a "Methodized, Explained or Corrected" (A4) account of the laws of *baron* and *feme* as set out in statutes and common-law and equity cases. The treatise's value lies in its clear enunciation of rules of law and legal principles. It is less interested in the obsolete details of legal history than in setting out current, established propositions and case rulings.

Its discussion of cases likewise seems designed to promote clarity. Like early modern abridgements, court holdings of significance (in particular, *Manby and Scott*) are abridged and reduced to propositions. In some areas of the law, rather than simply laying out the disparate holdings of a body of cases, the author provides a framework of specific rules to follow. For example, in explaining where and in what actions to join a husband and wife as parties to the suit, the author lays out eight rules so that "a Studious Mind may easily be directed how to advise in such Cases" (A5). *Baron and Feme* does not generally provide lengthy historical discussions of moot cases, as do *The Lawes Resolutions* and *A Treatise of Feme Coverts*. The note to the reader suggests that "[w]hoever has a mind to be curious about them, may with great Satisfaction consult the first Institutes, where they are largely and most excellently handled" (A4–A5).

Like collections of sample writs and pleadings published in the period, *Baron and Feme* reproduces several sample declarations and pleadings used in actions routinely brought by or against a husband and wife. These sample pleadings would have provided legal practitioners with the basic procedural mechanism needed to initiate most cases involving husbands and wives. The majority of these actions involve debts upon obligations, annuity, dower and jointure rights. These pleadings, although appearing in Latin in the first two editions of the treatise, are translated into English in the third edition. This translation was clearly made as a response to the statute passed in 1731 that substituted English for Latin as the official language of the English courts.[95]

The author of *Baron and Feme* seems to have written the treatise primarily for the edification of those in the legal profession. In the note "To the Reader", the author identifies both students and practitioners of the law as the intended audience for the treatise. Unlike the authors of *The Lawes Resolutions* and *A Treatise of Feme Coverts,* he does not claim that he wrote the treatise for the edification of women. The treatise's practical approach, clear rules, sample precedents and attempt to avoid moot cases also suggest that the author intended the treatise to serve as a handy reference manual to those either bringing causes of action or advising clients. The straightforward tone of the treatise is not punctuated by any of the moralizing asides or entertaining anecdotes that characterize the other two treatises.

Content

The treatise, at 485 pages in length, differs from *The Lawes Resolutions* and *A Treatise of Feme Covert* in its scope and organization. It does not explicate the laws relating to the different stages of a woman's life but instead seeks to summarize those concerned with the relations between husbands and wives from the solemnization of marriage through divorce and widowhood. The treatise also considers "Collateral By-blows" (A4) of relations between the sexes, such as bastardy. The treatise describes in some detail *femes covert* acting outside the strictures of coverture, notably queens, executrices, administratrices and *femes-sole* merchants. In thirty-three separate chapters, the author moves not chronologically but topically, generally dividing the treatise into chapters that detail the statutory and case law of technical legal principles, such as Dower and Copyhold. The final thirty-three pages of the treatise print the sample precedents of pleadings.

The author announces on the title page that his discussions of cases derive from "the best books of reports" (t.p.). Unlike *The Lawes Resolutions* and to a lesser extent *A Treatise of Feme Coverts*, *Baron and Feme* focuses on cases in equity as well as in the common law, the change of the third edition's title (from *A Treatise of the Common Law* to *A Treatise of Law and Equity*) underscoring this focus. This previously un-compiled material would have been of enormous value to legal practitioners advising women on how to protect and enforce their property and inheritance rights in the equity courts and to law students who did not obtain systematic instruction on equitable principles at the Inns of Court.

The many cases in both law and equity added to the third edition attest to the many changes in the laws of coverture and inheritance during the course of the first half of the eighteenth century. The treatise includes several new cases involving marriage settlements, pin money, and trusts made for the sole and separate use of wives (see, in particular, 81–85) and separate maintenances settled on wives separated from their husbands (259–61). The treatise also discusses several cases brought in an effort to limit, bar or otherwise clarify widows' claims to dower and jointures (see, in particular, 87–90, 111–14, 121–24, 159–63). The most significant expansion in the third edition involves a revising and enlarging of the discussion of what acts done or contracts made by the wife were deemed binding on the husband. This section distills the various resolutions made by the court in the case of *Manby and Scott* and subsequent cases brought by tradesmen against husbands for money owed on goods delivered to separated wives (274–85).

Reception

The fact that the treatise was reprinted twice and both times with substantial additions in the eighteenth century strongly suggests that it was an important and authoritative reference in the period. Its influence on other legal treatises of the period, in particular *A Treatise of Feme Coverts*, likewise offers proof of its value to legal practitioners in the period. The first edition of *Baron and Feme* was reprinted in facsimile as part of Garland Publishing's series *Classics of English Legal History in the Modern Era* (1979).

This facsimile of *Baron and Feme* takes as its photographic copy text the copy of the third edition at the Bodleian Library. This copy, while tightly bound, contains interesting marginalia. The evident work of a practicing attorney or legal scholar, the handwritten notes interspersed throughout the treatise correct case names (for example, on pages 264, 306 and 307), citations (for example, on page 301) and fact patterns (for example, on page 267). The following libraries likewise own copies of the third edition: The British Library; Advocates Library, Edinburgh, Scotland; House of Lords Library, London; Dublin Honourable Society of King's Inn; York University Law Library, Ontario; Henry E. Huntington Library; University of Pennsylvania Library; University of Texas Law School Library; University of California, Berkeley, Library; Harvard University Law School Library; Cornell University Library; Columbia University Law Library; Folger Shakespeare Library; New York Public Library; Library of Congress; University of Florida Law Library; University of Georgia Law School Library; DePaul University Law Library; University of Chicago Library; Ohio State Law School Library; Tarlton Law Library, University of Texas; College of William and Mary Library; Southern Methodist University Library; University of Virginia Law Library; University of Wisconsin Law Library.

Notes

1. Tim Stretton, *Women Waging Law in Elizabethan England* (Cambridge: Cambridge UP, 1998) 25.
2. For further information about the different legal jurisdictions operative in the early modern period, see J. H. Baker, *An Introduction to English Legal History*, 3rd ed. (London: Butterworths, 1990) chs. 2, 6–8.
3. See R.C. Van Caenegem, *The Birth of the English Common Law* (Cambridge: Cambridge UP, 1973).

4. For further background on the administration of justice at the local level, see Cynthia Herrup, *The Common Peace: Participation and the Criminal Law in Seventeenth-Century England* (Cambridge: Cambridge UP, 1987).
5. *Earl of Oxford's Case* (1615) 1 Reports Ch. 1 at 6.
6. For further background on women's presence in the equity courts and the effect of equity on the legal rights of early modern women, see especially Mary Ritter Beard, *Woman as Force in History: A Study in Traditions and Realities* (New York: Macmillan, 1946) 136–44; Maria L. Cioni, *Women and Law in Elizabethan England with Particular Reference to the Court of Chancery* (Cambridge: Cambridge UP, 1982); Amy Louise Erickson, *Women and Property in Early Modern England* (London: Routledge, 1993); Eileen Spring, *Law, Land and Family: Aristocratic Inheritance in England, 1300–1800* (Chapel Hill: U of North Carolina P, 1993) ch. 4; and Stretton.
7. For further background on women's presence in the ecclesiastical courts, see especially Ralph A. Houlbrooke, *Church Courts and People during the English Reformation, 1520–1570* (Oxford: Oxford UP, 1979); Martin Ingram, *Church Courts, Sex and Marriage in England 1570–1640* (Cambridge: Cambridge UP, 1988); Sara Heller Mendelson, "'To shift for a cloak': Disorderly Women in the Church Courts", *Women & History: Voices of Early Modern England*, ed. Valerie Frith (Toronto: Coach House P, 1995) 3–10; and Chilton Latham Powell, *English Domestic Relations 1487–1653: A Study of Matrimony and Family Life in Theory and Practice as Revealed by the Literature, Law, and History of the Period* (New York: Columbia UP, 1917).
8. Many legal historians have considered the effects of custom on women's legal rights and the abrogation of these rights due to encroachments by the common law. No consensus exists, however, as to the overall effect of custom on early modern women's lives. For important discussions of custom, see Alice Clark, *Working Life of Women in the Seventeenth Century* (London: Routledge, 1982); Erickson, *Women and Property*; Doris Mary Parsons Stenton, *The English Woman in History* (London: Allen & Unwin, 1957); Charlotte Carmichael Stopes, *British Freewomen: Their Historical Privilege*, 3rd. ed. (London: S. Sonnenshein, 1907); Stretton ch. 7; and Barbara Todd, "Freebench and Free Enterprise: Widows and Their Property in Two Berkshire Villages", in *English Rural Society 1500–1800: Essays in Honour of Joan Thirsk*, eds. John Chartres and David Hey (Cambridge: Cambridge UP, 1990) 175–200.
9. Erickson, *Women and Property* 5.
10. Tim Stretton has observed that "women's rights were in flux in the sixteenth and seventeenth centuries largely because the jurisdictions that extended them rights were in flux". Stretton 232.
11. See Baker, *Introduction* ch. 12.
12. For further discussion of early modern legal education, see Baker, *Introduction* ch. 10.
13. For further background, see J. H. Baker, ed., *Judicial Records, Law Reports, and the Growth of Case Law* (Berlin: Duncker & Humblot, 1989); T. F. T. Plucknett, *Early English Legal Literature* (London: Seer, 1958) 19; and A. W. B. Simpson, *Legal Theory and Legal History: Essays on the Common Law* (London: Hambledon P, 1987) ch. 12.
14. Plucknett 19.
15. Simpson 277.
16. *The Lawes Resolutions* 2.

17. For discussions of women's petitioning activity, see Antonia Fraser, *The Weaker Vessel* (New York: Alfred A. Knopf, 1984) chs. 11–12; Patricia Higgins, "The Reactions of Women, with Special Reference to Women Petitioners", in *Politics, Religion and the English Civil War*, ed. Brian Manning (London: Edward Arnold, 1973) 179–221; Ellen A. MacArthur, "Women Petitioners of the Long Parliament", *English Historical Review* 24 (1909): 698–704; Ann Marie McEntee, "The [Un]civill-Sisterhood of Oranges and Lemons': Female Petitioners and Demonstrators, 1642–53", in *Pamphlet Wars: Prose in the English Revolution*, ed. James Holstun (London: Frank Cass, 1992) 92–111; Lois G. Schwoerer, "Women's Public Political Voice in England: 1640–1740", in *Women Writers and the Early Modern Political Tradition*, eds. Hilda L. Smith and Carole Pateman (Cambridge: Cambridge UP, 1998) 56–74; and Keith Thomas, "Women and the Civil War Sects", *Past & Present* 13 (1958): 42–62. See also the EMEW volume *Elinor James*, edited by Paula McDowell (2005).
18. J. Oldham, "On Pleading the Belly: A History of the Jury of Matrons", *Criminal Justice History* 6 (1985): 1–64.
19. Joseph R. Tanner, ed., *Tudor Constitutional Documents, A.D. 1485–1603, with an Historical Commentary*, 2d ed. (Cambridge: Cambridge UP, 1930) 123–4.
20. Pearl Hogreve, *Tudor Women: Commoners and Queens* (Ames: The Iowa State UP, 1975). See also Rose Graham, "The Civic Position of Women at Common law Before 1800", in *English Ecclesiastical Studies*, ed. Rose Graham (London: Society for the Propagation of Christian Knowledge, 1929) 360–77.
21. See Fraser 230–31.
22. Schwoerer 56–8.
23. Margaret J. M. Ezell, *The Patriarch's Wife: Literary Evidence and the History of the Family* (Chapel Hill: U of North Carolina P, 1987) ch.1; Barbara J. Harris, "Women and Politics in Early Tudor England", *The Historical Journal* 33.2 (1990): 259–81; Karl von den Steinen, "The Discovery of Women in Eighteenth-Century Political Life", in *The Women of England From Anglo-Saxon Times to the Present: Interpretive Bibliographical Essays*, ed. Barbara Kanner (Hambden, CT.: Archon Books, 1979) 229–58; and Merry E. Wiesner, "Women's Defense of their Public Role", in *Women in the Middle Ages and Renaissance: Literary and Historical Perspectives*, ed. Mary Beth Rose (Syracuse: Syracuse UP, 1986) 1–27.
24. For further discussion of wardship, see Leonare Marie Glanz, "The Legal Status of English Women Under the Early Stuart Kings and the Interregnum, 1603–1660", diss., Loyola U of Chicago, 1973, ch. 1.
25. Erickson, *Women and Property* ch. 9.
26. 5 Eliz., c. 4.
27. Amy M. Froide, "Marital Status as a Category", in *Singlewomen in the European Past, 1250–1800*, eds. Judith M. Bennett and Amy M. Froide (Philadelphia: U of Pennsylvania P, 1999) 236–69.
28. William Blackstone, *Commentaries on the Laws of England*, 4 vols. (London, 1765) 4: 208.
29. Ibid., 210. For background on the crime of rape, see Nazife Bashar, "Rape in England Between 1550 and 1700", in *The Sexual Dynamics of History: Men's Power, Women's Resistance*, ed. London Feminist History Group (London: Pluto P, 1983) 28–42.

30. *The Lawes Resolutions* 51.
31. Edward Cardwell, ed., *Synodalia: A Collection of Articles of Religion, Canons, and Proceedings of Convocations* (Oxford, 1842) 1: 142–54, 282–83, 286–87, 304–06.
32. C.H. Firth and C.H. and R.S. Rait (eds), *Acts and Ordinances of the Interregnum*, 3 vols. (London: 1911) 2: 715–18.
33. 26 Geo. II, c. 33. For further discussion of clandestine marriage, see John R. Gillis, "Conjugal Settlements: Resort to Clandestine and Common Law Marriage in England and Wales 1650–1850", in *Disputes and Settlements*, ed. John Bossy (Cambridge: Cambridge UP, 1983) 261–86; and R.B. Outhwaite, *Clandestine Marriage in England, 1500–1850* (London: Hambledon P, 1995). For further discussion of changing laws of marriage formation, see Chris Durston, "'Unhallowed Wedlocks': The Regulation of Marriage During the English Revolution", *Historical Journal* 31.1 (1988): 45–59; Ralph A. Houlbrooke, "The Making of Marriage in Mid-Tudor England: Evidence from the Records of Matrimonial Contract Litigation", *Journal of Family History* 10 (1985): 339–52; David Lemmings, "Marriage and the Law in the Eighteenth Century: Hardwicke's Marriage Act of 1753", *The Historical Journal* 39.2 (1996): 339–60; and Powell.
34. For further background on the history of divorce, see Powell ch. 3; and Lawrence Stone, *Road to Divorce: England 1530–1987* (Oxford: Oxford UP, 1990).
35. 1 Jac. I c. 11.
36. Firth and Rait 2: 387–89. For background on this statute, see Keith Thomas, "The Puritans and Adultery: The Act of 1650 Reconsidered", in *Puritans and Revolutionaries: Essays in Seventeenth-Century History Presented to Christopher Hill*, eds. Donald Pennington and Keith Thomas (Oxford: Oxford UP, 1978) 257–82.
37. 18 Eliz. I c. 3; 7 Jac. I c. 4.
38. 7 Jas. 1, c. 4.
39. 21 Jac. I, c. 7. For further background on the crime of infanticide, see Frances E. Dolan, *Dangerous Familiars: Representations of Domestic Crime in England 1550–1700* (Ithaca: Cornell UP, 1994) ch. IV; Peter C. Hoffer and N.E.H. Hull, *Murdering Mothers: Infanticide in England and New England, 1558–1803* (New York: New York UP, 1981); R.W. Malcolmson, "Infanticide in the Eighteenth Century", in *Crime in England 1550–1800*, ed. J.S. Cockburn (Princeton: Princeton UP, 1977) 187–209; J.A. Sharpe, *Crime in Early Modern England 1550–1750* (London: Longman, 1984) 49, 54–6, 60–2, 66, 109 and 170; and Keith Wrightson, "Infanticide in Earlier Seventeenth-Century England", *Local Population Studies* 15 (1975): 10–22.
40. *The Lawes Resolutions* 124–25.
41. Blackstone I: 430.
42. Only queens evaded the strictures of coverture, retaining certain proprietary rights and privileges of *femes sole*. For background on the legal status of queens, see Glanz ch. 4.
43. For further discussion of *Manby v. Scott*, see Susan Staves, *Married Women's Separate Property in England 1660–1833* (Cambridge: Cambridge UP, 1990) 164–65.
44. For a discussion of women acting as executrices and administratrices in the period, see especially Erickson, *Women and Property* chs. 9–10.
45. For a discussion of the increasing number of *femes covert* who made wills in

the seventeenth century, see Mary Prior, "Wives and Wills, 1558–1700", in *English Rural Society, 1500–1800: Essays in Honour of Joan Thirsk*, eds. J. Chartres and D. Hey (Cambridge: Cambridge UP, 1990) 201–25.

46. See Stretton.
47. For further background on women's roles in slander and defamation actions, see especially Laura Gowing, *Domestic Dangers: Women, Words, and Sex in Early Modern England* (Oxford: Oxford UP, 1996); Tim Meldrum, "A Woman's Court in London: Defamation at the Bishop of London's Consistory Court, 1700–1745", *The London Journal* 19 (1994): 1–22; Peter Rushton, "Women, Witchcraft and Slander in Early Modern England: Cases from the Church Courts of Durham, 1560–1675", *Northern History* 18 (1982): 116–32; and J.A. Sharpe, *Defamation and Sexual Slander in Early Modern England; The Church Courts of York* (York: Borthwick papers no. 58, 1980).
48. For further background on domestic violence, see Susan Amussen, "Being stirred to much unquietness: Violence and Domestic Violence in Early Modern England", *Journal of Women's History* 6 (1994): 70–89; Anna Clark, "Humanity or Justice: Wifebeating and the Law in the Eighteenth and Nineteenth Centuries", in *Regulating Womanhood: Historical Essays on Marriage, Motherhood and Sexuality*, ed. Carol Smart (London: Routledge, 1992) 187–206; Elizabeth Foyster, "Male Honour, Social Control and Wife Beating in Late Stuart England", *Transactions of the Royal Historical Society*, 6th series, 6 (1996): 215–24; and Margaret Hunt, "Wife Beating, Domesticity and Women's Independence in Eighteenth Century London", *Gender & History* 4.1 (Spring 1992): 10–33.
49. For further background on the crime of scolding, see especially Martin Ingram, "'Scolding Women Cucked or Washed': A Crisis in Gender Relations in Early Modern England", in *Women, Crime and the Courts*, eds. Jenny Kermode and Garthine Walker (Chapel Hill: U of North Carolina P, 1994) 48–80; and D. E. Underdown, "The Taming of the Scold: Enforcement of Patriarchal Authority in Early Modern England", in *Order and Disorder in Early Modern England*, eds. Anthony Fletcher and John Stevenson (Cambridge: Cambridge UP, 1985) 116–36.
50. For further background on petty treason, see Dolan ch. 1 and Shelly Gavigan, "Petit Treason in Eighteenth Century England: Women's Inequality Before the Law", *Canadian Journal of Women and the Law* 3 (1989): 335–73.
51. 21 Jac. I, c. 6.
52. 3 Will. & M., c. 9.
53. *The Lawes Resolutions* 6.
54. See, for example, the works of Cioni, Erickson, Finn, Gowing, Meldrum, Spring, Staves and Stretton cited in the References.
55. For further discussion of these devices, see especially Lloyd Bonfield, *Marriage Settlements, 1601–1740: The Adoption of the Strict Settlement* (Cambridge: Cambridge UP, 1983); Lloyd Bonfield, "Affective Families, Open Elites, and Strict Family Settlements in Early Modern England", *English History Review* 2nd ser. 39 (1986): 355–70; Cioni ch. IV; Erickson, *Women and Property*, especially 103–13, 122–4, 136–7, 183–4 and 200–1; H. J. Habbakuk, "Marriage Settlements in the Eighteenth Century", *Transactions of the Royal Historical Society* 4th ser. 32 (1950): 15–30; Spring ch. 5; and Staves, *Married Women's Separate Property*.
56. Erickson, *Women and Property* 130, 143.

57. See Susan Staves, "Pin Money", *Studies in Eighteenth-Century Culture* 14 (1985): 37–77.
58. *The Lawes Resolutions* 232.
59. For further information on the legal and economic status of widows, see Cioni ch. V; Sandra Dunster, "An Independent Life? Nottingham Widows, 1594–1650, *Transactions of the Thoroton Society of Nottinghamshire* XCV (1991): 29–37; Erickson, *Women and Property* chs. 9–12 and Erickson, "Property and Widowhood in England 1660–1840", in *Widowhood in Medieval and Early Modern Europe* eds. Sandra Cavallo and Lyndan Warner (London: Longman, 1999) 145–63; Pamela Sharpe, "Literally Spinsters: A New Interpretation of Local Economy and Demography in Colyton in the Seventeenth and Eighteenth Centuries", *The Economic History Review* 44.1 (Feb., 1991): 46–65; and Todd, "Freebench and Free Enterprise".
60. 27 Hen. VIII c. 10.
61. See Spring, *Law, Land and Family* ch. 4.
62. For further background on freebench, see J.H. Bettey, "Manorial Custom and Widow's Estate", *Archives* 20 (1992): 208–16; Stretton ch. 7; and Todd, "Freebench and Free Enterprise".
63. Erickson, *Women and Property* 178.
64. 22 Ca. II c. 10; 23 Ca. II c. 10.
65. For a more comprehensive analysis of women's changing legal position in the early modern period, see Stretton ch. 9.
66. See *The National Union Catalog Pre-1956 Imprints*, 754 vols. (London: Mansell, 1978) 319: 342; A.W. Pollard, G.R. Redgrave et. al., *A Short-Title Catalogue of Books Printed in England, Scotland & Ireland and of English Books Printed Abroad, 1475–1600*, 2d ed. (London: Bibliographical Society, 1976–91) 335; and Charles A. Stonehill, Andrew Block and H. Winthrop Stonehill, *Anonyma and Psudonyma*, 2d. ed., 4 vols. (London, 1927) 2: 1259. For biographical information about Sir John Doddridge, see Sir Leslie Stephen and Sir Sidney Lee, *The Dictionary of National Biography*, 66 vols. (Oxford: Oxford UP, 1921–22) 5: 1062–63.
67. W.R. Prest, "The Law and Women's Rights in Early Modern England", *The Seventeenth Century* 6 (1991): 173.
68. Leslie F. Maxwell, *A Bibliography of English Laws to 1650*, 6 vols. (London: Sweet & Maxwell, 1925) 1: 319.
69. Prest 174.
70. Prest 172–74.
71. Henry R. Plomer, *A Dictionary of the Booksellers and Printers Who Were At Work in England, Scotland and Ireland From 1641 to 1667* (London, 1907) 131–32. Biographical information about More derives from this source.
72. Prest 175.
73. Prest 180.
74. Prest 181.
75. Prest 181.
76. Prest n. 62.
77. In fact, scholars have assumed male authorship. See, for example, Todd, "'To be some body'" n.1.
78. Lance E. Dickson in his introduction to the Rothman Reprints edition of this treatise also emphasizes this fact. See *A Treatise of Feme Coverts: Or the Lady's Law*, ed. Lance E. Dickson (South Hackensack, N.J.: Rothman Reprints, 1974) vii.

79. Biographical information about Elizabeth and Richard Nutt and R. Gosling derives primarily from Anne Crawford, ed., et. al., *The Europa Biographical Dictionary of British Women* (London: Europa, 1983) 309; H.R. Plomer, *A Dictionary of the Printers and Booksellers Who Were at Work in England, Scotland and Ireland from 1668–1725* (Oxford: Oxford UP, 1922) 130, 221–22; and H.R. Plomer, *A Dictionary of the Printers and Booksellers Who Were at Work in England, Scotland and Ireland from 1726 to 1775* (Oxford: Oxford UP, 1932) 106, 184.
80. Biographical information about B. and H. Lintot derives from Plomer, *A Dictionary ... from 1668–1725* 189–90.
81. Erickson, *Women and Property* 21.
82. I am indebted to the late Janice Thaddeus for this attribution and also for providing me with the reference to Anna Hopkins' letter. My thanks as well to Amy Louise Erickson and Margaret Hunt for putting me in contact with Janice Thaddeus. For an earlier, tentative attribution of the text to Chapone, see Virginia Blain, Patricia Clements and Isobel Grundy, eds., *The Feminist Companion to Literature in English* (New Haven: Yale UP, 1990) 196.
83. Ballard Manuscripts, Bodleian Library (43, f. 146; December 14, 1741).
84. See Blain 196. Biographical information about Chapone derives from this source.
85. Schwoerer 60–1.
86. See Schwoerer.
87. Astell's *Some Reflection* and Chudleigh's *Female Advocate* are reprinted in a forthcoming EMEW volume, *Texts from the Querelle: 1641–1701*, II, edited by Laura L. Runge.
88. Reprinted in Ezell 192.
89. Todd, "'To be some body'" 345, n. 7.
90. Todd, "'To be some body'" 345.
91. For more detailed discussions of these cases and some of the sources from which the author learned of these cases, see Todd, "'To be some body'" 344–48.
92. *Gentleman's Magazine* (May–June, 1735) 5: 241–242, 284. This source was obtained from Todd, "'To be some body'" 343.
93. See Erickson, "Property and Widowhood."
94. Plomer, *A Dictionary of the Printers and Booksellers ... from 1668–1725* 300.
95. 4 Geo. II, cap. 26.

References

[This list includes works cited and suggestions for further reading. Entries preceded by an asterisk are particularly valuable works for further study.]

STC 7437 [*Lawes Resolutions*]; *ESTC* T72208 [*Treatise*]; *ESTC* T4343 [*Hardships*]; *ESTC* T93339 [*Baron*]

Amussen, Susan (1994), "'Being stirred to much unquietness': Violence and Domestic Violence in Early Modern England", *Journal of Women's History* 6: 70–89

Atherley, Edmond Gibson (1813), *A Practical Treatise on the Law of Marriage and Other Family Settlements*, London

*Baker, J.H. (1990), *An Introduction to English Legal History*, 3rd edn, London: Butterworths

Baker, J.H. (ed.), (1989), *Judicial Records, Law Reports, and the Growth of Case Law*, Berlin: Duncker & Humblot

Barrett-Lennard, Thomas (1883), *The Position in Law of Women*, London

Bashar, Nazife (1983), "Rape in England Between 1550 and 1700", in *The Sexual Dynamics of History: Men's Power, Women's Resistance*, London Feminist History Group (eds), London: Pluto Press, 28–42

Beard, Mary Ritter (1946), *Woman as Force in History: A Study in Traditions and Realities*, New York: Macmillan

Bennett, Judith M. and Amy M. Froide (1999), *Singlewomen in the European Past, 1250–1800*, Philadelphia: University of Pennsylvania Press

Bettey, J.H (1992), "Manorial Custom and Widow's Estate", *Archives* 20: 208–16

Blackstone, William (1765), *Commentaries on the Laws of England*, 4 vols, London

Blaine, Virginia, Patricia Clements and Isobel Grundy (eds), (1990), *The Feminist Companion to Literature in English*, New Haven: Yale University Press

Blum, Carol (1996), "Of Women and the Land: Legitimizing Husbandry", in *Early Modern Conceptions of Property*, John Brewer and Susan Staves (eds), London: Routledge, 161–69

Bonfield, Lloyd (1986), "Affective Families, Open Elites, and Strict Family Settlements in Early Modern England", *Economic History Review*, 2nd ser. 39: 355–70

——— (1983), "Marriage, Property, and the Affective Family", *Law and History Review* I: 297–312

*——— (1983), *Marriage Settlements, 1601–1740: The Adoption of the Strict Settlement*, Cambridge: Cambridge University Press

——— (1986), "Normative Rules and Property Transmission: Reflections on the Link Between Marriage and Inheritance in Early Modern England", in *The World We Have Gained*, L. Bonfield, R.M. Smith and K. Wrightson (eds), Oxford: Oxford University Press, 155–76

Brydall, J. (1703), *Lex Spuriorum; or, Law relating to Bastardy*, London

Bunny, Edmund (1610), *Of Divorce for Adultery and Marrying Again*, Oxford

Campbell, Ruth (1984), "Sentence of Death by Burning for Women", *Journal of Legal History* 5.1 (May): 44–59

Cardwell, Edward (ed.), (1842), *Synodolia: A Collection of Articles of Religion, Canons, and Proceedings of Convocations*, Oxford

*Chapman, A., Beatrice Wallis and Mary Wallis Chapman (1909), *The Status of Women Under the English Law*, London: Routledge

*Cioni, Maria L. (1985), *Women and Law in Elizabethan England With Particular Reference to the Court of Chancery*, New York: Garland

*Clark, Alice (1982), *Working Life of Women in the Seventeenth Century*, London: Routledge

Clark, Anna (1992), "Humanity or Justice? Wifebeating and the Law in the Eighteenth and Nineteenth Centuries", in *Regulating Womanhood: Historical Essays on Marriage, Motherhood and Sexuality*, Carol Smart (ed.), London: Routledge, 187–206

Clay, Christopher (1968), "Marriage, Inheritance, and the Rise of Large Estates", *Economic History Review*, 2nd ser. 21: 503–18

——— (1981) "Property, Settlement, Financial Provisions for the Family, and the

Sale of Land by the Great Land Owners, 1660–1790", *Journal of British Studies* 21: 18–38
Cleveland, Arthur Rackham (1987), *Women Under the English Law From the Landing of the Saxons to the Present Time*, Littleton, CO: F.B. Rothman
Coke, Sir Edward (1628–44), *The Institutes of the Laws of England*, London
Crawford, Anne (ed.) et al. (1983), *The Europa Biographical Dictionary of British Women*, London: Europa
*Dolan, Frances E. (1994), *Dangerous Familiars: Representations of Domestic Crime in England 1550–1700*, Ithaca: Cornell University Press
Dunster, Sandra (1991), "An Independent Life? Nottingham Widows, 1594–1650", in *Transactions of the Thoroton Society of Nottinghamshire* XCV: 29–37
Durston, Chris (1988), "'Unhallowed Wedlocks': The Regulation of Marriage During the English Revolution", *Historical Journal* 31.1: 45–59
Erickson, Amy Louise (1999), "Property and Widowhood in England 1660–1840", in *Widowhood in Medieval and Early Modern Europe*, Lyndan Warner and Sandra Cavallo (eds), London: Longman, 145–63
*——— (1993), *Women and Property in Early Modern England*, London: Routledge
Ezell, Margaret J.M. (1987), *The Patriarch's Wife: Literary Evidence and the History of the Family*, Chapel Hill: University of North Carolina Press
Finn, Margot (1996), "Women, Consumption and Coverture in England, c.1760–1860", *Historical Journal* 39.3: 703–22
Firth, C.H. and R.S. Rait (eds) (1911), *Acts and Ordinances of the Interregnum*, 3 vols, London
Fitz, L. (1980), "What Says the Married Woman? Marriage Theory and Feminism in the English Renaissance", *Mosaic* 13: 1–22
Foyster, Elizabeth (1993), "A Laughing Matter? Marital Discord and Gender Control in Seventeenth-Century England", *Rural History* 4: 5–21
——— (1996), "Male Honour, Social Control and Wife Beating in Late Stuart England", in *Transactions of the Royal Historical Society*, 6th ser., 6: 215–24
Fraser, Antonia (1984), *The Weaker Vessel: Women's Lot in Seventeenth Century England*, New York: Knopf
Froide, Amy M. (1999), "Marital Status as a Category", in *Singlewomen in the European Past, 1250–1800*, Judith M. Bennett and Amy M. Froide (eds), Philadelphia: University of Pennsylvania Press, 236–69
Gavigan, Shelly A.M. (1989–1990), "Petit Treason in Eighteenth Century England: Women's Inequality Before the Law", *Canadian Journal of Women and the Law* 3: 335–73
Gillis, John R. (1983), "Conjugal Settlements: Resort to Clandestine and Common Law Marriage in England and Wales 1650–1850", *Disputes and Settlements*, John Bossy (ed.), Cambridge: Cambridge University Press, 261–86
*Glanz, Leonare Marie (1973), "The Legal Status of English Women Under the Early Stuart Kings and the Interregnum, 1603–1660", Diss. Loyola University of Chicago
*Goody, Jack, Joan Thirsk and E.P. Thompson (1976), *Family and Inheritance: Rural Society in Western Europe, 1200–1800*, Cambridge: Cambridge University Press
*Gowing, Laura (1996), *Domestic Dangers: Women, Words, and Sex in Early Modern London,* Oxford: Oxford University Press
——— (1993), "Gender and the Language of Insult in Early Modern London", *History Workshop Journal* 35: 1–21
Graham, Rose (1929), "The Civic Position of Women at Common Law Before

1800", in *English Ecclesiastical Studies*, Rose Graham (ed.), London: Society for the Propagation of Christian Knowledge, 360–77

*Greenberg, Janelle (1975), "The Legal Status of the English Woman in Early Eighteenth Century Common Law and Equity", *Studies in Eighteenth Century Culture* 4: 171–81

Habbakuk, H.J. (1950), "Marriage Settlements in the Eighteenth Century", in *Transactions of the Royal Historical Society*, 4th ser. 32, 15–30

Harris, Barbara J. (1990), "Women and Politics in Early Tudor England", *The Historical Journal* 33.2: 259–81

Herrup, Cynthia (1987), *The Common Peace: Participation and the Criminal Law in Seventeenth-Century England*, Cambridge: Cambridge University Press

Higgins, Patricia (1973), "The Reaction of Women, with Special Reference to Women Petitioners", in *Politics, Religion and the English Civil War*, Brian Manning (ed.), London: Edward Arnold, 179–221

Hoffer, Peter C. and N.E.H. Hull (1981), *Murdering Mothers: Infanticide in England and New England, 1558–1803*, New York: New York University Press

Hogrefe, Pearl (1972), "The Legal Rights of Tudor Women and their Circumvention by Men and Women", *Sixteenth Century Journal* 3: 97–105

*——— (1975), *Tudor Women: Commoners and Queens*, Ames: Iowa State University Press

Holdsworth, W.S. (1923), *A History of English Law*, 3rd edn, London: Methuen

Horwitz, Henry (1984), "Testamentary Practice, Family Strategies, and the Last Phases of the Custom of London", *Law and History Review* 2: 223–39

*Houlbrooke, Ralph A. (1979), *Church Courts and the People During the English Reformation 1520–1570*, Oxford: Oxford University Press

——— (1985), "The Making of Marriage in Mid-Tudor England: Evidence from the Records of Matrimonial Contract Litigation," *Journal of Family History* 10: 339–52

——— (1986), "Women's Social Life and Common Action in England from the Fifteenth Century to the Eve of the Civil War", *Continuity and Change* 1: 176–83

Howard, George Elliott (1903), *A History of Matrimonial Institutions*, 3 vols, Chicago: University of Chicago Press

Hunt, Margaret (1992), "Wife Beating, Domesticity and Women's Independence in Eighteenth Century London", *Gender & History* 4.1 (Spring): 10–33

*Ingram, Martin (1988), *Church Courts, Sex and Marriage in England 1570–1640*, Cambridge: Cambridge University Press, 1988

——— (1994), "'Scolding Women Cucked or Washed': A Crisis in Gender Relations in Early Modern England", in *Women, Crime and the Courts*, Jenny Kermode and Garthine Walker (eds), Chapel Hill: University of North Carolina Press, 48–80

Jordan, Constance (1987), "Woman's Rule in Sixteenth-Century British Political Thought", *Renaissance Quarterly* XL.3 (Autumn): 411–51

Kanowitz, Leo (1969), *Women and the Law: The Unfinished Revolution*, Albuquerque: University of New Mexico Press

Kenny, Courtney Stanhope (1879), *The History of the Law of England as to the Effects of Marriage on Property and on a Wife's Legal Capacity*, London: Reeves & Turner

Laslett, Peter (1977), *Family Life and Illicit Love in Earlier Generations*, Cambridge: Cambridge University Press

Law Companion; containing an Extract from all the Laws relative to Domestic Life, etc.(1795), 8 vols, London
Lawrence, Basil Edwin, *The History of the Laws Affecting the Property of Married Women in England*, London, 1884
Laws Respecting Women, As They Regard Their Natural Rights Or Their Connections and Conduct; Also the Obligations of Parent and Child, and the Condition of Minors (1777), 8 vols, London
Lemmings, David (1996), "Marriage and the Law in the Eighteenth Century: Hardwicke's Marriage Act of 1753", *Historical Journal* 39.2: 339–60
MacArthur, Ellen A. (1909), "Women Petitioners of the Long Parliament", *English Historical Review* 24: 698–704
Malcolmson, R.W. (1977), "Infanticide in the Eighteenth Century", in *Crime in England 1550–1800*, J.S. Cockburn (ed.), Princeton: Princeton University Press, 187–209
Maxwell, Leslie F. (1925), *A Bibliography of English Laws to 1650*, 6 vols, London: Sweet & Maxwell
McEntee, Ann Marie (1992), "'The [Un]civill-Sisterhood of Oranges and Lemons': Female Petitioners and Demonstrators, 1642–53", in *Pamphlet Wars: Prose in the English Revolution*, James Holstun (ed.), London: Frank Cass, 92–111
McIntyre, Bronwyn (1972), "Legal Attitudes Towards Women in England 1558–1648", Diss., New Brunswick
Meldrum, Tim (1994), "A Woman's Court in London: Defamation at the Bishop of London's Consistory Court, 1700–1745", *London Journal* 19: 1–22
Mendelson, Sara Heller (1995), "'To shift for a cloak': Disorderly Women in the Church Courts", in *Women & History: Voices of Early Modern England*, Valerie Firth (ed.), Toronto: Coach House P, 3–10
The National Union Catalog Pre-1956 Imprints (1978), 754 vols, London: Mansell
O'Donovan, Katherine (1979), "The Male Appendage – Legal Definitions of Women", in *Fit Work for Women*, Sandra Burman (ed.), London: Croom Helm for Oxford University Women's Studies Committee, 134–52
Okin, Susan Moller (1983–4), "Patriarchy and Married Women's Property in England: Questions on Some Current Views", *Eighteenth Century Studies*, 17.2 (Winter): 121–38
Oldham, J. (1985), "On Pleading the Belly: A History of the Jury of Matrons", *Criminal Justice History* 6: 1–64
Outhwaite, Brian (1995), *Clandestine Marriage in England, 1500–1850*, London: Hambledon Press
——— (1986), "Marriage as Business: Opinions on the Rise in Aristocratic Bridal Portions in Early Modern England", in *Business Life and Public Policy*, N. McKendrick and R.B. Outhwaite (eds), Cambridge: Cambridge University Press, 21–37
Plomer, Henry R. (1907) *A Dictionary of the Printers and Booksellers Who Were at Work in England, Scotland and Ireland From 1641 to 1667*, London
——— (1922), *A Dictionary of the Printers and Booksellers Who Were at Work in England, Scotland and Ireland from 1668 to 1725*, Oxford: Oxford University Press
——— (1932), *A Dictionary of the Printers and Booksellers Who Were at Work in England, Scotland and Ireland from 1726 to 1775*, Oxford: Oxford University Press
Plucknett, T.F.T. (1958), *Early English Legal Literature*, London: Seer
Pollard, A.W. and G.R. Redgrave et al. (1976–91), *A Short-Title Catalogue of*

Books Printed in England, Scotland & Ireland and of English Books Printed Abroad, 1475–1600, 2nd edn, London: Bibliographical Society

*Powell, Chilton Latham (1927), *English Domestic Relations 1487–1653: A Study of Matrimony and Family Life in Theory and Practice as Revealed by the Literature, Law, and History of the Period*, New York: Columbia University Press

*Prest, W.R. (1991), "The Law and Women's Rights in Early Modern England", *Seventeenth Century* 6: 169–98

Prior, Mary (1990), "Wives and Wills, 1558–1700", in *English Rural Society, 1500–1800: Essays In Honour of Joan Thirsk*, John Chartres and David Hey (eds), Cambridge: Cambridge University Press, 201–25

*Quaife, G.R. (1979), *Wanton Wenches and Wayward Wives: Peasants and Illicit Sex in Early Seventeenth Century England*, London: Croom Helm

Rushton, Peter (1982), "Women, Witchcraft and Slander in Early Modern England: Cases From the Church Courts of Durham, 1560–1675", *Northern History* 18: 116–32

*Salmon, Marylynn (1986), *Women and the Law of Property*, Chapel Hill: University of North Carolina Press

Schwoerer, Lois G. (1998), "Women's Public Political Voice in England: 1640–1740", in *Women Writers and the Early Modern Political Tradition*, Hilda L. Smith and Carole Pateman (eds), Cambridge: Cambridge University Press, 56–74, 179–221

*Sharpe, J.A. (1984), *Crime in Early Modern England 1550–1750*, London: Longman

——— (1980), *Defamation and Sexual Slander in Early Modern England: The Church Courts at York*, York: Borthwick papers no. 58

——— (1981), "Domestic Homicide in Early Modern England", *Historical Journal* 24.1: 29–48

Sharpe, Pamela (1991), "Literally Spinsters: A New Interpretation of Local Economy and Demography in Colyton in the Seventeenth and Eighteenth Centuries", *The Economic History Review* 44.1 (February): 46–65

Simpson, W.B. (1987), *Legal Theory and Legal History: Essays on the Common Law*, London: The Hambledon Press

*Spring, Eileen (1983), "The Family, Strict Settlement, and the Historian", *Canadian Journal of History* 18: 379–98

——— (1990), "The Heiress-at-law: English Real Property Law From a New Point of View", *Law and History Review* 8: 273–96

——— (1993), *Law, Land and Family: Aristocratic Inheritance in England, 1300–1800,* Chapel Hill: University of North Carolina Press

*Staves, Susan (1990), *Married Women's Separate Property in England 1660–1833*, Cambridge, MA: Harvard University Press

——— (1985), "Pin Money", *Studies in Eighteenth-Century Culture* 14: 37–77

*——— (1979), *Players' Scepters: Fictions of Authority in the Restoration*, Lincoln: University of Nebraska Press

——— (1996), "Resentment or Resignation? Dividing the Spoils Among Daughters and Younger Sons", in *Early Modern Conceptions of Property*, John Brewer and Susan Staves (eds), London: Routledge, 194–218

Stephen, Sir Leslie and Sir Sidney Lee (1921–22), *The Dictionary of National Biography*, 66 vols, Oxford: Oxford University Press

*Stone, Lawrence (1977), *The Family, Sex and Marriage in England 1500–1800*, New York: Harper & Row,

——— (1990), *Road to Divorce: England 1530–1987*, Oxford: Oxford University Press
Stonehill, Charles A, Andrew Block, H. Winthrop Stonehill (1927), *Anonyma and Psudonyma*, 2nd edn, 4 vols, London
Stopes, Charlotte Carmichael (1907), *British Freewomen: Their Historical Privilege*, 3rd edn, London: S. Sonnenshein
*Stretton, Tim (1998), *Women Waging Law in Elizabethan England*, Cambridge: Cambridge University Press
Swinburne, Henry (1686), *A Treatise of Spousals or Matrimonial Contracts*, London
Tanner, Joseph R. (ed.) (1930), *Tudor Constitutional Documents, A.D. 1485–1603, with an Historical Commentary*, 2nd edn, Cambridge: Cambridge University Press
Thomas, Keith (1978), "The Puritans and Adultery: The Act of 1650 Reconsidered", in *Puritans and Revolutionaries: Essays in Seventeenth Century History Presented to Christopher Hill*, Donald Pennington and Keith Thomas (eds), Oxford: Oxford University Press, 257–82
——— (1958), "Women and the Civil War Sects", *Past & Present* 13: 42–62
Todd, Barbara (1990), "Freebench and Free Enterprise: Widows and Their Property in Two Berkshire Villages", in *English Rural Society, 1500–1800: Essays in Honour of Joan Thirsk*, John Chartres and David Hey (eds), Cambridge: Cambridge University Press, 175–200
*——— (1998), "'To be some body': Married Women and *The Hardships of the English Laws*", in *Women Writers and the Early Modern Political Tradition*, Hilda L. Smith and Carole Pateman (eds), Cambridge: Cambridge University Press, 343–61
A Treatise of Feme Coverts: Or the Lady's Law (1974), Lance E. Dickson (ed.), South Hackensack, NJ: Rothman Reprints
Underdown, D.E. (1985), "The Taming of the Scold: Enforcement of Patriarchal Authority in Early Modern England", in *Order and Disorder in Early Modern England*, Anthony Fletcher and John Stevenson (eds), Cambridge: Cambridge University Press, 116–36
Van Caenegem, R.C. (1973), *The Birth of the English Common Law*, Cambridge: Cambridge University Press
Von Den Steinen, Karl (1979), "The Discovery of Women in Eighteenth-Century English Political Life", in *The Women of England From Anglo-Saxon Times to the Present: Interpretive Bibliographical Essays*, Barbara Kanner (ed.), Hamden, CT: Archon, 229–58
Wiesner, Merry E. (1986), "Women's Defense of their Public Role", in *Women in the Middle Ages and Renaissance: Literary Historical Perspectives*, Mary Beth Rose (ed.), Syracuse: Syracuse University Press, 1–27
Wrightson, Keith (1975), "Infanticide in Earlier Seventeenth-Century England", *Local Population Studies* 15: 10–22

LYNNE A. GREENBERG

The Lawes Resolutions of Womens Rights (*STC* 7437) is reproduced, by permission, from the copy at The British Library (shelfmark 1481.b.46). The text block of the original measures 150 × 85mm.

The following pages are mis-numbered in the original: 22, 23, 27, 92, 138, 141, 168, 169, 305 and 308.

Because the following pages were blotted or bled through, they have been substituted, by permission, from the copy at the Bodleian Library, University of Oxford (shelfmark Douce WW 110): 74, 87, 91, 95, 149, 217, 218, 233, 258, 262, 293–95, 308, 317, 329, 393.

Readings where the copy is blotted or bled through:

4.21	reafon
23.22	againft
26.26	connect
185.18	Joynture
197.29	them
197.30	ten pound
214.36	battery
218.4	exigent
232.5	is
232.6	say, cleane
233.31	upon a plea of
233.32	A speciall verdict was found
233.33	the Defendant had recovered
236.1	forfeiture
236.4	of the Realme:
236.5	dyed intestate
236.6	pious uses, he might seise
236.8	intestate
243.3	day,
243.4	Terminer
243.5	6.Edw.6.fol.76.
244.3	part
244.4	diftraine
244.5	recover*
245.4	the
245.5	feofees
247.6	widow
247.7	Gardine in
248.6	Fitzherbert
248.7	se maritandum
251.7	againft
252.7	without any fuch faying
253.12	words
291.31	of necessity
291.32	upon the issue, to whom for all that the widdow shall not
291.33	bee attendant, till hee have recontinued the estate tayle,
291.34	If the Tenant whilst hee li-
291.35	ved held of his Lord by fealty, and a nag of forty shillings
293.37	awarded
299.32	how a wo-
299.33	loft his land
305.15	Of Wafte
308.2	the Writ
308.3	Forreftor
308.4	boscum
311.5	lease for life, and dye, and his
311.6	reversion to B.
317.2	or he, or they,
317.3	haue
317.4	recoueries, where the
318.2	may enter
318.3	minde that this
318.4	litterall interpretation
393.1	factun recensest, and with Hue and Cry

THE LAVVES RESOLVTIONS OF WOMENS RIGHTS:

OR,

THE LAVVES PROVISION for WOEMEN.

A Methodicall Collection of such Statutes *and Customes, with the Cases, Opinions,* Arguments and points of Learning in the LAVV, as doe properly concerne WOMEN.

Together with a compendious Table, whereby the chiefe matters in this BOOKE contained, *may be the more readily found.*

LONDON;
Printed by the assignes of IOHN MORE *Esq.*
and are to be sold by IOHN GROVE, at his Shop neere the *Rowles* in *Chancery-Lane*, over against the *Sixe-Clerkes Office.*
1632.

A PREFACE TO THE READER.

VArious are the Conceipts and Judgements of Men: Nature teacheth each to preferre his Owne; Hence it is, that the number of Bookes multiply, insomuch, that, according to the Wise-man; Thereof, is no end.

To expect new Matter, were to give the old Proverb the Lie; Nihil jam dictum,&c. *It's enough, if what was before, be now so changed by Me-*

 thod

thod and Application, that it ſhewes as new, and becomes more ready for Uſe. Habit and Apparell alter the Shape, ſometimes the Conditions of Men. An old Theame in a new dreſſe ingenuouſly contrived makes the Compoſer an Author. Why then ſhould this Booke bluſh to ſhew it ſelfe? or doubt to bee ſervant to the Printer, whoſe Maſter neverthelеſſe it is?

To give it as abſolute, or free from faults, were to make it more then the Worke of Man, whoſe incident is Error: Such as it hath, are rather accidentall then originall, and may bee fairly excuſed; Not to inſiſt, That the Author's dead, That it was long ſince collected, Alteration of ſome Caſes by Moderne Statutes, Or this the firſt Impreſſion. Goodneſſe is the Parent of Confidence; The Act is crowned by the

the End, which was this, A publique Advantage and peculiar Service to that Sexe *generally beloved, and by the Author had in venerable estimation. To implore their Patronage, and prevaile, were to guard this* Booke *beyond Opposition. The strong neither needs nor desires a Champion; Meeknes protects it selfe: What here you finde reall and perfect, therefore accept; It will subsist; Remit the rest, the rather for that nor the* Tract, *nor* This *is peremptory, But onely proposed for your favorable sense and Approbation.*

I. L.

TO
THE READER.

BY whom this following DISCOVRSE was Composed I certainly know not, neither by what inducement the Authors paines therein was procured: But if for no other consideration then to make this scattered part of Learning, in the great Volumes of the Common-Law-Bookes, and there darkly described, to be one entyre body, and more ready, and clearer to the view of the Reader, his love deserves thanks, and his endeavours kinde acceptance. The VVorke hath beene carefully, and with much labour and diligence collected: The Theame, as the ſubject, is, *The Lawes Reſolutions of Womens Rights*; which comprehends all our Lawes concerning VVomen, either Children in government or nurture of their Parents or Gardians, Mayds, VVives, and VVidowes, and their goods, inheritances, and other eſtates. It is profitable and uſefull Learning to be well knowne. I am ſure it will pleaſe all them whoſe actions are guided *virtutis amore*, and offend none but thoſe ill manners, who can have no other antidote made them, then *formidine pœnæ*: for it ſets forth Law, and Iuſtice, things honeſt, and things convenient. I had ſuch a good conceit of the matter and frame of the

whole

whole Worke, that having a Copie thereof lying by me somtimes, within the Compasse of a Lent vacation, I pluckt my intentions from my own course of Studies, and cast them upon this. And those *vitia Scriptoris*, and *Authoris*, which I found, I amended, and haue added many reasons, opinions, Cases and resolutions of Cases to the Authors store: wherfore those oversights or neglects that thou maist impose upon the Printer or mee, (which I suppose wil be some (if not many) thou shalt have thanks to supply or amend, which is all I expected, and more then the Author, as I beleeve, had (or now being dead can receive:) and perhaps thou maist have a better reward; for the old Adage is true, *pretium non vile laboris.*

Vale,

T. E.

THE TABLE.

Mar-

THE TABLE.

Wooing

The end of the TABLE.

THE

THE WOMANS LAWIER.

SECT. I.

All Law, saith Iustinian in his Imperiall institutions, belongeth to persons, to things, or to actions: which division I acknowledge to bee good: and so in his method of the Civil Law, doth a Doctor and very learned man, Conradus Lagus, yet the same Lagus saith, it is too strait for his purpose, and therefore not feeling himselfe at ease in so narrow a distribution, to drive the formes of Civill Law to certaine heads, according to their materiall varieties, hee confesseth hee is compelled to constitute a pluralitie of Law members more then the very Law setteth down as appeareth in the 2. Part of his Method the 2. Chapter, yet a curious Caviler (I perceive) might find in Iustinians partition a very great redundance rather then any defect, for Res is a transcendente, comprehending actions, persons, and what not. And actions in the widest signification seeme alone to bee the theame and right subject matter of Lawes and all Humane Constitutions: as for persons they are so many, and so differing, that I thinke there is no use, Custome, Injunction or decree, but it appertaineth to some person, and that in some peculiarity of difference, either in state, age, sex, function, profession, merit, or some other like severall regard, so that in mine opinion, Law might bee dispersed into apt titles of this personall difference, in such sort as both Students, might come to the easier knowledge: the one of their learning generall, and the other of their particular duty. I though I bee farre unable to produce a perfect method of the Lawes of England, as Lagus following his owne artificiall project hath framed an excellent Deliniation of the Lawes of Rome, and though I bee unworthy to have the Marshalling of the titles of Lawe to bring all matter cohering under them, yet I will make a little assay what I am able to doe if I were put to it in a popular kind of instruction: following a frame by distinction of persons, chasing the primary distribution of them made before the World was seven daies old, *Masculum & Fœminam fecit eos*, of which division because the part that wee say hath least judgement and discretion to bee a Law unto it selfe, (*Women onely Women*) they have nothing to do in constituting Lawes, or consenting to them, in interpreting of Lawes, or in hearing them interpreted at lectures, leets or charges, and yet they stand strictly tyed to mens establishments, little or nothing excused by ignorance, mee thinkes it were pitty and impiety any longer to hold from them such Customes, Lawes, and Statutes, as are in a maner, proper, or principally belonging unto them: Laying aside therefore these titles which include onely the masculine, as Bishop, Abbot, Prior, Monke, Deane and Chapter, Viscount, Coroner, together with those which bee common to both kinds, as Hereticke, Traitour, Homicide, Felon, Laron, Paricide, Cutpurse, Rogue, with Feoffor, Feoffee, Donor, Donee, Vendor, Vendee, Recognisor,

Recognisée, &c. I will in this Treaty with as little tedious-nesse as I can, handle that part of the English Lawe, which containeth the immunities, advantages, interests, and duties of women, not regarding so much to satisfie the déep learned or searchers for subtility, as woman kind, to whom I am a thankfull debter by nature.

SECT. II.

The Creation of Man and Woman.

GOd the first day when hée created the World made the matter of it, separating light from darkenesse: the second day hée placed the Firmament which hée called Heaven, betwixt the waters above the Firmament and the waters under the Firmament: the third day hée segregated the waters under the Firmament into one place, calling the waters Seas, and the dry land Earth, which hée commanded to bring forth fructifying herbes, plants and trees: the fourth day hée made the Sun, the Moone and the Stares in the Firmament, to bée for Signes, Seasons, Daies and Yeres, and to give light upon the earth: the fift day he made by his Word the Fishes of the Sea, Whales and every fethered foule of the ayre, commanding them to increase: the sixt day he made Cattle, créeping things, the beasts of the Earth: and now having made all things that should be néedfull for them, hée created Man, Male and Female made he them, Bidding them multiply and replenish the Earth, & take the joynt soveraigntie over the Fishes of the Sea, the Foules of the Ayre, and over all Beasts moving upon the Earth, Genesis 1.

In the second Chapter Moses declareth and exprefseth the Creation of Women, which word in good sense, signifieth not the woe of Man as some affirme, but with Man: For so in our hasty pronouncing wee turne the preposition with to woe, or wee, oftentimes: and so shee was ordained to bee with man as a helpe, & a companion, because God saw it was not good that Man should bee alone. Then when God brought Woman to Man to bee named by him, hee found straight way that shee was bone of his bones, flesh of his flesh, giving her a name, testifying shee was taken out of Man, and he pronounced that for her sake man should leave Father and Mother and adhere to his Wife which should be with him one.

Now Man and Woman are one.

NOw because Adam hath so pronounced that man and wife shall be but one flesh, and our Law is that if a feofment bee made joyntly to Iohn at Stile and to Thom. Noke, and his wife, of three acres of land, that Tho. and his wife get no more but one acre and a halfe, quia una persona, and a writ of conspiracy doth not lye against one onely, and that is the reason, Nat. br. fo. 116. a writ of conspiracy doth not lie against baron & feme, for they are but one person, & by this a married Woman perhaps may either doubt whether shee bee either none or no more then halfe a person. But let her bee of good cheare, though for the neere conjunction which is betweene man and wife, and to tye them to a perfect love, agreement and adherence, they bee by intent and wise fiction of Law, one person, yet in nature & in some other cases by the Law of God and man, they remaine divers, for as Adams punishment was severall from Eves, so in criminall and other speciall causes our Law argues them severall persons, you shall finde that persona is an Individuum spoken of any thing which hath reason, and therefore of nothing but Vel de Angelo, vel de homine, fol. 154. in Dyer, who citeth

no

no worse authority for it then Callepinus owne selfe, seeing therefore I list not to doubt with Plato, whether Women bee reasonable or unreasonable creatures, I may not doubt but every woman is a temporall person, though no woman can be a spirituall Vicar.

Of Hermaphrodites.

Of Hermaphrodites I have some kind of doubts, not whether they bee persons, but what persons they bee, If a man die seised, leaving 3. children which bee all Hermaphrodites, whether the eldest shall have all his land, or that it bee partable as among coheires. Also if the eldest bee a Hermaphrodite, and the other 2. faire young Virgins which way jetteth the discent. Bracton in his first Booke, Cap. 7. saith, Hermaphroditus comparatur masculo tantum, vel feminæ tantum, secundum prævalescentiam sexus incalescentis, that is, it must bee deemed male or female, according to the predominance of the sex most inciting.

And as I remember I have read the like division, Bracton in his fifst book the 30. Chapter fol. 438. where hee sheweth that a man shall not be tenant by the courtisie Si partus declinaverit ad monstru, & cum clamore emitteret deberet, emisit rugitũ, saith, it is not partus monstrosus, licet natura membra minuerit, vel ampliaverit, ut si quis habeat digitos, aut articulos sex vel plures. Now then if these creatures bee no Monsters, but are in conjunction to take on thẽ the kind which is most ruling in thẽ, this must needs be understood in matrimony, and consequently they may have heires, which being granted, why may they not be heires according to the prevalescence which Bracton speaketh of: if I were to furnish my selfe a house, I would place no picture or Image in any parlour, dining or bed-chamber, but it should be of good seemely and natural proportion, Satyres and Centaures should come no nearer then the post Vi. Brit. Cont. fol. 1678.

at my doore. And at the threshold of this my treatise, or as it were a little behind the doore: I will leaue these deformed Children of Mercury, or Venus, suffering them to enter no further.

SECT. III.

The punishment of Adams sinne.

REturne a little to Genesis, in the 3. Chap. whereof is declared our first parents transgression in eating the forbidden fruit: for which Adam, Eve, the serpent first, and lastly, the earth it selfe is cursed: and besides, the participation of Adams punishment, which was subjection to mortality, exiled from the garden of Eden, injoyned to labor, Eve because shée had helped to seduce her husband hath inflicted on her, an especiall bane. In sorrow shalt thou bring forth thy children, thy desires shall bee subject to thy husband, and he shall rule over thee.

Sée here the reason of that which I touched before, that Women haue no voyse in Parliament, They make no Lawes, they consent to none, they abrogate none. All of them are understood either married or to bée married and their desires or subject to their husband, I know no remedy though some women can shift it well enough. The common Law here shaketh hand with Diuinitie, but because I am come too sóone to the title of Baron and feme, and Adam and Eue were the first and last that were maried so young, it is best that I runne backe againe to consider of the things (which I might seeme to haue lost by the way) that are fit to be knowne concerning women before they be fit for marriage.

SECT.

SECT. IV.

The Ages of a Woman.

THe learning is 35. Hen. 6. fol. 40. that a Woman hath divers speciall ages, at the 7. yeare of her age, her father shall have aide of his tenants to marry her. At 9. yeares age, shee is able to deserve and have dowre. At 12. yeares to consent to marriage. At 14. to bee hors du guard: at 16. to be past the Lords tender of a husband. At 21. to be able to make a feoffement: And per Ingelton there in the end of the case, a woman married at 12. cannot disagrée afterward, but if she be married younger, shee may dissent till shee be 14.

The age of 7. yeares, when Bracton wrote this aide, for making the sonne a Knight, or marrying the daughter, was due de gratia & non de Iure, and pro necessitate & indigentia domini capitalis: measured by the indigence of the Lord, and opulence of the tenants: But West. 1. Cap. 35. in the third yeare of Edward 1. the Law was made certaine, the Lord shall have aide of his tenants, as soone as his daughter accomplished 7. yeares age, for the marriage of her. Viz. xx. s. of a whole knights fée, and xx. s. of xx. l. land in soccage, and so forth, according to the rate more or lesse.

The King shall have this aide according to this proportion, by a Statute made 25. Ed. 3. and for this aide every Lord may either distraine or bring his writ de auxilio habendo at his election, but tenant by grand serjeanty, or petit, shall not pay this aide. Mich. 21. He. 4. fol. 32. no more shall coppy-holders, as séemeth by the writ, both in Fitzherbert and Bracton, for it is, Precipimus ut habere facias rationabile auxilium de Militibus, et libere tenentibus. Now if the Kings writ runne for it before the Statute, how is it that Bracton saith it was due, but de gratia, That perhaps he meant but for the quantity, ipse viderit, if the father dye, the daughter being unmarried, shee shall recover so much as was gathered and not paied her at the hands of the executor or heire, but this aide is onely for the marriage of the eldest daughter, and not for no daughter, where many make but one heire: But see Bracton fol. 36. b. Where he saith, primæ genitæ filiæ non dabitur auxilium tale, quia istud auxilium pertinet ad Cap. dom. sicut pertineret si non esset nisi unus hæres cum omnes sunt quasi unus hæres.

SECT. V.

A Woman compellable to serve.

THe next age of a Woman is 9. yeares when shee is dowable, but wee will stay a while with the virgins, concerning whom, if they be in the power and governance of parents, masters, or prochein amies, or if they bee poore, the Law differeth little or not much from the common forme apperteyning unto males, unlesse it bee in cases of rape, which I reserve to the end of my discourse, where the poore have least need of subsidie, onely this I observe here, By a Statute made 5. Eliz. ca. 4. Two Justices of peace in the Countrie, or the head officer and 2. Burgesses in Cities, &c. may appoint any woman of the age of twelve yeares, and under 40. being unmaried, and out of service, to serve and bee retained by yeare, weeke, or day, in such sort and for such wages as they shall thinke meet, and if she refuse, they may commit her to prison, till she shall be bound to serve.

SECT. VI.

Of Heires.

BUt leaving this sort to the title of day laborers, come wee to women wards in the custody of their lords. And take

take for the foundation here the Statute it selfe West. 1. Cap. 22. This Statute expresly reciting the materiall point of the Statute of Merton, willeth it in every of them to be observed, Merton Cap. 6. and the Statute of Merton is this, Whosoever lay person shall bee convicted hee hee parent or other, to have detained, abduced or married puerum aliquem, he shall yeeld the value of the marriage and be imprisoned untill yee have both made amends to the partie damnified, if the ward bee married, and satisfaction to the King for the transgression hoc de hærede infra 14. &c. but if any heire of 14. yeares age, or upward till 21. shall marry himselfe without greeing with his Lord to defraud him of the marriage, where the Lord offered him a convenient marriage, and without disparagement, there it shall be lawfull to hold the inheritance untill and after the full age of 21. yeares, by so long time as shall suffice to reape and receive the double value of the marriage, secundum estinationem legalium hominum et secundum quod pro eodem maritagio prius fuerit oblatum, sine fraude & malitia, et secundum quod probare poterit in Curia Dm. Regis. Let us speake of heires, and see a litle in what cases a woman shall inherit, It is knowne to all, that because women lose the name of their ancestors, and by marriage usually they are transferred in alienam familiam, they participate seldome in heireship with males, and therefore Bracton is bold to say, Nunquam ad successionem vocatur femina quâdiu hæres superfuerit ex masculis, but to this rule he subjoyneth exception and examples, the very same which are in Litleton, To wit exception of right line, right bloud and maner of giving.

Sect. VII.
Of the right Line.

A Female may be preferred in succession before a male by the time wherein she commeth: as a daughter or

daughters

daughters daughter in the right line is preferred before a brother in the transversall line, and that aswell in the common generall taile, as in fee simple, for example, land is given to a man, and to the heires of his body, who dyeth having issue two sonnes, of which the eldest dieth, leaving issue a daughter, this daughter shall inherit by the right of blood, also a woman shall bee preferred propter jus sanguinis: Example, a man hath issue a sonne and a daughter by one venter, and a sonne by another venter, the first sonne purchaseth in fee, and dieth without issue, the sister shall inherit. So it is where a man seised in fee hath issue, ut supra, and dieth, his eldest sonne entereth and dieth without issue, &c. Bracton who hath both these cases, disputeth here as if he were seeking a knot in a bulrush, and he findeth a difference where the inheritance is Discendens and Perquisita. But Littleton is plaine though the second sonne bee heire to the father in the last case, and therfore should have had the land, had the eldest sonne never entered, yet the case being as it is: possessio fratris de feodo simplici facit sororem de integro sanguine esse heredem. & whether the fee was descended, or perquisit what skils it, here it must needs be, if the brother was heire of the blood of the first purchasor, that the sister of the whole blood is so too, yet there is a great difference betweene land purchased by him that died seised, and land discended unto him, for the first may goe to the heire on the fathers side, & for default of such to the heire of the mothers side, but land discended must alwaies goe to heires of the blood of the first purchaser, and the case may bee such that a female shall cary away inheritance from a male, though there be no difference of right line, or in the integrity of blood, which Bracton calleth jus sanguinis duplicatum: as where John Stile purchaseth in fee, & dieth without issue, an ant or ants, or uncles daughter on the father side, shal inherite before an uncle, or uncles sonne on the mothers side, where they be both collaterall and the integrity or neernes of blood is alike. Put case, that the purchasor died leaving

issue

issue only Iohn the yonnger, and this Iohn married or unmarried dieth without issue, now cannot the land goe to the heires on the part only of the mother of young Iohn, and therefore ye must ascend a step higher to the marriage of the father and mother of the first purchasor, if ye will finde who shall inherit, where if there be neither brother nor sister to the purchasor, a daughter to the eldest uncle on the fathers side may inherite before any of the mothers side, yea and before a sonne of the second uncle on the part of the father, and this by the worthinesse of blood. I will not examine the crainkes of discent, but turne to the case, where possession of the brother excludeth a brother and taketh in a sister: If a man hath issue a sonne and daughter by one venter, and a sonne by another, and give land to the eldest sonne in taile, now if the father die and the reversion in fee discend to the eldest sonne, who likewise dies without issue of his body, the second sonne shall have this land: For here was no possession, but an expectance of fee simple in the eldest. Per omnes Iusticiarios de Communi Banco. 24. E. 3. fol. 13. For it is possessio fratris & non reversio fratris, &c. Yet Thorpe Iustice of the Kings Bench thought the land should goe to the daughter, Brooke con. Brooke discent. 13. Againe, a fine was levied to I. and A. his wife in taile, the remainder in fee to A. they had issue a sonne, and the husband died, the wife tooke another husband, by whom shee had issue another sonne and died: the eldest sonne entered and died without issue, the collaterall heire to him entered as into the remainder in fee, and the youngest sonne of the halfe blood, to execute the fee, brought a Scire facias, which was holden good, for though the eldest might have charged, forfited or given the fee simple by atteinder, yet it was not actually in him, and therefore the demi sanke none impediment but the younger sonne might have it, as heire to his mother, 24. E. 3. fol. 30. Which cases prove, that the possession of a brother to convey the fee to a collaterall heire, if it be not apprehendeth actively, the generall heire to the

common

common ancestor may enter, Therefore where there is a son or daughter by one venter, and a puisne sonne by another venter, if the father die seised of an advouson or a rent, and the eldest son died before he present or receive the rent, the daughter shall not inherit, and if the father die seised of an use in fee, possessio fratris facit sororem esse hæredem: by taking the profits of the ground. 5. E. 4. 7. Where it is said that if the father by testamēt bequeath the profits for tearme of yeares, this letteth not the possession of the eldest brother: otherwise it is, if it had beene for tearme of life, and the like difference is (by this booke) if a lease be made for yeares or for life of lands not in use, &c.

SECT. VIII.
Where the manner of gift altereth the discent.

BRactons first exception to his general rule, that a Woman shall not inherit, when there is an heire male, is, Nisi contrarium faciat modus donationis. His example is, A man giveth land to one in mariage with his daughter, to them two and to the heires of their bodies, they have issue a daughter, and the husband dying, the wife taking another husband, hath by him a sonne and dieth, the daughter shall inherit per modum donationis, the case is plaine.

But Littleton hath a limitation, where modus donationis, doth cleane exclude Women from inheriting, That is, where lands are given to a man & the heires male of his body: now if he die having issue a sonne and a daughter by one wife, and a second sonne by a second wife, the daughter can never inherit, nay, if he die having issue a daughter onely, which daughter hath a sonne, neither daughter nor son shall inherit, for whosoever shall inherit by force of an intaile made to heires males, must (per modum donationis) be males & cōvey his discēt to it per heirs males, which because

the

the sonne cannot doe here, the donor may reenter. But Littleton saith also (lest women should take the matter unkindly at his hand) that where land is given to a man, & to the heires females of his body, his issue female shal inherit per formā doni & not the issue male: for the will of the giver must be observed. He hath another case which I may not omit: When lands are given a man, & to the heires males of his body, which have issue 2. sonnes, & the eldest dyes having issue a daughter, if hee lease the land for tearme of yeares, the reversion descendeth to the sonne: but if the lease bee for tearme of life of the lessee, the reversion and the fee simple descendeth to the daughter, the discontinuance is the cause, & here the daughter is in not in the per, but contra modum donationis by violating the will of the giver.

SECT. IX.

Where a woman comming to lands shall retaine them, &c.

NOw I will shew you where a female having gotten inheritance: per modum donationis, or otherwise, shall retaine it, and where not. Marke well this case, Iohn died seised of fee, leaving issue Robert the eldest sonne, and Richard the puisne: Robert entred, tooke a wife and had issue Alice, which Alice dies, hee tooke another, and leaving her great with childe hee died, the Lord seized the land and ward of Alice, and granted the custody to one which indowed the wife of Robert, she was delivered of a sonne William, The Lord seized William his ward which lived ten yeares, and died without issue, Henry the sonne of Richard the second sonne of Iohn entereth, Alice entereth upon Henry, and hee brings an assise: now because the possession of the Lord was seisin and possession of William, to whom Alice was but

of

of the halfe bloud, it was awarded that Henry should recover. But by the opinion of the Court, the land which the wife held in dowre should goe to Alice: for therein William had no more but a reversion 8. Assisa pl. 6. Againe, Henry seised of tenements deviseable in Winchester (where the Custome is, that hee which is seised by devise may not with warranty or without warranty make alienation to barre the reversion or remainder (deviseth them to his wife Alice for tearme of life, the remainder to Th. his sonne for life; so that Th. should make no alienation: quo minus tenementa devenirent propinquioribus hæredibus de sanguine puerorum post mortem predicti Thom. Henry died having issue Steven an elder sonne, and Maud a daughter, which had issue Eliz. Steven died without issue Alice, the wife entered and died seised, Tho. entereth and alieneth in fee with warranty: Maud dieth, Elizabeth maketh claime by taking the haspe of the doore in her hand: Tho. dieth without issue, Eliz. entereth upon the alienee, he puteth her out shee, bringeth an assise.

Broke dispent. pl. 19.

It was holden that the heires of Henry had nothing in the fee simple by the limitation, which went not to his children, but to the next of blood to his children, excluding ses infants demesne, And by Wilby, if B. make a lease to Alice for life, the remainder to the neerest of blood, if he die having issue 2. sonnes, and the eldest dye having issue a sonne (though this issue be heire to B,) the other sonne after the death of Alice shall have the land as neerest of blood, and (by Greene and Seaton) if there had beene severall issues, of divers sonnes and daughters to the devisor, when the remainder vested it should have gone to them all. But here because the daughter of him had issue a daughter when the tenant for life died, and there was not issue of any sonne, at the instant to take from her, or with her, this Daughters Daughter shall have all, and though there came an after borne sonne of any of the brethren, she may detaine all, &c. for a remainder vested is not like to fee simple discended

to

to a daughter, where a sonne Posthumus may enter. And if lands be letten for life, the remainder to the right heires of I. & if I. dye having issue a son, which entereth after the death of the tenãt for life, & then dieth, his son shal have nothing, because he was not capax at the fal of the remainder, likewise where there is a brother & sister, & lands are let for life to an estranger the remainder to the right heires of the brother, if he and the tenant for life die, the sister may enter, and retaine the possession and fee, though the brothers wife bee afterward delivered of a sonne: in like sort did the remainder rest in the child of Maud in Eliz. viz. which recovered by award, 30. Assi. p. 47. But where there is father and sonne, which sonne purchaseth and dieth without issue, and an uncle entereth, if two yeares after the father hath a sonne by the mother of the purchasor, this sonne may enter and put out the uncle, and the reason of Law is that hee that comes in by purchase must be capax, at the time when the purchase vest in him, but in case of discent it is not so requisite. Perk. in his Chapter of devises saith, that if a devise bee made to a colledge, which is not a colledge at the time of the devise it is a void devise, although afterward it be made a colledge: & upon the same reason, is Dier 13. Eliz. 303. of a devise to an infant in ventre sa mere: And where a man dieth seised and his daughter entereth, &c. a son borne afterward may enter, but it is not so in case of purchase, &c. for if a woman consent to a ravishor, & her daughter and heire enter by the statute, 6. R. 2. ca. 6. the son Posthumus shall not put her out, no more shall he, where a daughter and heire entereth for condition broken, and where a daughter hath a villain by discent, which purchaseth & she entereth into the perquisits an after borne sonne her brother shall have that which discended, viz. the villien but not the land: these cases hath Brook Discents, 58. out of the Doct. and Student, 5. Ed. 4. fo. 58. in the case of Elizabeth Venor, agreeth concerning entry made by 6. Ri. 2. And so doth Hales and Mountague, in the case of Wimbish and Talbois, yet Mountague Chiefe Justice taketh there a

lear-

learned difference if a man devise land for life, the remainder to the right heire male of the devisor, & the heires of his body, &c. now if the devisee for life die, and a woman which is heire generall to the devisor entereth, and hath afterward a sonne, the sonne shall never out the mother in whom is vested the inheritance for want of other persons to take the falling remainder: per le melior opinion 9. H. 6. yet (he saith) the cases of ravishment possession of a brother, abatement of a bastard, &c, are all to bee understood of fee simple: for where the entry gaineth but estate taile, one may beate the bush and another take the bird, so if a man seised by discent from his mother make a feofment with condition, &c. and die without issue, if a woman heire on the father side enter for condition broken, an heire male or female on the mothers side may oust her. Plow. &c. fo. 56. a. b. & 57. a.

West. 1. ca. 22.

THen West goeth on with heire females, that so soone as they come to the age of fourteene yeares if the Lord for covetousnes will not marry them, yet he shall not keepe their land above two yeares after they have accomplished 14. within which two yeares if they be not married by their Lord, they may take action against him for their inheritance, to recover it without paying any thing for the custody or for marriage. If so be that of their proper malice or through the mischievous counsell of others, such women refuse convenable marriage offered by their Lord, he may in this case retaine their land untill they be of 21. yeares, and longer untill he shall receive the value of their marriage.

Littletons words upon this statute in his 2. booke cap. 4.

BY Littleton if tennant by service of Chivalry die, his here female being 14. yeares old or more: the Lord

Lord shall have custody neither of the land nor body, for at that age a woman may have a husband able to doe knights service, but if such an heire be under 14. and unmaried at the time of her auncestors death, the Lord shall have ward in her land untill she be of 16. yeares age, West. 1. cap. 22. which getteth the Lord 2. yeares to tender marriage without disparagement, and if during these two yeares the Lord tender no such marriage shee may enter and oust the Lord. If such an heire female be married under the age of 14. in the life of her ancestor, which ancestor dieth before she accomplisheth 14. yeares, the Lord shall have no more but the wardship of her land till shee be 14. yeares old, and then her husband with her may enter into her land and put the Lord out, for this is out of the Statute, because the Lord may not tender marriage to her that is already married, for before the Statute of West. such an heire female that was under the age of 14. at the death of her ancestor, and had atteined afterward to the age of 14. yeares, without any tender of marriage by her Lord made unto her, might well enter into her land, and put out the Lord, as appeareth by the rehearsall and very words of the Statute, which as it seemeth (so saith Littleton) was made altogether for the advantage of the Lord.

A suspition of Littletons *error.*

NOw saving Mr. Littletons inspiration, I am greatly afraid that ye shal not finde by the text of the Statute, That an heire female, being under 14. at the death of her ancestor, might by the common law before this Statute, enter and oust her Lord, as soone as she had accomplished 14. yeare of age without tender of marriage. The law perhaps was so, but this Statute proves it not: Againe, I doubt, Littleton was deceived, in taking this Statute to be all for the advantage of Lords, yet it is likewise said by Dyers

13.H.7.11. that this Statute was made for advantage of the Lords.

Glanvill ibro.7.cap.12.

HEare what Glanvill saith, women shalbe in ward untill they be of ful age & the Lord shal mary them being of ful age, euery one of thē, with their reasonable portion, & though they be of ful age they shal remaine notwithstanding in their Lords custody until they bée married by his aduise, for by the law of the land, no woman heire can be married, but by her Lords disposing and assent. In so much, that whosoever having a daughter or daughters heire or heires, shall in his life time without grée of his Lord marry any of them, he suffereth by the right and generall custome of the Realme perpetuall disinherison, without ever recovering any thing, but by the grace & méere mercy of his Lord. If it be proved that any woman holden in ward do forfit with her body, she shalbe deprived of her heritage, & her portion shall goe and accrue to her parceners. And if they all offend, the whole heritage shall fall as escheate to the Lord. But after such heires be once lawfully maried, though they become widdow afterwards they shall no more be holden in ward, nor then by their incontinency can they forfit any inheritance. But yet they may not remarry without their Lords assent. Thus far Glanvil.

Bracton *his 2. Booke cap. 37.*

BRacton, who (as it may very well be gathered) wrote one halfe hundred yeares after Glanvil, and but very little before the making of West. 1. In his 2. Booke and 37. Chap. finding it a question, at what time an heire female should bee out of ward, whether at 14. or 15. or at 21. acknowledgeth a greater capacity of deceipt, and maturity of desire

desire, to be in women then in men.

And that therefore, a woman might be out of ward at 14, and marry, because at that age she is able *disponere domui suæ et habere cone et key, et virum sustinere*, that is to order and dispose, a to have, the key clog at her girdle, and to be a jolly stay unto a man. But this early emancipation of women heires he taketh to be onely of such as inherit lād of socage tenure: for drawing toward the end of the Chapter he falleth in with Glanvil, And saith of heires coparceners in Chivalry, *si ab initio omnes maiores extiterunt nihil ominus in custodia dominorum erint donec per consilium et dispositionem eorum maritentur: quia sine ipsorum cōsilio et assensu, mulier hæreditatē habens maritari non potest non etiam in vita antecessorum, &c: quod si olim fecissent, hereditatem amitterent: sine spe recuperandi nisi solum per gratiam. Hodie tamen aliam pænam incurrent.* And presently hee sheweth the reason why they might not marry without their Lords assent viz. lest the Lord might be constrained to take homage of his capitall enemy, or of a man altogether unfit or unworthy.

SECT. X.

How the law came to a certainty in the point of a womans being out of ward.

Choose now whether ye will learne of Glanvil and Bracton, what the law was in their time, or of Mr. Littleton, that wrote many score yeares after the making of Westm. 1. In mine opinion, neither did this law bring any advantage to Lords, neither doth it shew that heires females, of tenants in Chivalry, might enter at 14. yeares, neither is there any cleere proofe that the law was cleerely so taken. The letter of the Statute doth not expresly giue 2. yeares to tender mariage, but restraineth couetous Lords, that they shall not hold the land aboue 2. yeres after the 14. which seemeth plainly to import, as it is reasonably taken both by Needh. & Billing 35. *H.6* that before the making of this law, the age of male and female in this point, tooke no difference. I may be asked, how it commeth then to passe, that the law is so cleere in that which Littleton concludeth withall, vizt. That the Lord shall not haue two yeres to tender his woman ward marriage, saue onely where she is under 14. and unmaried at the death of her ancestor: before the Statute, it was either out of doubt, that a daughter and heire, should not be cleane out of ward at 14. or at the least it was doubted, whether she should or no: and the words of the Statute whatsoeuer Mr. Littleton saith, maketh not the matter plaine enough. But we haue the helpe of Reuerend Prisor, in the Booke aboue mentioned. 3. 5. Henrici 6. Westm. 1. (saith he) was made in the time of Edward the first, who purposing to put all the law into certainty, and in writing, begun to makes Bookes thereof, by helpe of the most sage men of the law in this Realme, Iudges and others. And he made a Booke two yeares after the making of this Statute in which all the Statute is rehersed, which booke goeth on, and saith by expresse words: that no woman shalbe said to be under age, thereby to be in ward after she is past the age of 14. Thus saith Prisot. By him therefore and by other Iustices in the Eschequer chamber it was ruled cleere, that where the Kings tenant in Chiualry died leauing his daughter and heire of the age of 15. yeare, she should not be in ward. And Billing saith for law, that if betweene the 14. and 16. yere, when an heire female is in ward another ward falleth which holdeth in Chiualry of the first, the Lord shall not haue gard, per cause de garde, for the first ward is out of his power to all intents excepting onely tender of mariage. And another Iustice saith, if a tenant hold of one lord by priority, & of another by posteriority, the daughter heir under 14. shal

be

be in custody of the anteriour Lord till she be 16. but shee may enter upon the land by posteriority, as soone as shee commeth to 14. likewise if the Lord hath once maried this woman-ward, after the age of 14. she may presently, enter into her land: for now the Lord hath had all that, which to him belongeth, the marriage. And the course of the Chancery is to make livery, before: 14. cum exitibus, but after 14. livery tantum: vid. 4. Eliz. 213. Dyer. & Dyer. 20. Eliz. 362. 1. Hen. 720. on livery for then such an heire is to have the profits by the law. To come to an end of this matter, I will not forget, that even in Mr. Littletons daies very neere two hundred yeares after the making of West. 1. by the last Statute, that ever Hen. 6. made in the yeare of his reigne. 39. ca. 2. it was established by Parliament that women being of the age of 14: yeares at the death of their ancestors, without question or difficulty shall have delivery of their lands and tenements discended to them: for so the Law of the land wils.

SECT. XI.

A search for the true reason, why a woman is hors du garde, *at the age of* 14. *yeares.*

The principall reason that mooved our law founders, so soone to set women out of ward is none other then hath beene already declared, she is quickly able domui preesse, viro subesse, and her husband for her shall doe Knights service, or some other for him, and in his stead, the cases are therefore 26: *H.* 8. fo. 2: If the Kings tenant in chiefe, having feoffees to his use, marry his daughter, under age, to a man of full age, and dye, this daughter, being heire, is out of ward for her body though not for her land: for that shalbe in ward in this case, an the Kings possession must bee voided by suite and livery. But had she beene of full age of 14. yeares at her fathers death, no such thing had needed, neither should she have bin in ward, nor the King have any primer seisin: For that was not as yet seene into by the Statutes of *H*.7. which had given ward, reliefe and herriots upon the death of him, which died intestate and seised of onely a bare use: againe, if the King have a woman ward which he marrieth before she be 14, she shalbe to all intents out of ward at 14. and may immediatly sue her livery, 28. *H*.8. for as a ward masculine, married by his Lord under 21. shalbe *sui iuris* at 21. so shall a ward feminine being maried before 14. bee out of ward at 14. altogether. In the old *Natura brevium* in the writ *de eiectione custodiæ*. it is said, that where the tenant marieth his daughter being under age, to a man of ful age, & dieth, the daughter shalbe out of ward. But if he mary his daughter, being of full age, to a man under age, and die, she shall be in ward. This Mr. *Brooke* taketh to be no law: even so doe I: his reason is, that no Lord can have the marriage of her that is already married, or compell any heire to be twice married. For if a tenant marry his son and die, and then the sonnes wife dieth holden, the Lord shall not have his body in ward to marry him. Which is cleare: specially if the sonne were *infra annos nubiles* at the time of his fathers death. But certainely, if the Lord couple his ward to a wife which dieth, the ward is at full liberty for his body, and shall not be married by his Lord.

The reason why an heire female of full age married by her father to a man under age, should not be out of ward, must be because the supposition of law faileth: her husband is not able *arma portare & officiis fungi militaribus, vel pro iisdem faciendis cum alio pacisci*. But this notwithstanding, me thinketh a woman married, should bee out of ward for all her husbands nonage, though the woman bee but twelve yeares old a boy knight shall be out of ward for his body: shall a woman *innupta & matura viro* be in keep-

ing

ing of any but her husband, shall shee at 14. yeares age bee ward because she hath a husband but 19. yeare olds, who should not have beene in ward had she had no husband at al: non videtur. The husbands ability to doe souldiers service, is neither the onely nor the principall cause in mine opinion, why a woman is by law out of ward at 14. yeares age. But law going with the trace or tide of nature, that hath made women (as Bracton saith) fit to carry cey and key cloge betimes, suffereth them to mary very early: And it should be a mischievous, inconvenient, unjust, and unnatural law, that should hold a woman from her husband, or from her inheritance, which is without offence of law maried, & fully able to bring forth children, because her husband is not fully fit for all mannor of horsemanship. Be not therefore good woman absterred from a young husband, by old natura brevium.

SECT. XII.

How a woman that hath beene in ward, shall come by her land.

A Woman past 14. yeares of age at her ancestors death shall not be in ward: And where she is in ward till 16. she may have action at 16. against her Lord for her inheritance, according to the Statute. By Littleton, she may enter which standeth with reason, for the Statute giving action to her affirmatiuely, doth not disaffirme the entrie which she might have had, by the auncient catholicke Common law: if shee cannot or dare not enter, she may have alone (if she be alone) or with her fellowes (if she be a coheire) a writ of mortdancester, as well against her Lord as against any other abator. Marlbridg ca. 16.

But if shee be ward to the King, against whom a mortdandancestor, writ of Aile, Besaile or Cosinage then it melts into petition, and she must sue for livery. And where the King hath a woman in ward with some lands holden of other Lords in socage, such a ward shall not so soone as shee is 14. yeare old have livery of that socage lands, but she must arry unlesse she be married, in the meane while till she be 16. because livery must be at once parcell, & not by percels. Yet if 3. copartners be in ward to the King, she which first commeth to age, shall sue her livery, and have partition upon it.

SECT. XIII.

Of Parceners.

FOr, it must not be omitted there where a man dieth seised of any manner of inheritance, having issue none but daughters, to whom such inheritance descendeth, when they have entered by Litt. they are parceners, one heire to their common ancestor, & so are the heires of females parceners and they ought to come in by descent, for if by purchase they are jointenants: & they are called partners (saith he) because they are compellable by a writ de partitione facienda, to divide the inheritance amongst them. Like, or the same law is, where a man dying seised having no issue, his land goeth to his sisters, or aunts, that are partners, if one of them dye before partition made, her part shall descend to her issue, and for want of issue to her coheires, which shalbe deemed and adjudged in, by discent and not by survivour.

SECT.

SECT. XIII.

Difference betweene partners and jointenants.

FOr although partners have a conjoyned estate, yet law maketh a great diversity betwixt them and jointenants: Partners by the cōmon law, are onely females or the heirs of females, which also must be in, by descents, for if sisters make a joint purchase they are jointnants, and not partners. Betwixt whom observe here the germaine & apparent difference: If two coparceners be of lands in fee simple, wherof one before partition made chargeth her part with a rent & dieth without issue, her coparcener taking as heire and by discent, shall hold the land charged. But it is otherwise betwixt jointenants.

Also partners may devise and give away their part by testament, so cannot jointenants.

SECT. XV.

Difference betweene partners and tenants in common.

AND as in the cases precedent, parceners are like tenants in common, so in that which followeth they are like jointenants. If two sisters enter into their deceased fathers lands, and every of them having issue a sonne, dieth before partition, so that one moitie descendeth to one sonne, and one moitie to another, which sons enter and occupy the lands in common, if they bee now disseised they shall have but one assise and not severall assises. Because although they come in here by divers discents, yet still

still they are partners, and that not onely in regard of the seisin & possession which their mothers had, but rather in respect of the estate which descended to their mothers from the common ancestors, the grandfather, to whom they are but one heire, so that of a disseisin before partition, they shal have but one assise.

SECT. XVI.

Difference of partners from both jointenants and tenants in Common.

By Bryan, 10. Ed. 4 fo. 3. one copartner may in feoffe another copartner, for though their possession bee joint, yet their right and interest is severed, so that if one sister die, the other shall claime a moitie by discent from her, and not the intire inheritance from the Common auncestors.

Partners in this therefore are like tenants in Common, whose title and right are separated, and therefore they may infeoffe one another.

But it is otherwise with jointenants, whose right is intire and goeth with the possession by survivour. Againe, partners may release the one unto the other, and in this they are like jointenants only, for if one tenant in Common release to his fellow, his moitie passeth not, because that hee to whom the release is made, hath in the franck tenemēt of this moitie no possession. But partners whose right is from one roote have a more connect possession then tenants in common, and may release one unto another.

To conclude this point, partners differ from both jointenants and tenants in common in this, that partners are and allwaies were compellable to make partition, so was neyther

ther of the other two before the Statute 31. *H.* 8. cap. 1. which ordaineth that jointenants & tenants in common of inheritance, which in England or Wales in the right of themselves or their wives, shalbe compellable by writ de participatione, to be devised in Chancery to make partition: And that after partition, they and their heires shall have mutuall aid one of another, for the deraigning of a warranty peramount, to recover pro rata, as is used betwixt partners at the common law.

Afterward. 32. H. 8. cap. 32 it is ordeined, that if any have equal estate with others or in common jointly for tearme of life or for yeares, or unequal estate, with such as have an adhering inheritance, they shall likewise be cōpellable to make partition: Provided, that this shall not bee prejudiciall to any person, other then the parties to it, their executors or assignes.

SECT. XVII.

Of the Nuper obiit.

BUt ere wee goe any farther in partition, let us see what actions may lie betwixt partners for their inheritance before they have divided it.

And first, of the Nuper obiit, This is a writ and commandement of the King to the sheriffe to summon a coheir to be befors the Kings iustices at a day certaine, to shew why she or he (for it lieth betwixt parceners in Gavell kind also) deforceth the plaintiffe coheire from her reasonable part belonging to her, of the inheritance of I. S. their grandfather, father, uncle, brother, grandmother, aunt, sister, or cousin (as the case requireth) whose heires they be: & qui Nuper obiit, ut dicitur. This writ lieth for lands holden in fee simple, onely betwixt coheires, where one or more of them

them deforceth or holdeth out his or their fellow coheire or coheire, &c. It must be brought in the name of all those which be deforced though in verity there be but one that sueth. And this 1. may haue a writ of summoneas ad sequendū against her negligent copartners, who if they appeare not, the sole plaintiffe shall be receiued to sue for her portion against the deforcer: If after the ancestors death, a kinsman enter claiming by descent, the Nuper obiit lieth not against him, but after entry and ouster, an assise of novell disseisin or a writ of right, for though coheires may haue Amordancester against a stranger, yet can they not haue it against one of their owne parenteale, priuy in blood, and claiming by the same descent, and where a writ of right sometimes is betweene sisters, as where one is infeoffed by deed and another claimeth by discent, battaile lieth not, nor the grand assise, but an inquest in lieu thereof. Thus far, V.N:B.

The New.Na,Bre. not disagreeing saith further. That if one sister deforce another of the land whereof her ancestor died seised in estate of fee taile, the remedy must bee by forme done, and not by Nuper obiit, a Nuper obiit may bee brought of the seisin of the aile, besaile or the tresaile, and if it be brought of the seisin of the grandfather, Darreigne seisin in the father is no good plea without shewing that hee died seised.

This writ may be brought, by the aunt against her sister and niece, or by the aunt and niece, against another sister & niece, or by one sister against another, that is but of the halfe blood. But if the father giue part of his land in francke mariage to one daughter and dye seized, &c. the donee in francke mariage, shall not haue a Nuper obiit against her sister for her part in residue of her fathers fee simple lād, unles she put her land in hotch pot which was giuen in francke mariage. A nuper obiit must be brought by a coheire deforced, against all the other coparceners, though some of them haue nothing to doe in the demand.

A villein and his wife, shal not haue a Nuper obiit against the

the coparceners of his wife, for hee is not infranchised by marriage with one of those seigniorеsses to whom hee was bound. If a coparcener be deforced by a coparcener and by a stranger, the deforced may haue a Nuper obiit against her coparcener, and ioint tenancie abateth not the writ, no more shall non-tenure of parcell of the thing demanded, by rule of the register. If two coparceners enter after the ancestors death, and deforcing a third parcener, doe afterward make partition, and then one of them alieneth her portion in fee, the deforced partner may by a Nuper obiit against her two coheires (notwithstanding the alination) recouer a third part of that which is not aliened and a third part of that which is aliened by a morrdancester or writ of Aile (as the case lieth) and in her owne name, and in the name of her two coparceners against the alienee.

If one coparcener infeoffe a stranger in fee, and take backe an estate in fee or for life, it seemeth a Nuper obiit is maintenable still against her so long as she disclaime not in the blood, &c. But 21.Ed.3. and 45.Edw.3. is contra. But severall tenancy, or non-tenure is no plea in a Nuper obiit for the priuity of blood. But a sister may claime by purchase, and disclaime in the blood, and this is a good plea. If one coparcener die leauing issue a sonne, which sonne infeoffeth a woman in all the land, &c. & then marrieth her, now cannot the other parcener haue a Nuper obiit against the baron & feme. But she may haue a mordancestor in her owne name and in the name of the seisure which the father had the day of his death, for that amounteth to a dying seised see Novel nat.br.197.&c.

Sect.

SECT. XVII.
Of the writ of right de rationabili parte.

There is also another Writ, called a writ de recto, de rationabili parte that never lieth but betwixt privies in bloud as betwixt brothers in gavell kinde, or betwixt sisters, nephewes, nieces, &c. It is also for lands in fee simple, as where the ancestor leaseth land for tearme of life, and dieth having two daughters, and after the death of tenant for life, one of the daughters entreth into the whole inheritance and deforceth her sister, the deforced may have this Writ, it is maintenable by two or three sisters against the fourth, or by an aunt, or niece against a sister that deforceth, and this writ lieth as wel where the ancestor dyed seised, as where he died not seised. It is in nature a writ of droit patent, & must be directed to the Lord of whom the land is holden, from before whō it is removeable by a Tolt, as the Naught writ is, where the ancestor dieth seised, and one coheire deforceth another (whether it be in gavell kinde, or amongst partners at the common law) the deforced hath election of this writ or of the nuper obiit. But when he died not seised, and a coparcener afterward deforceth, the Nuper obiit lieth not: The forme of this writ is, Precipimus to the Lord, ut sine dilatione plenum rectum teneas A. de decem acris cum pertinentiis, quas clamat esse rationabilem partē de libero tenemento quod fuit I. patris, vel &c. & tenere per liberum servititum tertiæ partis, &c. for it must be seene what rent and service the whole land yeeldeth to the Lord, & according there to shall the plaintiffe be rated in his, or her writ. If after the death of their ancestor two coparceners enter, and the one doe then deforce the other of something appendant or appertenent to that which is holden in coparcenery, she may have a writ de rationabili parte of this appendant or appertenent which shall say, quod clamat tenere ad liberum tenementum.

If

If a man dying seised of lands intailed haue two daughters whereof the one entereth and deforceth the other, the remedy is by formedon, and neither by Nuper obiit or Rationabili parte: If a sister, aunt, niece or cousin, claime from her ancestor by feofment in fee, & one which should haue bin coparcener (had the feofment not bin) deforceth her, she may haue a writ of Droit patent, and joine the mise by battaile, or graund assise, come semble, saith Fitzherbert, because shee claimeth not as heire. But where there is no impediment, intaile, feoffement, or such thing, & all the partners deforced bring a rationabili parte against all the copartners, terre-tenants (for so it must bee) and the heire of an heire may sue for part of the seisin of the cōmon ancestor, there battail, or grand assise, voucher or view lie not, neither is nōtenure any plea, for the writ lieth only betweene privies in blood: finally, the demand in this writ must bee of a portion certaine as of x. acres, if xx. discend to two sisters, and the demandant if she recouer, shall haue iudgement of so many to hold in seueralty.

SECT. XVIII.

Of Partition.

NOw of Partition, it may be made in diuers maners, as first for example by agreement amongst two copartners or more which accord to diuide the inheritance into certaine parts of equall valew to bee holden in severalty, and alwaies the part which the elder hath is called Ini ia pars, though in this kinde of partition, there bee no prerogatiue of primer election giuen to the eldest.

Another manner of partition, is where they cause certaine friends to make the parts or diuision, & here the eldest shall first chuse, & then the next eldest, and so succeedingly.

If

If by their whole agréement the eldest make the diuision it is said (saith M. Littleton) that she shall last make election, which is as much to say (say I) as she shall haue none election at all, Littleton hath another maner of alotment wherein after partition made of the lands euery part being written in a scrowle, and lapped vp in a bale of wax, is put into a bonnet, which must be holden by some indifferent body, and then (as wee vse to choose Valintines euery partner pulleth out a part, the first borne first, the rest after her in degrée of ancientry and euery one shal hold her to her chance.

Also partition may be made in Chancery, as when one copartner of full age, and another remaineth in ward to the King, &c. in such case if she which resteth in ward at full age haue not her full part, she may sue a writ of partition by Scire facias vpon the record returnable in Chancery, to shew why a new partition shall not be made, and partition may be of a reuersion, or of an aduowson.

Of a reuersion thus, that A. shall haue reuersion of such such lands, B. the reuersion of such other lãds, & of an aduowson, that A. shall haue euery 2. 3. or 4. auoidance, &c. & this is good without déed, where partition is made of a mannor without mention of the aduowson it remaineth in common sée that case of aduowson and partition of aduowson, 2. Hen. 7. 5. a.

Partition by agréement of parceners is good in law, as well by paroll as by writing, and if vnto two copartners there doe descend two houses, whereof the one is worth xx. s. and the other x. s. annually, the best house may bee allotted to one copartner, and she and her heires to pay to the other and her heires, (for owelty or equalities sake) v. s. rent issuing out of her house, and all this is good without writing, so that the partner that shall haue this rent, and her heires may distraine for the same when it shalbe arere, of common right in whose hands soeuer the house charged shall come, and this shall be a rent charge of Common right had and recei-

received for equality of partition, Fitzherb. fol. 252. & Plow. 134.

Partition of lands, that one partner and her heires shall haue and hold them from Easter to the gule of August, alone and by her selfe; and the other and her heyres from August till Easter in the like manner, was awarded a good partition in the time of Ed. 1. and by similitude of reason (saith Fitzherbert) it is a good partition, where two Mannors descend to two Copartners: that the one shall haue one Mannor by name, and the other the other for a yeare, to change possession the next yeare, and so forth from yeare to yeare commutatiuely, betwixt them and their heyres for euer, No. na. br. 62. l. & m. Et auxi. partic. que lun. auera le terr. in ta. & laut. le ter. in fee simple est bone partic. And partners may make partition for terme of life or for terme of yeares, and if one Copartner lease her part to another Copartner for terme of yeares, yet shée may sue a Writ of partition against her partner the Lessée, though the terme be vnexpired. 33. Hen. 8. Dyer 52. is a quære. If the one of two Copartners lease for terme of yeares, that which to her belongeth, and after the other bringeth a Writ of partition against the Lessor, to whom in this partition there is alotted a lesse portion then the due, some thinke (saith he) that the Lessée without remedie must hold himselfe contented, aswell as the partner which leased; But if the partition had beene without writ, quære.

Sect. XIX.

Of partition by Writt.

VVHen Copartners cannot all agree to make partition amongst themselues, the aptest meane to compell them, is a Writ of partition. And if there be foure

D Co-

Copartners, one may haue this writ against three, or two against two, or three against one.

The gist of it by the old Na. bre. is where the one entereth keeping out the other, and refusing to make partition, but Litt. layeth it where they be all in possession, and so soundeth the Writt it selfe; for it is a commandement to the Sheriffe, Si A. fecerit te securum, &c. summoneas B. that she come and shew why she refuseth or permitteth not partition of a Mannor, or a wood, or such like, the which with the appurtenances, the said A. and B. doe hold together, vndiuided of the inheritance of I. their father, Mother, or, &c. Fitzherbert in his Writt of partition, setteth downe the forme as a Carpenter should set vp a frame of a Cottage, being both to shew on what soile it should stand, for he sheweth not the generall gist of his Writ, and that his President might make plaine, which is not doubtfull, that when Partners are in possession, one or more may haue a partitione facienda, yet he toucheth not the question, whether a Partner ousted, or not suffered to enter, may haue it.

40. Hen. 7. fo. 9. in a Writ of partition, Keble pleadeth for his Clyent, that the defendant was sole seised, sans ceo, that he held pro indiuiso, with the Plaintiffe: by Vauisour that is no good plea, for admit that shee bee sole seised, yet partition lieth well enough, but by Brian Chiefe Iustice, it is & hath been adiudged a good plea, in our bookes, for one shall not come to diuide that with another wherein he hath no part. And (saith Keble) in a Writ of waste betweene tenants in Common it is a good trauerse, Non tenet insimul & pro indiuiso, likewise is it here where we haue trauersed the point, and supposall of your Writ, and the partie by nuper obijt, may recouer in seueraltie, and partition shall be made, and it was said that the seisin of one parcener, is the seisin of both, and so the reporter thinketh, if one enter, &c. Where she which entereth claimeth in the name of her selfe, and of her partner I can well

well agrée, or if she enter not denying the right of her fellow: And if after the death of the common Ancestor, A. which is one Coheyre enter silent into the whole inheritance, B the other Coheyre may now perhaps (without other entry) in the name of her selfe and her Companion maintaine a possessorie action, against a stranger, but when a Sister entereth vindicating all to her selfe by purchase, or obiecting against her Sister, Bastardie, or Attainder, and keeping her out of possession, this I trow is no entry of both, but such a deforcing as the Writs de rationabili parte, and the nuper obijt, were made to redresse: If every seisin of a partner must néeds be the seisin of all those that can claime as coheyres, then there is no deforcing or néed at all of the forenamed writs.

But séeing that law hath appointed them for lands in fee-simple, and a formedone for land in taile against deforcers of their coparceners, I say, that seisin of one of them is not seisin to all of them, and hauing a chiefe Justice on my side, I dare hold, that non tenet pro indiuiso is a good plea in a Writt of partition, which if it be brought by her that is deforced and out of possession, it commeth preposterously out of kind and season, and out of the order that our Law-founders at the first ordained, See Brooke Coparceners per totum, ou entrie de vn est le entrie del auter vers estrange pur lour advantage, mes nemie pur disaduantage 43. Ed. 3. 19. & lentrie d'un nest l'entrie de ambideux entre eux mesmes. 40. E. 3. 8.

By whom, and how the Writt of partition must be brought at this day.

COheyres in Gauell kinde, may compell one another to make partition by Writt, but then they must mention the custome in their declaration, If one Coparcener dye hauing issue, &c. her husband being tenant by the courtesie is compellable to make partition, but he cannot compell, &c. by the Common Law, for the Writt lieth naturally, for none but parceners. Fitzherbert, and the old na. bre. haue a note out of the Register, that in the 12. of King Ed. (they tell not which) there was sealed a Writ of partition at Barwicke betwéene strange persons, and there it was said it might bee granted betweene any Coheyres or fellow tenants, without naming de hereditate in the Writt, where it was likewise affirmed that such a Writt before that time was neuer séene, aswell the other bookes of Law, as the Statutes of 31. H. 8. make it out of question, that this Writt by the Common Law was onely betwixt Coheyres, as the two Writts which we haue passed, were by custome in some speciall places: ioynt-tenants, and tenants in Common might haue a Writt of partition, as Fitzherbert setteth downe: by the Custome of London, Writt of partition lyeth against tenant by the curtesie Littleton 264. Dyer 1. M. 98. Brief de partit. at this day lye against the Feoffée of one Coparcener, but not for a Feoffée: mes. vide Dyer 3. M. 128.

Likewise before the Statutes, if a man were both tenant in Common, and tenant in Copartnerie, as hauing one third part by purchase from one Sister, and another in the right of his Wife, he and his wife might bring a Writt of partition, which see Na. br. fol. 61

It hath béene much doubted, whether partition by agréement betwixt tenants in Common, or ioynt-tenants were good without déed: But by the better opinion, 3. Ed. 4. f. 9. & 10. such a partition is good enough if it be vpon the ground: but see the bookes of 2. Eliz. Dyer. 179. 18. Eliz. Dyer. 350. There is also a prety case of a mill parted betwéen two brethren ioynt-tenants by an award of a third, that one should repaire the mill on the one side of a certaine poste, and the other on the other side imperpetuum, & . which was awarded a good partition without any writing. 47. Ed. 3. 24. & 19. Assi. p. 1.

It hath béene also much doubted whether iudgement may

bee

be giuen to hold in seuerall when in assise of nouell disseisin, brought by one ioynt-tenant or tenant in common against another, it is found for the plaintiffe, as it is cleare it may be if the action were betwixt partners 7. assi. p. 10. Herle would not haue giuen iudgement to hold in seueraltie, had the parties béene ioynt-tenants: But 10. Assi. p. 17. such a iudgement is giuen and no bones made of it, yet 28. assi. p. 35. R. Thorp in like case, would giue no iudgement but generally to hold a moity per my & per tont, though he were besought in the Country at the assises, & at West. again and again for Judgement to hold seuerally, 7. H. 6. fo. 4. Weston glanceth on such a iudgement, and Strange denyeth that it may be, for it destroyeth the suruiuor: But Chine saith, that it may be, and hath béen often: the reason why the Law was more scrupulous in those points betwéene tenants in Common, and ioynt-tenants, then betwéen partners, was (as I guesse) because coheyres haue their estate by course of law, and the other are in either by the act of some body which made the estate, or by their own doing, so that though for necessity they may alien that which belongeth to them, or charge it yet otherwise the Contract made by consent may not without manifest assent be vndone: Bract. saith, fo. 206. sufficit semel voluisse, nec dissoluitur mutua voluntas nisi mutua voluntate contraria. It is perceiued how the law was before the Statutes, 31. & 32. H. 8. a summarie of which is set downe already, now that it may the better in part be vnderstood, how the law hath béene taken since those Statutes, obserue the causes following, out of my Lord Dyers Reports.

The puisne of thrée Coparceners of a reuersion vpon estate for life gauel-kind alieneth by a fine, the lessée dieth, the eldest parcener entreth into all his Inheritance, the middlemost, and the Alienée bring a ioynt Writt of partition vpon the Statute, the eldest pleadeth the generall issue, non tenent insimul & pro indiviso, the case appearing by the euidence, it was holden vpon a demurrer cleere, that the action was not maintainable, for the one ought to haue her Writt by the Common Law, and the other by the statute, but ioyne they could not, Quære (saith Dier) if the entry of the eldest giue seisin to the rest, that it should giue it to the stranger were hard 2. & 3. Phi. & Ma. fol. 128.

One of three Coparceners alieneth that which to her belongeth, one of the other two bringeth a Writt of partition against her fellow parcener, and the alienée, vpon the statute, because in this case, she might haue had a Writ by the Common Law, this Writ vpon the statute abated: But if the two Coparceners had ioyned against the alienée, and the one had beene at non-suite, she should haue been summoned and seuered, and her part beene diuided as well as the others, quære, by the Register, when the husband vnto one of thrée partners purchaseth one part, &c. he and his wife may haue a speciall Writt against the third, euen so it séemeth if one of thrée Coparceners purchase a fellowes part, the purchaser may haue a speciall writt against the third parcener, 7. et 8. Eliz. 243. in Dyer, by Anthony Browne and Dyer ioint-tenants, cannot at this day make partition by paroll out of the countie where the land lieth, for 31. and 32. &c. change not the law in this point: But the partition must bee by Writt out of Chancery. Humfrey Browne and Weston: 2. Eliza. Dier. 179. a man deuised socage lands to his two daughters, and to the heyres of their two bodies loyally engendred, and died, the two daughters tooke husbands, and at full age, &c. partition was made by paroll, one husband had issue by his Wife, and shée dyed: By the opinion of the whole Court the other Husband, and his wife shall haue the whole Land by suruiuor, for partition by word onely betwixt ioint-tenants or tenants in Common of estate of Inheritance is voyd: yet of a tearme peraduenture (saith Dier) such a partition is good enough fo. 350. in Dier: If ye doubt now of any thing somthing more then you did before, yée are the better learned and warned to worke surely.

The manner of partition by Writ, &c.

The Iudgment vpon a writ de partit. faciend. if that diuision be made betweene the parties; and that the Viscount in proper person going to the lands and tenements by the oath of 12. loyall men of his Countie, make the partition, deliuering one part to the plaintiffe, or to one of the plaintiffes, and another part to another parcener, &c. making no mention in the iudgement more of the eldest then the youngest Sister, The Sheriffe must giue notice to the Iustices of the partition which he hath made, aswell vnder the seale of the 12. men as vnder his owne seale, And in this partition there is no primer election giuen to any: but the second may haue liuery before the eldest, or the younger before either of them euen as it pleaseth the Sheriffe.

And this difference is betweene partition by Writ here, and the other partition which is by agreement: In the first the Viscount shall make to euery partner, her distinct share, but in the other they may agree, that one shall hold in seueraltie, and the rest shall occupie that which remaineth in common. Thus farre Littleton.

Bractons partition.

There is in Bracton a large discourse of partition, which I see not why, (for the forme) at this day should not be good, if not of all other the best: And this partition is by commission to men either chosen by the parties, or appointed by the King as Iustices or extenders, with commandement to the Sheriffe to make them come before those Commissioners or extenders tam milites quam alios legales homines nulla affinitate attingentes, per quos negotium melius expedire poterit. He hath also a precept to the Coroners where the Sheriffe is negligent: Tepidus & re-

remissus in executione preceptorum domini Regis, with a rule for valuation of an aduowsan, viz. that a marke annuall to the parson shall be rated a shilling to the parcener to whom the aduowsan shall be alotted.

And when the extent and diuision is made, euery part being written by it selfe should be deliuered to a Lay-man altogether vnlettered, which should distribute to euery coheyre her part at aduenture, wherwith she should stand contented: But this might be otherwise, by their agréement amongst themselues, to elect according to the prerogatiue of their age. Bracton discendeth déeper into examination what things may be parted amongst coheyres, exempting neither lands, tenements, homages, villinages, seruices, seruitudes, or any thing belonging to lands and tenements from diuision, vnlesse it be seriantia (quæ diuidi non debent, ne cogatur Rex seruitium accipere per particulas) or a castle, or the head of some Earldome or Barrony, quod propter ius gladij diuidi non debet sit illud castrum vel aliud edificium, & hoc ideo (saith he) ne sic caput perplures particulas diuidatur & plura iura comitatus & Baroniarum deueniunt ad per nihilum quod deficiat regnum quod ex comitatibus & Baronijs dicitur esse constitutum. Therfore Caput comitatus vel Baroniæ resteth indiuisible, and shall go to the eldest copartner, though where there are many chiefe and great Mansion-houses, euery one may haue one perhaps, and if there be but one, euery one may haue part thereof, where the frank-tenement is holden by seruice militarie, for if a frée soke-man die, whose heritage it is, ab antiquo partibilis, the eldest son (by Bracton) shall haue his house, and the rest shall haue allowance: Amongst other things, Bracton standeth long vpon the bringing to a common heape (which we call Hotchpot) Lands giuen in marriage to a coheyre, shewing that though lands giuen in marriage (whether the Inheritance be discendens, or perquisita, and whether shee to whom the land is giuen, be at the time of the gift a maid or a widow) must needs fall into partition, when part of the other lands

is

is claimed (& hoc quamuis homagium interuenerit & post tertium hæredem:) yet for all that, she to whom there is giuen in marriage already more then an euen portion, may well retaine it, and is not compellable to any confusion vnlesse she demand a share in that which remaineth, so that she to whom all is giuen, may likewise retaine all. And where a daughter was infeoffed pro homagio & seruitio, or where a stranger was infeoffed of part of the inheritance, which afterwards married a daughter, &c. they might be made parcell of the other lands, without any Hotch-pott: of these things ye may read more in Bract. li. 2. c. 33 and 34 with a Writt of habere facias seisinam, for he saith, possessio non pertinet ad hæredes nisi naturaliter fuerit apprehensa animo et corpore proprio vel alieno; sicut procreatorio prius ad ipsos non pertinebit, & vnde cum in curia Regis facta fuerit particio statim habeant breue de seisina sua habenda.

SECT. XX.

Of Hotch pott, according to Littleton.

FOr putting of lands in Hotch-pot, there is no where so full, and plaine learning, as in M. Littl. third booke c. 2. If (saith he) a man seised in fee-simple lands, hauing issue two daughters, of which the eldest is married, giue parcell of those lands to his daughter and her husband in franke-marriage, and die seised of other lands, exceeding in value those which are giuen, &c. the husband and wife shall haue no part of this remnant vnlesse they will put the land giuen vnto them in Hotch-pot: for example, If the father had 30. acres, and gaue 10. now after his decease if the donées refuse to make commixtion, the other daughter may enter and occupie the whole 20. and hold it to her selfe: But putting all in Hotch-pott, to finde the intire value, (for it is but an estimation or valuation) finding the acres to bee of like goodnesse, the Donées in franke-marriage shall haue an accreasement of 5. acres to hold all 15. in seueraltie, so that

allwayes

alwayes, the land giuen in frank marriage, must remaine to the donées and their heyres, for else (saith Littleton) should follow a thing vnreasonable and inconuenient, which alwayes the Law detesteth, there is the same Lawes betwixt the heyres of Donées in frank marriage, and the other partners, if the Donées themselues die, before their ancestor, or before partition.

This putting of Land in hotchpot is where the other lands descend from the Donor onely, and not from any other auncestor, for if they descend from the father or brother of the donour, from the mother of the Donée, that which is equallie so discended, shall be without Commixtion equally diuided: Also (by Littleton) if the land descended be of equall valew with the land giuen in franke Marriage, Hotchpot should be then in vaine and to no purpose, and sée Littl. Chapter of parceners more concerning such Hotchpot.

How partition may be auoyded.

Partition made betwixt two Sisters tenants in fée simple, they both being of full age, is not defesable, though there want oweltie, and equall valew in their parts.

But if the land were in fée-taile, the parties making the partition should bee bound and concluded onely for their time, the issue of her which had the meaner value, might enter after her mothers death, into her Aunts part, and occupie with her in common, and she againe with her niece in the part alotted to her Sister: If two Coparceners in fée, both married, together with their husbands make partition, it shall stand in force during the coverture, but after the death of a husband, his wife hauing a meaner part, may enter and defeat the partition, not so if at the time of the alotment, the parts were both of equall annuall valew.

If two Coparceners, whereof the one is vnder 21. yeares age

age, make partition so that a meaner valew is allotted to the puisne partner, she may enter and defeat the partition either in her minoritie, or when she is of full age: but let her take heed when shee commeth once to full age, that shee take not the whole profit of that which to her selfe was alotted, for that is an agreement to the partition, and maketh it indefeasable, peradventure a moietie of the profits shee may take.

Three acres of land are given to one in taile, which hath other three in fee, and after his death, his two daughters make partition, so that one hath the land intailed, and another the land in fee, if shee which hath the fee-simple, alien her part and die, her issue may enter into the land tailed, and hold occupation in Common with her Aunt, whose folly was to make such a partition, for since shee is without remedie, against the alienee of her mother, and without recompence, for the lands intailed, whereunto she is an heyre, by descent from the first Donee, it is reason she may enter, specially considering, that the state taile is not discontinued, yet 20. Hen. 6. it is holden, that she is put to her Formedon.

A man seised of two carues of land, one by iust title, another by disseisin of an infant, dieth seised having issue two daughters, they divide so that one hath the carue gotten by disseisin, & the infant entereth upon her possession, &c. she may enter into the other carue, and hold in parcenarie with her Sister: But if shee had aliened her part in fee before the entrie of the infant, this had beene a full dismission of her selfe out of Copartnership which she could not have recontinued by entrie, as she might perhaps, had she made onely a lease for yeares, generally if after partition one part be evicted from her which hath it, by loyall entrie, she may enter into the other lands, and occupie with the other Coparceners, compelling them to a new division: all this saith Littleton.

How

SECT. XXI.

How Partition shall bee auoided when it is by Iudgement.

MUch of that which Littl. hath taught for the auoyding of partition (as I collect) must bee vnderstood of partition in pais, and by agréement, for when it is made by Iudgement in a Writ of rationabile parte, nuper obijt, or assise to hold in severalty, or by livery in the Chancery, or else by Writt, de partitione, in which cases there is commission or authority derived from the Prince to extend and to make partes by the Oath of 12. men, &c. there is now no reason, that a matter of this substance, circumstance and solemnity, should be all layd on the ground, by a bare entrie, yet that silly poore women altogether ignorant of the law, might not feare that that Partition which is made by the Law, that by law there were no meanes to reverse it, but that still it must stand impugnable, whatsoever iniquitie or inequality it had, Old Breton saith in the end of his 17. Chapter, Si ascum percenersoit que se tient dient paie de cel partison si ferres nous vener le process & le record deuant nostre iustices de banke, &c. ilonques soient les errors redresse, &c. He concludeth somewhat like Bracton. Et apres le Assignement des purparties fuit per sort ou per election: soit le seisin per iudgement de nostre court: But to the matter. There is occurring in many of the yeare bookes, remedies against partitions, as if iudgement be given in a nuper obijt, of purpartie, and seisin granted to hold severally, yet the partition may be avoyded by error in the first iudgement. If partition bee made in Chancerie, and a lesse value then is due alotted to a puisne Sister, which remaineth still in ward, she may haue remedy by scire facias when shee commeth to full age: So whether partition be of it selfe altogether vniust

vniust, or in part inequall, through malice, ignorance, or negligence of the Sheriffe or extenders, there is remedie alwayes, so the parties be not hurtfull to themselues.

And although partners of estate in fee, being all of full age, making purpart by agreement, bind & conclude themselues and their heyres for euer, yet when partition is compulsatorie, and the parts are deliuered by the Sheriffe, who with his extenders maketh diuision (which may be without the presence of the heyres) I see no great reason here, why acceptance should be a barre in the issue perpetuall, or to the parceners for terme of life, yet Littletons bien soi garde is good counsell, vide Dyer 33.H.8. 52.

SECT. XXII.

Of the coherence betweene Partners after diuision.

But admit now that partition is so made that there remaineth neither cause nor intention to vndoe it, yet the partners are in a kinde of confederacie and combination amongst themselues, by the very Law and custome of this Realme, Et lour droit est cy connex nul de eux ne doit respondre sans le autre: pur le contribution. Et si ascun se face ceo ne serroit in preiudice des auters partners. Britton cap. 73. so that if any of them will sue for any inheritance that was their Common Ancestors, the suit must be in all their names still, and if any of them be sued, for any such Land or inheritance, she may pray ayde of the other coheires, which may come with her to pleade a feoffment, fine, or release, or deraigne warrantie, and if in this sort she lost some or all her part, she shall recouer that which her partners hold her equall portion. But if a parcener put her selfe in defence, and will not pray ayde of her fellowes, which may strengthen

strengthen and assist her, she shall then recouer nothing against her coheyres, though she lose all her purpart and liuelihood: They continue therefore still in a sort one heyre tyed together like bundles of rods, for their mutuall strength, and by Bracton and Britton, if one of them die without issue after partition, her part shall goe to the rest, *per ius accrescendi*, But is crossed by Littleton aboue, which telleth you that their title shall be in this case by discent, though the dying be before partition, therefore if partition be betwixt two Sisters of the halfe blood, and one of them dyeth without issue, hauing an vncle of the whole blood to the Father, that Vncle by Bractons partition shall haue her Inheritance, &c.

SECT. XXIII.

By what manner of acquisition the ouer-liuer taketh the part of a Co-heire when she dyeth.

FOr your better instruction in this point, marke this Case, a man hath issue three daughters, by one venter, and one daughter by another venter, and dyeth seised, &c. they all enter, and two of the daughters by the first venter die, the third daughter by the same venter shall be heyre alone to their two parts, and the fourth daughter of the halfe blood getteth therein nothing, 10. Assi. p. 27. yet 4. Assi. p. 10. if a man die seised hauing issue two daughters by diuers venters, both vnder age, and a stranger abateth, and one of these daughters in their infancie, releaseth all her right, and dyeth without issue, the other may haue a mortdancestor, and recouer the whole Inheritance, as heire to her Father, though she can by no meanes be heyre to her Sister: But if she which released, had beene of full age when shee released, she had giuen away her moitie. And if shee had entered

tered at full age, or under age, nothing had accrewed to her Sister: But not entring, the mortdaucestor to which they were both intituled, goeth for all to the suruiuor. And this I thinke to be a good case, making nothing on Bractons side, and not plaine any thing on Littleton.

SECT. XXIIII.
Of Contribution

THat which Britton toucheth aboue, of Contribution, I vnderstand to be in case, where one partner prayeth ayde of another, the sequell whereof I haue shortly told you: There is another Contribution by Statute, Marlebridge, c. 9. which willeth, Si hæreditas aliqua de qua vnica tantum secta debeatur, ad plures participes eiusdem hæredit. devoluatur, ille qui habet eineciam partem vnicam faciet sectam, & participes pro portione sua contribuant. The writ for this Contribution, when the young copartners will not performe the ordinance, hath cum de communi consilio prouiso, &c. reciting the Statute.

This Statute reacheth not to the King, at whose Court all the copartners shall giue their seuerall attendance, suite, and seruice. And if any of the lands partable be holden in Ca[illegible] euery Coheyre shall and must haue a part of that in her alotment, for the Kings profit, The statute of Ireland which is a receipt of Hen. 3. 14 of his reigne to Gerrard Fitzmorrice Iustice, sheweth that by those dayes, the first borne partner did alwayes homage for her selfe and her fellowes to euery common Lord of the fee who tooke all his seruice, per manus primogenitæ, which primogenita, had in recompence; (saith the Statute) no homage, wardship, or subiection of Copartners, nor any thing but the Capitall Messuage, ratione einecia: Glanuil (which writ before the Statute) saith, that homage and all other seruices, were done to the chiefe Lord by the hand of the eldest parcener for all the rest, without guerdon from them or their heyres,

in

in the first or second degrée: But (by him) their heyres in the third degrée were bound to doe homage, and pay reliefe to the heyres of the eldest daughter, &c. Because forsooth (as Bracton maketh the reason) issue being had and continued to the third and fourth degrée, the heyre of the eldest, might now take homage without feare of being excluded from inheriting that which was altogether vnlike to descend vnto them: But by Bracton the youngest Sister should presently doe fealtie to the eldest, and by Britton (who wrote after Marlbridge) the matter rested méerely in the Lords election, (for thus saith he) Election le Seignior aprendre tiels seruices per vn mayne ou per les mains de toutes les parceners, Car autrement per droit les gardes & marriages des auters parceners pur les parols in le briefe de gard ou le plaintiffe dit que launcester, l'infant soit son tenant & lui fist seruice de chiualer. cac. 68. fo. 175.

Now séeing that Glanuile, the Statute of Ireland, Bract. Britton, and al do agrée, that euery Lord might take his seruices by the hands of the eldest partner, (the reason whereof was a desire which the Law had to conserue Seignories in their intierties, & that Lords should not take or diuide them into mynnomes, and Crotchets) what was it that caused the making of this ninth Chapter of Marlebridge? It should séeme that Lords in those dayes played vpon the aduantage, And though they were scrupulous in taking of homage, by which they were shut from succession, and yet willing enough to take intirely all other emoluments incident or annext to the tenure, from one paire of hands: yet suite of Court, which is burdenous or inconuenient to none but to the tenants, they would be and were content to dissipate, and it should séeme also that in puisne Sisters and Coheyres, though they were easily intreated, that the eldest should do all suit and seruice, yet they could be well content to giue them nothing for their paines, and therefore a Statute was needfull, for other things I will not accuse old writers of error, they erred not perhaps if they take it

as

as it was taken by Lawyers then, though that taking staggered from Lawes conformitie.

This I say, (to me) the statute of Ireland is sufficient to proue that the eldest Sister shall haue no gard, marriage, or subiection of the yongest, and neither homage nor fealty (by Litl.) can be taken otherwise, then a seruice incident to a tenure, for which it is lawfull to distraine. As therefore when a Mannor descendeth to two partners, each one may haue parcell of the demesne, and parcell of the seruices, and so of one there may step vp two Mannors: And if the diuision be that one shall haue the demesnes, and another the seruices, the suite is now in a very hant suspention, and the Mannor for a time broken in pieces: but it shal be a Mannor againe, if she which had the seruices die without Issue, (per Thiru. 12. H.4. fo.34. 35) So I doubt not but when a tenement, holden by seruice military, descendeth vnto two coparceners, and diuision is euenly made, each of them may pay rents and do seruice for her part to the Lord, who may take fealty and homage of either of them, if he will: And may be compellable to take homage of one of them at the least, which for the warrantie shall be auailable to both.

SECT. XXV.

What seruice belongeth only to the eldest parcener to doe.

THere is some thing besides suite of Court that shall lie only vpon the part, which by an Alcumized tearme we call einitia: Fitzherbert titulo partition. 18. hath this note, If the Earledome of Chester descend vnto two parceners, it shall be diuided betwixt them, As other lands vse to be, and the eldest shall not haue the Seigniory or Earledome whole to her selfe, quod nota: adiudged, per totam curiam, 23. H.3. But this notwithstanding if law should haue the course, which she had in her state of innocencie, I thinke the capitall Messuage of a Knights fee, and the head of an Earldome or Baronie in partition ought euer to goe to the eldest. And if because there is not else perhaps wherewith to make purparte to the youngest coheyre, or not any other thing, holden in Capite, to be distributed for the Kings aduantage and so for necessity, (quæ nullis vinculis legum continetur) the head of a Barony be diuided, yet the indiuisible seruice by which it is holden, as scutage and grand-serjeantie, I meane the very actuall seruice, falleth by right vpon the eldest parcener. Et vbi est commodum, ibi debet esse onus, and so vbi est onus debet esse commodum: whether the case following proue mine assertion or no, I will set it downe out of my Lord Dyer, and then prepare me to speake of another partnership: Humfrey Bohune, sometime Earle of Hereford and Essex, held the Mannors of Harefield, Newman and Whitenhurst by seruice of Constableship of England (which is grand-serjantie) and dyed seised, hauing issue onely two daughters, they entred, tooke husbands, and the husband of the youngest became King, then partition was made, in which the King and his wife did choose Whitenhurst and Harefield, and Newman fell to the other partner: By the opinion of all the Justices of England, the reseruation of the tenure at the first was good, the two daughters before marriage exercise this office by sufficient deputie, and after marriage the husband of the eldest might execute alone, And per omnes iusticiarios, as when there are two daughters, and the Father dyeth seised of lands holden of one of them, the whole seruice, if it be entire, (as homage) is reuiued after partition: so here vnitie of parcell of the tenancie in the King, did not determine the office, but it continued in the other parcener, so that the King might exact the seruice, or refuse it at his pleasure, as euery Lord may refuse the homage of his tenant, if it be not ancestrell. Mes pur ceo que le office fuit haut & dangerous, & auxi verri chargeable al Roy in fees, le Roy voile declaimer de auer le seruice execute Dier 11. Eliz. fo. 285.

THE

THE WOMANS LAWIER.

The second BOOKE.

NOw that I haue brought vp a Woman, and made her an Inheritrix, taken her out of Ward, helped her to make partition, &c. me thinks she should long to be married: Fœmina appetit virum, sicut materia formam, And I did not meane when I begun, to produce any Vestall Virgin, Nunne, or new Saint Bridget. Following therefore my first intention, I will begin to instruct Women growne, first such as are, or shortly shall be Wiues, and then Widdowes.

SECT. I.

Of Marriage, according to the Ciuill and Common Law.

MArriage is defined to be a Coniunction of Man and Woman, containing an inseparable connexion, and vnion of life. But as there is nothing that is begotten and finished at once, so this Contract of coupling man and woman together, hath an inception first, and then an orderly proceeding. The first beginning of Marriage (as in respect of Contract, and that which Law taketh hold on) is when Wedlocke by words in the future tence is promised and vowed, and this is but sponsio, or sponsalia. The full Contract of Matrimonie, is when it is made by words, de praesenti, in a lawfull consent, and thus two be made man and wife existing without lying together, yet Matrimonie is not accounted consummate, vntill there goe with the consent of mind and will Coniunction of body.

SECT. II.

Of Sponsion or first promising.

THe first promising and inception of Marriage is in two parts, either it is plaine, simple and naked, or confirmed and borne by giuing of something: the first is, when a man and woman binde themselues simply by their word only to Contract Matrimonie hereafter: the second, when there is an oath made, or somewhat taken as an earnest or pledge betwixt them on both parts, or on one part, to be married hereafter. There is not here to be stood vpon, the age definitiuely set downe for making of marriage irreuocable, but all that are seuen yeeres old (betwixt whom Matrimony may consist) may make sponsion and promise. But if any that is vnder the age of seuen, begin this vow and betrothing, it is esteemed as a mist, and vanisheth to nothing.

SECT.

SECT. III.
Of publike Sponsion.

This Sponsion (in which as it stands, is no full Contract of Matrimony, nor any more, saue onely an obligation, or being bound in a sort to marry hereafter) may be publique or secret: publique, either by the parties themselues, present together, or by message or Letters when they be distant one from another: Neither is there herein any curious forme of paction or stipulation required, but onely by words, howsoeuer expressed, a plaine consent and agreement of the parties, and by the Ciuill Law, (with which the ancient Canons concorded) of their parents, if the Contractors were *sub potestate parentum*: the like reason seemeth to be for consent of tutors, &c. But it is now receiued a generall opinion that the good-will of parents is required, in regard of honestie, not of necessitie, according to the Canons which exact necessarily, none other consent but only of the parties themselues, whose Coniunction is in hand, without which the conclusion of parents is of none effect: note further, that *sponsalia* may be made pure or conditionall, and whatsoeuer is else adiected (as earnest, pledge, or such like) is but accidentall.

SECT. IIII.
Of secret Sponsion.

Those Sponsals which are made when a man is without witnesse, *Solus cum sola*, are called secret promising or desponsation, which though it be tolerated, when by liquid & plaine probation it may appeare to the Judge, and there is not any lawfull impediment to hinder the Contract, yet it is so little esteemed of, (vnlesse it be very mani-

manifest) that another promise publique made after it, shall be preferred and preuaile against it. The cause why it is misliked, is the difficultie of proofe for auoyding of it, when for offence her iust cause of refusall, the one or other partie might seeke to goe loose, and perhaps cannot, but must stand haltered from any other Marriage, and the Iudge in suspence what to determine.

SECT. V.

The validity of the Desponsation.

THough this Sponsalia be allwaies made with intent that Matrimony should insue, yet the Contracter cannot therunto be compelled, vnlesse there were another thing ioyned to the Contract of Spousals, neither are they compellable to marry, though an oath accompanied the promise, vnlesse it were made pure and without Condition, for in conditionall sponsion of Marriage, the bond of performance is suspended in the Condition, till that be performed, vnlesse there follow a relinquishment of the Condition, by copulation of bodies, or a new consent by words of the present.

SECT. VI.

The nature of the Condition.

AND here in the quality of Conditions it is obserued, that if the Condition annexed to the promise be repugnant against the right of Matrimony, the disposition of the whole Spousals are void: As if a man promise a woman to marry her, if she poison the child which she conceiued, the promise is of none effect, as towards Marriage. But a

Con-

Condition, though it be otherwise unhonest or impossible, corrupteth not promise of Marriage if it be not aduersant, and against the Law of wedlocke.

SECT. VII.

How long the performance of promise is to bee excepted.

Now it may bee demanded what time must be tarried and expected by the Law Ciuill and Common, for perimplishing of promises made of future Wedlocke: It is answered, that if the limits of time prefixed when the sponsion was first made, be once passed and expired: if the vow were made without limitation of time, then (where there appeareth not any weighty cause of stay) if both the parties be residing in one Prouince, the woman quæ non vult sua vota diutius deludi, may after two yeares marry to whom she listeth, But if her Spouse be commorant in another Prouince, then she must tarry three yeares, Though indeede these times of expectance, may be prolonged and lengthened, by a Judge, as he shall finde cause iust and reasonable.

SECT. VIII.

In what case the betrothed may refuse one another.

If after the Sponsion or first betrothing, and before Matrimony contracted, some euill disease (as leprosie, or some violent cause or casualty) make one of the parties unfit for generation, the other may repudiate and abandon him or her, which shall be so diseased or unabled. Spousals are also dissolued for fornication, specially if it be committed by either of the parties with their kindred: likewise Spousals which are made a pupillis may be dissolved by a bare renuntiation, but by no meanes they are rightlier avoided, then by a dissention of both the Contractors, from their first consent, for by such dissent also society is or may be broken in sunder. There are other causes for which the bond of desponsation may be taken away, as devulgation of kindred unknowne, and opportunity of nuptialls sought by detestable meanes, for which cause not only Spousals, but Marriage it selfe, when it is contracted, may be dissolved.

SECT. IX.

By what authoritie Spousals are to bee undone.

TO all these causes of undoing the first vowes of marriage, there must be added the authority of the Bish which hath power to absolue, yet the Canons doe without the authority of any Bishops make free from the Obligation of onely promised marriage, all those which abdicate themselues to Religion. And Hostiensis contendeth that without authority of any Judge, Spousals are undone ipso iure, by a post-marriage, made by words of the present time, sed nemo sibi ipsi ius dicere debet, no man may bee his owne Judge: And it is certaine, that espousals ought neuer to be undone, but by publike authority, unlesse the cause for which wee will haue them undone be so well knowne, that it needeth neither proofe nor sentence, such as is fornication when it is notorious, and publike to all the world.

SECT.

SECT. X.

Of Matrimony contracted in the present time, and who may contract.

THose which the Latines call puberes, that is, they which are come once to such state, habit and disposition of body that they may be deemed able to procreate, may contract Matrimony by words of the time present, for in contract of Wedlocke, pubertas, is not strictly esteemed by number of yeares, as it is in wardship, but rather by the maturity, ripenesse, and disposition of body: There is further required in them which contract Matrimonie, a sound and whole minde to consent, for hee that is mad, without intermission of fury, cannot marry: But hee that is deafe and dumbe, may contract Matrimony, quia non verbis tantum sed nutu & signis sensa mentis exprimuntur, and as they which are impuberes, cannot for infirmity of age, make any firme knot of Wedlocke, so likewise they which by coldnesse of nature, or by inchantment, are impotent, be forbidden to contract.

The impediments Ecclesiasticall, as vowes, Compaternitie and spirituall kindred, I will not meddle with: But come to kindred of bloud, which containeth a principall let and prohibition of Marriage.

SECT. XI.

Impediment of Marriage by Kindred and Consanguinitie.

IN the worlds infancie men were inforced by necessity to marry with owne kindred, propter hominum paucitatem, But that necessity is taken away and long since by the very voice of God, they which are in certaine degrees of bloud

bloud are forbidden to marry, Leuiticus 18. And because Marriage is an aboundant seminarie of charitie and loue, it is wisely and profitably ordeyned that it should be dispersed into many families.

Therfore by Naturall, Ciuill, and Common Law, Marriage is cleane forbidden betwixt all those, which are as Parents or Children one towards another in infinitum; and betwixt those persons, which are of kindred in the transuerse line, Marriage is forbidden till the fourth degree bee past.

SECT. XII.
The impediment of Marriage by Affinitie.

THere is further a certaine nigh alliance called affinity, quasi fines duarum cognationum coniungens, this riseth betwixt them which are married, and the kindred of one of them, as betwixt the husband and the kindred of his wife: now affinity prohibiteth Marriage onely to the persons contracted, &c. for the Cosins or Consanguinity to my wife, are of affinitie onely to me, and not to my brothers or children by a former Wife; and my bloud and consanguinity are kindred of affinitie onely to my Wife, and not to her brothers or former children: here is it that the Father and the Sonne may marry the Mother and the Daughter, and two Brethren may marry two Sisters in another Family: for the Consanguinity, of which one is of bloud to the husband, and another to the wife, are betwixt themselues in no bond of affinity: And obserue that in what degree a man or woman is to one of them that are married, by Consanguinity, they are accompted in the same degree to the other in affinity: As the wiues brother, who is in primo gradu to his Sister, is in the same degree to her husband, and their children in the second, &c.

And

And so forth their Children Children, which after the fourth degree, are againe by all lawes permitted to marrie, contrahitur & affinitas per illicitum coitum.

SECT. XIII.

Diuersitie of Religion.

AMongst the hinderances of marriage, note this also, that by Constitution of holy Church, marriage is forbidden betwixt persons of divers Religions, as Jewes and Christians.

SECT. XIV.

Of feare and constraint.

ALso Matrimonie holdeth not when it is extorted by force, or by such a feare as may cadere in constantem virum; quia matrimonia debent esse libera.

SECT. XV.

Of Marriage detestable made.

ALso Marriage holdeth not, when it is sought or made with wickednes: And if a man promise to a woman which he hath adulterously polluted that he will marry her when his wife dyeth, &c. Or if a man haue sought to abridge the dayes of his lawfull wife to marry another: These villanies are such perpetuall cankers in marriage, that they doe not onely hinder it to be made, but also rend it in sunder when it is made.

There

There are other crimes, quæ distrahunt Matrimonia contracta, as Incest cum cognata, and rauishment, yet if any man rauish a Maide, or other vnmarried Woman, the Canons doe admit him to marry with her if she consent: But otherwise shee shall be rendered to her Father, vpon whose suite and accusation, the rauisher is put to Capitall punishment.

There are by the Ciuill and Common Lawes many other impediments of Marriage, as susceptio propriæ sobolis, publica pœnitentia, cædes Sacerdotis, interdictum Ecclesiasticum, &c. which I will not trouble Women withall.

SECT. XVI.

Marriage forbidden by publique Constitution.

BY Ciuill ordinance also Marriage is sometime restrained and forbidden, as betwixt him which adopteth, and her which is adopted: for seeing that they which are adopted are in the place and stead of Children, there resteth a League, as of kindred betwixt them and the bloud of him which adopteth, by the Ciuill Law and Canons both.

But this Ciuill Kindred lasteth no longer then the adopted are in potestate adoptantis, Neither is it any obstacle to a Marriage, saue onely betwixt the adopted and adoptant, and those which are in his power. And as adoption hindereth Marriage by the Ciuill Law: so by the same lawe, a man may not marry her whom hee tooke exposed, as a cast-away or a foundling, and brought her vp as a Daughter. Marriage is also forbidden, sometime ratione publicæ honestatis, as if a Man be diuorced from

from his wife, and afterwards shee hath a Daughter by another man, this is no Daughter in Law to the husband, yet hee should doe impudently to marry her. Those prohibitions of Marriage that were sometime betwixt a Tutor and Pupill, betwixt a President and a Woman in his subiection, betwixt a Senator and a freed bondwoman, betwixt a Senators Daughter and a freed bondman, betwixt a woman Comedian or one whose parents used some lasciuious or light Art, and a Senator: lastly, betwixt free and seruile, are all either by long publike Custome or by Common Law taken away.

SECT. XVII.

Of Polygamie.

There are examples in Scripture of Poligamy (viz.) where men had more wiues then one at once, as Abraham, Iacob, Dauid, and Salomon had: And it seemeth 21. of Deuteromie 15. that it was sufferable by Moyses his law, But it was said at the first, man and wife shall be one flesh, and the examples were rather permitted then lawfull. The Ciuill Law Canons, and all Christian Common wealths doe utterly condemne Polygamie, and so much did the wise Emperors of Rome detest all petulancie of Marriage, that they made and ordained Lawes, that Women which within the yeare of mourning for their husbands betake them to wedlocke againe, should be reputed infamous and defamed. But this also the Canons haue taken away, Contracts of Matrimony ought to be publike. Nuptials de presenti ought alwaies to be made publike at the Church, or at the least, in presence & Congregation, del bon gents, yet is it not of necessity, that they which marry stipulate by thẽselues, or be present in person at the contract making.

making, but it may be well enough by Proctor, so that the Contractors themselues be willing and witting, or that they ratifie it when it is done.

SECT. XVIII.

What words are requisite.

THere needs no stipulation or curious forme of Contract in Wedlocke making, but such words as proue a mutuall consent are sufficient, and it may be made by Letters. If question rise about words, recurrendum est ad communem intellectum, & vsum loquendi, & indubio pro matrimonio iudicandum, for there is more doubtfulnesse in construing of words, vt res magis valeat quam pereat,&c.

SECT. XIX.

The Accidents of Marriage.

THose things which are of solemnitie or beneuolence, as prouision of Dower, earnest, giuing pledges, nuptiall benediction,&c. are not of the essence of Matrimony which is made by consent: for though Dower cannot consist without Marriage, yet Marriage may very well stand without dower: And so it is of all Donations propter nuptias: In onely one case written instruments are required in making of Marriage, and that is where a man marrieth her whom he hath holden a long time as Concubine, here instrumenta dotalia are behouefull, that the children had before Marriage, may be esteemed Legitimate: But this holdeth not in England.

SECT.

SECT. XX.

Wherefore Marriage ought to be made.

THe causes of Matrimony principally are two: The first is *susceptio sobolis*, increase of Children, for euen by *Plato* euery good man ought to desire that he may leaue behind him worshippers of God, and propagators of piety: The second cause is the euiting of fornication and vncleannesse 1. *ad Corinth. ca. 7* Saint *Paul* biddeth, that to auoid fornication euery man haue his owne wife, and euery woman her own husband, and whosoeuer marryeth for beautie, age, order, splendour of birth, or for riches, rather then for these two causes, doth very peruersly, though it be not expresly disallowed, but Marriage may be for the other things also, and the Consent may be giuen for them.

SECT. XXI.

The Consummation and indiuiduitie of Marriage.

WHen to the Consent of minde, there is added Copulation of body, Matrimonie is consummate, the principall end whereof is propagation or procreation: But where the course after going is not obserued, there riseth no lawfull Off-spring, the Children which are had, are not in power and commandement of them which beget or beare them, neither are they taken by Law for any other, then *vulgo quæsiti*. Otherwise it is in lawfull Wedlocke, the knot whereof is so straight and indissoluble, that they which are yoked therein, cannot the one without the consent of the other, (neither was it euer permitted) abdicate themselues, or enter into Religion, for Saint *Paul* in the aboue titled Epistle and Chapter, saith plainely, that the hus-

husband hath not power of his owne body, &c. And there cannot chance any fedity or uncleannesse of body so great, as that for it a man and wife ought perpetually to be segregated, yea so unpartible be they, that law saith, they may not utterly leaue coniugalem consuetudinem, though one of them haue the very leprosie it selfe.

And here is moued a question not impertinent, That is, whether a woman be bound to follow her husband wheresoeuer he goeth, if he require it, whereunto it is answered by Bartall and by some other, That if the wife before shee married knew the negotiations and occasions of her husband, would be such, that he must of necessity euer be trauelling, she is bounden, and in the Contract seemeth to haue consented to go with him at commandement, but if after the bargaine made he take up a new tricke of circumuagari, she may let him goe when he list, and tarry at home when shee will.

SECT. XXII.

Of Diuorce.

PActis pœnarum cogi potest nemo ad Matrimonium contrahendum: And as no man can be compelled by any conuention of paine or penaltie to contract Matrimony, so is it impossible, when it is once lawfully and euidently contracted, to distract it by any partition, couenant, or humane tradition, Quos Deus coniunxit, homo non separet, yet there are Causes, for which diuers are permitted: But Diuorce, that onely separateth a consuetudine coniugali, taketh not away the bond of Matrimony, and therefore Diuorces are sometimes perpetuall, as long as the parties liue, sometimes for a season limited, and sometime, till reconcilement be had, and he that maketh Diuorce with his wife being only separated a Toro, is forbidden to take another wife.

SECT.

SECT. XXIII.

Causes of Divorce.

THe Civill Law hath many causes of Divorce, but by Divine and Common Law, the onely sufficient cause is adultery and fornication, which by the Canons is carnall and spirituall: the spirituall is heresie and Idolatry: They dissolve Matrimony for spirituall fornication onely, where one of the parties is converted to Christian faith, and the other for hatred of his religion will not cohabit, &c. And this is taken also from Saint Paul 1. ad Corinth. 7. where he saith, If the unbeleeving depart, let him depart, a Brother or Sister is not in subiection.

SECT. XXIV.

Impotencie or Disabilitie of Procreation.

THere is admitted also, in dissolution of Marriage, the complaint of impotencie: And Iustinian very discreetly, willed that in that exploration or proofe of the defect there should be expected three yeares: but the Canons ordeine that Matrimony is dissolued by probation of impotencie, without mention or limits of time. And this is more then a bare divorce or separation, a Toro, for it dissolveth Marriage, avoyding it as if had never beene: so that he or shee whose fellow is convicted of impotencie, may choose a new friend, and presently marry againe.

But this is to be understood of impotencie which was before the Marriage made: for indeede where the impediment was so precedent, there could not any Matrimony exist or have being, &c.

Otherwise it is, when this disability betideth after Marriage perfected and consummate, for in that case, he or she which remaineth potent, shall not leaue and depart from the impotent, but be compelled to beare the discommodity, aswell as any other ill fortune. And that which is here taught of Coniugall impotencie, stretcheth to all impediments of Marriage which are perpetuall, vt per ea Matrimonium nunquam extitisse iudicetur.

SECT. XXV.

Marriages inter ascendentes & descendentes.

Those Marriages that are made betweene ascendentes and descendentes, are so detestable, that by the Ciuill Law they deserue exile and confiscation of goods. And there is a glosse that would extend this to all vnlawfull Marriages: but by Bartell and others, it is to be inflicted only vpon those, which are contra iura sanguinis.

SECT. XXVI.

Captiuitie or long absence of one which is married.

It falleth out not seldome, the one of them which are married to be taken captiue, or otherwise so deteined, that it is vncertaine if he liue or no.

Therefore because it is in some sort dangerous to expect long the incertaine returne of an absent yoake-fellow, here the Ciuill Law did ordaine, that after a husband had beene gone fiue yeares, and nothing knowne whether he liued or no, the wife might marry againe, and so might the husband, that had expected his wife, &c. But the Common Law commandeth simply to forbeare Marriage till the death of him or her that is missing be certainely knowne.

SECT.

SECT. XXVII.

That no crime dissolueth marriage.

Of old time, some Crimes were numbred amongst the Causes of Dissoluing marriage: but Iustinian changed the Law here in part, and the Canons vpon the saying of Christ, Quos Deus coniunxit, &c. will not by any meanes that Matrimony rightly made and consummate, can bee dissolued, quoad ad vinculum Matrimonij, though for fornication they suffer a parting, quoad Torum. So that nodus legitimi Matrimonij, is neuer dissolued but by death, and the wife as long as she liueth is subiect to the law of her husband by Saint Paul.

Yet saith Lagus, seeing that in Contracts of Wedlock we regard as well what is decent and conuenient, as what is lawfull, I cannot tell why we be not bound in dissoluing of it to follow the like equitie: and for example, if a Wife cannot dwell with her husband without manifest danger of death, because he is cruell and bloudy, why may not shee be separated iudicis ordinarij cognitione precedente.

SECT. XXVIII.

The Authoritie of the ordinarie Iudge, &c.

For if Spousals of future Marriage cannot be dissolued without publike authority, it must néedes follow, that without like authoritie, there can bee no repudiation when Matrimony is fully contracted and consummate: But in pursuing of diuorce the strict order of Iudiciall procedings is not alwayes seuerely kept: for regularly production of witnesses before contestation of suite, non adiuuat producentem, yet if Cornelia sue a Diuorce against Sempronius, causa consanguinitatis, and Sempronius being cited will not appeare, if now Cornelia bring her witnesses, the Judge may receiue them.

Marry this religious obseruation the Canons giue him euer, when he commeth to point of Judgement, That the danger is lesse, in leauing men contrary to the Statutes of men, then in separating (contrary to the Statutes of God) those which are lawfully conioyned.

Thus farre haue I run my selfe in debt to Doctor Conradus Lagus, of whom in the third part of his Method, ca. 22. may be further learned the difference betwixt Scortum, pellex and Concubina, Our English comprehendeth them all in one word, and I would they dwelt all in one House, beyond Seas, Concubinatus speciem conjugij——habet; Et ex Concubinæ natis conceditur beneficium legitimationis. If maid, wife or widow, aske what I meane to tell them so much of Ciuill and Canon Law, seeing they be none of those Country women, I pray them not to looke for the Regions in mappa mundi, but for their owne Regiment in Christian dutie: The spirituall Law is here an Oracle to the temporall, which euermore sendeth to the Ecclesiasticall Judge, viz. the Bishop, for certification of lawfulnes or vnlawfulnes of Wedlocks when Accouplements come in question.

SECT. XXIX.

Statutes concerning Marriage.

For it is true that Newdigate saith, 12. He. 8. fo. 6. that marriage and Diuorcements with the circumstances of them be properly no parcell of Common-Lawes learning.

Yet it is very needfull here that I shew you here what the Lawes of England haue needfully concerning Marriage established. 32. H. 8. ca. 38. declareth all persons lawfully to marry

marry, which are not prohibited by Gods Law. And it was ordeyned, that all Marriages contracted and solemnized in face of the Church, and consummate with bodily knowledge, should remaine indefeasable, notwithstanding any pre-contract, &c. Further, that neither dispensation, prescription, law, reseruation, prohibition, or any thing (Gods law excepted) shall trouble or impeach any Marriage made without the Leuiticall degrées, nor any man bee receiued in spirituall Court to processe, plea, or obligation, contrary to this Act. This Statute, though it seemed to be made vpon good and great considerations, (because precontracts too too slenderly proued, and sometime but onely surmized, helped the Romish oppression, and separated those which were at quiet in an honest coniunction) yet many did after the making of it, very dissolutely come from their first vowes, and, as it were in spight of conscience and Ecclesiasticall censure, coupled themselues bodily with such as they newly fancied, slipperily leauing their former Contracts: it is repealed 2. & 3. Ed. 6. ca. 3. only in the points of pre-contracts: And they are left in the validity which they were of, by the Kings Ecclesiastical lawes, immediately before the making of 32. with prouiso that all the rest of the said Act standeth whole and in strength. So is it now againe by 1. Eliz. cap. 1. See also 5. & 6. Ed. 6. ca. 12. that the Marriage of Priests and Ecclesiasticall persons is lawfull, their Children legitimate, a Priest may be tenant by the courtesie, and his Wife haue Dower.

It is a sport to behold how some of the Canonists & Glossographers refreshed themselues in their disputes about Nuptiall questions, how cleare they make it, that, If Adam our first Father were now aliue and a Widdower, he could not take a Wife, quia, all Women are his Children, and that in the right line: Then what a question it is, whether vnlawfull copulation cause any affinitie or no.

In hoc articulo, (saith one of them) non parcam in foro verecundiæ, that is to say, hee will handle the quidditie without shame or honestie, and then in the plainest that may be, he findeth a difference betwixt a dogges necke in the Collar, and his nose in the Ring, betwixt knocking at the Barrels head, and setting it abroach: but the curious learning was that of spirituall kindred, caused either by holy Baptisme, or by the blessed Chrisme, and this had power impediendi Matrimonium contrahendum, & dirimendi matrimonium contractum: yea, this was such a matter, that 39. Ed. 3. fo. 32. Bastardie is pleaded against the Plaintiffe in assise, and the cause was, that the father married a woman, before which Marriage he had christned one which was his Wiues cousin, and for this cause, after one of them was dead, Diuorce was sued, and Judgement thereof giuen in the spirituall Court, though indeed by Justice Thorpe, and the greatest opinion in the temporall Court, the Issue could not be bastardized, unlesse the Parents had beene called, and the Nuptials destroyed by sentence, which was now impossible to doe, for death had determined them.

Out of question therefore, if the parties had liued, a little or no Kindred, had marred great good acquaintance: But howsoeuer, by those dayes secular Marriage was forbidden in spirituall men, and secular men were straightly prohibited by spirituall. Spirituall Kindred, the Statutes afore-going, haue now welcommed Wedlocke, cleane out of the Popes stockes, And the 18. of Leuiticus alone, doth in a manner sufficiently demonstrate, with what persons Women are restrained to marry.

SECT.

SECT. XXX.

With what persons Women may not marry.

SUch are her Grand-father, her Father, her Sonnes Sonne, &c. her Brother, though it be but the one part, her Fathers or Mothers Brother, her Brothers or Sisters Sonne, or her Sonnes Sonne. Brothers or Sisters Children (saith Ramus in his Commentaries of Christian Religion, lib. 2. ca. 9.) are forbiden to inter-marry, sed more, non lege Diuina vel Romana: Christians, he saith further, which haue abrogated the Law, 25. of Deuteronomy, whereby a Brother might bee challenged to raise vp the house of his deceased brother, haue also constituted a prohibition, within certaine degrées of affinity, and therefore a man may not marry with the widdow of his Grandfather or of his Father, or with the widdow of his owne Sonne, or of his Sonnès Sonne, or with the widdow of his Brother, or of his Brothers Son, or of his Brothers Sonnes Sonne, &c. Nor with the Grand-mother, Mother, Daughter, Neece, great Aunt, Aunt or Sister of his deceased wife.

SECT. XXXII.

Of Wooing.

I Am affraid my feminine acquaintance will say I write as I liue, I talke much of Marriage, but I came not forward: stay a while yet I pray you, I know many an honest woman more repenting her hastie Marriage ere she was wooed, then all the other sinnes that euer she committed. It were good reason we speake a little of wooing, but to handle that matter, per genus & species, would take vp as much roome, as the Indian figge-tree, euery third whereof, when it falleth to the ground, groweth to a body. I will slip by it, onely obseruing that the giuing of gloues, rings, bracelets, chains, or any thing that is ex sponsaliorũ largitate (as a man would say, of loues liberality) or as a pledge of future Marriage betwixt them that are promised, haue a condition (silent for the most part) annexed vnto them, that if Matrimony doe not insue, the things may be demanded backe and recouered, yet there is a distinction of like, for I haue authoritie in it, Si sponsus dedit aliquid, & aliquo casu impediuntur nuptiæ, donatio penitus rescinditur, nisi osculum intervenerit: marry if he had a kisse for his money, then the one halfe of that which was giuen, is the womans owne good: And she hath yet more fauor in the case, for whatsoeuer shee gaue, were there kissing or no kissing betwixt them, she may aske all, and haue all againe. Quære of this in the Consistorie.

SECT. XXXII.

The Condiments of Loue.

There are with vs, as wel as with the Ciuilians, many kinds of Donations propter nuptias, and some ex sponsaliorum largitate: Good meats are the better for good sauce; venison craueth wine, and Wedlocke hath certaine Condiments, which come best in season in the wooing time, and serue (as Breton saith) pour doner fees come melier talent d'aymer Matrimonie. A husband per se, is a desirable thing, but Donements or Feoffements, &c. better the stomacke, though of it selfe it be good and eager; And because the first Marriage made in Paradice, if you marke it well, had a Jointure, I cannot but allow the circumspection which is had.

SECT. XXXIII.

Of Franke Marriage.

IT was, as I suppose, more frequent in the old time, that men gaue Lands with their Daughters in Marriage, then it was at this day: But now as then, if a man liberally and freely, without money or other considerations, saue onely loue and naturall affection, giue Lands or Tenements to another man, with a woman which is Daughter, Sister, or Cousin to the Donor, in Franke Marriage, whether it bee tempore Matrimonij, vel ante vel post, this word Franke Marriage maketh an estate of Inheritance, viz. to the Donees, and the heyres of their two bodies, and they shall hold quite of all manner of seruices (except the pure fealtie) till the fourth degree bee past. But the Issue in the fift degree, and his Descendant, shall hold of the Donor and his Heyres, as they hold ouer.

SECT. XXXIV.

The Gift must bee Franke.

PEr *Rich.* 16. assi. p. 66. if a man giue land in Franke Marriage, rendring a rent, the reseruation is voyde, till the fourth degree be past per Martine Iustice, 4. H 6. 22. such a reseruation is meerely voyde, for it is contrary to the nature of Franke Marriage.

By the old tenures, such a reseruation is good, and the Donee shall hold in Common estate taile; by Brooke in his Abridgement, it cannot be any estate taile, for want of the parol heyres. And where such a gift is made to a woman, not

not cousin to the Donor, there passeth but estate for life, for it is by a maxime or ground, that Franke Marriage maketh inheritance, and this case is out of the principall: By Bracton fo. 28.& 29. Si terra detur in maritagium viro cum vxore, & eorum hæredibus pro homagio & seruitio viri, licet detur in liberum maritagium (quæ sunt sibi ad inuicem aduersantia,&c.) tunc prefertur homagium & erit ac si donatio fieret tam viro quam vxori, he deliuereth the like learning before, fo.22. and this rule withall ex tacita conditione & pacta incontinenti opposita insunt contractibus, & legem dant eis & illos infirmant.

SECT. XXXII.

The gift must be to a Woman,&c.

IT was deliuered for a Law in tempore H. 8. that Lands cannot be giuen to a man in Frank Marriage, though he be Cousin to the Donor.

SECT. XXXVI.

It may be tempore Matrimonij, ante, vel post.

WHat if after the gift made, the man refuse to marry, the Cousin of the Donor marry else-where?

If two Donees in taile after the Common forme be diuorced vpon a pre-contract made by the woman, they shall remaine ioyn-tenants of the Franke Tenement, and the Inheritance is gone Taile 9. But per Dyer fo. 147. and 12. assi. p. 22. and 19. assi. p. 2. If Tenants in Franke Marriage be diuorced, the Woman shall haue all the Land, for the Land was giuen for the womans sake, and for

for her aduancement; and by Iohn Bracton, her husband hath no more in it but Custodiam, as he is the wiues tutor and Guardian: By the same reason therefore that the wife shall haue the land, if she be diuorced, by the same, I should thinke, she should haue it, if her Sponsus refuse to marry her: But where I giue Land to one to marry my Daughter, or, if hee marry my Daughter, there, if hee marry another woman, I may enter.

SECT. XXXVI.

The word Franke Marriage maketh Inheritance.

IF a man giue lands with his Sister to I. S. in Franke Marriage, habendum eis & hæredibus suis in perpetuum. By Kniuet, Mowbray and Finchden, 45. Ed. 3. fo. 19. this maketh neither Frank Marriage nor estate taile, with an expectance of fee, (as in Case where Lands are giuen expresly in taile, habendum eis & hæredibus, but the fee-simple passeth presently by the gift, for Frank Marriage must be holden of the Donor, which here hath nothing left in him, but all is holden of the Lord Paramount, and the words doe not make any other estate taile: yet 13. Ed. 1. lands were giuen to one, with the Cousin of the Donor in Franke Marriage, habendum eis & hæredibus, and it was taken for good Frank Marriage: This, saith Brooke, was in the yeare, that estates taile were made in. But for all that, if yee look the case in Fitzherbert, Formedone 63. whither Brooke sendeth you, you shall perceiue that at the time of the gift, it was Franke Marriage in fee-simple, for by those dayes the Donee had potestatem alienandi post prolem suscitatam: But in a gift made after the Statute of quia emptores, on such a fashion, I take it the Law will be, as before in the case 45. Ed. 3. According as it was also holden in the yeares of H. 8. that if a gift bee made in Franke Marriage, the remainder to I. S. in fee: this is no good Franke Marriage, for warrantie and acquitall that are incident, &c. bee only in regard of the reuersion to the Donor, and they cannot be had when the fee-simple is presently conueyed to a stranger.

SECT. XXXVIII.

The Accompt of the Degrees.

Litl. accounts the Degrees from the Donor to the Donees, the first Degree; from the Donees to their Issue, the second; from the Donees Issue to his Issue, the third, &c. and the Issue in the fift Degree shall doe seruice. And this (saith he) because the Issue of the Donor and the Issue of the Donee after the fourth Degree past, may inter-marrie by holy Churches Law. Bracton accompts thus, donatarius facit primum gradum; hæres suus facit secundum; hæres hæredis facit tertium; hæres secundi hæredis facit quartum, qui tenebitur ad seruitium, yea, hee maketh it an expresse rule, that onely the Donee and two heyres succeeding lineally, shall enioy the immunitie of being acquitted. And hee seemeth to vnderstand no other reason of the acquitall so long, but onely an abstenancie from homage, lest the taking of it should hinder a reuerting, if it betided the Donee, or the Issue to die without Issue. Fitzherbert titulo droit 55. and 60. citeth 6 H. 3. and 15. H. 3. in warrant of Bractons Computation, which I thinke he fetched not any further then out of the Author himselfe, in whom fo. 21. I find it. And fo. 22. hee answereth a doubt of his owne asking, that is, Whether all other seruice shall follow and continue, if homage be done ante tertium hæredem. Wherein he concludeth, that the seruice euer followeth homage, quamuis ad damnum soluentium: And I conclude, whether it it be the third heyre, or the fourth, that shall doe seruice, he may still vouch, haue a Writ of meane, as if the fourth Degree were not past, and if he bring a Formedone, the Writt shall be Dedit in liberum Maritagium.

SECT. XXXIX.

A Woman giues Lands to one to marry her.

AS Frankie Marriage maketh Inheritance without the words Heyres, and is allwayes made to a woman, and for her sake: so there is another Donatio propter nuptias. that is conditionall without words of Condition made euer by a woman to a man. That is, where a woman giues Land to a man in fee-simple, or for tearme of his life, to the intent that hee marry her, who if hee afterwards when hee is thereto within conuenient time required, refuse, &c. there is now an ordinary Writt for remedy granted in this case, to reduce the Land, which Writt may be sued in the per cui, or post, after one or more alienations, either by the woman sole, or by her and her husband married, against such a one as should haue married her, after the refusall, or after her death by her Heyre, whether it bee Sonne or Daughter, or Daughters with the child of another, and there needs no scripture or writing to proue that the feoffement was for intent of Marriage: nay, if a woman infeoffe a stranger, to the intent to infeoffe her, and one which she intendeth to marrie, if now the espousals take not effect, she may haue Writt causa Matrimonij prelocuti, against the stranger, though the deed of feoffement were simple and sans Condition, an. 34. Ed. 3. li. assi. and 40. Ed. 3. li. assi. a woman enfeoffed one which had a wife, and entred for non-performance of the Condition.

tion, vpon the second feoffée, and her entrie was adiudged lawfull.

Also, where a woman maketh feoffement, rendring rent, if by written déed she can both shew and proue that it was to the intent he should marry her, she shall maintaine her Writt, for causa Matrimonij prelocuti, notwithstanding the reseruation. But if a woman giue Lands in taile vpon prelocution of Marriage, &c. by Fitzherbert she cannot haue this Writt, for the strong streame of Westm 2. de donis conditionalibus, will not be turned by an intendment or matter onely auerrable. To conclude, it is cléere by Iustice Dyer and Fitzherbert both, that if a man giue Lands to a woman, &c. to the intent that shee shall marry him, the fee-simple after Marriage remaines in the woman, and if the Baron alien and die, she may haue a cui in vita, and if shee refuse to marry with him, he shall neuer haue the Writt, causa Matrimonij prelocuti.

By the old Natura breuium Conditions that shall auoyd a feoffement, by a woman thus made, causa Matrimonij, must be expresse, and by indenture, which if it were true, there should not need any Writt at all in the case, I am out of doubt therefore the law is as I haue already deliuered.

But I am demanded a reason, why a womans feoffement is here priuiledged more then mans, to challenge a Condition onely by intendment. Of like there was in the old time, some knaues abroad (as there are now) that with colour of loue and collocution of Marriage cozened heyres and poore wemen of their ground, and gaue them the bootes, when they had done, carrying the gaine to their better beloued, which perhaps could cretisare cum cretensi, and in fauour of women, and in ayde of simplicity sprang vp this Law of auerment for women, not permitted to men, because they be in lesse danger of circumuention in this point, and also better able, when they will haue conditions in their grants considerately to expresse them. Another question is, how

how it commeth to passe that this kind of largition by women, though it be in strength, is not in use as it was wont: are women in our dayes, lesse liberall or lesse louing unto men then they were in former ages? I cannot tell, But I feare craftie fellowes perceiuing they cannot cozen the uncouert to get their lands by faire words first, and let them get husbands afterwards as well as they can, require now a dayes no preludes of feoffements at their hands, but marry them first and cozen them afterwards. Such are Tenants by cozenage: I cannot but mislike them the more, when I consider the great liberalitie, that law useth towards them which marry women Inheritors: yet if they use them with all honest regard, loue and true kindnesse, as they ought to doe, my reason perswades for fauour and forgiuenesse.

Sect. XL.

The courtesie of England.

For Sir, in the Married life Children are some token of true loue, and honest life and kindnes in a husband, breedeth increase of liking in a wife, and where affection hath her right repercussion (if secret imperfection be none impediment) there is like to follow fecunditie, which hath this priuiledge, whosoeuer taketh a Wife seised of lands, or tenements, in fee-simple, fee-taile generall, or as the Heyre of fee-taile speciall, and hath Issue by her, a Childe borne aliue, that by possibility might be heyre of the estate which the mother hath, though the Childe die afterward, he shall haue and hold his wiues Inheritance after her death, in estate of Franke Tenement during his life: and this is called an estate by the Law and courtesie of England; because it is this Realmes priuiledge peculiar: I giue it place in my booke, because it is taken out of the Inheritance

heritance of woman, and in this part because it resembleth the Donations, that are propter nuptias, the Doctrine of it being something like that of Dower.

SECT. XLI.

Marriage.

THis Courtesie is in the Inheritance of a Wife, therefore a consequent of lawfull Marriage, and exceptions of Concubinage, or such like, which are impediments of Dower, must needs be good exceptions here.

SECT. XLII.

Seisin.

THere must be in the wife a seisin and possession; for if she were but heyre in appearance, & die before her Ancestor, this auaileth her husband nothing. Similie, If the Father (being seised of Lands) dye, and soone after his Daughter and Heyre dyeth before actuall seisin had by entrie either by the husband, wife, or other person for them, so that no possession and a naked possession in law here is all one: yea, the law is taken, that if a man dwell in Essex with his wife, and lands descend to her in Yorkeshire, if she die the next day after, before entrie, the husband shall not bee Tenant by the Courtesie, for euen in this case is found a default in him, that he did not constitute one to make entrie for him maintenant after the Auncestors death, & yet if rent descend to a woman Couert, &c. which dieth before day of payment, or after the day, and no demand made of the rent by her husband, hee shall haue Courtesie in the rent notwithstanding. So it is if an Ad-

bouson

vowson in grosse descend to a woman married, hauing Issue, &c. though she die afore auoydance, the husband shall present, and though the Bishop after the descent present by lapse, yet the husband shall haue the second presentment, for there cannot in these things possession be taken maintenant and at all times, as they be in Lands: And take with you here these Cases out of Dier, 1. Ma. fo. 95. Tenant per Cheualrie in cap. dieth, his Daughter and Heyre being vnder age office is found, and the King grants the wardship of body and Land to me which marrieth the ward and hath Issue by her, and after shee accomplisheth the age of sixteene yeares, and the King is satisfied for the two yeares profit, they tender a generall liuerie, and before it be past, the Wife dieth, the Baron shall haue the Courtesie come semble, saith the Booke.

And 6. Eliz. Dier, 229. the like descent is to a Daughter, and married, hauing Issue by her husband, and she dieth ten dayes after her Father, no Liuery being sued that is found by office, the Baron shal be Tenant by the Courtesie, and shall sue liuery.

SECT. XLIII.

No Courtesie of reuersion after estate for life.

THe seisin must be to the Wife in estate of Inheritance not mangled or cut off from the Frank Tenement, and therefore (by Parkins) where a Woman an Heyre enters after her Fathers death, and being seised in fee-simple, makes a Lease of her Land to I. S. for terme of his life, if she now marry, haue Issue, and die during the Lease, the Husband shall neither be Tenant by the Courtesie of the Land when it reuerts, nor of the rents in the meane while: Also 8. assi. p. 6. If a Daughter and Heyre enter, endow her Mother, take a Husband, haue Issue, and dies, the Mother still liuing, the husband shall neuer be tenant by the Courtesie, of that which the Mother held in Dower: for the tenant in Dower here, is in by her husband of his possession, and that possession which the Daughter had, is by the Indowment turned to a reuersion. Note also this case, 19. Eliz. Dier, 357. William Chicke seised in fee, made his Will, vt sequitur, I giue the fee-simple of my house in Soper-lane to my Cousin Alice Ludlam, and after her decease to William Ludlam her sonne (which was Heyre apparant) the Testator died, Alice entred, and married, and died, hauing Issue by her husband: the opinion of the Court was, that Alice had but estate for life, the remainder to her sonne for life, the remainder in fee to Alice Ludlam, but her husband might not be Tenant by the Courtesie.

SECT. XLIV.

No Courtesie of right onely.

If a woman seised in fee of Lands, bee disseised, take a Husband, haue Issue, and die before re-entry, here shall be no holding by the Courtesie: But if during the Couerture the wife entred, and the Disseisor re-entred, here the Husband vnderstanding (after his wiues death) the entrie which she made, may enter and hold by the Courtesie. And if a man seised in fee in the right of his Wife, be disseised before hee haue Issue by her, and after hee hath Issue, and the Wife dies before re-entrie, &c. he may notwithstanding enter and hold by the Courtesie. Parkines 91, 472.

SECT.

SECT. XLV.

Discontinuance.

If the Lachesse of a husband, not carefull to reduce his wiues land pulled away by Disseisin, put him by the Courtesie, it is good reason that his owne discontinuance suffer no lesse punishment: Therefore, if a man make a feoffement in fee of his Wiues Land, and take an estate backe againe to himselfe and his Wife, by whom (being thus remitted) he hath issue & dyeth, he shall not now be Tenant by the Courtesie; for though the wife her selfe were remitted, yet the Baron was not remitted to his wiues Right, so as he might be receiued to plead it; But hauing giuen away his right that he had or might haue, hee was estopped to claime otherwise then from the feoffee, or to make his owne title, contrarie to his owne grant and act, vide By Parkines likewise if before Issue had, the husband make a feoffement of the Wiues Lands, vpon condition of the part of the Feoffee, and then hath Issue by the Wife, and the Wife dieth after the Condition broken, though the Baron now re-enter, hee shall not hold by the Courtesie, vnlesse hee made the feoffement whilst hee was vnder age.

SECT. XLVI.

No courtesie of an estate suspended.

If the Tenant inter-marry with her of whom he holdeth his Land, &c. and she dieth, he shall not haue Courtesie in the Seignorie that was suspended by the couerture: likewise, where the Tenant makes a feoffement of his Lands to a stranger, sur Condition, and the Feoffee intermarry with the Seigniorešse, of whom the Land is holden,

den, and haue Issue by her, and the condition being broken, she dyeth; if now the Feoffor enter, the Feoffee shall not be Tenant per le Curtesie of the Seignorie: But if a feme sole haue a rent or common in or out of certaine Lands, and the Tenant leasseth the Land to a stranger, during the life of I. S. and the woman intermarrieth with the Lessee, hath Issue, and I. S. dyeth, now if the wife die, the Baron shall haue Courtesie in the rent or Common. And if the Tenant leased his ground for 20. yeares, and a woman hauing in the ground a rent charge in fee, intermarrieth with the Lessee, &c. dieth during the terme, it is a question in Parkins, whether the husband shall haue Courtesie in the rent after the terme determine, see Parkins, cap. By the Courtesie.

SECT. XLVII.

No Courtesie of a bare vse.

IF a Woman sole seised, &c. make a feoffement to the vse of her selfe & her heyres, and then she marrieth, hath Issue, and dieth before any estate in the same lands be againe by entry or otherwise executed to her, her husband shall not be Tenant by the Courtesie, and this aswell after the Statute of 27. H. 8. as before, if the Feoffement were since the Statute.

SECT. XLVIII.

What Husband may be Tenant by the Courtesie, and of what estate.

WHere the Wife is actually seised of Lands in fee-simple, fee-taile generall, or as Heyre of fee-taile spe-

speciall, the second Baron may bee Tenant by the Courtesie, as well as the first, for so is the Maxime.

And Parkins, Fitzherbert, and Brooke have all of them the Case, 21. H. 3. viz. A woman Inheritour hath Issue by her Husband, and he dieth, she takes another Husband, hath Issue by him, and that Issue dieth, the woman dieth, her second Husband shall be Tenant by the Courtesie: Bracton agreeth also, who when hee hath shewed this Civilitie of England, concludeth. Quod dicitur de primo, dici poterit de secundo, siue de primo viro hæredes apparentes exciterunt siue non plenæ ætatis vel minoris. But hee addeth, Quod iniuriosum est secundum Stephanum de Segraue, qui dicebat quod lex illa male fuit intellecta, & male visitata: Nam quod dicitur de lege Angliæ, intelligi debet de primo viro, & communibus hæredibus, & non de secundo, maxime cum hæredes apparentes exciterint de primo.

My mind giues mee that hee said truth, and that Law turning a little out of her Channell here before Justice Segraues time, could neuer since bee brought to her course.

SECT. XLIX.

Of speciall Taile.

BEfore West. 2. cap. 1. all the Estates which wee now call tailed (that is curtailed or cut off) were fee-simple Conditionall, If Lands had beene giuen to a man and a woman in Franke Marriage, or to them and to the Heyres of their two bodies (which gifts make now a speciall Taile) as soone as they had Issue, the Condition was thought to be performed. And as a woman suruiuing her first Husband in this case might alien the Land, so might she by bearing a Childe to her second Husband, &c. this makes him Tenant by the Courtesie.

And as West. 2. by the Clause in the end, ad dona prius facta non extenditur, did expresly saue feoffements and alienations made by the Donees post prolem suscitatam, and before the Statute, so the expounders of the Law by equitie, as ye may perceiue, Formedone 66. in Fitzherbert, haue not denied the Courtesie to a second Husband of a woman Donee in Franke Marriage, if he married her before the Statute, though she died after it, wherein it is too late to call them to account whether they did well or no: But I find a replication in Bracton against him that in bar of an assize maketh this title, per legem Angliæ, to say that the land was giuen in Marriage with the first Husband, &c. the Statute therefore I dare affirme, doth but make that cleare which to many was thought reason and Law before. And now out of doubt the second Husband cannot be Tenant by the Courtesie, where the Wife is seised but in speciall taile.

And where a woman is concluded from claiming other Estate, the Baron shall be concluded likewise. As 46. Ed. 3. fo. 5. A man seised of Lands taketh a Wife, they leuie fine, and take backe an estate to themselues and their heyres of their two bodies, they haue Issue Eliz. and die, Eliz. taketh a husband, and shee and her husband leuie a fine, and take backe an estate to them and to the heyres of their two bodies, they haue issue, which being vnder age, the Land being holden in Chiualry, the Baron dieth, Eliz. takes a second Husband, hath Issue and dieth, the Lord seiseth the first Issue as Ward, and entreth into the Land, the second Husband entreth vpon the Lord, claiming by the Courtesie, pretending a remitter to the first estate taile made by the first fine, which to his wife was generall taile, and euery Issue of hers might by possibility inherite it, and for her Issue it is true, but by the better opinion, the wife was estopped to claime contrary to the fine leuied by her selfe and her first husband, whereby they tooke estate but in speciall taile, and being seised as of that and none other during the second Couerture, the husband was concluded likewise and could not bee Tenant by the Courtesie, though the Statute haue taken courtesie d'Angleterre from a second Husband to the Donée in Franke Marriage, or other speciall taile, it hath not taken it from a second Husband, to a Daughter and Heyre of that Estate: for as ye perceiue in the case afore-going, such a Daughter is in as generall taile, and any Childe of hers by any husband begotten, may by possibilitie be Heyre, &c. The words therefore, or as heyres of the speciall taile, are well put in Littl. Canon or Maxime: And I suppose they are not so narrowly to be understood, as if it were not possible a man should be Tenant by the Courtesie, where the Wife is Donée in speciall taile, for if Lands be giuen to a married woman, and to her heyres begotten by her Husband, this I take for speciall taile in the wife onely, and this Husband I thinke may be Tenant by the Courtesie. Also, if lands be giuen to a woman and her heyres begotten by her husband, and her husband die without Issue, shee becomes Tenant after possibilitie of Issue.

And if Fée-simple descendeth to Tenant after possibility, she is now Tenant in fée-simple executed, and her second husband or tenth husband may be Tenant by the Courtesie, otherwise it is where the speciall taile continueth, and the fée-simple is but in pendenti, 9. Ed. 4. fo. 18.

SECT. L.

No Courtesie without a Childe.

I Haue read of some places in England, where by a speciall custome the Husband may be Tenant by the Courtesie, though he neuer had childe by his wife: But the generall Law of the Land is, that there must be Issue borne aliue. By Bracton he that claimeth by the Courtesie, may be inforced to proue, that the Childe sent forth some voyce or cry arguing life and naturall humanity: for if it bellowed, bleated, brayed, grunted, rored, or howled, there accrued no courtesie by getting such an vnciuill vrchin.

By him therefore there must be a naturall crie heard inter quatuor parietes, for (he saith) though a Child be borne mutus & surdus, tamen clamorem emittere debet, siue masculus sit, siue foemina, nam Dicunt E. vel A. quotquot nascuntur ab Eua:

E. or A. all crye that from Eue come,
Though they be borne both deafe and dumbe.

Non sufficit igitur tantum baptizatus & sepultura: yet 28. H.8. Dyer fol. 25. sets downe Fitzherberts opinion, that a man may be Tenant by the Courtesie though the Childe neuer crie, car paraduenture lissue soit nee dumbe, And so saith Parkins 9. 4. 7. viz. that if the issue bee borne aliue, though it die before it be heard crie, or before it be baptized, for that is a matter also with Bracton, if there were no lachesse, contumacie or contempt in the Baron, he may be Tenant by the Courtesie: But by negligence or by contempt he shall preiudice himselfe alcuns diont.

SECT. LI.

A Childe borne beginneth the title of Courtesie.

Now this hauing a Childe, is such a matter (as it seemeth) that maine tenant thereupon the title of Courtesie beginneth: for example, if a bond woman purchase Land and marrie, if the Lord enter before Issue be had, no Childe borne afterwards shall make the husband tenant by the Courtesie: But if the Baron haue Issue by his wife, before the Lords entrie, he shall be tenant by the Courtesie, and the auowrie from that time forward shall rest vpon him solement, And the possession in Law if the wife die, shall

shall not light vpon the Heyre, but vpon the Baron, which shall be tenant to euery præcipe. Ceo est cleere lei, Brooke out of the Doctor and Student, vide Brooke villenage, 35.

And if a woman Heyre haue issue by her husband, commit felonie and be attainted, it hath béen mostly holden, that the husband shall be Tenant by the Courtesie, notwithstanding, and that after Issue had, the Lord may auow for homage vpon the husband without the wife 21. Ed. 3. 49. By Parkins, 91. 475. Likewise if the Wiues Inheritance be recouered against Baron and feme, by false oath, or erronious Processe, and execution is had and sued of this recouerie, if they haue Issue afterwards and then the wife dieth, the Baron now reducing the Land by attaint or error, shall hold per le Courtesie.

Sect. LI.

What if the Childe die.

If a man haue Issue by his wife, that is here in possession, the death of the Issue is no losse of Courtesie, and by Parkins, if a Daughter and Heyre apparant take a Husband, haue Issue by him, and the Issue dieth, if now the Father die, and the Baron and feme enter, he may be Tenant by the Courtesie without hauing other Issue, Brooke makes it questionable.

Also by Brooke, if a man die, his wife being priuement enseient, a Daughter entreth as heyre, taketh a Husband, and hath Issue, if a Sonne post-humus enter vpon the Baron and feme, and the Issue of the Daughter dieth, and the posthumus dieth without Issue, the Baron clærely shall not be Tenant by the Courtesie, vnlesse hee re-enter in his wiues time, and he doubteth, though the Baron enter sans other Issue.

Sect.

SECT. LIII.

By what Acts a Husband shall lose the Courtesie.

If a Woman sole seised in fée take a Husband, haue issue by him, and the Baron is attainted of felony, and pardoned by the King, he shall not be Tenant by the Courtesie (saith Keble, 13. H. 7. 17.) vnlesse hee haue other Issue afterwards: By Bracton, he that séeketh or goeth about the destruction of his Wife, shall not be Tenant by the Courtesie.

SECT. LIV.

Of Dower.

I Haue hitherto handled onely those gifts, causa Matrimonij, which come from Women or their Auncestors, as if English men were so dainty, and coye, that they must be enticed, or our women so vn-amiable, that vnlesse it were by purchase, they could haue no Husbands: But I could neuer heare of any woman that néeded buy new bootes to ride on wooing. Contrariwise, so swéet, faire and pleasing are they, or so very good and prudent (vt eas præcipue quærimus) that though some men get Lands by them, most men are faine to assure part or all of such Lands as they haue (in ioynture or otherwise) to them, ere they can win their loue, and where there is no such assurance, the Christian custome and Law of the Realme giueth euery good Wife part of her Husbands Lands to liue on when hee is dead, which wée call Dower, and of which we come now to speake.

SECT.

SECT. LV.

What Dower is.

THe word in Latine imports no more, but a bringing, giuing, or bestowing, And with the Ciuilians Dos is no other thing, then that which a Wife or some other body in her name, or for her sake giueth to her husband to be his during Couerture. Though Bartol more fine will haue it to be ipsum ius rebus vendi. Dos profectitia (with them) is that which commeth from the Brides Father or her Fathers Father: aduentitia Dos, is from her Mother or other Kindred of their liberalitie. And paraphernalia bona, or such things as the wife bringeth in ædes Mariti propter Dotē, as it were in stead of Dower, and into the Husbands Custodie, but not into his full dominion, for vnlesse shee make a gift of them, shee may aske them, and haue them againe.

Bracton saith, Dos profectitia is the Land giuen in Franke Marriage by the womans Auncestors, aduentitia the Lands which some other Kinsman giueth, and paraphernalia that which is giuen to a man or woman before or after Marriage for other considerations then Marriage. There is further with the Ciuilians a gift pro Dote, giuen in recompence of securitie of Dower, and this doth somewhat resemble our Dower, because it proceedeth from the Husband, as Homer, Tully, and Saint Paul, are called, the Poet, the Orator, the Apostle, carrying a name of generalitie for their speciall excellencie; so in my opinion for the like excellencie among the estates which are made causa Matrimonii, that which women claime in their Husbands Inheritances when they be dead, by a speciall and vniuersall largenesse of the Law is called Dower, concerning which the plainest and most plentifull rule is that of M. Littleton, viz. where the Husband is seised of Lands or Tenements of such estate, that the Issue which by possibility

bility his wife may beare him, may by possibilitie be heyre of that estate Si le possession le Baron ne soit loyalment auient) As addeth Parkins the Wife shall be endowed.

SECT. LVI.

The Husband must be seised.

Dower is of the possession of a Husband, the ground of it therefore is Marriage, a Concubine then shall haue no Dower, no more shall shee which is but onely contracted, and it was holden by some, 10. H.3. that she which was married in a Parlor or Chamber should haue no Dower but it is now taken otherwise.

Also where Marriage is cleerely voyde and vnlawfull, there groweth no title of Dower: But if a woman first contracted to E. I. intermarry afterwards with T. K. this Marriage is voydable, but not cleerely voyde, and if it be not frustrated, otherwise then by death of T. K. the Wife shall haue Dower of his Land. Here yee may perceiue that which destroyeth an absolute true Marriage, destroyeth Dower also: for though by Bracton there may be by speciall Constitution a Dower appointed, that shall stand good against the tempest of diuers assaults, yet by ground of the Common Law Matrimonium est fulcimentum dotis. And Bracton saith in his second booke and 39. Chapter, Vbi nullum omnino Matrimonium, ibi nulla dos: igitur, vbi Matrimonium, ibi dos, quod verum est si Matrimonium in facie ecclesiæ contrahatur.

SECT.

SECT. LVII.

Matrimony may be, and yet no Dower.

Though Matrimony doe allwayes precede Dower, yet doth not Dower allwayes follow Matrimony: for first where the husband had no Land, the Wife can haue no Dower by the Common Law, Bracton and Breton which giue a woman Dower in a certaine somme of money or in other Chattels, speake rather as Ciuill Lawyers then méere English: Also Dower is not granted, vnlesse the Husband is aboue 7. yeers old, and the wife aboue nine, 13. Ed. 1. Fitzherbert Feme perdera Dower, si son Baron moruft deuant 9. ans d'age Dyer 14. Eliz. fo. 313. Also if a man marry his bond-woman in grosse and die, she shall not recouer Dower against the Heyre, for shee is his bond-woman, but against the Feoffée of her husband she shall recouer Dower, vnlesse she be regardant to the Mannor whereof the Feoffement was made.

SECT. LVIII.

What Seisin is requisite in a Husband.

Where the Huband hath neither possession in fact, nor possession in Law, during the Couerture, nor any thing saue onely a right or title, the wife shall not haue Dower, as also if the Baron suffer a Disseisin, an abatement, a Condition broken, an alienation in Mortmaine, or cesser of his rent or seruices by two yeares space, &c. and then he take a wife, dieth before reduction of his Land, or if iudgement be giuen for him in a plea of Lands, and hee marryeth afterward, and die before entry or suing of execution, the wife shall not haue Dower of these Lands: So is it if I. S. exchange Lands with T. K. and I. S. entreth, but T. K. taketh a wife, and dieth before entrie, his wife shall not haue Dower in any of the Lands exchanged, but where

where a husband is once actually seised, the wife shall bee endowed notwithstanding any disseisin afterward done to him, or feoffement made by him either absolute or conditionall: And if before or after Marriage celebrated and not dissolued a possession in Law be cast vpon a Husband by descent, escheate, or fall of some remainder, the wife shall be endowed though the Baron die before entrie, as if the Kings Tenant die seised, and his Heyre being married dieth before office or entrie, the wife of the heyre is dowable: so if rent descend to a husband which dyeth before day of payment, &c. for there is not requisite in the husband such a seisin as whereof an assise lyeth: but if a precipe quod reddat might lie against him, it sufficeth 4. He.7.fo.1. Brooke 65. in Dower.

A husband may haue possession in law by descent of a villaine in gros, or possession in law of a rent charge, by excepting the deede of grant, and hereof the wife shall be endowed, although the Baron doe afterwards refuse receit and seisin of the rent. But iudgement in a Writ of annuity for the Baron taketh away Dower of a rent charge from the wife, and a woman may haue Dower of an estate that was suspended, as if the Lord married with his Tenant, now is the Seignorie suspended, but if he die, the wife shall haue Dower, a third part of the rent per retaigner: for the Seigniorie, though it slept, yet there was still a possession in Law of it in the husband: Here it must not be forgotten that it seemeth doubtfull whether an abatement of a stranger which is a possession in fact destroyeth a Possession in Law, it appeares by Park. fo.72. sect.371. & 372. & 4.H.7.1. per meux that it doth not.

But 21.Ed.4.fo.60. which is accorded for good Law, 4. H.7.fo.1. where in a Writt of Dower the Tenant pleadeth ne vnques seisie in dower, &c. the demandament sheweth that Lands descended to her husband, she being then his wife, and that he dyed before entry made either by him, or by other person, & issuit & est donable per le ley, and shee

was

was inforced by the Court to plead that none entred: for if a stranger had entred, she had not béene dowable: And if she had pleaded issuit seisie que Dowre la P et, this had wayned the speciall matter, but the other conclusion puts it to the Law and Courts consideration. Yee sée now of what possession of Law a woman is dowable per Brian 4. H. 7. 17. if the Kings ward die under age, and the next heyre being married, die before deuenerunt sued, his wife shall not haue Dower, But by Dauers and Hussey, if the Kings Tenants Heyre haue a wife, and after office found, the Heyre doth not enter, but dieth, the wife shall be endowed of the possession in Law before office, for the Statute of prerogatiue cap. 13. is intended onely where the Heyre taketh a wife after office, and intrudeth.

SECT. LIX.

There must be in the Husband an Inheritance not cut from the Franke Tenant.

A Woman shalll haue no Dower in Lands, whereof the Frankement and Inheritance was neuer conioyned in her husband, during Couerture, therefore where the Husband had but a reuersion after estate for life, the wife is not dowable: under this rule commeth one other, dos de dote peti non debet: And if a man seised, &c. take a wife, and alien with warrantie, and then both the feoffor and feoffée die, if the wife of the feoffée bring a Writt of Dower against the heyre of the feoffor, which voucheth to warrant the heyre of the feoffor, and hanging the voucher, the wife of the feoffée demands Dower against the heyre of the feoffée, if shée bring her Writt, not for a third of two parts, but for a third of all that whereof her husband dyes seised, she shall not haue iudgement till the first plea be determined: Litleton. If there be father and sonne both

both married; and the Father seised of one acre, &c. dieth, and the sonne entreth and dieth: if now the sonnes sonne enter and endow his Grandmother which dieth, his mother is not Dowable of that which the Grandmother held in Dower, for of that his Father had no more in meere right, but a reversion upon or after a Franke tenement, and the Grandmother endowed was in of her Husbands possession, yet if the father had in his life time infeoffed the Sonne, &c. the sonnes wife might well have Dower after the Grandmothers death, of that very Land which the Grandmother held.

And if the sonnes sonne voluntarily or compulsarily by Writ of Dower had endowed his mother, against whom the Grandmother had then received her Dower, and dies after execution, the mother might well have entred into the land which the ailesse recovered against her, Parkins 63. The Franke tenement and Inheritance may be both in a sort in the Husband, and yet not sufficiently knit and united together to give Dower: for example, the Lands bee given to two, and to the heyres of the body of one of them, if hee which hath the inheritance die first, his Wife is not dowable, no not after the death of the survivor, for the state taile was not executed, in her husband to all intents, though the Issue in a Formedone against an abater might alleage seisin, and esplees (as we call them) in his father. Likewise, if by fine sur graunt & render, estate be made to a husband for terme of life the remainder to I. S. his sonne in taile, the reversion to the right heyres of the husband, and the fine is executed, if now the Baron die, living I. S. or any of his Issue, the wife of the Cognusee is not dowable: But if a Lease be made for yeares, the remainder to I. S. for life, the remainder to his right heyres, &c. the wife of I. S. shall have Dower of this estate, though execution of Dower cannot be lasting the terme; And if a Lease be to the Husband for life, with a remainder to a stranger for yeares, the remainder to the Husband in fee, the inheri-

tance

tance and Franke Tenement are sufficiently connexed to giue the wife Dower, but execution shall cease during the terme: for when an estate for yeares is more ancient, or as ancient as the Inheritance, which the Husband had during Couerture, there the execution of Dower to the Wife must néeds tarrie the termes expiration: And so it is if a man grant me a rent in fée by Indenture, with Condition that the rent shall cease during the non-age of mine heyres, my Wife shall not bee endowed during mine heyres minoritie.

What if a man that is seised in Fée-simple make a lease for life rendring rent, &c. and then taking a Wife he dieth, the heyre shall haue this rent incident to the reuersion, and it shall be alets to him in a Formedone in Descender: but the wife gets here no Dower; and saith Parkins, a woman shall not be endowed of a rent reserued by her Husband to himselfe and his Heyres vpon a Lease for yeares, 1. Ed. 6. titulo Dower in Brooke accordeth. If the Law be so, Dower hath lesse fauour in this case then the estate per Courtesie d'Angleterre.

But Cléere if a man take a wife first, lease his Lands for yeares or for life, and die, now the Wife may recouer Dower of the Land it selfe, and by Breton, if the woman recouer the third part of Lands leased for yeares de office, de iustice il serra a gard que el tertia remnant, les deux parties: que demorent de terre iesques atant que il eit receiue al value de le tierre partie que il auera perdue, &c. But if she recouer all the Land leased from the termer, he shall haue recouerie per plea de garranti, either of such other Lands as the Lessor had, or if he had no other of the Lands seised, when the widdow is dead, by scire facias out of the Court where the Judgement was inrolled. Note, That though the Law be as is abouesaid, where Lands are giuen to two, and to the Heyres of one of them, yet if the Husband purchase to himselfe and his wife, and to the heyres of the Husband, the wife may relinquish the purchase, and disagrée by bringing her Writ of Dower: Like Law séemeth to be, where the purchase is to the Baron and feme during the life of the Baron, the remainder to his right heyres.

SECT. LX.

Of what things Dower is granted.

LIttletons ground is of Lands or tenements, But a woman is Dowable also of all manner of rents which are rents of Inheritance, Also of Offices, as for example, of a Bayly-wicke in fée, a woman may haue the third part of the profit in Dower, and be contributary to the charge: Also at this day where the Baron hath but an vse in fée-simple or fée-taile generall, vnlesse it be in case where the Husband may and doth disagrée, the wife shall haue Dower, and if a bargaine and sale be made of Lands to the Husband which dieth before inrolement, the wife notwithstanding shall haue Dower, and by the inrolement einsement, it shall be indefeisable against the Vendor and the Heyre of the Vendée: Also a woman is Dowable of Villaines regardant to a Mannor, and if a villanie in gros, a woman may haue Dower by taking his seruice euery third day, and if a mill by taking the third part of the profit, and shee shall grinde tole-frée, and if a House, a woman is Dowable by a Chamber or rent assigned out of the house. Note that if such a rent be assigned out of the Land wherein Dower is claimed, the woman may haue Assise without Deed, contra, if it be assigned out of other Land, 33. H. 6. fo. 2.

Also a woman may hold an Aduousan appendent, in Dower of the third part of an Aduousan in gros, by presenting at euery third auoydance, or the third part of the moitie of an Aduousan, by presenting at euery sixt auoydance: And

And of a Common in gros which is certaine a woman is Dowable. Likewise if any grant to I. S. that hee and his heyres shall take yearely in his Meadow three load of Hay, &c. For Common appendant, Parkins saith, If a woman accept two acres parcell of a Mannor in allowance of Dower, she shall haue no Common appendant: aliter, if a moitie bee assigned her. Et 5. Iacobi le Countesse of Oxfords case cited in Harpers case, Coke 11. Rep. fo. 256. Dower shall be of prediall Tythes, &c.

SECT. LXI.

Of what things Dower is not granted.

OF naked seruices, as homage and fealtie, there is none endowment, nor of a bare annuity granted in fee, nor of things uncertaine as of Common without number. And if it be granted to I. S. that hee and his heyres shall take so many Estouers in Metholo wood as they will burne, in &c. this will yeeld no Dower, no more then a License or grant de coylor bois in auter bois: By the old writers, if in the first establishment of Dower speciall mention be not made of Aduousons or third presentments, the wife cannot haue Dower of any Aduouson pur ceo que aduouson de esglyse vest mi departible: But when a Mannor with the appurtenances is ordained for Dower, if an Aduouson be appendant to the Mannor, and the Church become voide, after the Husbands death the Wife may present.

Also by them a woman cannot challenge a Castle, chiefe Mease, or head of any Baronie or Countie, or any thing within the close or Circuit of the chiefe Mease, to be assigned her in Dower: But for her habitation she may choose aliquod honestum Messuagium de villenagijs, that is, some bond Tenements within the Mannor-house.

And where there is none such to choose, shee shall haue one clapped vp for her in aliqua platea competenti de communi bosco: as long and broad as the third part of her husbands chiefe house: A cottage of clay and splints set close in a corner of a cold Common, which is but a rewmaticke Lodge to welcome Suitors to. But how if the Common and all things bee so inclosed that there is not roome to swing a Cat in, women are not put in Rogum with their Husbands any where but in the Indies, and I thinke that custome is left there also by this time: If there be neither base tenement, nor wood, nor ground wherewith & whereon to build a Widowes habitacle, she may bee endowed (for necessity) of the principall Messuage, and without necessity alwayes if the heyre be so contented: The reasons which Breton and Bracton doe expresly alleadge, for nicenesse of Law, making dainty in their time to endow Widowes in Aduousons and great Messuages, is onely the indiuiduity or impartablenes of the things. Of an Aduouson because it is but ius quoddam, and not corporall, and great houses, &c. for the dignity and strength which the Realme was thought to haue by their conseruation: But considering that the end of Dower is chiefly the maintenance of a Wife, Si vir premoriatur: it may further bee colourably said, that Law at first did neuer meane to trouble Widdowes with presenting of Clarkes, for that either is not, or ought not to bee a matter lucratiue or of gaine, though indeede Bracton prize a Benefice of an hundred Markes at one hundred Shillings valew.

SECT. LXII.

Of what estate of Inheritance the Husband must bee seised.

THe Learning here is not discrepant from that which went before in title of Courtesie: Of fee or fee-taile generall a Woman shall have Dower, so shall she of fee-farme or of a base fee-simple, but not of Coppy-hold unlesse the Custome serve for it: And if Tenant for life make a feoffement in fee, the wife can have no Dower, 3. H.4. fo. 6.

The which Littl. inserteth in this Chapter of Dower, viz. where the Husband is seised, as heyre of speciall taile, &c. is no interdiction of Dower in all cases to her which is married to the Donee of speciall taile. Littletons own example is, That if Lands be given to a man, and the heyres which he shall ingender of his wife Alice, if he dies, Alice shall be endowed of this estate; for no Issue of a second wife could be heyre of speciall taile, and that makes the difference.

The case 41. E.3 fo.30. is this, A man seised in generall taile by fine made a feoffement and tooke backe an estate in speciall Taile to himselfe and his first Wife, and died, the King seise by Tenure in capite, and endowed the second wife, the Issue of the first Wife came, shewing the speciall taile, and by scire facias against the Wife recovered for default: she tooke a second Husband, who with his wife brought a quod ei deforceat against the Heyre, and hee pleaded the speciall taile, the woman by remitting the heyre to the ancient taile, would have concluded him to say, that her husband was seised of any other estate. Et non allocatur.

Parkins makes this case somewhat more austere against Dower, for as he putteth it fo. 60. the Issue is sonne to the

Woman which claimeth Dower, yet the mother by him not Dowable, because the sonne though hee be Heyre is in of another estate then that which was in the Baron during Couerture, so likewise 44. Ed. 3. fo. 26. in a Writ of Dower against the Heyre Tenant, hee sheweth that the band was giuen by fine to his father and mother in speciall taile, and that afterwards his father & mother discontinued the taile by fine to a stranger, and taking backe an estate in generall taile, they had Issue this heyre, then his mother dyed, and the father taking the demandant to wife, he died, so the sonne was now in per lun taile & per lauter, and being adiudged in his eigne right by remitter, the wife was barred of dower, this Case in my conceit fringeth the generality of Littletons rule, for the Issue which by possibility the second wife might haue had, might by possibility haue inherited, though not indefeisably in such estate as was in the Husband during Couerture.

To conclude, where Lands are giuen to the Baron and feme in speciall taile, the remainder to the Heyres of the body of the Baron, and the Wife dies without Issue, there a second wife may be endowed, for after the death of the first wife the remainder in generall taile vesteth maine tenant and is executed: 50. Ed. 3. fo. 4.

Newton saith, 7. He. 6. fo. 11. if a man make a lease for yeares with Condition, if the Lease pay an hundred pound at the end of the terme, that then he shall haue fee, etsi nemy que il auera que terme: that in this Case by paying an hundred pound at the end of the terme, the termer shall haue fee from the beginning, and his wife is Dowable: quere, for it seemeth tunc hath relation but ad tempus solutionis. If Tenant in Dower lease her estate to the Heyre for her life, and the Heyre dieth, his wife shall bee endowed notwithstanding the life of the first dowager, 45. Ed. 3. fo. 13. In action of Dower the tenant shewed that Tenant per Courtesie granted his estate to him in the reuersion, rendring rent with clause of re-entry, for non-

payment

payment, he in the reuersion marry the demandant, the tenant per le Courtesie re-entreth for the Condition, he in the reuersion died, his wife was barred Dower, for the surrender might well be vpon Condition, 14.E.4. fo.6.

SECT. LXIII.

Where Dower is giuen or not giuen of an estate determined.

VVHere the Husbands estate is loyally euicted or determined, Dower for the most part faileth, As thus, two men make exchanging of two acres executed in fee, one of them dieth, his sonne takes a wife and entreth, and the otherpartie being impleaded, voucheth the sonne which entreth into warrantie, so that the Tenant recouereth in value the acre, which he deliuered in exchange, the sonnes wife shall neuer be endowed of this acre, for the title of recouerie in value, is from time of the exchange by way of relation, and so before the Marriage.

Likewise if two Copartners in gauell kinde make partition, one of them marrieth, and the other being impleaded, prayeth ayde of his partner which ioyneth, &c. if the demandant recouer, and the Tenant haue pro rata of the partners part which afterward dieth, his wife shall not haue Dower of that which is recouered, for the title of recouery pro rata is from the death of the common Ancestor, saith Parkins. As a Villeine takes a wife, purchases lands in fee, his Lord enters, the Villeine dieth, his wife shall haue Dower, for the Lords title begun by his entrie, and the wiues by seisen in the husband, the Tenant alieneth in Mortmaine, or erecteth a crosse (see thereof, W.2.c.33.) and the Lord entreth, the tenants wife shall haue Dower notwithstanding. So if the Lord recouer in a Ceßauit, the tenants wife shall be endowed, yet if the tenant had made a Lease for yeares, the Tenant should haue lost his terme, W. enfeoffeth R. vpon Condition, that it should be lawfull for him to re-enter if hee pay ten pound at Michaelmas, and he dieth before payment: now if the Heyre of W. pay ten pound after Michaelmas & redeeme this land, the wife of R. should haue Dower notwithstanding: If a man giue Lands in taile reseruing a rent to him and his heyres, and for default of payment a re-entry, if the Donor take a wife and die, and his heyre re-entreth for Condition broken, the Donors wife is Dowable neither of rent nor of Land, neither is there here any Dower for the wife of the Donee, yet if the Donee in generall taile take a wife and die without Issue, his wife shall haue Dower notwithstanding the Donors entry, and a man that hath Issue by his wife Donee in generall taile, shall be Tenant by the Courtesie, if the wife and Issue both die, so that the estate is by the act of God determined, a woman that is Donee in taile rendant rent, takes a husband, hath Issue and dieth, if now the Issue faile, so that the rent of Inheritance becomes a rent but for life, before execution of Dower to the wife of the Donor whose husband during Couerture was seised of the rent, she shall neuer be endowed of this rent, 9. Ed. 3. I doubt whether it be Law or no, for I see not why the possession or seisin of a husband should not be as fauourable a title to the Donors wife to haue part, as the hauing a child is to the Donees husband to haue all, nor why there may not as well bee an imaginary continuance of inheritance for the one as for the other: But execution maketh the difference, and therein le Courtesie hath a greater prerogatiue aboue Dower.

Ye haue in Fitzherbert titulo Dower placito 127. That if the Baron be infeoffed with a Condition which is performed by the feoffor in his life time, so that he or his heyre re-entreth, yet the wife of the feoffee shall be endowed: And if I infeoffe one vpon Condition to infeoffe another before Easter, if he make the feoffement ouer accordingly yet his

wife

wife shall recouer Dower: The first Case saith Fitzherbert is no law: So also doth Parkins hold it, plea 321. And in my conceit the second is Law like the first, the land had not beene transferred but for the condition: for if after Easter according to the Condition the feoffer might at all times haue entred vpon the feoffée, and then by Parkins, his wife should neuer haue beene endowed, or vpon his heyre, or vpon his wife, if she had beene endowed: Now then if by keeping the Land vniustly the feoffée could haue gained no estate to himselfe, to his heyres or his wife, but such as must alwaies haue beene defeasable at the feoffors pleasure, it shall be pulled in part backe againe, and not pay tole vnto Dower.

The Condition was good, no maxime or ground of law broken in mouing or remouing of the estate, so it is you will say perhaps where a man selleth his fée-simple lands, yet his wife shall recouer Dower against a lawfull purchaser, for where the Baron was seised in fée, the wife shall haue Dower, she shal indéed when the husbands estate was pure and absolute: But when in the very creation of his estate there was matter annexed to it, that went in destruction of it and of Dower, or that went but in retardation of it, then it must passe as it was made subiect to those natiue debilities that are accompanying it, if they be not repugnant to Law: As therefore the Condition vnperformed would haue destroyed Dower if the wife had once obtained it; so here being well performed and all things deriued according to the first meaning & intention of the Condition, she shall neuer haue Dower, yet indéed the case, 28. assi. fo. 4. making against it sauoreth of equity and conscience, for there a man seised in fée, made a feoffment to one vpon condition that he should infeoffe his owne son, & his owne wife, he did so and died; now when the shrewd boy perceiued that his mother tooke nothing by her husbands feoffement, but all was his owne good, he would admit no partner, the woman séeing she could not get halfe, gaue a venture for a third

part,

part, and brought a writ of Dower, it came to issue, ne vnques seisie, &c.

The Jury found the speciall matter, and being asked what they thought of it, they answered, because there was neuer any permanent seisin in the husband, that she was not Dowable. Your thinking (said Justice Thorpe) is contrary to your verdict, for here was a possession whereof she is Dowable, Et ceo fuit opinion de toutes. Littleton also seemeth to be against me in Estate sur condition, but it is not ipse dixit, but plusiors ont dit: Therefore if hee were aliue, I might perhaps intreate him to bee on my side.

SECT. LXIV.

How much and how a woman shall hold in Dower.

THe Common Law alloweth for Dower the third part of that whereof the Husband during Couerture, had such seisin as is before declared to haue and hold (if it be in lands) by limits and bounds. But this Indowment per metes & bonds cannot be where the husband is Tenant in Common.

If one of two Copartners in gauell kinde take a wife, and die before partition made, the Heyre may assigne his mother a third part of his moity to hold in Common, or he may first make partition and then endow her per metes & bonds.

Generally, when a woman recouers Dower the Sheriffe shall put her in possession per metes & bonds, and it hath beene holden, that wheresoeuer the heyre assigneth Dower a third part, per mi & per tout, to occupie in Common, if the widdow accept it accordingly, that this should be a good endowment: The Law seemeth to be otherwise, By Common right Parkins saith, a woman shall haue Dower, the third auoydance of euery Aduouson, and the third

third part of euery Mannor that was her husbands, for if shee take it in another forme by assignment from the Heyre she may suffer preiudice.

As if a man seised of three Mannors takes a wife, and grants a rent charge issuing out of all three Mannors, and dieth: now if the wife by assignment of the heyre, accept one Mannor in Dower for all, the two parts of this Mannor remaine subiect to the distresse of the granter, because the woman (for the two parts) accepted here her Dower in counter comen droit. But had shee vpon recouery of Dower béene assigned this Mannor by the Uiscount, she should haue held all discharged.

Yet if a married man seised of thrée Aduousons of thrée seuerall Churches, grant to I. S. that he shall present to the Church which next becomes voyde, and the granter dying his wife recouers in a Writ of Dower against the heyre before auoydance, and the Uiscount assigneth to her the Aduouson of one Church for all, &c. if now the Church thus assigned become voyde alcuns diont, saith Parkins, the grantée shall present, and not the woman, for she is endowed incounter common droit, and I. S. the grantée which is a stranger to the assignement cannot otherwise take aduantage of his grant. But in the first Case after assignment of one Mannor by the Uiscount, the grantée might distraine in the other two Mannors.

SECT. LXV.

Lesse or more then a third part.

Though by the Common Law a woman is to haue no lesse then a third part, yet if a widdow will be so foolish as to accept a fourth or fift part or moity of her husbands Inheritance assigned in allowance of all his Franke Tenement, it is a good assignement: And by custome in some

places

places, a woman shall claime and haue of right a moity of her husbands lands, and in some Towne or Burrough she shall haue the intierty in Dower.

Prerogatiua Regis, endeth with these words, that by custome of Gauell kinde in Kent, Mulier habebit post mortem viri medietatem pro dote sua: Et si mulier fornicetur in viduitate, perdet dotem, vel si sit disponsata viro, Therefore in a Writ of Dower for a moity the Demandant must alledge the Custome and that she is sole; 2. Ed. 4. fo. 17.

And where the Custome giueth a moity of Lands and Tenements in Socage, &c. this must be taken strictly not extendable to a Bayly-wicke or a Faire, vnlesse they append to the Mannor or Lands within which there is a custome, for if they be so appending during Couerture, though they be disappropriate after, yet the wife shal haue Dower, a moitie of the profit.

SECT. LXVI.

Dower is of the Husbands best possession.

FOr, as soone as the Baron hath such a possession, ius dotis spreadeth vpon it for the wife, who shall be alwayes indowed of the best possession of her husband: As where there is Lord Mesne and Tenant, the Tenant holding by three pence rent, and the Mesne by three shillings, if now the Tenant being married the Mesne release to him all his right in the tenancie, and the Tenant die, his wife shall be attendant to the heyre by no more then a penny. So if a Disseisor infeoffe a stranger of the Land with warrantie, which takes a wife, and then the Disseisie brings a Writt of entry in le per against the feoffee, which voucheth the feoffor, &c. after recouery had on both parts with

with execution, the Feoffee die, his Wife shall haue Dower, not of the Land lost, but of that recouery in value.

SECT. LXVII.

Election of Dower.

Sometime a woman may choose whereof she will bee endowed in Cases where the Baron exchangeth Lands, and the exchange is executed; or where he purchaseth Lands, out of which hee had issuing some rent charge or seruice: But where a Tenancie escheateth to the husband, and hee entreth, she hath no election, but must needs take her to the Land and to the seruices againe if the land be recouered; yet where a Tenancie escheateth, after a Woman is once endowed of the rent which it yeelded, she shall retaine her rent, and distraine for it of Common right, for she can by no meanes haue part of land, wherein her husband had neuer any possession.

SECT. LXVIII.

Dower of Land and of rent issuing of the same Land.

IN some cases some hold a woman may haue part of Lands in Dower, and rents issuing out of the Lands, as if the Baron being seised of foure acres make a feoffement reseruing by Indenture foure shillings rent to him and his heyres, with clause of distresse the rent (say they) comes not in liew of the Land, and when the feoffers wife, hath one acre and a third part of an acre assigned in Dower, the whole rent still goeth out of the residue. And if a man seised

seised of three acres in fee, marry and die, and a stranger which hath but two of these acres entreth by abatement into the third, and after hee hath married the Widdow hee infeoffes a stranger of all three acres by indenture, reserving vt supra, and dieth, the rent goeth out of all the acres, but if the heyre of the first husband recouer his acre and assigne it to the woman in Dower, shee is Dowable also of the rent, for indeed it is entirely issuing out of the two other acres: And if a man seised of three acres in fee make a feoffement of two reseruing rent out of those two acres, vt supra, the wife hauing the acre which remained in Dower, may haue Dower also of the rent reserued; quære saith Parkins, car il est incounter le conscience de diuers homes, And making the acres to be of equall value, it must needs bee against law also, for one acre of three equally valued, or of euery acre one third part is a iust Dower. But if the acre vnsold were inferior in value, there is both conscience and law for the woman to claime Dower of the two acres, or of the rent, for a woman must be endowed of the best possession, and not according to the number of acres, but according to the value of the Inheritance whilst it was the Husbands. Therefore if I make a feoffement of my lands, and dye, and the feoffee builds a house vpon it, or otherwise improoues it, my wife shall be endowed no otherwise then according to the value of my possession; yet if a disseisor or a feoffee sur condition, doe edifie, the disseisie or feoffor re-entring, shall haue the building. If being married I make a feoffement, and the feoffee ruinateth a house which was vpon the Lands before the feoffement, and that was worth foure or fiue pound annually, my wife shall be endowed according to the value that the land was of, at time of my death, because a woman hath no right to possession of Dower before the death of her husband: But Parkins dares not let this Case goe without a quære.

SECT.

SECT. LXIX.

Of Dower at the Church doore.

The old kind of endowment at the Church Doore commeth now a dayes seldome in use: But for all that I would have women better learned then to be ignorant of it, it is when a man seised in fee-simple, being of full age, comming to the Church doore to be married, doth there affirme affiance and endowe his spouse of all his lands, or of part, as of halfe or a lesse quantity openly and with certainty, the woman thus endowed may enter into her Dower, after the husbands death without assignement, and this Dower may be at the Church doore in one County of Lands in another County and without deed, Parkins, sect. 217. Vide Plowd. in Sharington, ca. fo. 304. b. it is good without livery of seisin, Et per Shelly 28.H.8 Dyer fo. it may be done within view, and the puisne sonne of Land in borow English may not make such a Dower.

Also a sonne and heyre apparant when he is espoused by consent of his father, may endow his wife at the Church doore in part of such lands and tenements as are the Fathers in fee-simple, and the sonnes wife after his death (the father living) may enter presently without further assignement into the parcels, thus certainly appointed: But if shee enter after her husbands death and agree to any of these endowments ad ostium ecclesiæ, she is concluded from claiming any other Dower. Thus farre Littleton. By Bracton none can endowe his wife in this manner, unlesse hee bee Liber homo; for in his time if I bee not much deceived, the greatest number of bond-men held in manurance Lands of their Lords, which they occupied to the Lords use and profit, in pure villeinage. These having none other lands, could not endow, &c. Also by Bracton, Quis posset dotem constituere, & sciendum quod tam minor quam maior masculus. Cui vxori, tam maiori

maiori quam minori, poterit enim ille qui infra ætatem est vxorem suam dotare, quamuis existentem infra ætatem, dum tamen possit dotem promereri & virum sustinere, & quamuis vir infra ætatem moriatur, vxor sua, siue infra ætatem, siue non, dotem obtinebit, de hac autem materia inueniri poterit de termino Paschæ, Anno 9. H. 3. in causa Saræ quæ fuit vxor William Burnell. But Littleton 8. A. requireth full age in him which shall endow his wife in his owne lands, ad ostium Ecclesiæ. And Parkins fo. 85. Sect. 438. saith, If an Infant eight yeares old endow his Wife, ad ostium Ecclesiæ sans suit: the endowment is void, although he agree at fourteene, &c. for though the Spousalls were good till fourteene, yet that which should binde his inheritance was voyd, and things meerely voyd cannot be made good.

Concerning the age of the womans marrying, Littleton doubteth whether she shall haue Dower or no in these kinds of dowments if she be vnder nine yeares age. Againe Bracton saith semper quod tertiam hereditatis partem exuperat per admensurationem dotis amputabitur, Glanuile is with him quia minus tertia parte tenementi sui dare, quis potest in dotem, plus autem non, Bracton agreeth, and by all of them, a Constitution of Dower lesse then the third part shall binde the fee. But Littleton alone will counterpaise and weigh downe all their authoritie, by whom the Wife hath election to refuse or accept this endowment post mortem viri. Also he saith shee may be endowed of all or of a moity, &c. And with him accords Fitzherbert fo. 150. n. & Q. And one saith, Assignetur pro dote tertia pars totius terre mariti nisi de minori fuerit dotata ad ostium Ecclesiæ.

Also Bracton, Clandestina coniugia heredibus & vxoribus nihil valent sed cum solemnitate & publica debet esse hæc dotis constitutio. Fitzherbert likewise saith, that a woman married in a chamber shall not haue Dower at the Common Law, Nat. bre. 150. n. Of espousals in

Chap-

Chappels not dedicate, quære if Marriage be by Licence of the Bishop semble reasonable que le feme auera Dower. 10. *H.* 3. a man looking every day for death married his Concubine and endowed her at the Chamber doore, this was holden no good endowment, yet the Banes were first proclaimed in three parish-Churches: The same yeare a man languishing in his bed married, his wife could not be endowed Patch. 9 *H.* 3. 202. Titulo Dower in Fitzherbert: there followeth a speciall Case. That if the King give Lands to a man with a woman in Marriage, the husband if he had none Issue by her shall not have the land after her death, but the Issue which the wife had before, shall presently inherit. Also by Bracton, Vxorem dotare quis potest in certa summa pecuniæ, siue terras habuerit siue non. Et si se tenuit contentam de tali summa excludetur ab omni alia dote, & dos constitui potest in rebus consistentibus pondere & mensura, & tam in liquido quam in solido, & sicut in isto vel in illo, sic in vtroque. But 7. *H.* 4. fo. 13 & 14 is cleane against this learning: for though with the Civilians Dower may bee in goods and not in lands, yet here in England it must be in lands and not in goods.

All moueable treasure which the wife or husband hath, are the husbands to spend as he list, dum vilem redigatur ad assem.

Further the Ancients did hold that Dowment ad ostium Ecclesiæ, might bee de assensu fratris, sororis, vel amici.

And that by these endowments a woman might have Dower of lands revertible to the husband or to his father, after the death of Tenant for life; I think there is scarcely any piece of our tradition wherein the old and late writers interfier and dash more one against another then in this. But it is cleere and without all contradiction, that in both these endowments Frank Tenement passeth by them without livery of seisin: If a man make a Deed of Feoffement to Alice at Stile, and then comming with her to the

I Church

Church doore to be married deliver the Deed to her, shewing her the lands, saying, his will is, she haue them according to the deede, if the Baron neuer claime otherwise, then in right of his wife that is a good feoffement.

But he may endow her, of his owne lands ad ostium Ecclesiæ, without deede, though the Land be in a forraigne Countie, marry when the Dower is of the fathers Land, ex assensu, there must bee a deed, for assent lieth not in auerment 40. Ed. 3. 43. yet this is contrary to Bracton, and in old Bookes the consent hath beene tried by proofes, Dowment may be good, ex consensu matris, but as they say now, not ex consensu fratris, sororis, vel consanguinei, The assent ought to be at the Church or Church doore, yet 2. *H.* 3. the sonne married against the will of his parents, and eight weekes after indowed his wife, of his fathers lands, ex assensu patris per curiam, it was holden good, Fitzherbert 199.

Of the head of a Baronie, or the Capitall Messuage of a Knights fee, Dowment ad ostium, &c. is not good, but it may be of a moity of all such Lands as the Baron shall hereafter purchace in fee, or of all such Lands as the Barons mother holdeth in Dower: But if the Father lease his Lands for life, and the Sonne and Heyre apparant endow his wife, ex assensu, &c. of the reuersion: now if the Lessee die, the Lessor enter, and the sonne die, the wife shall not haue Dower, because she was not Dowable of the reuersion at the Common Law, though it had beene in her husband during couerture; so is it if the Father were seised for life, or iointly with another in fee: But if the father had beene Tenant in taile, the endowment by consent had beene good during his life, though no conclusion after his death to his Issue, or his wife claiming Dower, euen as by Election if tenant in taile, being himselfe in actuall seisin, endow his wife ad ostium Ecclesiæ, & die, if his wife enter, the Issue may out her, and so may hee in the reuersion if issue faile: If the Father at time of endowment ex assensu

he

hee seised none otherwise then in his wiues right: Yet Parkins argueth, hee shall bee bound during his life, quære.

I haue held young Maides now indeed somewhat long in the old endowments, and I would proceed to instruct them in the dower of the new learning iointures, I meane, for my desire is, that they should be able to haue when they are Widdowes a coach or at the least an ambler, and some money in their purses. But they are of the minde for themselues I perceiue, that Themistocles was in for his daughter, He desired a man rather without money, then money without a man, here is a wise adoe yee say, I tell you of Dower, of the Widdowes estate, and God knowes whether ye shall euer haue the grace to be widdowes or no, yee would know what belongeth to wiues, on then in a good way, I haue brought you to the Church doore, if ye be not shortly well married, I pray God I may.

FINIS.

THE WOMANS LAWYER.

The third BOOKE.

AS soone as a man and woman are knit, and fast linked together in bands of wedlocke, they are become in common parlance coniuges & consortes, yoke-fellowes, that in a euen participation, must take all fortunes equally. Yet Law permits not so great an interuallum betwixt them as society, which must alway consist among two or more, rather it affirmes them to be vna Caro, regarded to many intents meerely as one indiuided substance.

SECT. I.

When or how soone Barron et Feme are said to bee one person.

IF Titius and Sempronia, by words de presenti in a lawfull consent, contract Marriage, they are man and wife before God.

But

But they cannot doe all that married couples may, yee know my meaning, id possumus quod de iure possumus, but they may (saith Parkins) infeoffe one another; for they are not yet vna persona in the eye of the Law.

If it fall out that the woman chance to die before nuptials celebrated, he which is no more but betrothed, shall not haue her goods, vnlesse it be by her last will and Testament, which she might without crauing Licence of any body, haue ordained according to her pleasure. If a man affianced to Sempronia, know her carnally, infeoffe her of a carue of Land, and then marry her in facie Ecclesiæ, the old world would haue iudged this feoffement voide comming post fidem datam & carnalem copulam, but at this day it is good enough: Publike Celebration therefore according to Law is it which maketh man and wife in plaine view of Law, Consensus non Concubitus facit matrimonium: But one naile keepeth out another and a firme betrothing forbiddeth any new Contract, yet they which dare play man and wife onely in the view of heauen, and closet of Conscience, let them be aduised how they shall take the aduantages or emoluments of marriage in conscience, or in heauen, for on earth if the Priest see no celebrated Marriage, the Iudge saith no legitimate issue, nor the Law any reasonable or constituted Dower. Now if Titus and Sempronia were Christianly married in facie Ecclesiæ, but Titus soone after Dinner or a little before night, leauing his wife a Virgin, tooke his way ad campos Elysios, shall Sempronia haue a Child of his bodie? videtur quod sic, 22. Ed. 3. fo. 30. in a Writ of Dower, the tenant saith the demandant was not of age to deserue Dower, Tempore mortis viri sui: viz. 9. annorum &c. for Littleton is plaine in the affirmatiue, a woman shall haue Dower, if she were past the age of nine yeares, the third part of that which the husband had during Couerture, and ye shall not take couerture here like a master Stallion or breeder of Colts, but a woman is Couert Baron as soone as she is ouershadowed with her Husbands protection and supereminency: Now the Law that giueth Dower to her that is able to deserue it, and enableth at so greene yeares, knoweth well enough that women are at their Husbands commandement: If Titus being dead haue left his wife her maidenhead, immunis a culpa, a pœna immunis erit, This I might dilate as in probabilitie or likelinesse of reason at Common Law, but it seemeth the matter resteth otherwise determinable.

For in action of Dower the Tenant shall not plead nunquam carnaliter cognouit, nor the demandant be driuen to auerre a knowledge, &c.

But the case may perchance bee drawne to an issue of ne vnques accople in loyall Matrimonie, and that must be tried by the Bishop: Therefore for the better direction of Brides, take the case verbatim, as it is propounded with the solution 22. Eliz. Dyer 369. A woman of full age contracts Matrimonie by words of the present instant, with a young man of twelue yeares age, and this being solemnized in face of the Church with consummation after a sort, the young man being put to bed to her died vnder age, quære if the Ordinarie ought to certifie an accomplement in loyall Matrimonie, Solutio doctorum quindecem.

We be all of opinion that she is to be taken for a loyall wife coupled in loyall Matrimony, and in question of Dower, that the Bishop ought so to certifie; for albeit that in other regards these were but Sponsalia de futuro, yet in case of Dower, and the priuiledge thereof, they are extended to Matrimony consummate, Et iudicium datum pro dote; heere ye say was the Law as cleere as Christall on your side, when supper is done dance a while, leaue out the long measures till you be in bed, get you there quickly, and pay the Minstrels to morrow.

SECT. II.

Baron and Feme one person.

NOw that Matrimony is celebrated and consummate, here is so strait a fellowship or rather identitie of person, that if a feoffement bee made to a man and his wife iointly with I. S. the Baron & Feme take but a moity, and in a feoffement to Baron and Feme, and I. S. and T. K. they take but a third part, and where a feoffement is made to a man and his wife ioyntly, they take not severall moities, as other ioynt Feoffees doe, but the Baron and feme take intirely together, and in Law they are said to be seised by intierties, and there is no halfing betwixt them: For if the Baron charge the whole land or part of it with a rent, the wife shall hold it discharged after his death, and if he sell all or part and die, the wife shall recover all by Writt of cui in vita. See 40. assi. pla. 7. If a Villeine and his Wife purchase land ioyntly, the Lord enter, and the Villeine die, the Feme or her Heyre shall have the whole Land, Eadem lex videtur, where the Husband ioyntpurchaser is an Alien borne, or attaint in premenire, or of fellonie. But the booke of Assises goeth not so farre.

The videtur is Parliament 43. in Brooke, where likewise ye shall see it was holden 5. H 7. fo. 31. that if T. infeoffe W. and A. his wife, & afterward it is by Parliament enacted that all estates, made by T. to W. shall bée voyde, that the feoffement shall be voyd as well towards the wife as towards the Husband, because they are but one person in Law, and the Feme taketh nothing but by agréement of the husband. And upon the like reason is the case Dyer 3. Eliz. fo. 196. Sir Rob. Catline purchase land held in capite to him and his wife and his heyres without licence, and the Queene pardons all offences, pro quacunque alienatione sibi facta, and doth not speake of the wife in the pardon, and yet it was allowed in the Exchequer.

But if the feoffement had beene to W. and I. S. this I. S. should haue held his moity, notwithstanding the Parliaments decrée, and this seemeth to bee the better opinion, though there were in manner equall number to maintaine, That if the feoffement were before couerture, the Parliament should voyd it for a moity, but if it were after couerture, it should voyde for no part against the Feme, when shee was discouerte, leauing to Parliaments their omnipotencie, it is cléere the husband cannot seuer the Joynture betwixt him and his wife, as an other Joynttenant may, if the Joynture were made during Couerture, because there is then no moity: Otherwise it is if the Joynture were made before the Marriage: And if lands be giuen to a man and his wife, habendum one moity to the husband, and habendum the other moity to the wife, now they bee seised of moities as Tenants in Common: But for this I finde no other authority, then the opinion of Knightly in Dyer, 28. H. 8. 10. b.

SECT. III.

Baron & feme cannot infeoffe one another.

MOreouer, this Conglutination of persons in Baron and feme, forbiddeth all manner of feoffing or giuing by the one vnto the other, for a man cannot giue any thing vnto himselfe, therefore 27. H. 8. fo. 27. In action of debt vpon an obligation to performe couenants, where it passed for the Plaintiffe, because the Defendant had not paid annually seauen pound to his wife, it is alleaged in arest of Judgement, that the Couenant was impossible in it selfe, &c. But Chomeley, Shelley, and Fitzherbert moued the husband to agrée with the Plaintiffe Car le exception

fert

sert de riens, for although in strict intelligence of Law, money and Chattels, paid, delivered, or given to the wife by the husband, are still his owne, yet a man may give his wife a paire of hose (saith the booke) as a man is bound by honesty, so he may be bound by red waxe and parchment to finde his wife sustenance, and to bee bound to give her money for her securitie, is all one; from this Lanthorne I thinke he tooke his light, which bound a gentleman of mine acquaintance to give his Wife the Obligée his Daughter, yearely such and so many gownes, Kertles, &c.

And the meaning must bee taken and observed: in the booke of 4. H. 7. fo. 4. is another memorable Cause, A man was bound to I. S. by obligation to make a sure estate to a woman in certaine tenements within three moneths after his fathers death: The Obligor marrieth the woman in his fathers life time, and the Matrimony continueth, till the three moneths be expired; the obligation is forfeited, Vauisor said, the husband might well have performed the condition by fine levied, upon a writt of Covenant brought by a stranger, against the Baron and feme. Fisher said he might have performed it by making a Lease unto a stranger, the remainder to the wife, quære of that. Vauisors performance had beene good I thinke, if there had beene in the beginning a full purpose and intent of intermarriage betwixt the woman and the Obligor: But that appeares not, and therefore being that hee hath brought himselfe to an impossibility of performance either of words or meaning, the Obligée must néeds be allowed the advantage. If the obligation had béene to the woman her selfe, the condition by inter-marriage had béene dispensed with; for where the Obligee is a cause that the condition cannot be performed, the not performing is without penaltie to the Obligor, as if in the old dayes, I had béene bound to an Abbot that A. should infeoffe him, &c. before Christmas, if A. had presently entred into Religion, my bond

bond had presently beene forfeited: not so, If A. had beene professed, vnder the obedience of the Obligée.

And if I bee bound to C. that A. shall marry B. before Easter: If I marry B. and our Espousals continue till Easter, my bond is forfeited. Similiter, If C. marry B. or if A. and B. cannot marrie, because one of them dieth or wareth mad before the day.

I finde none other cause in our Yéere-bookes alleaged why things may not passe by gift, betwéene Baron and feme, saue only vnitie of person.

But vndoubtedly the restraint springeth from a politique consideration, rather to bréed, cherish and maintaine the vnity, then in iudging of an impossibility because of the vnitie.

But the Ciuill Law, vir non potest dare vxori, ne fœminæ amorem coniugalem in quæstu habeant, & prohibentur inter coniuges donationes, quia si liceret coniugibus inuicem donare matrimonia fierint venalia & sæpe distraherentur, &c. And because it would amount to arguing inter coniuges, there is a restraint by that law. Ne priuignus dare queat nouercæ vel nouerca priuigno. What if the Matrimonie be inualidum & legibus non consistens, yet non valet inter coniuges putatiuos facta donatio, ne melioris sint conditionis quam illi qui recte faciunt: But a gift to a plaine Concubine is good enough: vnlesse the giuer be a Soldier. By old Iohn Bracton, lib. 2. ca 5. Non valent donationes inter virum & vxorem; non enim poterit vir dare vxori, nec e conuerso constante Matrimonio, quia huiusmodi donationes prohibitæ sunt inter tales personas, nec in fraudem facere possint constitutioni, veluti si Maritus donet extraneæ personæ ea mente vt redonet in vita viri vel post mortem: hee maketh his reason in the 14. Chapter, Si tales donationes fieri possint ob amorem inter virum & fœminam posset alter eorum egestate & inopia premi.

But at this day, though lands cannot passe betwixt Baron and Feme, right out by plaine livery, or bargaine, yet in in the obliquitie of fines, recoueries and vses, there is an Expedite transporting of Inheritance betwixt them, to the vndoing perhaps of the partie whose Lands are transferred and auferred, with not so much as coniugall loue alwayes in recompence.

SECT. IIII.

In what sort things may passe betwixt Baron and Feme.

Lands cannot passe from the Baron by feoffement to put the state from him immediately to the wife, though he were infeoffed to that intent and vpon such a condition: But one man may infeoffe another vpon condition to infeoffe the wife of the Feoffor, (whatsoeuer Bracton say) and the condition good. Also a feoffement, fine, or recouery may be made, knowledged or suffered, to the vse of her and her heyres which is wife to the Feoffor, Conusor or sufferer, &c. And as I may make another man the instrument to conuey lands to my wife, so may I be the meanes to conuey Lands to my wife, from another man, for by Letters of Atturney-ship I may deliuer seisen of Lands to my Wife for another, and the feoffement shall be good by Parkins 41. And a man may deuise in his last Will and Testament, either by the custome, or by the Statute, 32. H. 8. Lands to his Wife in fee, fee-taile for life, or for yeares, because this taketh none effect, till the Couerture be dissolued.

It is said in Scolasticus case, If I deuise that he shall haue greene acre after the death of my wife, my wife shall haue estate for life by the intent, &c. And although a wife by the generall rule hath no will but her Husbands, and all Testaments of a feme-couert to deuise any Mannors, Lands, Tenements and Hereditaments are ineffectuall, by expresse declaration of 34, *Henrici* 8. capite 5.

Yet

Yet ye may see 12. *H*.7. fo. 22. 23. 24. that as a Woman may make her Will by consent and agreement of her husband, and by Church Law, without his consent for some things, so by the very Law of England a Feme couert hath free power to make either a stranger or her husband her Executor for all such duties as were due to her before shee married, which are not yet come to a possession but rest still in action, specially (as some say) if they be by writing: for example, A Feme sole makes a Lease for terme of her life rendring rent, the rent is arere, and she marrieth, or a woman Executrix to one unto whom were owing many summes of money marrieth: This wife dying may make her Husband or a stranger her Executor for the things not come to possession, otherwise the duties should perish, and the husband prouing the testament consenteth to the Executorship: See also in Scholasticus Case, Plowd. 414. That cesti que vse, made his Wife Executrix, and deuised that she should sell his Lands, &c. the woman tooke a second husband, and sold the Land to him, this was adiudged good sale, and the Feoffees held bound to make feoffement according, which some of them refusing to doe, were committed to the Fleete, 10. H. 7. fo. 20. Yet see Cui. in vita Brooke, a Land was giuen to a woman upon condition to sell it and distribute the money for the Feoffees soule, she tooke a husband, they two sold the land and distributed, in this case there lay no cui in vita or sub; oena post mortem viri, for the sale was good according to the condition. But per Justice Brooke, the woman might haue sold the Land to any saue to her husband, Et hoc per fait mes nemy per fine.

The next thing that I will shew you is this particularitie of Law, in this consolidation which we call Wedlock is a locking together: it is true that Man and Wife are one person, but understand in what manner.

When a small brooke or little riuer incorporateth with Rhodanus, Humber, or the Thames, the poore Riuolet loseth

seth her name, it is carried and recarried with the new associate, it beareth no sway, it possesseth nothing during couerture. A woman as soone as she is married is called couert, in Latine nupta, that is, vailed, as it were, clouded and ouer-shadowed, &c. she hath lost her streame, she is continually sub potestate viri. Bracton termes her vnder the scepter of her husband, and that which the same Author is bold to say of the King in a Paradoxe, his fellowes Earles and Barons are aboue him, nam qui habet socium habet magistrum, I may more truely farre away say to a married woman, her new selfe is her superior, her companion, her master: The mastership shee is fallen into may be called in a terme, which the Ciuilians borrow from Esops Fables, Leonina societate.

SECT. V.

The Woman marrying changeth her name, Dignitie, &c.

THe Wife must take the name of her Husband, Alice Greene becommeth Alice Musgraue; She that in the Morning was faire weather, is at night perhaps Rainebow or Goodwife Foule, Sweet heart going to Church, and Hoistbrick comming home.

But a thing something worse is Vxor censetur dignitate Mariti.

The Lady Anne Powes, and her Husband Randolph Hayward Esquire brought a Writt of partition against the Duke of Suffolke, and his Wife for part of the Inheritance that was Charles Brandons: because the Writ was per Ranulphum & Dominam Annam, &c. they were inforced to bring a new Writ ad respondendum to Randolph and his Wife late the wife of Lord Powes; for per Mountague chiefe Iustice, and Hales, by Law of England whatsoeuer

soeuer be the courtesie among Dames of honor, a womans name of dignitie changeth with the degree of her husband, and of such women as haue not their honor by birth, but acquire that by Marriage the rule of Law taketh order, Si mulier nobilis nupserit ignoblem, desinet esse nobilis when she taketh a second husband.

But what though the scrupulositie of the Common pleas were obserued throughout the Realme, that Esquires Ladies should be no Ladies in Court and Country, whereunto I will neuer giue voyce what inequality were in this depressing? shall not likewise a Knights widdow marrying with a Baron or Earle as be much exalted verament, yet you see the dignitie hangeth meerely on the male side, carrying the scepter of Wedlocke.

Sect. VI.

Touching seruitude.

Now touching the state of freedome or bondage, Littleton saith, that if a free-man marry a bond-woman, the Lord cannot seise her; but there is remedie by action, for taking her sans gree or licence.

Fitzherbert in his libertate probanda agreeth 78. G. that she should be freed perpetually: But the Law seemeth to be otherwise. And so you may find the opinion of Doct. & Stud. fo. 139 b. And that indeed it is no more but a Temporarie priuiledge and exemption from seisure of her Lord, during time of couerture, for if the Seigniour of a Mannor marrie his Niefe regardant, the best authority that I can finde is, that this Niefe is no more but shrined in the honour of her Lord, if he die she shall haue no Dower, but remaine still in her niefitie regardant to the Mannor. And to say truth, I perceiue not how a womans being married can in any sort be an infranchisement, no not for a time: it is no more but a sconsing or hiding of the seruitude. Bracton

cton saith elegantly manumission is a detection or laying open of the freedome which is a natura. A womans liberty is free licence to doe what she list unlesse shee be letted by force or by Law, it is not restored to Niefe when she marrieth, Marriage rather pulleth it from her which before was free: When a Seignieur therefore marrieth with his bond-woman she must not turne her bumme to him and say, heretofore my Lord; I lay in your bed, and now I lye in mine owne, as the French Concubine said being married newly to her French Lord, but let her bee buxome and mindfull of her subiection, for if this louing Seignior of hers die, she may right well be an apparant Niefe againe to her owne sonne for ought that I know, why not as well as causes may happen that the father to sonne, or one sonne to another may be a villeine, the case did happen 3. Ed. 3. that the villaine married his Lords mother, and so the father in Law, and the brother de demi sank were villeines: If a free woman marry a villeine, her naturall freedome is not otherwise infringed then by subiection to her husband: If the villeine purchase Lands and die before seisure made by the Lord, the wife shall haue Dower: But if a free-woman seised in fee or fee-taile, take a husband which is a villeine and die, the Lord may enter upon the husbands possession per le Courtesie, or upon the Issue being Tenants in fee-simple or fee-taile: See the Booke 22. H. 6. fo. 18. & 19.

But may the Lord enter upon the Land during Couerture, quære. If a villeine be possessed of certaine goods, and the Lord make seisure of them by poll, this is sufficient without seisen in fait: But if the villeine die before any seisin, and ordaine Executors, these Executors shall haue his goods, 3. H. 4. 15. 16.

And a Villeine shall retaine goods which hee hath as Executor against his Lord; yea hee may bring Action of debt against him as an Executor, all to the use of the Testator. Also if a Feme gardian in Soccage marrie with a villaine, villeine, I take it the Lord shall haue nothing to doe in this gardianship: If a Seignioresse of a Mannor marry her bond-man, he is made free, and where before hee was her footstoole, he is now her head and her Seignior, here is part of the particularitie.

SECT. VII.

The Baron may beate his Wife.

THe rest followeth, Iustice Brooke 12. H. 8. fo. 4. affirmeth plainly, that if a man beat an out-law, a traitor, a Pagan, his villein, or his wife it is dispunishable, because by the Law Common these persons can haue no action: God send Gentle-women better sport, or better companie.

But it seemeth to be very true, that there is some kind of castigation which Law permits a Husband to vse; for if a woman be threatned by her husband to bee beaten, mischieued or slaine, Fitzherbert sets downe a Writ which she may sue out of Chancery to compell him to finde surety of honest behauiour toward her, and that he shall neither doe nor procure to be done to her (marke I pray you) any bodily damage, otherwise then appertaines to the office of a Husband for lawfull and reasonable correction. See for this, the new Nat. bre. fo. 80. f. & fo. 238. f.

How farre that extendeth I cannot tell, but herein the sexe feminine is at no very great disaduantage: for first for the lawfulnesse; If it be in none other regard lawfull to beat a mans wife, then because the poore wench can sue no other action for it, I pray why may not the Wife beat the Husband againe, what action can he haue if she doe: where two tenants in Common be on a horse, and one of them will trauell and vse this horse, hee may keepe it from his Companion a yeare two or three and so be euen with him; so so the actionlesse woman beaten by her Husband, hath retaliation left to beate him againe, if she dare. If he come to the Chancery or Justices in the Country of the peace against her, because her recognizance alone will hardly bee taken, he were best be bound for her, and then if he be beaten the second time, let him know the price of it on Gods name.

SECT. VIII.

That which the Husband hath is his owne.

BUt the prerogative of the Husband is best discerned in his dominion over all externe things in which the wife by combination devesteth her selfe of proprietie in some sort, and casteth it upon her governour, for here practice every where agrees with the Theoricke of Law, and forcing necessity submits women to the affection thereof, whatsoever the Husband had before Coverture either in goods or lands, it is absolutely his owne, the wife hath therein no seisin at all. If any thing when hee is married bee given him, hee taketh it by himselfe distinctly to himselfe.

If a man have right and title to enter into Lands, and the Tenant enfeoffe the Baron and Feme, the wife taketh nothing. Dyer fol. 10. The very goods which a man giveth to his wife, are still his owne, her Chaine, her Bracelets, her Apparell, are all the Goodmans goods.

If a Woman taketh more Apparell when her husband dyeth then is necessarily for her degree, it makes her Executrix de son tort demesne, 33. *H.6.* A wife how gallant soever she be, glistereth but in the riches of her husband,

band; as the Moone hath no light, but it is the Sunnes. Yea and her Phœbe borroweth sometime her owne proper light from Phœbus.

SECT. IX.

That which the Wife hath is the Husbands.

FOr thus it is, If before Marriage the Woman were possessed of Horses, Neate, Sheepe, Corne, Wool, Money, Plate and Iewels, all manner of moueable substance is presently by coniunction the husbands, to sell, keepe or bequeath if he die: And though he bequeath them not, yet are they the Husbands Executors and not the wiues which brought them to her Husband.

SECT. X.

The Husbands interest in Chattels reall.

A Tearme or Lease for yeares, made to the wife before or after Couerture hath somewhat peculiar in it selfe: for if Tenant iure vxoris of a terme grant it or surrender it and die, the Wife is without remedy; but if hee continue possession vntill his death, it shall remaine to the Wife, Parkins 107.

If Tenant iure vxoris, for twenty years lease the Land to a stranger for ten yeares rendring rent, with re-entry

for

for default of payment, if the Baron die, the Wife shall haue the rent, and not the Barons executors, for the Wife shall haue the remainder, but she cannot re-enter for Condition broken. Parkins 165. And see the bookes of 21 *H.7.* 29.b.& 2.Eliz.Dyer 183. If a woman haue a terme as Executrix: and the Husband submit himselfe to arbitrement, vpon which the moity is awarded to the pretendor of the Title, and the Husband dye, yet the wife shall be thereby bound.

If a Feme lessee for yeares, take a Husband which neuer makes any alienation, the Suruiuor shall haue the terme, for though it were neuer deuised out of the Woman during Couerture, yet if she die, the Husband shall haue it as a thing setled in possession, Plowden 191. 192.

In Brackbridges Case Plow. 418. is a whole Lecture of the Barons interest in the Chattels that are not the wiues: The Case is, Sir George Griffeth Lessee for yeares, granted his terme to Anticle Brackbridge, and to Iocosa the wife of Thomas Brackbridge tenant of the reuersion in fee, &c.

The principall learning deliuered, by opinion of the full Court in this, If a man grant a terme to a Feme Couert, and to a stranger, or if a Feme sole that is ioynt-tenant of terme with an other, take a husband, the ioynture is not hereby seuered, but the suruiuor shall haue all: And in suit of eiectment of ferme against a stranger, the wife shall ioyne with her husband, and haue iudgement together with her husband; for if a Feme sole Lessee for yeares take a husband which in his life time grants a rent charge, &c. or by his testament bequeatheth the terme, the wife who had an estate at and before her husbands death, shall by suruiuing preuent the testament and auoid the Charge, But of Chattels personals, the Law deuesteth all propertie out of the wife, and puts them meerely to the husband, and to his

Executors; if such chattels bee given to the wife and to a stranger, the husband alone is tenant in Common of them with the stranger. Secondly, the Court did hold cleerely, that in Brackbridges Case, and such like, the immediate inheritance in the Baron, did not drowne the interest of the Feme, for the one he had in his owne right, and the other in his wives: But by an expresse act, as by feoffement or grant of a new lease, he might haue giuen away the interest of his wife.

But leauing all to Law, the Law shall saue that interest distinct, and preserue it: And it was holden in this Case, that Baron & feme might not ioyne in an eiectione firmæ with Anticle, but he alone might bring his action and the Baron chased to more higher and more reall Writt.

Also it was holden the Baron might distraine or haue action of debt for a moity of the rent, and as I comprehend the end of Brackbridges case, a feoffement by Thomas Brackbridge made of the Mannor whereof the Land seised was parcell, and might well drowne all interest Executory which his wife had, but not a Lease executed except livery had beene made in the very Lands seised, for a Lease in possession of three acres maketh them to bee no parcell of a Mannor during the Lease, but a rent charge, or a lease executory which is but an interest, leaueth the possession entire, and no reversion in the Baron, there is further in the Commentaries the Case of Dame Hales, viz. Sir Iames Hales Lessee for yeares, in his owne right taking a new Lease for twelue yeares ouer in remainder to himselfe and his Wife, died felo de se, the whole interest was iudged forfeite, for the felonye had relation from the act done, id est, from entrance into the water, &c. At which time the Baron had power to grant, and consequently to forfeit it.

If

If the Wife haue a ward by reason of her Seignio-ry, this likewise is a Chattell reall, and the Hus-bands interest in it shall be as in a terme or lease for yeers: But if the wife be gardian in socage, no lease of the infants land, though it be made by Baron and feme, per Indenture shall binde the wife, but she may enter after the husbands death, and if she die, the husband shall not haue the Gardianship.

For in this Case, the wife hath nothing to her owne vse, but she is an officer appointed, vpon confidence in her natu-rall loue, and this office is not grantable nor forfeitable. vide nat. bre. 145. I haue hitherto, but shewed what is wrought as it were ipso facto, vpon marriages consumma-tion while it is gréene, not past a day or a wéeke old, and I thought it methodicall to insert the learning of battery, be-cause in my poore opinion it were better to combat for hou-shold mastry in the beginning, then to bring a Writt of right for it, when it hath gone too long, by title of rusty pre-scription.

SECT. XI.

Of the Wiues interest of affaires before Marriage.

NOw let vs looke backe a little and see what shall become of the dealings which Mistris Titus had whilest shee was Sempronia, an agent in the world, widdow or maide sola and vncouert.

SECT. XII.

Of Infancie.

TO debate matters of infancie would aske a whole volume per se: But breefly know that all deeds, gifts, grants, &c. made by an Infant which take not effect, by deliuery of the infant be absolutely void. By matters in fait or writing, which take effect, by hand and deliuery are onely voydable by the infant, or by them which haue the infants estate.

Out of this rule are excepted acts apparently of necessity or profit to the infant, or which can be no disprofit to him, for manger boire, necessarie apparell and schooling, the obligation or couenant of an Infant is good.

Also an Infants presentation to a Church is good enough for danger of lapse, and because it is no matter of emolument, and things done by vertue of office, as giuing of goods, or payment of debts by an infant Executrix, are good, so are acts which concerne the infants proper purchace. As if estate be made to an Infant of two acres, to haue and to hold, the one for life, the other in fee, a feoffement of one acre made by the Infant is a good election: And it is said fo. 104. in Dyer, that an Infant is bound by all

all Statute Lawes, if there be not an expresse exemption; Now whatsoever a Feme sole might avoyd by infancie, she and her husband may avoid it by entry or action after Marriage, if they take the time, else not.

For example, An infant feme sole hath title to enter for Mortmaine, within a yeare after alienation, or title to enter into the purchase of her villeine before his alienation, if by lachesse she let slip her advantage, as she may doe notwithstanding her infancie, no wise husband that she taketh afterward can mend it, for here was but a title to that which neither she nor her auncestor ever had: But if an infant Feme sole have a right, as upon disseisin done to her or her auncestor, she may alwayes enter, whilst she is sole, notwithstanding any descent during infancie; And so may her husband which marrieth her after the descent: Littl. teacheth us, fo. 95. Chap. Descents, that lachesse of a husband which suffers descent, shall not toll the entry of a Feme covert, or her heyres after Marriage dissolved. But there is an addition to Littleton, that it is otherwise where a title is already given to a Feme sole which taketh a husband, and suffers descent, &c. for it shall now be accounted the Womans folly that shee would take such a husband.

Howsoever it be Law, or howsoever it be understood, the Case before must needs be good Law, for an infant Feme hath as much favor as an infant Male: And taking of an husband cannot toll an entry which was saved to a Feme sole by infancie, neither doe I perceive, how the husbands lachesse at the time of descent, can toll the Wives Infancie to make any imputation of folly, where infancie might excuse it.

By Parkins, If a man lease two acres to me for life, the remainder of one of these acres to a Feme sole, which afterwards takes a husband, and then the Lessee dying, the Baron entreth into one acre, and thereof enfeoffes a stranger by mets and bonds, the wife shall not after his death enter into the other acre to make a new election, but it shall be iudged her folly whose title begun in a sort before couerture, that shee would take such a husband. And I agree it, for in this case, if the Feme had beene sole and vnder age, the election which shee had made in her infancie should not haue beene auoyded, for the fall of a remainder will not tarry the time of an ebbe and flowe. But presently vpon the death of the Lessee, the free-hold of one acre vesteth in her, and when she hath as a Purchaser decided which acre she will haue, the other acre is returned, and cannot be called backe.

Againe 4. & 5. Philip & Mariæ Dyer fo. 159. the Case is, that Baron and Feme made a lease by Indenture, for yeares, rendring rent, the Lessee entred, the Baron dyed before day of payment, and before day of payment likewise the wife tooke another husband, and he died after he had accepted the rent: Now by Dyer, Stamford & Browne (for Brooke was contra) the Woman within her viduitie before payment of the rent, might at her pleasure haue ousted the Termoar, by her second husbands Marriage, had giuen her election to her husband by resignement or assignement in Law, as strongly as if she had expresly acknowledged her selfe content to accept the rent, if *I. S.* did thereto agree.

But can this reason in a case of Inheritance, be inforced against an infant which being disseised tooke a husband, and whilst she was yet vnder age the disseisor died seised? I suppose it cannot: If before marriage, she had appointed I. S. to enter for her or she had Couenanted with the disseisor, that none should enter for her, to what effect had this beene by the Common Law.

The Baron may by liuery discontinue the wiues possession, but he cannot doe it by grant, may he then doe it by holding his peace, onely by a sufferance? No. But a descent is equiualent, and this is not the act of the Baron, but a forbidding of Law, to which the Baron must submit himselfe

selfe; true: But the wife is vnder age, will you now in fauor of a wrong descended, toll the entry of an infant, heare her speake for her selfe.

My good Lord, saith shee, it is true, I had right before I married a good while, and it was my folly to take a Husband that neuer entred; but seeing this Atturney in law of mine hath failed in his office, I hope I shall be allowed the aduantage of my yeares, and that Law weighing the weakenesse of nonage of any, shall not punish me for folly, but helpe my want of prudence, and supply the defect at last. If I may not enter during my husbands dayes, yet I hope I shall if hee die: Litticton makes a quære, If the Baron being himselfe vnder age makes a feoffement of the wiues Land, whether the wife may enter after his death or no. The Baron himselfe, he saith, might enter notwithstanding his feoffement, and his entry must be in right of his wife, and cleerely his heire cannot enter because the Baron had nothing but in right of his wife, and seing that his owne feoffement lies not in his owne way, what Iustice is it, that his feoffement should grieue another body. So I say seeing the Barons feoffement is voydable by his infancie, why should not the wiues right by her infancie be saued, where there was no feoffement or act done but onely a taciturnity or sufferance.

By Fitzherbert, if the Baron and Feme being both vnder age alien the inheritance of the Feme, she may haue at her full age after the husbands death, a dum fuit infra ætatem,

And this opinion is, though hee dares not confidently deliuer it, that where the Baron of full age with his Wife vnder age, makes alienation of his Wiues inheritance: shee may haue a dum fuit infra ætatem, or cui in vita, at her election; for when they ioyned in a feoffement of the Wiues Land, this hee saith was the feoffement of the Wife vntill her disagreement,

and

and if Baron and Feme make a gift in taile or lease for life of the wiues Land rendring rent, so soone as the Baron dies the reuersion is onely in the wife, who by accepting the rent shall bind her selfe and her heyres: But if shee will refuse the rent because she was vnder age at time of the feoffement, it seemes she may be receiued to a dum fuit infra etatem, wherby she affirmes the feoffement to be her owne. If this be infallible Law, I doubt not then if a Feme infant disseised doe marry, and during her infancie the husband suffereth a descent, but her entry is saued, and she may enter, after Couerture dissolued if not before: But Fitzherbert concludeth with a quære, and so must I.

SECT. XIII.

Acts, &c. of a Feme sole being full Age.

Vnderstand now by a Feme sole, a Woman of full age. If a Feme sole become indebted, and marry, the Baron and Feme may be sued for this debt during life of the Feme: If the Creditor sue and recouer, the Baron shall be charged with it after the wiues death, aliter non.

A Feme sole, Lessee for life, rendring rent takes a husband, the rent is arrere, the wife dieth, though here be no recouery in the wiues life time, yet because the Baron tooke the profit, he is still chargeable in a Writt of debt for the rent, for qui sentit commodum sentire debet & onus, If a Feme endowed of rent take a husband and die, the husband shall haue action of debt for the rent arere, for it was a duty accrued during couerture: But if a man be bound to a Feme sole, and she takes a husband, and the day of payment comes during Couerture: now if she die, her husband cannot haue an action of debt vpon the obligation, for this was a thing in action before marriage, Nat. bre. fol. 120. & 121. And agreeing to that is 39. H. 6. 27. Br. Testaments

ments 10. but by that booke the Wife may make the Baron her Executor and so saith the Booke of 12. Hen. 7.22.

If a Feme sole being made Executrix, take a husband, she remaine still a disposer of the Testators goods to his use: and after payment of his debts she may deliuer Legacies, and after all that giue the rest for Gods sake maugre le test sa Baron. But upon such a giuing of goods or deliuering of Legacies before payment of debts the husband may haue an action of trespasse, for gift before payment is not a right administration, but a deuastation of the Testators goods, Par. fo. 2. and 18. H. 6.

A feme sole seised of a carue of land, grants out of it a rent Charge by déed, and deliuers this deed to a stranger with Condition to deliuer it to the grantée as her déed, if he goe to Rome and returne before Easter, the Woman takes a husband, the grantée performes the Condition, the déed is deliuered to him, he hath a good rent Charge, yet the Baron was seised of the land before the grant tooke effect, what though, if the Feme had infeoffed a stranger of the land, he should haue held it charged, for to some intent the grant hath relation from deliuery of the deed as an escrow though for the rent, the grantée cannot haue that but for the dayes incurring after the darraine deliuery, and if the Feme at the deliuery of the escrow had béene marryed all had béene voyd, Par. fo. 2, & 3. and fo. 29. some hath maintained, he saith, where a Feme sole deliuers an obligation or other déed of grant, as an escrow with condition, &c. vt supra; that it should haue no relation at all saue onely to the last deliuery; for if hée to whom an obligation is so made, release all action to the Feme sole, before performance of the condition, and before deliuery of the déed by the baylée, he may notwithstanding sue upon the obligation, when it is deliuered, which proues that it takes none effect till the last deliuery; and then it must néeds bee void if the Woman be married at time of this deliuery, if all were

were not countermanded presently by taking a husband. But Parkins will not yeeld to these reasons, for the Feme sole was a person able to oblige her selfe in any manner of Contract, and her couenants and agreements made vpon consideration, she could not countermaund though she would.

If a Feme sole seised of Land, infeoffe a stranger by deede indented reseruing rent to her and her heyres, to be paid annually at Easter, with a conditionall clause of entry for non-payment, and then they two inter-marry, &c. heere can be no failing in performance of payment during couerture, for all this while the rent and condition are suspended.

If the condition had beene to pay ten or an hundred pound, it had beene drunke vp by the inter-marriage, for if a feme sole make a feoffement to a stranger vpon condition to pay her ten pound, and then she marrieth with I. S. I. S. before the day of payment may release all manner of conditions, duties and demands, and the condition shall be determined. But such a release comming after the day wherein the condition should haue beene performed at what time the wife hath a title of entrie will not binde her or her heyres, after the husbands death. Par. fo. 148.

There followeth a question, if a Feme sole infeoffeth a man of blacke acre by indenture with Condition, that hee shall infeoffe her of green acre before Easter, and they two marry and continue married till after Easter, whether the husband be maine-tenant seised of blacke acre in the right of his wife, There followeth in Par. fo. 149 a case ayding towards solution of this doubt. If I be bound by obligation to a Feme sole to marry her by munday next, if shee marry a stranger and the espousals continue till tewsday, I need not tender my selfe to her.

A Feme sole makes cognizance of her right to leuie a fine before Commissioners per dedimus potestatem, hauing the Writt of Couenant (vt oportet) and at the

day

day giuen in banke, when the Concord should be recorded, the woman is married, but notwithstanding the fine was recorded and ingrossed, as leuied by a Feme sole: the question was whether it should binde the Husband, or not, it was said, death of a partie, &c. which as the act of God dissolues the whole busines, by abatement of the Writ, but marrying after the teste of the Writ of Couenant, and dedimus potestatem, and Cognizance made, doth not so: The woman therefore and her heyres are bound for euer; and the Husbands release of all his right to the Conusee, makes all cleere 7. & 8. Eliz Dyer 246. the Lord Keeper of the great seale of England his case.

SECT. XIII.

Of Acts done by a Feme Couert.

EUery Feme Couert is quodammodo an infant, for see her power, euen in that which is most her owne: A wife may be seised in her owne right with her husband in estate of Inheritance: but if she make liuery and seisin to another in any parceil of this Inheritance by her selfe alone without gree of her Husband it is voyd, yea her Husband and shee together may maintaine an assise vpon the entry: but where onely the Baron is seised, and the Feme maketh liuery, the assise must bee onely by the Baron in his owne name: Par. 38. Likewise fo. 2. he telleth vs, where a man is seised in the right of his wife, and the wife grants a rent charge out of her owne Land, the Husband not knowing it, or the Husband knowing, but not consenting; but the deed is onely in the name of the wife, this grant is voyd. Admit the Husband be vagrant out of the Countrey, and the Wife (ignorant of his life or death) grants a rent Charge by deede reciting that shee is sole; yet if the Grantee enter and distraine for the rent, the husband may maintaine an Action of Trespasse for this entrie.

Admit that this vna caro Baron and Feme through false loue or iealousie, bee set at nine miles asunder variance, and certaine Lands are assigned to the Wife by the Baron for her maintenance, if the Wife grant a rent Charge out of this Land, it is meerely void.

If a Feme Couert grant a rent Charge out of her land by fine, as though she were sole, this bindeth not the Husband; but if he die before hee and his Feme haue reuersed their fine by error, the Feme shall be bound.

And if to a Feme Couert there be a feoffement made (a feoffement and liuery is of great celebritie) yet a naked disagreement of the Baron auoydeth it 1. H. 7. fo. 16. If a Feme Couert (her Husband being beyond the Seas) bee enfeoffed of an acre of Land, and the Husband comming home refuseth, and causeth the Wife likewise to relinquish all manner of seisin or taking any profits of the Land, this in a Writt of entry, sur disseisin in le per brought against the Baron and Feme will discharge the Husband of damages from the time of the refusall, but not for the occupation before refusall, tamen quære, Par. fo. 10. yet (saith he) they remaine Tenants (for all the refusals) of the Franke Tenement to vse any action so long as none other person entereth: but if a Tenant when his Seignior is beyond the Seas, doe infeoffe his Lords wife ioyntly with a stranger of the Tenancie, and the Lord comming home distraines the cattle of the stranger for his rent, this distresse is a compleat disagreement, and puts the Wife out of seisin, so that now the possession remaines intirely to the stranger the ioynt feoffee; otherwise the husband should be at a shrewd mischiefe viz. without remedie for his rent, for all the time incurred before the distresse, Par. 10. Note that in these Cases, it is no plea, for the grauntor to say that the

the Baron did not agrée, but hee must shew the disagréement.

A Feme Couert may be a disseiseresse without assent of the Baron, and hee shall be charged with damages, in assise against him and his wife: But if the Baron doe a disseisin to the vse of his wife and she agrées to it, the Franke Tenant for all this setleth not in her, for the entry of a husband gaineth nothing to his wife, but where she hath either right of entry (as vpon disseisin) or title of entry as vpon a Condition, &c. A Feme Couert makes a Testament of the goods of her husband, she dieth, the Executors proue the testament, if the Baron now will deliuer the goods to the Executors, this maketh the Testament good; for howsoeuer it might be accounted voyd, being made without the husbands consent, yet being once proued, it gathereth spirit (as it were) and the deliuery of the goods, shall imploy an assent before the will was made, note that licence or assent here, is sufficient per paroll, Par. 97.

A Feme Couert may take an assumption from any man for her Husband, shee may take an obligation or feoffement to her selfe, she may commit a disseisin, and her husband by his assent shall be a disseisor, ab initio: Shee may giue, sell, or charge her husbands Chattels, by his assent, as a horse or such like, and she is not so like a Monke that all her acts should haue an impossibility of taking any strength, but her husbands agréement comming after them, shall make them good whether they be to his aduantage or disaduantage, 27. H. 8. fo. 24. But the acts of a Monke cannot be made good by agréement of the Soueraigne.

And in the end of the case, Fitzherbert affirmes, that when a Woman makes a gift of her husbands goods, the Husbands post-assent is a new gift. One thing I will adde, That though a gift made by a wife of things which are quickly gotten, and quickly gone, (chattels I meane which require no solemne conueyance) and the Wife hath

Q

a medling with them may bee made good by agreement, yet a feoffement made by the Feme, cannot be made good by the Husbands bare consent succeeding.

Now for Executorship of a Feme Couert note that per Brian, 2. H. 7. fo. 15. b. she cannot be an Executor without the agreement of her Husband, and per mesme le reason, she cannot giue goods of the Testator without his consent; for vpon returne of deuastauerint, the Husbands goods shall be put in execution: The case in the booke, is of an Executorship, before Couerture. And remember that Fitzherbert saith, 28. H. 8. Dyer fo. 7. If the wife haue a Lease by Executorship, the husband cannot sell it, sed tota curia contra eum: But a Feme Executrix to her first husband may retaine goods against the Executors of her second Husband, if hee neuer did alienate them. 21. H. 7. per Fineux.

SECT. XIV.

Of Elopement.

AMongst the acts of a Feme Couert, I must not forget to admonish her that she take heed of Elopements, A woman shall not forfeit Dower by not suing appeale of her Husbands death, or by not visiting her husband, or not comming to comfort him when he is wounded or exceeding sicke in a forraigne shire; but if he be in his home Countie where he dwelleth, quære: A woman in her frenzy may cut her husbands throat, and it is no forfeiture of Dower; but if she make an Elopement (which is a mad tricke) Dower is forfeited. Elopement by the sound and quality of the offence might seeme to be derived from alopex a fox, for it is when a woman seekes her prey farre from home, which is the foxes qualitie. But the word seemeth to bee

French,

French, there is a faire Statute against Elopement, West. 2. ca. 34. Si vxor sponte reliquerit virum & abierit & moretur cum adultero suo, amittat in perpetuum actionem petendi dotem, quæ ei competere posset de tenementis viri sui, si super hoc conuincatur, nisi vir suus sponte & absq; cohertione Ecclesiastica eam reconciliet & secum habitare permittat, in quo casu restituatur ei actio. A Woman that leaues her husband, goeth away and abides with her adulterer, if she be conuicted thereof, loseth for euer her command of Dower, &c. vnlesse the Husband of his owne free accord without ecclesiasticall compulsion suffer her to be reconciled and to cohabite with him, in which case her action is restored for Dower.

It is commonly holden (saith Parkins) that a Woman shall lose her Dower by voluntary Elopement, though her abiding be inuoluntary, and though she make none abode at all with her Adulterer: But if she be rauished, and demurre with the Rauishor, against her will, she loseth no Dower. If when the husband is commorant at one mannor, his wife depart to another of his mannors, and there liue in adultery, this is none Elopement, for it cannot but be intended, she cannot abide there without gree and goodwill of her Baron; ye shall haue a case for your erudition out of my Lord Dyer concerning this matter: of Dower was demanded of a Mannor, ex dotatione Domini Powes by R. H. and Anne his Wife, it was pleaded that the said Anne in vita Domini Powes.

Frankly of her owne accord,
Left her Husband and her Lord,
And from *Bednall Greene* she ran
With *Mathew Rochlei* Gentleman

To the parish of Saint Clements Danes, where she liued in adultery, all the life long of Lord Powes, abiq; hoc that euer she was reconciled, the demandants pleaded a reconciliauit

L

ciliauit & cohabitare permisit, the reioynder is non reconciliauit modo & forma.

To prove the reconciliation, a lying together divers nights at divers places was given in evidence with demeanure, as Baron and Feme; against this it was obiected that they never were resient or abiding in one house together, but alwayes in sunder, and that the woman continued in adultery with one or other continually, as long as her husband lived. Et non allocatur, for there may be many Elopements with many reconciliations, and the Defendant at his perill must take issue upon one, 1. & 2. Phi. & Mariæ, Dyer, fo. 107. But me thinkes here wanteth equality in the Law, women goe downe stile, and many graines allowance will not make the ballance hang even: A poore Woman shall have but the third foote of her Husbands lands when he is dead, for all the service she did him during the accouplement (perhaps a long time and a tedious) and if she be extravagant with a friend vt supra, this is an Elopement and a forfeiture, &c. But as the saying is, men are happy by the masse, they may goe where they list I warrant yee, and because they are enforced to travell in the world, they will pay deare abroad for that which they esteeme of no value at home. Their adulterous soiournings is not discerned, they may lope over ditch and Dale, a thousand out-ridings and out-biddings is no forfeiture, but as soone as the good wife is gone, the bad man will have her Land, not the third, but every foote of it.

Have patience (my Schollers) take not your opportunitie of revenge, rather move for redresse by Parliament, and in the meane season be perswaded that liberty or impunity in doing evill by immodest life and lascivious gallops, is no freedome or happines: no, but rather act thus farre your Husbands duty of instruction, namely, to learne him to leave his incontinencie abroad, by your modest and chast life at home. And if this will not produce you, the comfort of your Husband, yet a farre greater comfort the effect of Balaams desires, Let me die the death of the righteous, and let my end be like his.

SECT. XV.

The Husbands power in Lands, which the Wife holdeth in Dower or otherwise for life.

The Husbands Soueraigntie ouer his wife, her goods, and chattels personall or reall, is no lesse then hath been declared. The dominion likewise ouer, all manner of Franke Tenements his owne or his Wiues, is supereminent in him during Couerture, but so that he standeth well bridled from doing any thing a per luy, whereby either the Dower which his wife had by a former marriage, or expecteth by the present or any other estate for life or in fee, can be taken from her when hee is gone: If a Widdow tenant in Dower marry, and her new husband surrendreth, &c. this is good during Couerture, but if the Feme suruiue, or if there be a Diuorce causa præcontractus, the Feme may enter and defeate the surrender, though he to whom it was made be dead, and his Heyre in by descent, yea and the Law differeth not heere though the Wife had ioyned with the Husband in the surrender: But if Baron and Feme will surrender Lands which the wife holdeth for life by fine, this shall bind the wife, for the wife which is giuer shall be examined, &c. for no particular Tenant can surrender by fine without being named in the writt, whereupon the fine is leuied, Par. 117.

If a lease be made to Baron and Feme for life, and the Baron make alienation in fee, the Lessour may enter for a forfeiture, and maintaine an assise, if he be ousted: but the Wife suruiuing, may haue a cui in vita post mortem viri, for her title is from the first demise, but the title of entry is onely from the alienation. 11. assi. p. 11.

The like Case is, 43. assi. p. 17. Baron and Feme tenants for life, the remainder to A. in taile, the Baron alieneth in taile, A. dyeth hauing issue, his issue may enter for the alienation, though the Feme Lessee be liuing, for shee may haue her cui in vita, &c. Brooke 9. & 10. in cui in vita.

Yet see Couerture & Enfancie Brooke 5. Newton said for Law, that if a Feme sole be infeoffed with a condition, or a lease be made to her, rendring rent with condition of re-entry for non-payment, if she take a husband that breaketh the Condition, the Woman shall bee bound for euer by the Feoffors or Lessors re-entry, 20. H. 6.28.

And per Martine 9 H. 6.52. if the Baron claime fee in a quid iuris clamat, or disclaime in auowry, so that the Lord recouer in the quid iuris clamat, &c. the wife is without remedie. But 15. Ed. 4. 29. If a Woman Lessee for life take a husband, and being impleaded pray ayde of a stranger, if the Baron die, hee in reuersion cannot enter: And if a Feme Tenant for life take a husband which alieneth in fee, though he in reuersion enter, the woman shall haue the land againe if her husband die, 29. assi. p. 43.

SECT. XVI.

The Husbands power in his owne Lands to preiudice his Wife in right of Dower.

A Feoffement or other plaine alienation here is to small purpose, and therefore it should seeme, That a great while agoe Husbands, either for the little loue they bore towards their Wiues, or for great affection to the price of their Dower, had gotten a vse of suffering lands to to be recouered from them by iudgements, concords and translations in the Kings Court: Against this a Statute declaratory was made West. 2. c. 4. anno 13. Ed. 1. Quod si vir implacitatus de tenemento & reddat tenementum petitum aduersario suo de plano, post mortem viri iusticiarij adiudicant mulieri dotem si per breue petat, &c. And where Iudgement is against the husband by default, the Wife may recouer in a Writt of Dower also by this Statute, vnlesse the tenant can shew that he had right, and the Husband none: And at common Law (some haue said) euery recouery bound the wife vnlesse it were by render, and that the Statute aydes onely against recouery by default, and I take their ground partly to be vpon these words of the Statute which are put in the conclusion of the clause touching default, namely, vt de cætero huiusmodi ambiguitas amputetur. Which I thinke is not true, but that the Statute is a common-Law Ordinance: for Bracton lib. 4. cap. 13. fo. 310. who wrote tempore H. 3. before the Statute, is that against recouery pleaded in barre of Dower, the demandant might reply, quod si per iudicium recuperauit, hoc fuit per dolum vel per negligentiam viri, vt si vir scienter, & in odium vxoris suæ defaltam faceret, & ita amitteret, vel alio quocunque modo, hoc mulieri non nocebit si probatum fuerit, quia dolus vel negligentia viri non præiudicat mulieri. And a little while after he sheweth, that a fine leuied by the husband in fraudem vel odium mulieris, vel propter lucrum habendum, is no obstacle in a Writ of Dower, vnlesse it be ante desponsationem. I agrée therefore with Parkins, that the Statute is in affirmance of the Common-Law, whereby recoueries against the Husband were & are falsifiable. Si le baron auoit droit, & le recouerer nul droit: As for example, The Husband being disseised by I. S, re-entreth, I. S. arraignes an Assise, the Husband confesseth a disseisin, I. S. releaseth damages and hath iudgement to recouer, the Wife shall haue Dower notwithstanding by the common Law, mesme lei, If he which is by a husband disseised, release all his right to the husband, and afterward notwithstanding the release brings a writt of entry in nature of an Assise, and recouereth against him by default, the wife of the releassee shall bee indowed. But if the Heyre of a disseisor being in by descent, the disseisee re-enter, and take a wife, now a recouery against the Baron by default or reddition in a writt of entry in nature of Assise taketh away Dower from the wife, for the recoueror had right according to the nature of his action, and the possession which the Baron had during Couerture is destroyed: But it falleth out otherwise where a man is married, and then there is a disseisin, descent, entry and recouery, vt supra.

If a Precipe be brought against the Baron which pleadeth misnosmer, or iointenancy, and it is found against him, whereby the demandant recouereth, this ousteth not Dower, vnlesse the Demandant had right.

In a writt of entry in le post against the Baron, hee voucheth himselfe to saue the state taile, and sheweth how his father gaue him the land in taile, and that the feesimple is descended vnto him, and vpon a trauerse of the gift in taile, it is found for the demandant which recouereth, and the Baron dieth: Now if so be that the Baron might well haue pleaded a release of all actions or all right of the demandant, the Wife may falsifie this recouery in her writt of Dower: Tenant in taile hauing Issue dieth, a stranger abateth, dieth, his heyre entreth, and takes a wife, the Issue of tenant in taile, arraignes an assise of Mortdancestor, against the Baron which trauerseth the points of the writt, and they are found against him; so that the demandant recouereth, and the Baron dieth. It hath beene holden that the wife shall not recouer Dower heere, vntill the heyre haue reuersed the verdict by attaint. But it seemes (saith Parkins) he may falsifie the recouery in a writt of Dower maine tenant; for the husband might haue pleaded to the action of the demandants writt, and if the Feme (which by

no

no meanes might haue attaint) must tarry till the Heyre haue defeated the verdict, perhaps he will neuer sue attaint, or he will release, & so the wife which once was intituled to dower by her husbands possession, neuer defeated but by his owne lachesse, should lose her Dower maugre sat est, which seemeth vnreasonable: Yet quære (saith he) for the iudgement is upon a verdict, comprehending matter repugnant and contrary to that which should bee pleaded against the writt: But if the demandants entry had béene congeable: then out of doubt the wife had had no power of falsifying, for the entry had wrought a remitter.

The Heyre of a Disseisor entreth, taking a wife, and the Disseisée in a writ of entry, ad terminum qui preterit, recouereth against the Baron by default, the wife may falsifie this recouery in a writ of Dower: But it is seldome that the demandant in Dower shall falsifie a recouery against the husband, had by his lachesse in not pleading a plea, which went méerely in abatement of the writt.

And therefore to say that the Baron might haue pleaded misnosmer or ioynt-tenancie will not serue to falsifie a recouery: But if she can proue that the demandant had no right nor cause of action, but jointly with a stranger, which stranger by his deed shewed forth to the Court had released before commencement of suit all his right to her husband being in possession, this will serue to falsifie the recouery for a moity.

Thus hath Parkins in his treatie of Dower at large discouered, that a title neuer tryed against the Baron in his life time, may be tryed by his wife when he is in his graue: And so further 36. H. 6. titulo fauxifier de recouerie in Fitzherbert, 15. That a woman may falsifie a recouery had against her husband by action tried, but it must be in another point, and not in the very same which was tried by the recouery.

SECT. XVII.

Losse of Dower by the Husbands attainder.

HEe that hath a notable grudge against his wife, and would be sure to delude her hope of Dower, hath a direct way, though it be somewhat dangerous, and I will not be of his Counsell: Hee needs doe no more but imagine, compasse, and conspire some detestable renowned treason of the old stampe; and if he be once attainted thereof, according to his desire, &c. But if he doe but pingle, as suffer himselfe to bee outlawed, in action of trespasse, this was neuer any forfeiture of Franke Tenement: The Law was in the late dayes of Littleton and Parkins that euery attainder of murther or felonie done by the Baron, was an ouster of dower to the wife. The first Solons of the English Law be like thought that tender regard of a wiues estate, should restraine a husband from all inormious transgression against the sacred Crowne and dignitie Royall, would God it might: but the true reason why the law was so penall for such offences of the husband toward the wife, (in whom perhaps was no fault) that thereby shee should haue no Dower: and towards the children that they should haue no descent of inheritance, but the hereditary blood should be corrupt) was vpon these reasons grounded vpon the Law of nature, and giuen by Iustice Stamford in his booke fo. 194. saith he to this effect, men will now eschew those Capitall crimes when they shall see those persons who in nature and affection are neerest and dearest vnto them, and most to bee beloued, shall be punished with themselues: so that if themselues will not refraine such crimes for themselues, yet they should the rather refraine for the loue of their wife & children vpon whom they bring so perpetuall losse and punishment and staine of so infamous a note as that their stocke, blood,

blood and Lineage shall be corrupted and attainted, their children disinherited, and the wiues of their bosomes because the wiues of such impious and foolish Husbands, by their defaults depriued of all their meanes and liuelihood. And Breton fo. 258. makes another reason why a wife of a man attainted, &c. shall lose her Dower est pur ceo que est a supposer que el scauoit del felony son mary, and by him a woman lost no Dower, in case the felony were committed before Couerture.

King Edward the first in the first yeare of his Reigne abrogating some Statutes concerning treasons or felonie, for their austerity, and making some new decrees concerning treason, preserued Dower against all perpetrations of an euill husband: But 5. & 6. eiusdem regis ca. 11. by the last prouiso, It was againe enacted, that no Wife of any person attainted of treason should bee receiued to demand or haue Dower, &c. Yet for felonie 1. Ed. 6. is still in force.

And treasons by Act 5. Eliz. ca. 1. for assurance of her Maiesties royall power, or by the Act eodem anno cap. 11. against clipping, washing, rounding or filing of Coynes, or by the Act 18 Eliz. ca. 1. against diminishing or impayring the Queenes Coyne or other coyne currant here, doe none of them make any corruption of blood, or forfeiture of Dower.

Note, if after attainder the Baron purchase his pardon, this is so farre forth a new birth vnto him, that his Wife shall haue Dower of the Lands which come to him after pardon, if his Issue by her may per possibilitie inherite. Par. 75.

And remember this Case, 3. & 4. Phi. & Marie, Dyer 140. b. Marie the wife of Sir Iohn Gate, attainted of treason brought a Writt of Dower, against Wiseman the attainder of Sir Iohn; was certainly pleaded in barre, she replyed, that long time before the attainder and before the treason committed, after the Espousals, the said Sir Iohn Gate

Gate was seised in fee of the Land whereof she demands Dower, and thereof enfeoffed A. B. whose estate the tenant hath vpon a demurrer, without argument at barre or bench the Councell of the parties being heard in Iustice Brookes Chamber, the demandant was barred of Dower, by opinion of all the Iustices, because the Statute is, The Wife of a man attainted of any manner of treason whatsoeuer shall in no wise bee receiued to aske, challenge, demand or haue dower of any her Husbands Lands during the force of that attainder: And by Stamford, 195. this extendeth to petty treason: But nota, (saith Dyer) the Lands here sold and gone before treason committed, were neuer subiect to forfeiture or escheate, vt in causa Vauisor, M. Litleton in the Chapter of Dower: And therefore Antho. Browne Serieant was angrie at the heart for this Iudgement: See Littleton fo. 11. per Vauisor. If a man commit felonie, aliene his land, and then be attainted, the Wife shall haue action of Dower against the Feoffee, but not against the King or Lord, if it be escheated.

SECT. XVIII.

The Husbands power in his wiues inheritance, and of discontinuance.

A Womans Inheritance is Lands of Inheritance which she hath by descent or purchase, and her Marriage such as was giuen her in Franke Marriage by learned M. Littleton: But take heere all fee-simple or fee-taile, which she hath sole by her selfe, or ioyntly with some other to be her Inheritance.

Then know that at Common Law a man seised in the right of his Wife of greene acre, may make a feoffement

of

of it to a stranger, and this is such an interruption (called a discontinuance) of the wiues estate, that not onely the Baron is bound whilest he liueth, but the Wife also when he is dead is by common Law forbidden entry into her owne land, and put to her action of *cui in vita*, but if a man seised in the right of his wife be disseised and release to the disseisor (though it bee with warrantie) this is no Discontinuance.

If a man seised in fee in the right of his Wife, haue Issue by her a sonne and die, and then a second Husband makes a Lease of the Land, for terme of his life, and the Wife dyeth, if now the Lessee surrender to the second Baron, it is a question, whether the sonne can enter during the life of lease for life: But cleere (saith *Littleton*) when he is dead, the son may enter for the discontinuance which was but for the life, was determined.

If Tenant in the right of his Wife make a Lease for his owne life, the reuersion in fee is in the Baron: If hee die in the life time of his Wife and of the Lessee, and his heyre grant the reuersion with atturnament, now though the grantee enter, after the death of the Lessee, yet the wife may re-enter: for as an estate taile cannot be discontinued, but by one which is seised by force of the intaile, so the estate of a Wife, is not discontinuable but by him which is seised in the wiues right.

SECT.

SECT. XIX.

Of a Remitter.

YOu must vnderstand somewhat also of a Remitter. And because women learne faster by example then by precept, I will not stay to define a Remitter: Baron and Feme seised together in speciall taile, haue Issue a daughter, the wife dyeth, the Baron catcheth another wife, hath Issue by her another daughter, discontinueth the taile, disseiseth the discontinuee and dieth, now is the Land descended to the two daughters, the eldest daughter is remitted (that is remaunded and setled in the ancient estate) for a moitie, and driuen to a Formedone against her Sister for the other moity, for here the Sisters are by seuerall titles tenants in common not parceners.

If Tenant in taile infeoffe a Feme sole and die, and then his sonne being vnder age, intermarrieth with the Feme Feoffee, this is a remitter to the Sonne, and his wife which before had fee-simple hath now nothing at all in the land. But if the sonne had beene of full age at the time of espousals, hee had not regained the ancient estate, but stood seised onely in droit sa feme. If a Woman seised, &c. take a husband which alieneth in fee, and then takes backe an estate to him and his wife for life, this reprisall (though it were by Indenture or by fine) is meerely the act of the Husband, and the woman sans folly is adiudged in her Remitter, the reuersion of the Lessor running to smoke, rightly to smoke, which is something more then nothing: for if after all this the Lessor bring an action of waste against the Baron and Feme, the Baron cannot barre her by shewing her reprisall and remitter; but hee is stopped from speaking against his owne Feoffement and receipt.

So

So that here may bee an estoppell or conclusion by a matter not witnessed with specialty or any manner Scripture: But if in the action of waste the Baron will make default, at the grand distresse, the wife upon her prayer received to shew her matter shall barre the Lessor of his action right well.

For in every case where a woman is received to plead in her husbands absence, she shall have advantage as if shee were a Feme sole. And the reason why rendring backe the land by the Alien to Baron and Feme worketh a remitter, though it were by fine, is because a Feme Covert that taketh any thing by fine is never examined by the Justices.

But where somewhat is to bee conveyed, from a Feme Covert, by a fine, as if Baron and Feme make cognizance to another, &c. or a grant or render, or a release by fine, in all or such like cases, because the right of a Wife is passing, and she shall be eternally concluded, she must bee examined before the fine can be received: and if shee confesse that her husband menaced her if shee would not levie the fine, &c. it shall not be received. 15. E. 4. fo. 1. But where nothing is moved in fines, save onely a wives purchase and gaining, there is used none examination of her, and therefore such fines doe not conclude her.

If Tenant in taile discontinueth it and dieth, and the discontinuee makes a Lease to the Daughter and heyre of the Tenant in taile being of full age, and to her husband for their two lives, the daughter is remitted: If Baron and Feme Tenants in speciall taile be, and the Baron alieneth in fee, and takes backe an estate to him and his wife, for their lives, because they are but one person, and the estate is likewise one and intire without moities, and the Feme cannot be remitted here without the Husband be also remitted, they are adiudged both in their remitter: But the Baron himselfe is stopped from claiming so much contrary to his owne alienation.

If

If Lands be giuen to a Woman in taile, remainder to another in taile, remainder to a third in taile, with remainder ouer in Fee, if the woman take a husband that discontinueth in fee, all the remainders are discontinued, and if the Wife dyeth without Issue, there is no remedie but a Formedon by turne, if the first, second or third Donee die without Issue: But if after the discontinuance an estate be made to the Baron and Feme for their owne life or another mans life, or any other estate, the Wife is remitted and so are all they in remainder. If the Feme die, the next in remainder may enter, and so is it for them in the reuersion after the taile is ended.

A Lease of a house is made to a Feme sole for terme of her life, and in a faint or false action a stranger recouereth this house against her by default, so that she may haue a quod ei deforceat by West.2.ca.4. now is the reuersion of the Lessor discontinued, and hee cannot haue an action of waste. But if the woman marries, and the recouerer lease this house to the Baron and Feme for life, the wife is remitted to her first estate by the Lease, the first Lessor to his reuersion, and he may haue action of waste if there be cause.

Yet here if the other which recouered in the false action bring an action of waste, the Baron hath no other remedie but to make default at the grand distresse, and then the wife receiued, may bar him by shewing the faintnes or falshood of his action whereby he recouered.

If after discontinuance, &c. the Baron take backe estate to himselfe and his Wife, and to a third person, this is a remitter for a moity, and for the other moity the Feme must sue her cui in vita after the death of her Husband.

If after discontinuance of the Wiues estate, the Baron goe beyond the Seas, and the discontinued lease the Land to the Wife for life, and deliuer seisin; if the Baron agree thereunto at his returne, this is a remitter, for the Feme shall

shall be adiudged as an Infant, and not as a Feme sole in this Case, Quære (saith Littleton) if the Baron at his returne disagree, &c. whether this oust the Feme of her remitter.

If the Baron discontinue, the discontinuee be disseised, and the disseisor lease the tenements to the Baron and feme for life, this is a remitter to the Wife, though the Baron were consenting to the disseisin: But if the Baron and Feme were both of Conen and Consent to the disseisin, the wife shall be a disseiseresse and not remitted.

If the discontinuee make backe estate to Baron and Feme by indenture upon condition, viz. rendring rent, and for fault of payment re-entry, and because the rent is arreare, the discontinuee doth re-enter, upon this entry the woman may have an assise of novell disseisin after the husbands decease, for the condition by the remitter, was cleane extinct in truth, though during coverture the Baron was estopped, &c. so that he and his Wife could not have an assise together.

If the Baron discontinue, take backe estate to himselfe for life, the remainder after his decease to his wife for her life, here is no remitter till the husband be dead: but the Wife surviving, Franke Tenement is cast upon her maine Tenant will she nill she by act of Law, and shee is remitted, for though shee enter not, yet shee can have none action against any body for this land; but any man that hath cause may have action of it against her, because a recipe quod reddat is maintainable against tenant in ley, and that is the widdow here: But Tenant of Franke Tenement in fait, is one which hath an actuall seisin, and upon disseisin thereof may maintaine an assise.

The Statute of Glocester perceived how by common Law a man may play fast and loose with his Wives Inheritance by feoffement to discontinue her estate, and to continue it againe by resumption, and so to make it Inheritance or not to his wives at his pleasure.

But

But a feoffement doth onely barre the Wiues entry, what if to his feoffement the Baron aimes warrantie, what if to his warrantie assets, what if he leuie a fine? Glocester, ca. 3. anno 6. Ed. 1. is,

If Tenant by the Courtesie alien, &c. his sonne shall not be barred in a Writt of Mortdanccster by the deed of his Father, from whom none heritage is descended, to demand and recouer the mothers land, although his Fathers Charter be with warrantie for him and his heyres: But if land descend to him de part son pere, he shall be fore-closed, for the value of so much as is descended.

If after the Fathers death, any heritage descend from the Father, the Tenant shall recouer against him of the mothers seisin by a writt of iudgement out of the rolles, &c. which the Iustices before whom the plea was pleaded, shall grant to re-sommon the warrantie, as hath beene accustomed in other cases where the voucher pleads riens a luy descendre from him vpon whose deed he is vouched, &c.

And in like sort, the Issue of the sonne shall recouer by Writ of Cousinage, aile, or besaile. In like manner the Wiues heyre shall not be barred after the death of his father and mother to demand by Writt of entry, his mothers heritage, which his father in her life time aliened dont nul fine est leuie in court le roy.

SECT. XVII.

Mr. Littletons *glosse vpon the Statute of Glocester.*

Before the Statute (saith M. Littleton) if Tenant by the Courtesie did alien, &c. in fee with warrantie, onely this, after his disceasе, should barre the Heyre: for this was a collaterall warrantie before the Statute. Since the Sta-

Statute it is cleere, that whether tenant by the Courtesie, or tenant in the right of his wife, doe alien the wiues heritace or marriage by his deede in pais, which warrantie leauing none assets, it is no barre to the heyre: But what if the Baron alien by fine leuied in the Kings court, with warrantie, shall this barre the heyre without any thing descended in value?

Newton Chiefe Iustice of the Common place, thought it should by implication of words: for hee tooke dont nul fine. &c. to be a generall exception, and therefore this alienation by fine with warrant to remaine a collaterall warrantie, as it was at Common Law.

But Littleton giueth his voyce with them of contrary opinion which thought it an obscure exposition to permit irreuocable alienation by Tenant in droit sa feme onely by his warranting concord without assetts when the Statute hath in the beginning taken it expressly from tenant by the Courtesie alienating by Feoffement. Nul fine therefore, is as much to say, nul loyall fine rightfully leuied, viz. a fine leuied by Baron and Feme, for it is true that before this Statute was made (and somewhat after it too) there was no estate taile come into England. A fine might then well and rightfully haue beene leuied by Baron & Feme, the Barons heire be bound with warrantie, and the wiues heire barred for euer: But now since the Statute if Baron and Feme had made a feoffement in fee by deede in the Countrey, the womans heyre after decease of them both may haue a Writ of entry, sur cui in vita, for all the husbands warranty. And this Statute of Glocester, had left a fine no more force then a feoffement here, if the finall exception had not beene; for when it comes with ensemente & in meime le manner giuing a writt of entry to auoyd the alienation made by the father in the mothers life time, this might be extended perhaps to a fine leuied by them both, for where the Baron and feme doth alien by fine, its true that the Baron doth alien:

Lest therefore a fine leuied by Baron and Feme should be thought to be infeeblished, this exception of a fine was necessary, and it is to be intended of a fine loyall: For when the Justices know once that tenant in right of his wife, commeth to leuie a fine onely in his owne name they will not receiue it.

SECT. XXI.

Dyers Exposition.

Litleton in this discourse seemeth to speake, as if hee tooke a warrant without assets made by tenant per Courtesie, or iure vxoris, to bee no collaterall warrantie now a dayes, whereat I maruell. A man may haue a veyne cut vnder his eare, that shall disable him from performing a great part of manhood; but he shall be a man notwithstanding, and a horse may be so foundred that he shall neither well goe or stand, and yet a horse still: So this kinde of warrantie gelt or foundered by Statute remaines collaterall nomine & specie, Dyer is so fo. 148. at Common Law (saith he) garrantie by tenant per le courtesie was collaterall & vncore est come ieo intend: But it it is no barre in Mortdancester, aiel or cousinage, without assets in fee simple descended re & facto, whereas before the Statute it was brought to bee intended and supposed, and this Statute is taken strictly: for the law at this day is come ieo intend, if the heyre doe not enter vpon the aliene of his father in vita patris, that he shall be bound and barred of his entry by the warrantie.

If the Father be disseised, and release with warrantie, the heyre shall be barred without assets both of entry and action also, for this is none alienation by tenant by the Courtesie. In the last point of the Statute of Glocester for alienation by the husband, in vita vxoris, &c. if he alien the

the purchase of his wife with warranty: this is out of the Statute, for heritage or marriage is not intended purchase by her.

So much my Lord Dyer, note that both he and Littleton stand upon the word Marriage, which indeed is not in the letter of the Statute.

SECT. XXII.

The Statute of 32. H. 8. ca. 28.

WEe haue passed the pillers, not of Hercules but of Littleton in the Husbands power ouer his wiues Inheritance, now let vs looke plus vltra with Columbus.

King Henry the eight and the Parliament ordained in the yeare aboue specified, That all Leases of Mannors, Lands, Tenements, or Hereditaments hereafter to bee made by Indenture sealed for yeares or for life, by any person or persons being of the age of one and twenty yeares and seised in fee-simple or fee-taile, in the right of themselues, their Churches or wiues, or iointly with their wiues of any estate of Inheritance made before Couerture or after, shall be good, &c. against the Lessors, their wiues heyres and Successors, &c. according to the estate comprised in such Indenture of lease, in like manner and forme, as if the Lessors and euery of them at time of the Lease making, had beene seised in pure fee-simple to her owne onely vses: prouiso, that this act extend not to Leases made of Mannors, Lands, Tenaments or Hereditaments, being in the hands of any fermor or fermors by vertue of any old Lease, vnlesse the old Lease be expired, surrendred, or ended within one yeare next after making of the new Lease, nor shall extend to any grantee of reuersion, &c. nor to any Lease of any Mannors, Lands, Tenements, &c. which hath not beene commonly let to ferme or occupied by fermors by space of 20. yeares next before such Lease, nor to any Lease made without impeachment of waste, nor to any Lease to be made for aboue 21. yeares or three liues at the most from the day of the making thereof: And vpon euery such Lease there shall be reserued yearly to the Lessors, their heyres and successors to whom the Lands should haue come after the Lessers death, if such Lease had not beene made, or to whom the reuersion shall appertaine so much or more, annuall ferme or rent as hath beene most accustomably yeelded, &c. within twenty yeares next before such Leases were made. And euery person to whom the reuersion shal appertaine after the death of such Lessors or their heyres, shal haue such remedies a aduantages to all intents, against the Lessees, their executors or assignes, as the Lessor might haue had: So that if the Lessor were seised in in speciall taile, &c. the issue or heyre of that speciall estate, shall haue the reuersion, rent and seruices, &c.

Prouiso, that the wife bee made party to euery Lease made by her Husband of any Mannors, Lands, Tenements or Hereditaments, being the wiues Inheritance, and that euery such Lease be by Indenture in the name of the Husband and the Wife, and she to seale the same: And that the ferme be reserued to the Husband and wife, and to the heyres of the Wife according to her estate of Inheritance: And that the Husband shall not in any wise alien, discharge, grant or giue any the rent, or any part therof, longer then during Couerture, without it be by fine leuied by the Husband and wife, but the rent shall remaine, descend, reuert, or come, &c in such sort and manner as the land should haue done if no such Lease had beene made: prouided that this act extend not to giue liberty of taking more fermes, &c. then before was lawfull, &c. nor inable Vicar, or Parson to make or grant their Lease of Messuages, Lands, Tenements, Tythes, &c, or Hereditaments belonging

ing to their Church or Vicarage: And it is further enacted that all Leases made within three yeares before the twelfth of Aprill in the 31 yeare of H. 8. made by Indenture sealed by person or persons of full age, of whole memory, not unlawfully coacted, nor under Couert Baron, for terme of yeares, of any Mannors, Lands, tenements, or Hereditaments, whereof the Lessor or Lessors were seised in any estate of Inheritance, to their onely use at the time of their Lease-making, and whereof the Lessees, their executors or assignes at time of this act making, were in possession by vertue of the Lease, no cause of re-entry or forfeiture being had or made, shall be good and effectuall in law against the Lessors, their heyres and successors according to the couenants and agreements specified in the Indenture, &c. so that there be reserued to the Lessors their heyres, successors, &c. as much yearely rent as was at any time yeelded within 20. yeares before making of any such lease, or else the Leases to be of none other effect then they were of before this act.

And moreouer it is ordained that no fine, feoffement, act or acts to be made, suffered, or done by the husband onely of any Mannors, Lands, &c. being the Inheritance or freehold of the wife during Couerture betweene them, shall in any wise be, or make any discontinuance or be preiudiciall to the said wife or her heyres, or to such as shall claime right, title or interest by her death: But that shee or her heyres, or they to whom such right or title shall appertaine, after her decease shall and may lawfully enter into such Mannors, Lands, &c. any such fine, feoffement or other act notwithstanding, except fines onely leuied by Baron and Feme, wherunto the wife is priuie and a partie. Prouided that this clause extend not to giue any liberty to any Wife or her heyres to auoid any Lease hereafter to bee made of any her Inheritance by her husband and her selfe for 21. yeares or under, or for three liues at the most, whereupon yearely rent shall be reserued vt supra: Prouided also that

 this

this act extend not to any Lease heretofore made by Ecclesiasticall or other person by Couent or Common-seale, which Lease is made voyd by act of Parliament, nor to make good any Lease of any Ecclesiasticall person made by couent, seale or otherwise, or of any other person attainted of treason, &c.

SECT. XXIII.

The Exposition.

This Law in the first part is affirmatiue, or I may say leasatiue, a leasing Law or Statute, Tenant in fee-simple, iure mero suo nothing restrained by it: No more is Tenant iure vxoris, but he may make a Lease for yeares, to continue till the last hower of Platoes great yeare, or till King Arthur come againe (for all this Statute) for no greater rent then thrée bundle of bulrushes, as well as he might before although her land were neuer leased before, since Noahs floud, and such a Lease shall bind him during Couerture.

But if the Husband make a Lease by paroll or by poll déede, or by Indenture, and the wife not partie; or if the Land were not in former times demised, or if the ancient rent or more be not reserued, then as the earth stayeth in the worlds center vpon nothing but Gods prouidence and permission, the Demisée leaneth vpon no Statute, but hangeth at the wiues courtesie, ponderibus librata suis, as at Common Law.

SECT.

SECT. XXIV.

Law before the Statute.

How that was, yee shall perceive by the cases following; If before the Statute of quia emptores, tenant in fee, iure vxoris infeoffed a stranger expressing no tenure, the feoffee was to hold of the Baron by such services as he and the Wife held by of the Lord Paramount. If the Baron and Feme had ioyned in a Feoffement to hold of the Baron, &c. th expressed tenure had beene voyd, and the Feoffee must have held of them both by such services as they held over, &c.

If the Baron in this case had died, and the Wife accepted the rent in her viduity, this acceptance here barred her for ever from avoyding the Feoffement by Writt of cui in vita. If Tenant iure vxoris and his Wife, had made a Feoffement to hold of the Wife, the Feoffor should have held of them both, and if the Wife had died, the Feoffor was to hold of the Baron till the feoffement were avoyded by sur cui vta, Par. 126.

Againe, if before this Statute of 32. H. 8. Tenant in fee iuro vxoris, and his wife had ioyned in exchange for other lands in fee, and the exchange being executed, the Husband had dyed; now the Feme by entring in upon the Land given her upon the exchange, should be barred for ever from defeating the exchange. But if it had beene made by the Baron alone, she might have defeated it notwithstanding her entrie; for that could give no seisin by force of the exchange to her that was neither partie nor privie to it, Par. fo. 8.

And if a man seised in right of his Wife, &c. make a Lease for life rendring rent with a letter of Atturney to his Wife to make livery, the Wife delivers seisin, the Baron dieth, she accepts the rent, she may have a cui in vita by the common Law, for the acceptance here maketh not the Lease good, because the livery which the wife made, was as servant to her Master and onely the act of the Baron, Par.41. we haue concerning acceptances some plentifull Learning, 21.H.6.fo.24. Ascu saith there, That if Lessee for yeares bee in arrerage of rent and die, his Executors shall pay the arrerages if they occupie the Ferme, contra, if they waive possession, and so if a Lease for life be made to Baron and Feme, the Baron commits waste and dies, the wife shall be subiect to an action for waste done by the husband if she occupie the land; contra, if she waive the possession, and by Paston in the end of the case, if Baron seised. ex. vxoris, make a lease for life of the land, and die, the wife can haue no action of waste, for she was not partie to the lease, & ex hoc sequitur, that a woman vpon acceptance of rent of lease for yeares made by her husband without being her selfe a partie, is not bound, but shee may enter: And albeit the lease were for life, yet acceptance barreth not a cui in vita, if she were not partie, &c. 26. H. 8. fo. 2. per curiam, if Baron and Feme sell the Wiues land, make feoffement, and the Vendee by the Indenture of sale couenants to pay ten pounds annually to the Baron and Feme during their liues, if the Baron die and the feme accept the ten pounds, this is no bar in cui in vita, no more then acceptance of rent after Marriage dissolued, where the Baron a per luy made a feoffement or lease.

But acceptance of rent, &c. where they both made a feoffement or lease for life is a barre of all actions. I will hunt for no farre fetcht learning of acceptances: but this I finde, if a man lease his land to I. S. to hold at will by certaine rent, none acceptance of the rent here, after the Leassors death can barre the Heyre of entrie, or make any affirmance of the lease, for acceptance can neither make good a lease determined by entry, or a lease already void without entry by the lessors death.

And he that leaseth to hold at will endeth that will when

he

he endeth his life: but a lease for yeares by an Abbot or Tenant in taile, is not by their death presently void, but voydable, and the successour or Issue by acceptance of the rent affirmes the Lease; So doth the Feme affirme the Lease made for yeares, by her husband of her Land, by acceptance when she is become sole: and see Dyer, 5. Mar. 159. by the opinion of three Iustices, Dyer, Stamford and Browne, if Baron and Feme had made a Lease by Indenture rendring rent, and the Baron before rent day die, and the Feme before the day take another husband, who accepts the rent and dies, this acceptance shall bind the Wife: but note and take with you this peculiar rule, where acceptance binds her that she be a partie to the Lease, and that by writing, for if a man makes a Lease for yeares without deed, of land, which he holdeth in right of his wife, this was meerly void towards the wife, so soone as the Husband is dead, and acceptance of the rent is to no purpose, Plo. 431. per Bromley.

Againe 9. H. 6. If tenant in Fee iure vxoris make a Lease for yeares and the wife dieth, the Lessee shall pay the rent untill the Wiues heyre enter, for so long there is a continuance of a Fermour by force of the Lease; but none avowry lyeth for the Husband, because he hath no reversion. And an action of trespasse vi & armis may be against him, but he cannot haue action of debt for the rent.

But to come home to the very brinke of the Statute, nota (saith Dyer) That the common opinion amongst all Iustices at this day is, If Baron and Feme make a Lease for terme of yeares, before the Statute of 32. Hen. 8. by Paroll reserving rent to them both, if the wife when shee is become sole, accept the rent at the Fermors hands, this binds her not from avoyding the Lease, if it were not by Indenture, for her assent was requisite at the beginning, and that ought to haue appeared by deed Dyer, 1. Mar. fo. 91. The same Learning is, 4. Mar. fol. 146.

When

When a Feme Couert departs from her Land the intent, consideration and cause ought to be expressed in scripture to proue her consent to the whole Mannor; for it is agreed for Law, That if before the Statute, Baron and Feme had made a Lease by paroll of the Wiues Land for terme of yeares, rendring rent, though after the Barons death she had accepted the rent, yet she might out the Termer, because her priuitie to the Lease appeares not per escript; likewise if a feme couert suffer a recouery or fine of her Land, it shall be intended by Law to be to her owne vse, if there appeare none other intent expresly by Writing.

And none auerment shall be taken of intent or consideration in such Case other then the Indenture specifieth.

SECT. XXV.

Obseruations vpon the very Statute.

I Haue shewed what strength a Demise or Lease for yeares made of the Wiues Land by Baron and Feme, or by the Baron onely was of before the Statute, and is of being made since the Statute without the appointed circumstance and solemnitie: Now a little to the very Statute, As I said before, the ordinance is that Leases shall bee good, &c. But not directly that any terme shal be voyd, though voyd of strength by this Statute they may be many wayes, as appeares by the prouiso.

Note that the forerunning Lease, Demise or occupation by Fermors must bee derived from one that had Inheritance (for if at the end of a primitiue Lease made by the Lord of whom the Tenancie is holden, or by the Kings grantee or committee of wardship, or by tenant in Dower, or by Tenant per le Courtesie, some of which may by good possi-

possibilitie haue had power to make Leases by space of twice twenty yeares, a tenant in tayle makes a Lease, this succeeding demise hath no vertue or ingredience of the Statute though it seeme to haue good correspondence with it; And it is doubted whether a Ferme continued twenty yeares by the Donors demise, be sufficient or no, to make roome for a new Lease.

This for ought I perceiue is by a prudent interpretation of the Constitution rather vpon equitie and intent, then vpon the Text, tenants in fee-simple or tailed which transmit their possession to their deere off-spring, will not make Leases to any great disaduantage of any of their owne babes or blood, and therefore their Leases may well bee imitated.

But like enough it is that Tenant per le courtesie, or in Dower, or in right of his owne or in another mans Seignory, may Lease away their estate, for a proud fine and a little rent: Nay yee may be sure, that if they might set the example, they should be gotten to make Leases for esperuiers annuall, and small yearely income in hope that my young Master at his full age, should be content with the old rent, and a kennell of hounds: King Henries and the Parliaments meaning was not therefore, that their Leases should be any patternes for reseruation of rent by Tenant in Taile, or as I suppose in the right of his Wife. If Baron and Feme make a Lease by Indenture for twenty yeares to commence at Michaelmas it might seeme doubtfull by the booke 7. & 8. Eliz. Dyer, 246. whether it be a good Lease, by this Statute.

If Baron and Feme by their Indenture make a Lease to commence after the Wiues death, I thinke this no good Lease, according to the Statute, for twenty one years ought to be from the making of the Lease, &c. If the Baron and Feme die, the Heyre is not bound to accept the rent or allow the Lease. And though he doe accept it, if the

Land

Land were tailed, he may enter notwithstanding: vide 10. Eliz. Dyer, 279.

If Baron and Feme make a Lease by Indenture, &c. for 31. yeares, quære, the Baron dying, whether this be a good Lease, for 21. yeares or no, I thinke it is not, but standeth meerely at Common Law. For the first Prouiso of this act is that it shall not haue respect or extend to Leases made for aboue 21. yeares.

When King Henry the eight in 31. of his Reigne by Parliament had made voyd all Leases to bee made of Lands, which should afterward come to him, if any Leases former were in esse, or being, with prouiso viz if he which had an old vnexpired lease, tooke a new that he should hold for 21. yeares, from making of the new Lease, so that it exceeded not twenty one yeares, it was admitted in Falmestones Case, that such a Lease made for fifty yeares, was good for 21. Plo. 110.

And when Thomas Vmpton after (32. Henry the 8) ca. 1. which gaue power to Tenant per Chiualrie to deuise two parts of his land, had deuised a whole mannor in fee, before 34. Ed. 3. 5. Hen. 8. of explanation, which will by the said Statute of explanation, was referred to the Law, the deuice was adiudged good for two parts, contra Kelwais opinion, as you may see 4. & 5. Phil. & Mar. Dyer, 150. But these cases differ farre from the former as yee may finde by the comparing the Statutes: If after a Demise by Baron and Feme for twenty shillings of vsuall rent, the husband release all his right, except twelue pence, &c. or grant that the Lessee shall hold dispunishable for waste, the Wife accepting twelue-pence post mortem viri, may distraine for the rest notwithstanding, and haue an action of waste, Dyer 304.

Note, before this Statute was made the Count Bridgewater being tenant in taile, the remainder to Basset in taile, he bound himselfe in recognizance to the said Basset to make no alienation, grant, sale, conueyance or exchange, other-

otherwise then for his owne life, it was a question after the statute, whereunto Basset and all men were parties, whether the Earle might now make a lease for xxi. yeares without forfeiture of his Recognizance, resolved by Bromely, Portman and Harris serjeants that he could not, but if hee did make such a lease, they thought that neither hee in remainder or the donour should ever avoid it by any dying sans issue, 33 H.8. f.49. in Dyer, who, concludeth and so shall the statute be expounded, for so was the intent, a meaning of the makers, yet the text hath no word of donours, or of them in remainder, I heare that law is taken now to bee cleane contrary in the last point viz, that remainders and reversions are freed from this act, and I beleeve it the rather because 34. H 8. ca. 20. that frustrateth fained recoveries against tenant in tayle, where the King is in reversion or remainder, in the provision for strength of leases, made according to the Statute, is only against the heyre or heyres of tenant in taile, &c.

The last part of the Statute.

SECT. XXVI.

THe Last part of the Statute is negative against discontinuance, which how farre it prevailed before or after the act, the former instructions, with the act it selfe, doe put in some cleerenesse. But a case or two will make it more plaine, Amy Townsend seised of a Mannor in tayle, take a husband, the husband made a feoffement, 29. of H.8. to divers persons in fee, to the use of himselfe and his wife for life of them two, with remainders of use over. After this Statute made, Amy and her husband made a Lease for 21. yeares of part of this Manuor, according to this act of 32. H 8 Amy died first, then her husband died; the question is, whether Amy were remitted to her former estate taile by vertue of 27. *H.* 8. ca. 10. and so the Lease good, it was

was argued on the one part, that reduction of the possession by the statute 27. &c. was of effect alone with their feoffement, and because this possession was regained without either tort or folly in the wife, whose agreement whether she would or no, was included in her husbands agreement during Coverture, she must needs when Coverture was dissolved, till disclaimer, or some act done to the contrarie be adiudged in possession, there was then no tenant against whom to bring her cui in vita, if she should not bring her cui in vita to purge the first wrong, she must needs be remitted, if she were remitted, this cause must needs be good. And although the Statute of 27. settle possessions according to qualitie and quantitie of the use, yet it seemeth not that so it shall continue, but they may change by a former ancient right, for the Act being affirmatiue takes not the Common Lawes operation in remitters: besides that, it hath an expresse sauing of eygne right: further, if that the wife should not be remitted, this inconuenience followeth, the Baron might charge the Wiues inheritance with a rent, to the whole yearly value, or be bound in a Statute merchant, &c. and then making a feoffement to his wiues use, shee should hold the land charged after his death. To this it was answered on the other part, that the feoffement at the time thereof made a discontinuance, which puts Amy to her cui in vita, which because she hath not used, but is come to possession onely by force of 27. &c. she must take it onely by the manner, order, and limitation of the same Statute, Couerture, or infancie, being no whit materiall, because the Statute hath none exception. The words are in manner, forme, qualitie and condition of the use, &c. and because this was a new Constitution of that which was not at the Common Law, it hath not the force of a negatiue implying in nul auter manner then is therein described: Amy is therefore a ioynt purchaser with her husband in estate for life, and not in or by descent of estate taile: Now to say that her right and estate should change by by silent operation of the Law after shee was repossessed, that cannot be, for the whole entry is tolled, and if she be not remitted by her first possession and reprisall, she is never remitted.

If a Disseisour make feoffement to the use of the Disseisee, and after the Disseisor enter, he shall be remitted, but before his entry he shall not be remitted, for he shall be adjudged in possession by vertue of the Statute, but so soone as hee entreth he is remitted, for his entry was never tolled: But Amy Townesends entry was cleane taken away, by the discontinuance, &c. further if she should be remitted by the Statute of 27. the remainders should be all destroyed contrary to the text of the same Statute. And to the inconveniencie alleadged, if she shall not be remitted shee shall hold incombred with the charges of her Husband, that is none at all, for Amy after her husbands death might have disagreed and relinquished the use with possession annexed to it, by bringing a cui in vita, against him next in remainder; for in him by such disagreement or user of action had the remainder vested, as though the woman had beene a Monke or dead person in Law, or never named in the limitation: If the use had beene to Amy Townsend in fee, she might have brought her cui in vita against the Feoffor or his heyre, by which they shall be Tenants to her action, and so might the incumbrance have beene avoyded; for when a feoffement is to the use of one which refuseth the use, it shall be in effect as if the use had beene limited to Paules steeple or to Charing-Crosse, all falling or reflecting because the Feoffor hath no recompence or consideration to his use, and hee shall be Tenant to every Precipe: It was further agreed, that as the Cause fell out, Amy Townesend could not be remitted, though her possession had returned by refeoffemẽt at the Common Law, because Sir Roger Townesend her Husband outlived her, for 21. Ed. 3. the Case is, Baron made a Feoffement, the Feoffee reinfeoffe the Baron and Feme and heyres of the wife, the

the woman dyed, the Heyre entred, the Baron brought an Assise, which was iudged maintainable: for whilest the Baron liued he was tenant to the heyres action; And the the Iudgement was, that Amy Townsend was neuer remitted; the reason was indeed because there is nothing in the Statute of 27. to make a remitter: for the clause of sauing of Droits, Titles and Actions, is of such right, &c. as was before the Statute, and not of any right, title, or action, risen since or after it: Now note that as a Lease made for twenty yeares by Baron and feme Tenants for life binds not any remainder by the Statute, which speaketh onely that Leases made by Tenants of Inheritance, shall binde heyres and Successors, so I would inferre that if the Leassors inheritance be determined, whether it were iure vxoris in taile or otherwise in taile, the remainder must be free from the Statute: But note that the point which made me choose this case for illustration of the Statute, is this, Amy Townesend was iudged not remitted, because she had no title of entry, but onely by the 27, &c. of vses, and therefore she must needs claime her possession, according to the vse.

But put Case the Feoffement had beene since the Statute of 32. the Law would then haue iudged a remitter; for by Littleton, where any persons entry is congeable, which taketh estate for life or in fee, it is a remitter, if the reprisall be not by Indenture, or record, or some matter of estoppell, for alwayes where there is a double right or title, the Law must iudge for the best, as well in the entry as in the possession, and an Indenture made by Baron and Feme is none estoppell to the Wife by the Common Law.

Concerning the Case 21. Ed. 3. Wilby which gaue iudgement, thought the Barons aduantage a hinderance to the Remitter, yet if he died the wife should be remitted: But if you looke, Brooke remitter 21. and 41. ye shall finde that

the

the Feme was maintenant remitted though to saue the husbands aduantage of warranty, they would not so iudge it, quod mirum saith Brooke, and quære quia contrarium acco iour.

SECT. XXVII.

Whether acceptance or taciturnity may not take away an entry at this day.

NO fine, feoffement or other act done by the husband onely shall make any discontinuance or be preiudiciall to the wife, but that she may enter, &c. what if Baron and Feme make a feoffement or Lease for life, by solemne Indentures with Liuery and seisin cleere, this takes not away at this day the wiues entry after Couerture ended. But admit when shee is a widdow, shee refuseth to enter and accept payment of rent or performance of couenants: is not now both her entry, and her action gone also, euen as in case of an Infant, which makes such a feoffement or Lease, and accepts the rent when he is of full age: The question must be answered out of the Statute, and in mine opinion there is nothing in it to ayde a woman after such ratification by acceptance volenti non fit iniuria, nec inuitis confirmantur beneficia. A Lease by Baron & Feme per Indenture is not voyd presently by the Barons death. But whereas before she was driuen to suit and action, shee may now enter by the Statute, yet it compels her not to enter, neither casteth any free-hold vpon her. In like manner if the Baron alone alien his Wiues Land by fine with proclamation, the Wife may enter by force of this Statute, but per opinionem totius curiæ Ed. 6. Dyer fo. 72. If she suffer fiue yeares to passe and expire without entry or vser of action she and her heyres shall be barred for euer, for this

Statute of 32. though it limit no time for the womans entry, yet it speaketh nothing of fines with proclamation, and therefore it takes not the generall Law made 4.Hen.7.cap. 24. of fines, with proclamation. And see Sir Ed. Cokes 8. Rep. fo. 72. in Grenlies case.

SECT. XXVIII.

Of Fines.

SEe further the case 18. Eliz. Dyer 351. Land holden in socage was given to a man and his wife in taile, the remainder in fee to the Barons right heyres, the Baron alone levied a fine with proclamation to his owne use, and afterward by his last will and Testament in writing, devised the Land to his wife for life, the remainder over to a Stranger upon condition to pay certaine rent annually out of the land with Clause of distresse,&c. the Baron died, the wife entering and claiming estate onely for life paid rent according to the will and died. Now the question is, whether the Issue in taile or Devisee of the remainder should have this Land, Ex per iudicium curiæ. Partly because his mother had waved the estate taile, and although shee had not done so, yet because he could not convey his title and discent, but aswell as heyre to his father as to his mother, the fine with proclamations levied onely by his father barres him: So farre goeth the Booke. And you may observe, that it barres the wife if she will.

See also 5.Eliz. 224 in Dyer, the husband levied a fine with proclamations of his owne land, and after five yeares died, his widdow continuing sole, of full age, whole memory, out of prison, within compasse of the foure Seas, and doth not make any demand or claime of dower, within 5. yeers after her husbands death (quære if he which pleadeth in barre

barre of Dower, ought expresly to auerre this:) The question was, if she were barred of Dower, Dyer telleth vs termino Hillarij 4. H. 8. rotulo 344. such a barre pleaded was admitted good, for the ground of Dower was the Husbands seisin, and the action giuen by his death. So that it is within the second sauing of 4. H 7. which preserueth to all which are not parties pursuit of right growne after the fine, by or vpon cause before the fine, so that they take it within fiue yeares.

In Plowden fo. 373. Iustice Dyer arguing Stowell and the Lord Zouches case, affirmes the learning which I haue recited out of his owne booke: But Plowden inserts his note, that he takes the Law to be otherwise, and that a woman is bound to no time of her Dower, after such a fine, for (saith he) the ayme of 4. H. 7. as against future droicts is wholly against such rights, as either suffered wrong before the fine, or by the fine, and in this case of Dower, the title is all after the fine, and standeth well in accord with it, not touched by the Statute, the woman therefore may demand when she listeth.

So if there be a cessor begun, a yeare before a fine with proclamations continued a yeare after, the Lord is not restreyned at the end of 5. or 15. yeares to bring a cessauit. so he saith likewise, if a morgage be disseised, a fine levied by the Disseisor with Proclamations passed, yet the morgager paying his mony to the Morgagee may at any time, within 5. years or more, after the payment re-enter. When Giants fight, Pigmées may not part them: but howsoeuer some incertainty arise in euery corner of the Law, this is here certaine, that a fine leuied by the husband onely, of his owne land, tolleth not the wiues action of Dower, if she come in time: And a fine so leuied, by him, of the wiues Land, taketh not away her seasonable entry; but the gulfe that swalles vp entrie, action right, and all possibility of reducement by Law is a fine lawfully leuied by baron and feme, where (forsooth) because a woman is examined by a Justice or one that hath a Dedimus potestatem, &c. and acknowledgeth her free consent and agreement, what cannot men get wiues to doe if they list, she shall be barred and for euer excluded of a great many acres of ground, for a few kisses and a gay gowne. That is a fine finem litibus imponens, for till it be done and dispatcht, the poore woman can haue no quiet her husband keepes such a iawling.

SECT. XXIX.

Of common recoueries.

AS for trickes of Common recoueries I perceiue not how that can be greatly preiudiciall to women: for first if a man will suffer a faigned recouery of his owne Land to defeate his wiues Dower, she may falsifie it, &c. see the Electione firmæ per Eare against Snow, Plowd fo. 515. the baron there being tenant in taile, his wife hauing nothing in the Land, he and his wife suffered a common recouery with voucher to his owne vse, &c. the opinion of all the Justices was, that though the woman suruiued, yet the estate taile shal be barred, for it was found precisely by verdict that the wife had no interest in the Inheritance: The baron therefore, which alone lost estate taile by the recouery, might recouer alone estate taile in value. But as for the wife, no man can say what estate shee had; nor whether she should haue a quod ei deforceat, or a Writt of right, if she had lost the land by default. So likewise hauing lost by the recouery, nothing or no man can tell what her recompence in value must be: She was named (said the Justices) vpon intent to barre her of Dower, and such is the meaning of husbãds which wil haue their wiues named in such recoueries: but cleere the estate taile is barred, if in his case the wife might sue execution in value against the voucher vouchée by estoppell, yet the issue in taile should not be concluded by the act of his Father, but he might oust her of that which she had so recouered in value, &c. see Sir E. Cokes 10. Rep. 43. a. in Mary Portingtons ca. that the usage hath béen alwayes upon common recoueries against Baron and Feme to examine the wife, and to grant a dedimus potestatem, to take upon her examination her Conusance as in case of a Fine.

But let the case be, Tenant iure vxoris is agréed with John a Stile to suffer a recouery of his wiues Lands to certaine uses comprised in Indentures betwixt them two, a Writ of entry in the post is brought against the Baron and Feme, which appeare in person or by Atturney, calling to warranty the common vouchée, a man well worth a couple of new rosted egges, which re-enters into warrantie, Then after declaration and imparlance, at the day of the appearance shall the demandant recouer against Baron and Feme, and they in right of the Wife shall recouer against the Vouchee of such lands as he hath, or is like to haue when time hath a hairy crowne: shall this recouery or possibility of unlikely recouery in value binde the wife when the Baron is dead whether she will or no: by Brooks nouell cases, 23. H. 8. pl. 37. it séemes that such a recouery did then bind the wife to: but without examination mee thinks it should not bind the wife: The Statute of 32. is that none Act of the Barons shall make discontinuance, &c. except onely a Fine by Baron and Feme, Ergo such a recouery notwithstanding though it be executed the wife may enter. See 23. Eliz. cap. 3. and there is a sauing to euery Feme couert or her heyres her Writt of error to be sued within 7. yeares after she become sole, for reuersing of Fines and recoueries past, if they must be reuersed by error, it séemes without error, they were very dangerous. For a rule to conclude withall, take this, That wheresoeuer the Baron doth any thing out of Court, which thing he and his Wife were compellable to doe, it shall be deemed and construed to be the act of both of them, as if the Baron seised in right of his Wife, or ioyntly with his wife, assigne Dower to another woman, it bindeth, and so granting of a rent for equality of partition and atturnement by the Baron alone, bindes the Wife.

SECT. XXX.

Of Iointures.

I Will enter no farther into the streame of Fines and recouerie, they require a cunning swimmer: And a short Discourse cannot possibly make any plaine discouery of them; otherwise this place would haue borne the Doctrine fitly about making of ioyntures, for all husbands are not so unkinde or untrusty as to endamage their Wiues by alienation of their Lands: but contrariwise the greatest part of honest, wise and sober men, are of themselues carefull to purchase somewhat for their Wiues, if they be not, yet they stand sometimes bound by the womans parents to make their Wiues some Ioynture.

If husband, Father, Mother and all would be unmindfull of prouision in this point, yet very many of our English women haue with their singular vertue, so much wisedome of their owne, as to foresee for themselues, and discerne the difference betweene that which wee call Dower and Ioynture: Ioyntures saith Dyer 4. M. fo. 148. are made for the most part to Baron and Feme ioyntly, or to the Feme onely, this also is comprehended under the terme Ioynture before Marriage or after, for sustentation of the charge and necessities of Espousalls; and they are made causa matrimonij & gratis, without the consideration of money, bargaine or any thing sauing for loue and affection of the Baron or his ancestors, and these Iointures are a present possession: But Dower must be tarried for till the

Hus-

Husband be dead: It must be demanded, sometime sued, for sometime neither with suit or demand obtained. Againe, Dower was subiect to forfeiture in times past, by felony done and proued in the Baron by the Barons treason, by the Wiues elopement, and euery question in the validitie of Marriage maketh a scruple of Dower, all which inconueniences being wisely foreseene, women did learne to become ioynt purchasors with their husbands of such estates, as would auoid all weathers, and a good while they did enioy Ioyntures and Dowers after their Husbands were dead; against which the Statute of 27. H. 8. of vses, ordeineth as followeth.

SECT. XXXI.

A part of 27. H. 8. ca. 10.

IT is prouided, &c. that where any persons haue purchased or haue estate of lands, &c. made to them and their Wiues, and to the heyres of the Husband, or to the Husband and wife, and the heyres of their two bodies, or to the heyres of one of their bodies, or to the husband and wife for terme of their liues, or for the life of the wife, or where any such estate hath beene or shall be made, to any husband and his wife or to other persons their heyres and assignes to the vse and behoofe of the said husband and wife, or to the vse of the wife for the ioynture of the wife, that in euery such case the woman hauing such a Ioynture, &c. shall not claime any Dower of the residue of any Hereditaments that were her Husbands, by whom she had such a Ioynture, or make any demand thereof against the Tenants of the said lands, &c. prouided that if any woman be lawfully expulsed or euicted from her said Ioynture or from any part thereof without fraud or Couen, by lawfull entry, action or discontinuance of her Husband, that euery such woman shall be endowed of as much of the residue of her Husbands hereditaments as the Lands or Tenements so euicted shall amount or extend vnto: Prouided that nothing in this act extend to hurt or preiudice any woman heretofore married, concerning her right, title, vse, interest or possession which she may claime or pretend to haue for her Joynture or Dower in any Lands, &c. of her late Husband being now disseised: Prouided also, that if any Wife haue or hereafter shall haue any Lands, Tenements, or Hereditaments vnto her giuen or assured after Marriage for terme of her life, or otherwise in Joynture (except the assurance be made to her by act of Parliament, and the Wife after that fortune to out-liue her husband, in whose time the Joynture was made, that the Wife so ouer-liuing, shall and may at her pleasure refuse the Lands appointed or assured in Joynture, and thereupon haue, demand and take her Dower by Writt or otherwise, according to the Common Law.

SECT. XXXII.

The Exposition.

THe first obseruance is that no estate gained by matter of conclusion, shall be deemed a purchasement within this Statute, or bee auerred to bee made pro iunctura: But the Statute must be intended of true and substantiall estates. Therefore if an owner or tenant of certaine land make answer to Baron and Feme in an action of waste, or if he pray ayde of them, as if they were seised of the reuersion, or if he bring a quod ei deforceat, against them as if he had none other then a particular estate; though these things were purposed for Joynture, yet they seclude not a Woman from right or demand of Dower: Releases such as inure to make estates, as where a ioynt-tenant releaseth

leaseth to his Companion, or such as goe to inlarge an estate, as where he in reuersion releaseth to his particular Tenant, may well make and accomplish a Joynture: but such Releases as worke no more but vn mitter le droit, as where he that is disseised by Baron and Feme, releaseth to the woman the disseiseresse, &c. are no purchase intended within this Statute, for it is meant onely of such purchases as the wife hath by gift either of her husband or of some other body, and not of such estates, as shee hath gained by her owne wrong: likewise is it of releases that goe by way of extinguishment, as where a Disseisor infeoffeth Baron and Feme, and the Disseisee releaseth to one of them, this is alike auaileable to both, but this release can make no Joynture, for there is no estate conueyed by it.

Per iusticiarios, 6. Ed. 6. Brooke titles Dower, a deuise of Land by the Husband to his Wife in his last will and testament, is no barre of Dower, for it is but a beneuolence and no Joynture: Yet in M. Brograues reading it was holden contrary, 5. Eliz. Dyer, 220. the case is, that a man seised of Lands in taile, and of some other in fee-simple, holden in socage, deuiseth the third part of all his Lands to his wife for her life, in full recompence of all such Joynture and Dower as she shall haue or may claime, &c. the Wife without any assignement or vser of Action of Dower entreth after his death, into that which was holden in Fee-simple to a value of a third part of all, and the opinion was, she had determined her election and barred her selfe of Dower.

But this Case maketh nothing to the variance or question, because the Legacie was with an expresse exclusion of Dower, &c. But see Sir Ed. Cokes 4. Rep. fo. 4. a. in Vernons case, resolued that vnlesse it be expressed in the will to bee for her Joynture it shall be no satisfaction for her Dower: See 38. H. 8. Dyer 61. William Whorewhod seised of Land, to the value of 360. pound, of which 60. pound was by ioynt purchase to him and his Wife during Couerture,

ture, deuised, that his wife should haue the third part of all his land during her life, with those Lands, which she had in Joynture, the assignement to be made by his executors, if it were not contrary to Law, this Widdow refused her Jointure of 60. pound, and demand a third part of the whole inheritance; viz. 120. pound as her Legacie, with a third part of that which remained for her Dower, viz. 80. pound: at last by agreement it was ordered and decreed in the Court of Wards, that she should haue the Legacie, vt supra, and forty pound ouer for Dower: This Case decideth the question, for it is against the latter opinion expresse, ideo quære. Brooke noteth also Dower 69. that per Iusticiarios, if a man make his Wife ioynt-purchaser with him after Couerture, of any estate of Franke Tenement, vnlesse it be to him and his Wife and their Heyres in fee-simple, it is a barre of Dower if she agree to the Joynture post mortem viri, otherwise it is of fee-simple, for thereof the Statute saith nothing. But M. Brograue in his reading did maintaine for all the foresaid opinion, that where fee-simple is conueyed to a Feme for Joynture expresly, it is a good Jointure within compasse of this Statute: for if estate in taile or for life be a good Jointure, and exclude Dower by acceptance, &c. a fortiore, fee-simple shall barre. And see in Vernons case reported by Sir Ed. Coke 4. Rep. fo. 3. b. that the case in Brooke is mis-reported and the Lord Dyer is against it, and confuteth Brooks reasons of this opinion.

Hee relied also vpon dame Dennis case, 8. Eliz Dyer 248. An Indenture was made 36. Hen. 8. Betwixt Sir Maurice Dennis and Elizabeth Statham, that in consideration of expected Marriage, and other things reasonable the said Sir Maurice and his heyres, should from thenceforth stand seised of certaine Lands, &c. to the vse of himselfe and his heyres vntill Marriage were had and solemnized, and then to the vse and behoofe of the said Maurice and Elizabeth, and their heyres after Marriage, Sir Maurice

rice dyed, entred into the Lands, and demanded Dower of his other Lands, it was a question whether this conveyance and matter, vt supra, with auerrement that it was for a Joynture, should barre her of Dower, Catline, Saunders, and Dyer were against the Dower by equitie of the Statute, which in the third prouiso is of Joyntures for terme of life or otherwise: Against them were Justice Browne and Whiddon, and they resembled this Statute to another of the 11. H. 7. ca. 20. which cannot be extended to fee-simple, but is meant and expressed onely of estate for Life, or in taile seuerally or ioyntly with the Baron.

But Justice Dyer as it seemeth by M. Brograue vpon diligent conference with sage men of Law, did strongly adhere to his former opinion, that this conueyance with auerment made a good Joynture: Yee shall finde againe, 14. & 15. Eliz. he affirmeth for Law, that where Fee-simple is limited ouer to a Wife, or estate made to Baron and Feme in fee, it is auerrable pro junctura, if the conueyance be not expressly contrary: See a question for auerment, Dyer 226.

One that had an vse in Fee of certaine Lands, to the value annuall of 100. pound, tooke a wife, 22. H. 8. and after espousals at request of his wiues friends and Parents, caused the Feoffees to execute estate to him and his wife, and to the heyres of himselfe of parcell of this Land to twenty pound value, &c. He then purchased other Lands, and after 27. dyed seised of all: The wife by taking rents and profits of the twenty pound land agreed to her estate therein, and afterward brought a Writ of Dower, de tertia parte residui omnium terrarum, &c. because the Statute is expressed of Jointure, and the deed whereby estate was made to the baron and feme hath no mention of Joynture or Dower, quære, whether this matter generally alledged without auerment, that it was pro junctura vel pro dote, shall barre or no: See the Institutions of Sir Ed. Coke, fo. 36. much matter concerning Joynture.

An

In all conneyance or purchase for Joynture, unlesse it be by fine, or common recouerie, he which makes the estate must be a person able to conney &c. at the time of Joynture making, or else it is not good.

He must not therefore be non compos mentis, attaint of treason, an alien borne, or under age; but the non-age of the Wife, is not materiall whether the Joynture be made, before Couerture or after, if she accept it, agréed at M. Finches reading.

SECT. XXXII.

The Words, Land, Tenement or Hereditament.

Land is intended as well of pasture, meadow, woods, heath, &c. as of arable, and lands couered with water or surrounded is within the Statute: So is a Towne an Isle, &c. but vestura terræ, or an upper Chamber cannot make a Joynture as Land.

Tenements assured in Joynture, may bee Aduousans, Rectories, Windmils, an upper Chamber, a Seigniory in Chiualrie, and a reuersion sur estate pur vie, all comming within the meaning of the Statute.

As for a reuersion upon or after estate for yeares, it is rather in account of law, land, then a tenement: for the Franke Tenement, which is the principall, is as the present substance of the Land it selfe: And the reuersion of either of these particular estates, if rent be reserued, may well be assigned for a Joynture.

Yea and whether rent be reserued or no upon a Lease for yeares, it might be somewhat doubted whether the reuersion be assignable for a Joynture, &c. because the Franke Tenement passeth presently, and a woman may haue an assise thereof.

But

But cleere a nude reversion, sur estate pur vie sans rent, because it is no present commoditie, cannot make a Joynture, yet if such a reversion be assigned, and it turne to a possession in the Husbands life time, it may be a good Joynture by matter of subsequent Hereditament, within the Statute may be a rent charge granted to a woman for life, though it were never in esse before; or a rent reserved upon a Lease for life: But the Hereditament assigned must bee a profit and commodity, or else it is not assignable, &c, for homage or fealtie, shall not make any Joynture.

Rent payable every five yeare may be assigned for Joynture, for is a profit though it be not annuall. And an ancient keepership of a Parke with a fee belonging to it, may be appointed or assigned in Dower.

But so is not a keepership newly granted and sans fee, which is a charge, without gaine or utility.

SECT. XXXIII.

Estates Taile.

ALl estates tayle, are within the equitie or compasse of this branch of 27. and the formes or species within the letter are but as patternes or examples of Joyntures. And therefore where an estate is limited to Baron and feme, and to the Heyres Males of their bodies, or to them and the heyres Males or Females of the body of one of them, although this be an abridgement or amputation of one sexe, from the examples within the very Statute; yet it is a good Joynture.

There is a Case in proofe thereof, Dyer, 97. 1 Marie the Duchesse of Somerset was ioynt-purchaser with her husband of estate to them two, and to the heyres Males of her Husbands body, betweene them begotten, which is none of the

the fiue estates expressed in the Statute, but the Iustices held cleare vnlesse it were refused it excluded Dower.

So is it if estate be made to Baron and Feme, to them and the heyres Males which the Baron shall haue of the body of his wife, vel e conuerso. Or if the gift be to Baron and Feme, and three heyres of their two Bodies, which is an estate determinable vpon death of the third Issue, or if it be to them and to the heyres de corpore, the sonne of both of them or of one of them all these estates limited for Ioynture are good enough.

SECT. XXXV.

Estate for Life, &c.

THese words, Or for life of the Wife, are intendable as well for an estate made to the Wife onely during her life, as of an estate made ioyntly to Baron and Feme during the life of the Wife: Therefore an estate made onely to the Wife for her life, or to the Baron for his life, with a remainder to the Wife for her life, is a good Ioynture within meaning of the Statute; yet it seemeth not to agree with the nature of a Ioynture by the etimology of the word, and the Statute speaketh not of any remainder, Dyer 14. & 15. Eliz. fol. 387. agreeth and saith that Ioyntures may bee conditionall, which if the Wife accept after the husbands death, she shall be barred of Dower, as where the condition is, that shee shall keepe her selfe vnmarried, and, saith he, a Conueyance to a wife during her life in remainder, after the immediate death of her Husband, vpon condition reasonable may well bee intended pro iunctura, yet he himselfe afterwards, fo. 340. thinketh that such a remainder to the wife for her life, after the death of her Husband, cannot bee termed a Ioynture, because the Etimologie serueth not, and 11. H. 7. ca. 20. & 27. H. 8. demonstrateth

strateth no such Joynture for women in possession or in use of any estate in remainder after the Husbands death, &c. quære.

If an estate bee conveyed to a mans Wife, and to a stranger for their two lives for the Wives Joynture, it is good enough; yet the Statute mentioneth onely estates betwixt Baron and Feme: And although the estate be not conveyed to the Feme by precise termes for her life; yet words that amount to as much, shall be of as great effect: As if Lands be given to a wife, untill I. S. hath levied an hundred pound, or till he be promoted to a Benefice: This maketh an estate for life, within the branch of 27. &c.

SECT. XXXVI.

Estate to the use of Baron and Feme.

If estate be conveyed to Baron and Feme to the use of a Stranger, this is no Joynture; but if it be to Baron and Feme, or to one of them, or to a Stranger to the use of the Feme, it is a good Joynture, and in every limitation of use to the Baron and Feme it is requisite that he or they that shall take the possession may be seised to an use, for if Lands be given to the King, or a Corporation, or to an alien borne to the use of Baron and Feme, this is no good Joynture, for these persons cannot stand seised to another bodies use, no more can a Rector or Parson of a Church, or a Bishop, unlesse it be in respect of their naturall capacitie; but a man attainted may take for another bodies use, and therefore a Feoffement to him, to the use of Baron and Feme may be a Joynture.

SECT.

SECT. XXXVII.

How a Woman may haue a Ioynture and Dower, and how neither Ioynture nor Dower.

A Woman may haue Dower notwithstanding her Jointure, by the kind ouersight of her Husband, or of his heyre: As if a Joynture assigned, the Baron himselfe will endow his Wife, ad ostium Ecclesiæ, or ex assensu patris; Or if after the husbands death, his heyre or Feoffee will assigne other Lands in Dower to her which hath a Joynture already: Or if the heyre plead to her in a Writt of Dower, ne vnque seisi q; Dower, &c. or nient accouple in loyall matrimonie; or any other plea saue Joynture, &c. in barre of Dower, for in such Case if it be found against him, the woman shall recouer Dower, and retaine her Jointure neuerthelesse, quia volenti non fuit iniuria. On the other side a Woman shall haue neither Joynture nor Dower, if by her owne folly or wrong done, she haue forfeited her Joynture: As by breach of a condition annexed to her estate, or doing of wast, or making a Feoffement: And if her Joynture by lawfull title, and without any folly in her, be euicted from her yet where the heyre is remitted to another estate then that which her husband was seised of during Couerture, she getteth no Dower. So is it if the estate whereof Dower is demanded, were conueyed to the Baron and his heyres during the life of I. S. But if it were to the Baron and his heyres, for so long time as I. S. had heyres of his body lawfully begotten, this estate may yeeld Dower.

SECT. XXXVII.

The first Prouiso *for Dower vpon euiction of Ioynture.*

This Prouiso is to be construed fauorably for women, as the premises be in fauour of the Heire: And therefore as well tayled Lands as Fee-simple are bound to render value and recompence; if therefore the Ioynture euicted were to the value of twenty pound per annum, and the heyre haue twenty pound per annum of Land tayled to his Father, the woman shall recouer euery whit of it in recompence of her lost Ioynture, for this latter and new Statute controlleth the ancient Statute, de donis conditionalibus.

SECT. XXXVIII.

In what case a Woman may refuse her Ioynture to demand Dower.

The Statute is plaine, that a woman may refuse a Ioynture made during Couerture, and take her Dower, or waiue Dower, and rest on her Ioynture, vnlesse the Ioynture were by act of Parliament, &c. And M. Brograues opinion was, that if the Ioynture were made by other assurance, and afterward confirmed by Parliament, that such ratification tooke away a womans election as well as if the originall assurance had been by Parliament: But if the Ioynture were made before Marriage, the woman must needs hold her to her Ioynture, sans election. And this is by implication vpon the third prouiso, as appeareth by the report of Anderson, &c. See Commentaries Plowden, 390. The Case 6. Eliz. Dyer, 228. is, That Richard Ashton Esquire in accomplishment of certaine Indentures betwixt him and Sir William Barenport, concerning Marriage to be had betwixt Richard Ashton the sonne and Elizabeth the daughter of Sir William, which gaue seuen hundred Markes with her in marriage, infeoffed certaine persons before Marriage of Land to the annuall rent of twenty pound to the use of the said Elizabeth for terme of her life: The Marriage being consummate, first Richard the Father, and then Richard the Sonne died, then it was found by office that Richard the sonne died seised in Fee of these Lands, whereof the Feoffement was made, and of other Lands holden by Chiualry, as of the Dutchie of Lancaster his heyre being under age, the first question was whether shee might retaine the twenty pound Lands, and haue Dower of the rest, because she was not Richard Ashtons wife at the time of the Feoffement first made, neither was it made of the barons lands, or by the baron resolued by Councell of the Court, that shee was barred of Dower: And it was so likewise resolued in Vernons Case, Sir Ed. Cokes 4. Report, wherein is much learning touching Joynture.

The second question in Eliz. Astons ca. was whether she were Dowable from the Queene, because the feoffement was not found by the Office.

The third question, whether it might be auerred for the Queene in stay of petition of Dower, that the Feoffement was made pro iunctura, no such matter being expressed neither in the deed of Feoffement or Indenture of Couenants.

The fourth question, whether the Widdow Elizabeth might be receiued to auerre, and proue by Commission in the Court of Wards, that the Feoffement was not meant for a Joynture. Here is enough to make Women beware how they take Joyntures before Marriage: Take another to admonish you, beware of fines after Marriage, Joynture was made to a Feme Couert by her Baron, shee and her baron aliened the land by fine sur connusance de droit,

droit, by the opinion of Justices, Wray, Bell, Manhood, and Dyer, she shall not demand Dower of the residue of her husbands Land after his death; for she aliened her Joynture before time of election was given her, by the Statute, quære. But if the fine had bene sur connusance de droit, come ceo que le connusee ad de done le Baron tantum, this had béene a better forme for the wife and lesse dangerous, 19. Eliz. Dyer, 358.

SECT. XXXIX.

What is a sufficient refusall or agreement of or to a Iointure made after Couerture.

See Sir *Edw. Cokes* 3. *Rep.* in *Butlers* and *Bakers* Case.

THe refusing or agreement, &c. because they are peremptory, must not bee clouded, darke, doubtfull or implicatiue, but plaine and expresse, a bare word or saying, by a woman, that she will refuse her Joynture or accept it, is not materiall, as diuers Justices doe hold it: But if shee come vpon the Land whereof she is Dowable, and there refusing her Joynture pray the heyre to assigne her Dower; this is such a refusall that the heyre by this shall be charged in damages from this time forth in a writt of Dower, and this refusall must be to the heyre himselfe, and not to a Stranger. If a Widow waiue the possession of a house or tenement assigned in Joynture by her husband, and get her to another place, this is no refusall: But if she haue any medling with the land assigned in Joynture, or doe any other act amounting to assent or dissenting, as for example, If she bring a writt of Dower and declare vpon it, this is peremptory although she bee vnder age, Couert or not Couert of a second Husband; for the Law saith, that they which haue discretion to acquire and get things, haue sufficient discretion to giue and preserue those things gotten. Therefore if an Infant come to any thing by purchase, hee shall not in that haue any aduantage, or bee in better plight then a parson of full age.

As where estate is made to an Infant of two acres, to haue and hold the one for life, the other in fee, &c. a Feoffement made of one whilest he is yet vnder age is a sufficient election. And if a rent charge bee granted to an Infant, whereupon he bringeth a Writt of annuity, he shall neuer auow for it, as a rent, when he commeth to full age: So if an Infant recouer debt, and sue execution by elegit, &c. he shall neuer haue a scire facias: And an Infant is subiect to an action of waste or entry for condition broken as well as any other person, These collections gathered, as I thinke, by some well learned and industrious Student out of M. Brograues reading, though they want of the fulnesse and perfection which the owne pen of so great a Lawyer might haue giuen them; yet are they pertinent and important. And I not a little beholding to him, from whose hands I obtaine them.

SECT. XL.

Of Actions brought by Baron and Feme, or by one of them.

NOw because the common sayings are found by common experience true, Qui capit vxorem, capit lites, and qui habet terras habet guerras, A Wife brings iarres, and wealth brings warres, quarrels, suits and controuersies at Law, sans ceo, that it hath any other intendment, it will not be amisse a little to declare how and in what manner actions at law must be commenced and pursued by baron and Feme, or against them, or by or against one of them.

them according to prescription of Law, and their severall and ioynt Interests, &c.

SECT. XLI.

Where the Baron shall sue onely in his owne name.

A Man shall sue for his Wives Marriage money onely in his owne name, but how or where, that is a matter of some obscurity: by Bracton, lib. 5. ca. 10. 407. money that is promised causa Matrimonij, is as a sequell of Marriage, and so being annexed to a thing spirituall, requires a spirituall suite; yet he confesseth that it is otherwise for Land promised or covenanted, &c. Fitzherbert in his Writ of Debt citeth 31. Ed. 3. that if a man promise one twenty pound to marry his Daughter, which marrieth her accordingly, he may have a Writ of debt upon his promise, but he forgets not the neere difference in the Booke of assizes; for in the Writt of prohibition, he tels us, if a man promise one twenty pounds if he marry his Daughter, after marriage if the promiser will not pay the money, the husband may not sue in Court Christian, if hee doe a prohibition lyeth; marry if I promise one twenty pounds with my Daughter in Marriage, &c. now upon nonpayment, he may sue in Court Christian, for this concerneth Matrimony. The same learning he insisteth upon his Writt of Consultation, adding that if he die which made the promise, the other may sue in Court Christian against the Executor, or Executors of Executors, 22. ass. pla. 70. is thus, upon Contract had betwixt two men, that if one of them will marry the others Daughter, hee shall have ten pound, &c. the ten pound after Marriage must be demanded in the Kings Court, because the promise was not with his Daughter in Marriage, but by Covenant,

 that

that he should, &c. But if he had promised the money with his Daughter in Marriage, it must haue béene demanded in Court Christian: And if a man promise vpon his faith to pay ten pound, the Ordinarie cannot compell him to pay it, but he may enioyne corporall penance, vnlesse the promiser will voluntarily redéeme it: Thus teacheth Iustice Thorpe in declaration of the Statute of circumspecte agatis 45. Ed. 3. fo. 24. The Demandant declares vpon a couenant betwixt him and the Defendant, that if he married the Daughter of the defendant, hee should haue an hundred pound, &c. It was moued that this demand of debt vpon a Couenant concerning Matrimony was not good, but the matter concerned the Court Christian per articulos cleri, Notwithstanding because the demand was vpon a déed, and a written déed maketh a lay couenant, the defendant was compelled to answer: But 14. of Ed. 4. fo. 6. in an action of debt the Plaintiffe declares that he had married the Defendants daughter, vpon agréement of twenty pound to be paid, &c. and all the Iudges of the common pleas (without tarrying the Defendants answer) awarded que le plaint prist rieu person brief, for the demand is, say they, of the same nature with the espousals, viz. ius spirituale, and determinable no where but in Court Christian, and yet the Booke of assises was there remembred 15. Ed. 4. fo. 32. the plaintiffe in a Writ of debt demanding fiue markes declares vpon a couenant quod nota, for fiue pound where he had marryed, &c. and 33. pound fiue shillings foure pence was paid, but the residue being 5. Marks, the defendant denyed to pay, yet I care not saith Catesby though he be discharged: for I know well enough that vpon such a matter, the action lieth not at common Law, quod fuit concessum per curiam: And the cause alledged was that there was not quid for quo 17. Ed. 4. fo. 5. The master of the Rowles asketh the Iustices of the Common pleas, if a man promise money to another to marry his daughter or seruant, which marrieth her accordingly, whether an acti-

on

on of debt will lye at the common Law or no: No saith Townsend, for it is but a nude promise of no more effect then if I promise you 20. pound to build you a new Chamber, and ex nudo pacto non oritur actio. But if I promise you sixe shillings every weeke for the bording of I.S. here is quid for quo, for law intendeth here, that I haue aduantage and profit by the seruice of I. S. But further in your case, the thing that is to bee done is spirituall which cannot bee sold, neither can the party be compelled to doe it: Rogers and Siliard were contrary to him in opinion, That a promise vpon Marriage is no nudum pactum, because the daughter cousin or friend is by intendment aduanced. And if I promise a Schoole-master money to teach my childe, he shall haue action of Debt. Likewise if I promise a Surgeon money to heale a poore mans wound, or a Labourer money to mend a high-way. But in the end Choke & Littleton agreed with the Master of the Rowles, that in the case by him propounded none action lyeth at common Law, because Matrimony whereupon the promise is founded is a thing spirituall, and by no manner of meanes vendable. 19. Ed.4.fo.10. in an action of debt, brought vpon such a bargaine: Collow saith, it is true, a man must demand a woman contracted to him in the spirituall Court, but money is a temporall thing: And when a Parson of a Church is to recouer tythes, he must sue in Court Christian; but if he sell his tythes, when they be seuered, hee shall sue for the money in the Kings Court, but then and afterward in the same or like case 20. of Ed. 4.fo.3. Bryan asketh him then, to what end serueth the Statute, that things touching Matrimony and Testaments must be tryed in Courts Christian, cui des vous quam vous purres achate les Sacraments, Sir, saith Neale, dismes are a thing spirituall, but if a Parson of a Church lease his Tythes, hee must sue for the rent in a temporall Court, and Collow stands to it, that per emptionem & venditionem res spirituales efficiuntur temporales, he neuer spake a truer word in his life.

Out of these opinions consorting together like harpe and harrow, may be gathered this sure learning. That hee which will wed shall doe well, (and according to the Statute of circumspecte agatis) to take as much as he can of his wiues marriage money before hand, with faire Indentures or good obligation for the residue. And by the aboue-said Bookes, as also by M. Plowden in that case he may haue action of debt, for euery deed sealed and deliuered carrieth sufficient consideration, to wit, the will of him that made it.

Concerning the old scruple, though money be a visible signe of inuisible grace Sacramentall and Spirituall, specially if it be in Angels; yet I trust it is not more spirituall then the woman her selfe with whom it is promised. And as there is no question made but a man may sue in Court Christian for his lawfull wife vnlawfully taken and witholden, vpon which suite if a prohibition be granted, a consultation may be had for proceedings, quatenus pro restitutione vxoris duntaxat prosequitur, &c. So by Fitzherbert in his Writt of Consultation an Action may be brought at Common Law, de vxore abducta cum bonis viri, or an action of trespasse for taking onely of the Wife. But for a cleare proofe that in these promissions of money vpon Marriage, neither the money is any Ghost, nor the promise any nudum pactum. See the case 10. Eliz. Dyer, 272.

An Action of the Case was brought vpon promise of twenty pound made to the Plaintiffe in consideration, that at speciall Instance and request of the Defendant he had married his Cousin: this was a good cause of action in the Queenes Court, although the Marriage were celebrated and perfected before the assumption, because the Nuptialls did ensue the Defendants request.

And as Lands may bee giuen in Franke marriage after the Espousals, and yet the Espousals be cause and consideration

sideration of the gift: so may money be promised after Espousals, and yet the Espousals be cause of the promise.

But Reader be not confident of the Law in that Case of Dyer, for I haue seene a report of a Case betweene Sandill Plaintiffe, and Ienny Defendant, entred in Banco Regis. Hillar. 2. Iacobi Rot. 571. where the Plaintiffe declared that the Defendant in consideration that the Plaintiffe had formerly married his Daughter at his speciall request, the Defendant promised the Plaintiffe to pay him euery yeere during the life of the Defendant ten pound, &c. and as my report saith, the Plaintiffe vpon non assumpsit pleaded, had verdict and iudgement in the Kings Bench, but vpon a writ of error in Exchequer Chamber, the Iudgement was reuersed, for that the Marriage was executed before the promise made, and yet the declaration supposed that the Defendant requested the Plaintiffe to Marriage, &c.

But let me not run so farre from my Text as neuer to finde the way backe againe: A man may sue for Marriage money in his owne name onely, and so is it generally where that which is in demand, or to be recouered, commeth meerely and onely to the Baron. Example, 43. Ed. 3. fo. 8. The Earle of Arundell brought a Writt of Trespasse against one, for chasing in a free Chace that he held in right of his Wife, and the Writt awarded good, though the Wife were not named in it, because nothing was to be recouered by damages.

Likewise is it if the Baron bring a Writt of Trespasse for strayes taken in Lands holden in right of his Wife. And eod. anno fo. 26. for breaking of a house and carrying away of timber, the Husband alone shall haue the action because hee may when hee list pull downe a house or fell timber standing vpon his Wiues Inheritance, or make a release to any body vpon such manner of trespasse, and the Wiues action is gone for euer.

There is also the same yeare fo. 16. another Case, wherein because a decies tantum was brought by Baron

and

and Feme, the Writt abated; for though the first action concerned the Wiues Interest, yet nothing is to be recouered in a decies tantum but damages, &c. See the Booke of 20. H. 6. fo. 1. a Writt of maintenance wherein nothing is recouerable, but damages, was brought by Baron and Feme vpon maintenance in a bill of fresh force against them, by the better opinion they might ioyne, &c. And the Defendant passeth Ouster, but not by award, 41. Ed. 3. f. 9. a Writ of Champertie brought by the Baron onely vpon an assise which had passed against him and his wife, was allowed good notwithstanding exceptions taken of the wiues Interest, &c. vpon the reasons before expressed. And by Finch, if a man haue a Ward in right of his Wife, Dower shall be demanded against him onely, because the gard is a Chattell vested: But if a Writt of Wardship be to be brought, it shall be against the Baron and feme, &c. because of voucher.

And in trespasse, if the Plaintiffe recouer against Baron and Feme by false verdict, they both must ioyne in the attaint; for that must be according to the record 46. Ed. 3. fo. 20. a man brought a Writt of rauishment de gard, declaring vpon a possession, iure vxoris, and the Writ held good: yet in this case there is more then damages to be recouered, for the Plaintiffe shall haue the Infant restored by the very words of his Writt. But there againe it was agreed, that an action to recouer a Ward must be against them both, because of voucher, though in a writt of Dower it be vt supra, because therein there is no voucher, &c. If Baron and Feme sell the Wiues Inheritance by fine for twenty pound, an action of debt for the money shall bee brought by the Baron onely, for the grant was onely the Barons grant, and if he die, the Executors shall haue the action and not the Feme. 48. Ed. 3. fo. 18.

And a replevin must bee brought by the Baron onely, because a Feme Couert cannot haue a propertie in any goods or Chattels: But for such goods as the Wife hath

as

as Executrix, it seemeth the Baron and Feme may ioyne in a r plenen: so shall they for goods of the Wife taken dum sola fuit, Fitz. in the title recaption. In trespasse at Common Law, or vpon the Statute, Anno 5. Rich. 2. the Baron alone shall haue action of trespasse, and so likewise for taking away Charters, concerning the Wiues inheritance. So is it if he alone deliuer such Charters, he alone may haue action against the Bayliffe, &c.

But a Writt of Detinue of Charters of the Wiues inheritance must be sued by both, &c. because the Charters themselues are to be recouered. And therefore vpon recouery of them the Baron and Feme must ioyne for recouery. A quare impedit was brought 50. of Ed. 3. fo. 13. and the Baron declared of an agreement betwixt thrée Sisters to present by turne to a Church, whereof they had the Aduousan, and this was the turne of his Wife, &c. The Defendant demands Judgement of the Writt, because the Wife being still aliue was not named, but this Writt also was awarded good, because nothing was to be recouered here but onely the Presentment and not the Aduousan. And if a Writt should be awarded to the Bishop against the Baron, the Wife thereby should not be out of possession, because she is not partie to the Judgement, besides that, she is ayded by West. 2. cap. 3. And for a generall rule where the Husbands release is good, the action may be brought in his name onely, as vpon cutting of trées, grasse, Corne, &c. And such actions may be brought in the name both of the Husband and the Wife. An assise of darraigne presentment is a mixt action, and the Aduousan it selfe, shall be recouered in it, therefore of necessity it must be brought both by Baron and Feme 15. Ed. 4. fo. 9. The Baron Seignior in right of his wife, ioyned in a writt of rescous, and it was argued that he alone ought to haue brought the writt: But it was awarded well brought by them both. Though per Littleton it were good enough in nosme le Baron tantum. And per Pigot, when an obligation is made to Baron and

Feme,

Feme, the Baron alone may haue the action, or they may ioyne eadem lex in trespasse, &c. maintenance, &c. for alwayes, where the action may suruiue to the wife, the wife may ioyne in the writt: They which shall read these two last Cases argued 50. Ed. 3. and 15. Ed. 4. in the yeares at large, shall not neede to repent it.

SECT. XLII.

When a Wife may sue or be sued alone.

IT is seldome, almost neuer that a marryed woman can haue any action to vse her writt onely in her owne name: her husband is her sterne, her primus motor, without whom she cannot doe much at home, and lesse abroad: But if her Husband commit felonie, take the Church and abiure the Realme, she is now in case as a Widdow inabled to make alienation of her owne land as a Feme sole, or to bring a cui in vita for her Lands aliened by her husband, quod vide cui in vita, Fitz. 3. Likewise 1. H. 4. fo. 1. The Kings writt of Ward against Sybill Belknap, is awarded good, though it were brought by the King; but iudgement was asked of it, because Sybill was a Feme Couert, iour del briefe purchase, and the husband not nemed; whereunto was answered, that for offence against the King and his Peeres, Belknap was banished to Gascoigne, there to remaine till he obtained the Kings Grace, &c. Iustice Gascoigne by the assent of his fellowes, commands the Defendants to answer, and she pleads in barre. Againe 2. H. 4. fo. 7. all the Iustices testifie, that the wife of Sir Robert Belknap who was banished, sued a writt alone without naming her husband, and by their common award it was holden good, for that as some said, the said Sibyl was the Kings Fermer.

But

But howsoeuer it were, Markham exclaimes Ecce modo mirum quod fœmina fert breue regis, Non nominando virum coniunctum robore legis. Some say it should be conuictum, &c. It is like a miracle that a wife should commence any suit without her husband, 18. Ed. 4. fo.4. If a feme Couert be impleaded without her husband and outlawed, the baron and feme may ioyne in a writt of error to reuerse the outlary, for the wife cannot sue without the Husband. If a fine be leuied to a feme Couert, yet she and her husband must ioyne in the quid juris clamat, as the book of 11. H. 4.7. telleth. If Baron and Feme be beaten, &c. they must Ioyne in action for battery of the Feme, but for his owne stripes the Baron shall bring his owne action by himselfe, or else his writt abates for that part, 9. Ed. 4 fo. 52. Because a feme Couert hath nothing to doe to participate in the suites of her husband, nor in the priuileges of her husband: Therefore a suite against the Wife of an atturney shall not be in the Court where hee serueth by bill, but by originall writt, and none essoine de seruitio Regis, or other essoine cast for the Husband, shall serue for the wife, for if in a præcipe quod reddat against baron & feme at the grand Cape the Baron be essoyned de seruitio regis, and the wife make default, shee shall lose her Land. So likewise if the Baron be a seruant of the Chancellor, &c. no writt of priuiledge shall serue for him and his wife, but actions against them both must be sued at the Common Law; But a protection cast by the Baron, dismisseth the plea sans iour for both, because the Feme cannot answer without her husband, 35. H.6.f.3 & 4. a feme couert shal not be receiued to disauow the atturney of her husband, but he shal make an atturney for them both 33. H.6.f.31. And eod. an. fo.43. If the wife will come into the Court & offer to plead any other plea then that which her husband hath pleaded, or to confesse the action, she shal not be receiued to it, but the husband may not forcher per essoin. And if baron & feme wage the law, &c. if the wife appeare not at the day giuen, the baron shall be condemned: But a wife shal neuer be receiued to disauow the

suit:

suite of her husband and her selfe, quod vide 39. Assisarum pla. 1. a good Case.

SECT. XLIII.

Of Felonies.

IN matters criminall and capitall causes, a Feme couert shall answere without her husband, 15. Ed.4. fo.1. And note, if a Feme Couert steale any thing by cohersion of her Husband, this is not felonie in her 27. lib. Assisarum 40. It was found that a woman had stollen bread to the worth of two shillings by compulsion of her husband, and awarded that she should goe quite. It seemeth to be all one if a woman steale by commandement of her husband, quære.

If a man and his wife commit felonie ioyntly, it séemeth the wife is no felon, but it shall be wholly iudged the Husbands fact, saith Stamford: Seuen men and a woman were arraigned of felonie, found guilty, and because the woman cryed out she was wife to one of the seuen, the Iudges sent to the Bishop to be certified of the Marriage. But a woman by her selfe without the priuitie of her husband may commit felonie to become either principall or accessary: As if shee steale goods, or receiue théeues to her house, &c. and if the husband so soone as hee perceiue it waiue and forsake their company, and his owne house, in this case the Womans offence makes not felonie in the baron. But if the baron commit felonie, his wife not ignorant of it may kéepe his company still notwithstanding, and not be deemed accessary; for a woman cannot bee accessary to her husband, insomuch as shee is forbidden by the Law of God to bewray him: note also that a woman cannot be thiefe of her husbands goods, if shee take and giue them away, the receiuer is no felon, Stanford. lib. 1. cap. 19. Briton allowes that the wife shall keep her husbands counsell,

sell, but yet so that if she acquit her selfe per pais del fait & consent, for felons wiues hee saith haue often held men whiles the husband killed them, and in that case it is reason and Law that they hang together, fo. 47. By Bracton, non debet virum accusare vxor, nec detegere furtum suum neque feloniam, consentire tamen non debet, nec coadiutrix esse, sed feloniam & nequitiam viri quantum potest impedire. And by him if goods stollen be found sub clauibus vxoris, she shal be culpable with her husband of his felonie. Item, si vxor cum viro coniuncta fuerit, vel confessa fuerit quod viro consilium vel auxilium præstiterit, tenebuntur ambo, nam licet obedire debeat vxor viro in atrocioribus tamen, & latrocinijs, nec est ei obediendum. Poterit vir ligare & tenere, atque vxor sponte & non coacta occidere, & ita tenetur de maleficio vterque: libro 3. ca. 32. In the end he sheweth how execution of iudgement shall bee deferred when the woman condemned is with child, siue ante delictum conceperit, siue post. Hee coteth ciuill Law for it. But Scanford hath it perfecter.

If a woman bee arraigned of felonie, it is no plea to say she is with child, but she must plead to the felonie, and if she bee found guilty, shee may then claime the benefit of her wombe, whereupon the Marshall or Vicount shall bee commanded to put her in a chamber, and cause some women to examine and try her, whether she be ensoint de vn infant, which if she be not, she shall be hanged maintenant: And though she be quicke with child, yet Iudgement shall not be delayed, but onely execution deferred. If after such respite when she is once deliuered, she become great againe, and obiect to prolong her life, the Iudge ought to command execution presently, for this benefit shall bee claimed but once. If the Iudge inquire further of it, it must be but to set a fine on the Marshall or Sheriffe for looking no better to her. Stanford, lib. 3. ca. vltimo. And by the bookes which he citeth the obiection must be not priuiment ensoint, but enseint de viue enfant.

SECT.

SECT. XLIV.

Of Treasons.

AND this obiection of enseintment is aswell to delay execution for treason as for felony. A woman for committing either grand or petty treason shall be burned. The latter part of the Statute 25. of Ed. 3. ca. 2. is, That if any seruant kill his Master, any woman kill her husband, or any man secular or religious person kill his Prelate to whom he owes obedience, this is treason, and every Lord shall haue the Escheates for such treasons of his owne proper fee, the Statute is but declaration of the common law titulo Coronæ, in Fitzh. A woman compasseth with her Adulterer the death of her husband, they assailed him riding on the high way, beating, wounding, leauing him for dead, and then they fled: The husband got vp, leuied hue and cry, came before the Iustices, they sent after the offendors, which were gotten, arraigned, and the matter found by verdict, the adulterer was hanged, the woman burned to death, the husband liuing, voluntas reputabitur pro facto, 15. E. 2. A woman seruant conspired to rob her Mistris, and brought a stranger to the bed-side where the Mistris lay asleepe, the stranger killed her, the seruant silent nothing doing but holding the Candle, the two chiefe Iustices and Hare thought the seruant a Traytresse, and a principall, 2. & 3. Eliz. Dyer, 128. yet Mistris is not verbatim in the Statute, Stanford was one of them against the chiefe Iustices opinion in this case; yet in his owne booke he teacheth that abettors & procurers, are within the meaning and intent of the Law: The seruant and the wife conspire the husbands death, he is killed by the seruant, in absence of the wife, this is petty treason in them both, by opinion of diuers Iustices, otherwise it is if the murtherer be no seruant, Dyer 16. Eliz 332. for Saunders wife which

pro-

procured Browne to kill her husband, but barely hanged as accessarie, because the principall was but a murtherer. 8. Eliz. Dyer 254.

SECT. XLV.

Actions by Baron and Feme together.

The baron and feme may ioyne in a writ of trespasse, quare vi & armis clausū fregit, &c. for trespasse done in the wiues land, either before couerture, or during couerture. Sée 21. H. 6. fol. 30. such a Writ brought of trespasse in the Close of Baron and Feme, and féeding vp blada sua. Iudgement is asked of the Writ, because a Feme couert hath no propertie in goods and chattels during the couerture. The Declaration, saith Markham, is blada sua dum sola fuit depastus fuit. That, saith Newton, is not possible, but it ought to be blada ipsius Katherinæ, &c. Yeluerton saith, that both the Writ and Declaration ought to haue béene Dum sola fuit, which Newton denies, and saith, that the Count ought only to be so, and affirmeth, that as the matter is brought forth, there is an intendment of depasturing before couerture, and of breaking the Close after couerture, of which the Baron and Feme may haue a Writ Clausum suum fregit, &c. So the Action séemeth to be by two seuerall titles: But in the end the record was viewed, which was Quod clausum ipsius Katherinæ fregit & blada eiusdem Katherinæ depastus fuit; and the Declaration Dum sola fuit, which made the Writ to be awarded good. And there it is said, that by the Register the Writ is not Dum sola fuit but generall, and the Declaration speciall. Yet 7. H. 7. fol. 2. vpon the like Writ of Quare clausum fregit & bona & catella sua cepit, which Declaration of trespasse to the Feme Dum sola fuit, iudgement being giuen, was afterwards found erroneous, for fault in the Writ which should haue

P béene,

beene not bona sua, but bona ipsius le Feme, and therefore a Repleader awarded. The baron & feme may haue a Writ of trespasse of assault made to the Feme, and imprisonment of her, untill the Baron compounded and paid a fine, and the briefe and count shall be ad damna ipsorum quod nota. 46. Ed. 3. 3. Nota per Curiam, saith Brooke, Baron and Feme may ioyne in appeale De rape le feme, for the husband alone cannot haue it without his wife, 8. H. 4. fol. 21. The case there is, A woman prisoner in the Marshalsey, makes a suggestion to the Court, that the Marshals man had ravished her in prison: Gascoigne commanded the Marshall to take his man to his custody, and his staffe from him, and the Court told the woman, that she alone could not bring appeale, sans son Baron, but if her husband would come, and they two together would proue the rape, the ravisher should be hanged. By this case it is plaine, that the wife alone cannot haue the appeale, but the Baron and Feme may haue it. But neither by this case, or any other statute, can I finde that the baron may not haue it alone, Whether ne vnque a couple in loyall matrimony be a sufficient plea in this appeale, and whether he which is but Baron in possession only, that is, that husband which is at the time of the rape may haue it, quære, and see 11. H. 4. 13. Baron and Feme may ioyne in a Writ of Debt, and 16. Edw 4. fol. 8. such a Writ brought for arrerages of account, with Declaration that the defendant was the wiues receiuer, Dum sola fuit pur account render, and that the Baron and Feme after espousals, assigned Auditors, which found the defendant in arrerages, &c. Insomuch as the ground of the Action begun by the wife, and the assignment of the Auditors was pursuing. And likewise by the wife they might ioyne. So if an Obligation be made to Baron & Feme, they may ioyne in a Writ of Debt, and if the Baron die, his wife and not the Executors shall haue the Action, 3. H. 6. fol. 37. Per curiam Baron and Feme may ioyne in a Writ of Debt vpon an Obligation made to them during couerture,

couerture. And Babington affirmes that the Baron may haue the Action alone if he will, 43. Ed. 3. fol. 10. such a Writ was brought, and exception taken that it ought to haue been by the husband alone, sed non allocatur, Though for chattels vested, as goods that are giuen to a man and his wife, the Baron alone must pursue his Action for taking them out of his possession: Otherwise it is of matters consisting onely in Action, &c. for they suruiue to the Feme, like to a Lease granted to Baron and Feme for yeares. So is it of rauishment, or eiectment of Guard, for these are Chattles reall: But if a man and his wife be bound by Obligation, a Writ against them both vpon that Obligation shall abate car fait del Feme couert est void. See 15 Ed. 4 fol. 10. that if an Obligation bee made to Baron and Feme, and the husband dieth, the wife or husbands Executor, which of them shall hap to haue the Obligation shall sue, &c. as it is said by Bryan. And Detinue of Charters shall bee brought by Baron and Feme for Charters concerning her ioynt possession, 38. H. 6. fol. 25.

If Baron and Feme make a Lease for yeares of the wiues lands, they must ioyne in an action of waste, or else the Writ shall abate, 7. H. 4. 15. yet 3. H. 6. fol. 53. a Writ of waste so brought was doubted of, because forsooth a Feme couert cannot make any Lease: But at the last the Writ was holden good, for the wife might accept the rent, or distraine for it, and make auowrie after the husbands death, at what time, and not before, shee hath power to agree, or disagree; but during the Couerture, the lease was the Act of them both, baron & feme tenants for yeares, may ioyne in an Action of couenant, against the Lessor that outeth them, for the wife suruiuing shall haue the terme, if the husband doe not aliene, 47. of Ed. 3. fol. 12. And where a remainder is to bee executed to a Feme couert by force and conueyance of a fine, &c. the Baron and Feme may haue a Scire facias, to shew why the land should not remaine to I. S. and to N. his wife, for the land cannot remaine to one of them, but it must remaine to them both: But a Formidon in Discender, or Reverter, or a Writ of Escheat differeth, 11. H. 4. fol. 15. 44. Ed. 3. fol. 10. a Writ of Dower was brought by Baron and feme, and the tenant pleaded, that the former baron had never any thing in the land during the espousals, which the Demandants did not deny, therefore the Tenant prayed they might be barred, and their confession recorded, but it would not be granted, because it should bee prejudiciall to the wife, yet at the request of the Tenant they were received to acknowledge their right by fine, and the woman was examined. Quod nota, for shee shall not be examined upon confession of an Action.

SECT. XLVI.

Actions against Baron and Feme.

As Actions are rightly pursued by Baron and Feme when right is withholden from her, or wrong done to her selfe, her interest or possession, so when the wife is, or is supposed a wrong doer, or her husband doth wrong under pretext of her interest, writs must be sued against them both; for as it hath béene shewed already, if a Feme covert bee condemned in any civill Action without her husband, shee and her husband may have a Writ of error. Therefore if a woman which is indebted take a husband, an Action of Debt shall be against her and her husband in the Debet, 9. E. 4. fol. 24. 7. H. 7. fol. 2. agréeth, and if any thing were owing to the Feme before marriage, the Writ of such a debt shall bee Quas eis debet. If a man baile goods to a Feme sole which marrieth afterward, an Action of Detinue shall be against her and her husband for these goods per curiam, 39. Ed. 3. 17. And 1. H. 4. fol. 31. a Writ of trespasse sur le case, was brought for not repairing certaine bankes, upon lands which the defendant

had

had in Dale, by reason whereof the plaintiffes ground was surrounded, and because the Defendants whole interest in Dale was only jure vxoris, which wife was not named in the Writ, it abated, for they ought to haue béen ioyned. 3. H. 4. fol. 1. Upon a Lease made to Baron and Feme for yeares, rendring rent, the Lessor brings a Writ of Debt, &c. against Baron and Feme, and Judgement was asked of the Writ, because it was not brought against the Baron onely: Thirning holdeth the Writ good, aswell as an Action of waste shall bee against both Baron & Feme upon such a Lease, and so doth one other Justice, but some pleaders argued contra. And in Actions against Baron and Feme, the woman must be named wife, 42. Edw. 3. fol. 23. A writ of trespasse is brought against Iohn and Alice with others, Alice saith shee was and is the wife of Iohn, iour del briefe purchase iudgement del briefe, and this is a good plea in abatement of the writ. So if a writ be against Iohn and Alice his wife, Alice if shée be single may plead, not the wife, Iudgement del briefe. But Iohn shall not haue that plea per totam curiam, for none as Brooke maketh the reason, shall plead Misnosmer, but the partie, 7. H. 6. fol. 9. In Assise against Baron and Feme the Vicount returned, that hee had attached the Baron per centum oues matrices, but the wife had nothing to be attached of, within his Balliwicke, nec est in eadem inuenta, the best opinion is, that the returne is not good, for he was commanded to attach the wife, which the Law would neuer command if the thing were impossible, but it is possible enough for the wife to be attached, by her husbands goods, and by him shee must bee brought into the Court. Babington saith, an Attachment must bee by a meere chattle, which shall be forfeited by Default, but not by any Chattell reall, as a Lease for yeares, or a ward, or by apparrell, &c.

Now note, it hath béene said, that in an Action of debt or trespasse, or other personall Actions, if the Baron appeare, and the wife make default, or if the wife appeare, and the baron make default, they shall not answer the one without the other, 44. Ed. 3. fol. 1. A Writ of debt was brought against Baron and Feme, the wife outlawed, the Baron rendred himselfe at the Exigent, at returne whereof hee appeared in ward, and the Plaintiffe prayed because the Processe was determined against the wife, that the husband might answer sed non alocatur. But see in the next leafe a writ of trespasse pursued against Baron and Feme to the Exigent, the Vicount returned that hee had taken them at the day, the Baron came in ward without the wife, &c. The Plaintiffe declared against him, he was compelled to answer, and pleaded not culpable le Vicont fuit charge de le corps le Feme. & amercie, and a writ went out to haue the wife at Westminster at a certaine day, with a Venire facias betwixt the Plaintiffe and the husband, returnable the same day, see 34 H. 6. fol. 29. A writ of trespasse against Baron and Feme, and the Baron as seruant to the Chancellor brought a Supersedeas for himselfe and his wife. Littleton said it was to be allowed for neither of them, no more than where trespasse is brought against one of the Chancery, and another man, &c. Nay not so much, saith Prisot, for in that case the Plaintiffe may take his bill in Chancery against him which is of the Chancery, and leaue out the other, but hee cannot doe so here, specially the trespasse being supposed to be done by the wife. The priuilege being dissolued, Littleton praieth that the Defendant may answer: Nay, saith Billing, the wife neuer yet appeared, therefore take your Processe against her, and we wil pray an Idem dies for the husband. In an Action of Debt, saith Littleton, against Baron and Feme, it is true that one shall not answer without the other, and in trespasse also the wife shall not answer without her husband, but the husband may answer without the wife, if she make Default. Truth, saith Prisot, all is one, in euerie writ of trespasse, whether it be of Battery, or otherwise, and in euerie other personall Action one of them shall not plead without the other. But in a

Præcipe

Præcipe quod reddat the default of a wife is the default of the husband and wife, aliter in trespasse or debt against baron and feme, for there if the baron appeare by cepi corpus or exigent, and the wife makes default, the baron shall haue an idem dies p mainprise, and if the wife waiue be, the husband shall goe sine die, for in euery case where the wife is party to the writ it must be intended prima facie, that the cause of action beginneth from the wife. Bryan a Protonotaries Clarke said it had béene holden by the Court before this time, that if the baron came in gratis, he should answer sans sa feme, but if he come by cohersion, &c. then vt supra. But saith Prisot all is one, and there is no diuersity, to whom all the Iustices, and many Serieants agréed, q̃ il ne respondra vnques sans sa feme en nul case: yet afterward 36. H. 6. fo. 1. in an action against baron and feme vpon the Statute 8. Hen. 6. of forcible entries, the Sheriffe returned the plur' capias mandaui balliuis, &c. which answered they had taken their bodies, etc the Bailiffes were demanded to bring in their prisoners, the Baron appeared, and the wife made default. It is a doubt whether the husband should answer maintenant, and a writ goe out to the Sheriffe ad habendum corpus vxoris, or whether the baron should haue an idem dies with the wife, and goe in the meane season sans mainprise, for by Wangford he might not answer without his wife, because of the imprisonment, etc. Prisot here asked, what was the supposall of the writ? and when he vnderstood it was of an entry by baron and feme ioyntly, hee affirmed the baron should answer presently without the wife. And so said he in trespasse & battery, when it is supposed by the writ that baron and feme together did beat the Plaintiffe, the baron appearing, sans le feme, shall answer, otherwise should it be here if the writ had supposed the forcible entry dum sola fuit, for it were vnreasonable when the action riseth and is caused from the wife, that then her default should bee her husbands default. And likewise is it in action of debt if the wife bee waiue, the baron appearing

P 4

ring at the exigent, shall goe sans maineprise, for it cannot be intended, but that the action riseth onely from the wife. But if an action of trespasse done by baron and feme joyntly, the baron appeare at the exigent, and the wife be waive, the husband shall answer, and if the issue bee found against him, and afterward the wife sue her Charter of pardon, it shall not bée allowed, unlesse shée bring her husband with her. By Prisot also in this case, a man cannot have a writ in the Chancery against baron and feme, supposing a forcible entry dum sola fuit, but the entry must bée supposed joyntly as in an action of trespasse. And Laycon declares against the baron in the end of the case. And note 40. E. 3. that in trespasse if the baron be outlawed, and the wife appeare at the exigent el alera sans iour, if the baron purchase a pardon, and sue scire facias against the party, he must bring his wife with him, or his pardon shall not bée allowed: But it is otherwise if the baron appeare, and the wife be waive, &c. for the baron alone may answer. There is much of this matter in the yéere bookes, 43. Ed. 3. fo. 18. in action of detinue against baron and feme, the wife was waive, the husband appeared at exegent, praying that the Plaintiffe might declare against him, which hee did upon a delivery to the feme dum sola fuit: Because the processe was determined against the wife, whose acts the baron alone could not answer unto. It was awarded que il alast quit, for though to losse of issues returned to baron and feme, the wives default is the barons default, yet it is otherwise upon a capias or exigent for the corporall punishment. But in a præcipe quod reddat a grand Cape shall goe out upon the wifes default, And sée 41. Ed. 3. fo. 24. in a writ of dower against baron and feme upon the default a grand Cape went out, and at the day the baron only appeared, and pleaded that he alone was tenant, &c. sans ceo, that his wife had any thing in the land, here the wives default was so far, a default of baron and feme both, that the demandant recovered seasin, 41. Ed. 3. 24. in libro veter.

But

But the Barons default is neuer any default of the wife, therefore 16. Assis. p. 5. In a præcipe quod reddat against Baron and Feme, the Baron made default, and the wife was here receiued and pleaded to issue, which being found against her, shée and her husband brought an attaint. Though indéed it were challenged, first, because the Baron (they said) by default had lost his Interest, and then because he was not priuie to the verdict, 3.H.6.fol.9. In a writ of debt at the pluries capias the Sheriffe returned Cepi corpus for the wife, and the Baron non est inuentus, the exigent here went out only against the Baron, and an idem dies was giuen to the wife. But it was said if the Sheriffe had returned, the husband taken, and the wife non inuenta, exigent should haue gone against them both; for the wife is to be brought by the husband.

For by Chok.& Danbie 9.Ed.4 f.23. if in an action of debt the Baron appeare, and the wife make default, capias shall goe against them both, quod mirum, saith Brooke, where corporall punishment shall bée, indéed it séemeth to be no law, for 9.H.6.f.8. in an action of debt, at the exigent the Baron and Feme sued a supersedeas, but notwithstanding they were returned outlawed, and at the same day the Baron appeared alone, and a new exigent went out against the wife only, and an idem dies giuen to the husband, car il nauera corporall paine, &c. and if he make default at the returne of the exigent, a distringas shall goe against him. Againe, 11.H.4. a pluries capias went against Baron and Feme, the Baron appeared, and the wife made default, the Plaintiffe could not obtaine exigent against them both, but he had it against the Feme, and an idem dies giuen to the Baron: For though in a præcipe quod reddat in regard of the grand Cape, and such like, and for losse of issues returned vpon Baron and Feme, the wiues default be the husbands default, yet the wiues default onely shall not bée so mischieuous to him as to driue him to a corporall punishment, as to the capias or exigent. Likewise 39.Edw.3. fol. 18. in trespasse against

Baron

Baron and Feme, at the exigent the Baron appeared, the wife made default, and because she was misnamed in the writ, a new exigent went out, and an idem dies to the husband, yet he was compelled here to answer maintenante, 8. H. 4. fol. 6. in appeale of Mayhem against Baron and Feme after exigent awarded, the Baron alone came and found suerty, and had a supersedeas, though the wife neuer appeared, 12. H. 4. fo. 1. in a writ of debt against Baron and Feme, processe continued till capias was awarded, then the Baron appeared of his owne accord, and the wife made default, an idem dies was giuen to the husband, and a capias sicut alias went against the wife, which came and finding suerties, had a supersedeas to the Sheriffe, then at the day of appearing the wife came, and the Baron made default, therein was awarded that the wife should haue another day of maineprise, and processe went out against the husband. But this, he said, should be no example in temps a vener.

Sect. XLVII.

Of Fourching.

This interchange or shifting of appearance and default by Baron and Feme is called fourching or fourcher: The terme being of no greater linage than from a hay forke or pitchforke, which in french is fourch: The Logicians call their dilemma a forke: And our Ancients haue giuen a like name to a subtill kinde of delay which parceners, ioyntenants, and married couples had at the common Law when suits were commenced against them called forcher, for euen as a cunning fighting bull when he is bayted, offering to the dog first one horne, and then another, might be said to forch, so these conioyned aduersaries were wont to play with both tynes, when first one should appeare, and his fellow be essoyned, and at the next day

day of appearance he should make default, which formerly appeared and be essoyned by him which first made default. Against this Westm. 1. ca. 42. complaining that demandants were greatly delayed by perceners, which might not answer but together and by ioyntenants which knew not their owne severall, that used to fourch by essoine, till every one were once essoined; Ordeineth that such tenants henceforth shall bee allowed no essoine more than at one day, and as one person. The Statute of Gloucester made 6. eiusdem Regis, scilicet Edw. the first reciteth the former Statute thus: Whereas it is established, that parceners and tenants in common shall not fourch by essoine, after they have once appeared in Court; It is ordeined that the same Law shall bee observed when a man and his wife are impleaded, &c. In the booke 11. H. 4. fo. 1. Culpepper affirmeth, that fourcher which was at the common Law in a writ of debt is not to be remedied by this Statute of Gloucester. And Thirne confesseth, that the Statute is only touching pleas of land, but yet saith he, at the common Law Baron and Feme might never fourch by distresses, insinet in a writ of debt, for that they are in a manner one person in law. Thus much of fourching.

SECT. XLVIII.

The Baron and Feme appeare.

But admitting that there is no delay used, how shall Baron and Feme plead? I suppose it is hardly comprehended within rules. Brooke setteth downe that in a quid iuris clamat against Baron and Feme they may deny the deed, by which the Feme should bee bound, and a quid iuris clamat was brought against a Feme couert, 18. H. 6. fo. 1. Titulo Baron & Feme 83. And where the Baron is estopped from pleading non tenure, the wife is so too, Titulo Ioyntes accompts Br. 17.

26.

26. assisar. p. 44. An Assise was brought against Baron and Feme, the Baron came in proper person, and pleaded the Plaintiffs release, the wiues Atturney was asked if hee would assent to the plea, who answered he would be aduised, therefore the deed was deliuered back againe to the husband, to the intent that it should not bee allowed, vnlesse the wiues Atturney consented, who afterward agreed. Thus doth Fitzh. titulo Assise abridge the case 243. very neere the originall, for Brooke mistooke it, or I mistake him, in the title of Baron and Feme, 72. In an action of debt against Baron and Feme executrix, It is a good pleading to say that the wife hath fully administred, and a good replication to say that the wife hath assetts sans patler del Baron, 28. Hen. 6. fo. 4. And there it is saie, that a wife executrix, may administer and distribute goods without the assent of her husband: And if that she sell the Testator goods and redeeme them, yet still they remaine assets. If a Feme tenant for life take a husband, and they two, being impleaded, pray ayd of a stranger, if the Baron die, he in reuersion cannot enter, for that is the act of the husband.

If a Feme tenant for life take a husband which alieneth in Fee, and hee in reuersion entereth, if now the Baron dye, the wife shall haue the land againe, 29. assisar. p. 43. Brooke 86. Titulo Baron and Feme. The case is of an estate made to baron and Feme in the booke of assises, in a writ of entry in nature of assise against Baron and Feme, the Baron pleaded non tenure for his wife, and for himselfe ioyntenancie with a stranger; This was holden a good plea per Curiam and not double, for he must answer for both, 16. H. 6. fo. 22.

12. Rich. 2. Baron and Feme were acquit in appeale, & it was found by verdict that they had beene imprisoned to dammages C. l. By Thirne & Hull Iustices, the dammages ought to be seuered, the Baron to haue one iudgement for himselfe, and he and his wife another iudgement for his wife, for if the husband should dye before execution,

tion, the wife ought to have execution of her dammages, and not the husbands executors, which could not bee if the recovery were in common, Fitzh. Titulo Iudgement 108.

SECT. XLIX.

Outlarie of Baron and Feme or of one of them.

44. Ed. 3. fo. 3. The Baron and Feme being outlawed in an action of debt, got each of them a severall Charter of pardon, sued scire facias against the Plaintiffe, and found maineprise joyntly, the Viscount returned that the scire facias came tardy, at which returne the Baron appeared without his wife, and praying to have scire facias sicut alias upon the first maineprise, or a new scire facias by new maineprise, neither of them might be allowed without his wife, yet it was agreed that if two men were outlawed, one might sue pardon and scire facies without the other, for in that case, the one may plead alone upon the first originall without his fellow, against whom the processe is determined: but the Baron cannot plead here without his wife, see the booke 11. H. 4. fo. 89. Baron and Feme being outlawed, the wife appeared and brought a Charter of pardon, shee was suffered to goe at large, but the pardon might not bee allowed because the baron appeared not, and the wife could not plead without him.

14. H. 6. fo. 14. Iune said that one kinde of divorce betwixt baron and feme is, when an action of trespasse is brought against them, and the baron only appearing, processe goes out against the wife till she be waive, &c. Shee can never purchase her pardon, unlesse her husband appeare, so that if he will he is divorced. The like subtilty hath M. Littleton 13. Ed. 4. fo. 4. where he affirmes, that if a woman be outlawed by erronious processe, if the husband will not bring a writ of error, hee may so be rid of a shrew; for that countervailes a divorce.

11.H.4. sheweth that a woman may be suffered to goe at large, though her pardon bée not allowed till her husband appeare with her. &c. And sée Dyer 10. Eliz. 271. In debt against baron and feme, processe was continued till the baron was outlawed, and the wife waiue, afterward the wife came in ward by processe, brought the quéenes pardon for her waiuery: Though the pardon could not bée allowed, because the wife without the husband could not sue scire facias against the plaintiffe, to make him declare vpon the first originall, for the pardon had a condition in law, ita quod ipsa staret recta in curia, which shée could not doe alone, yet by the opinion of the Court shée was to bee discharged of the imprisonment, I thinke the shrew went home. But that a woman outlawed by her selfe alone for an offence touching her in an action brought against her husband and her, and the husband appeared before outlagary was discharged of her imprisonment vpon sight of her pardon, I find not here nor no where else, and therefore it may be M. Iunes way will serue sometime to bee rid of a shrew, and that by a like manner a woman may be voided of a slouin, or vncumbred of a Churle. An action of trespasse is brought against baron and feme, and the baron outlawed, the wife appearing at the exigent, goeth sans iour: if a capias vtlagatum lay hold of the husband, I perceiue not well how he can get loose without his dames fauour.

SECT. L.

Of Diuorce.

BUt it is time to make an end of marriage since wee are come to matter of diuorcement, of which I reckon this of outlary for none. 47. Ed. 3. in the very end of the yeere setteth downe fiue wayes, Causa professionis, Causa præcontractus, Causa consanguinitatis, causa affinitatis, and

and Causa frigiditatis, with an obseruation, that when diuorce is Causa professionis, the wife shall be indowed, and the heire inherit, contra, in al the residue, Immaturitis also, or minoritie of age at the time of espousals, may be one cause of diuorce, as 29. Ed. 3. fo. 32. Iohn & Alice his wife brought an assise, the Tenant said that Alice had sued diuorce in the Archbishopricke of Warwicke, because she was vnder age of consent, tempore sponsaliū, neuer consenting afterward, and diuorce was had iudgement del briefe. And Broke titulo garde 124. remembreth that 5. Ph. & Mar. the Doctors of Law declared for diuorces vpon this case, That if an heire, or other body be married infra annos nubiles, and doe disassent at the age of discretion, or after (before assent) to marriage it is sufficient, and the party may be wedded to some other body, without either diuorce or testimony of the disagreement, before the ordinary, who though hee may punish p arbitrium Iudicis here, yet the second espousals are good, by Law of both Realme and Church: But when diuorce is had, for kindred, præcontract, frigiditie, or such like case, the Law is cleane contrary, for tryall of diuorce when it is pleaded in a temporall Court, must bee by certificate of the Bishop, and not p pais. 5. Hen. 4. fol. 2 and sentence of diuorce belongeth to the Bishop in his spirituall Court.

Of which there is authority, 2. Eliz. 179. in Dyer, This yeere he saith, sentence of diuorce was giuen Causa frigiditatis naturalis, in the Archbishops Court of Audience, and the woman was actrix & querulans de impotentia procreandi in viro, who was adiudged impotent by the Physitians: The same yeere, or next yeere, another case and iudgement hapned like, and the woman which complained married to a second husband of better stuffe, by whom she had children, and gaue him all her land by fine, &c. her first husband also was married to another woman, and had children by his second wife, (vt asserebatur) in which case the Doctors held that the parties diuorced were compellable to liue againe together, vt vir & vxor, quia

quia sancta Ecclesia decepta fuit in Iudicio priori, Therefore much adoe was made to stay the ingrossing of the fine, yet the Iustices made it be ingrossed, contra mandat dom Custodis,&c. But see Sir Edw. Cokes 5. Report. fo. 98. in Buryes case, that the Doctors were deceived, for the parties divorced causa frigiditatis cannot live together againe, and the issue by the second wife is legitimate, for a man may bee habilis & inhabilis diversis temporibus. Againe, 13. and 14. of Eliz. Dyer fol. 305. teacheth that right and lawfulnesse of marriage is ever to be iudged, not by the temporall, but by the spirituall Iudge: And therefore in an issue of ne vnques accouple in loyall matrimonie, if the Bishop certifie not the lawfulnesse of wedlocke, but the circumstances, hee shall be amerced, and a melius certiorando awarded. Seeing therefore right of marriage is to be discussed by the spirituall Iudge, they which are married ought in no case to sever themselves, and remarry without the spirituall Iudge: if they doe, the second marriage is no marriage, the children had in it are illegitimate, and the woman not dowable, except in the case first specified. And generally where espousals are not meerely void but defeisable, if they bee not avoided by divorcement, the issue which is had without defeiting that shall inherit: as if a man marry his cosin or his sister, saith the booke, and have issue by her, and die before divorce had, now nothing can bastardize the issue, for though the Commissary was wont in his visitation to make a kinde of divorce in such cases after death of one of the parties, it was never any more than an Inquisition of office, Ad inquirendum de peccatis, for the heire could not be bastardized, when the parents both or one of them were dead, and therefore not citable to appeare, &c. And it is holden strongly by Thorpe 39. Edw. 3. and in the Parliament 24. H. 8. see Brooke titulo Bastardie 23. 37. 44. 47. And a divorce cannot bee had but of a marriage consisting, and not yet by death dissolved, for there cannot wel be a reversing of any divorce when the parties divorced be dead, as

Brooke

Brooke understandeth Conningsby 12. H. 7. 22. for saith he, it was adiudged in Corbets case, where the baron and feme had issue, and afterward were divorced, the baron taking another wife, by whom he had issue and died, that when the first issue sued in spirituall Court to reverse the divorce and bastardize, the second issue, after his fathers death a prohibition lay: But it was said that the title and discent were comprised in the libell, or else the prohibition could not have beene granted. Thus saith Brooke titulo Deraignment. But titulo Bastardy 47. hee setteth downe the same case, that a man may be bastardized after the espousals, wherein he was begotten and borne, or by death determined. See Sir Edw Cokes 7. report Kennes case, that some divorces dissolue the matrimony, scilicet à vinculo matrimonii, and bastardize the issue, and barre the woman of her Dower, and some à mensa & Thoro, which dissolueth not the marriage, nor barre the wife of her Dower, nor bastardize the issue: And therefore if any action be brought and divorce pleaded, the cause of divorce ought to bee shewed: And there it is said that a divorce may be repealed in the spirituall Court after the death of the parties, but a suit after the death of the parties to divorce them, and to bastardize their issue may not be, for that the triall of bastardy, or not belongeth to the temporall Court, originally if sentence doe not hinder. And see Sir Edw. Cokes Institut. ca. Dower f. 33. & ca. Estates upon condition fol. 381. the deriuation of the word divorce à diuertendo or diuortendo, quia vir diuertitur ab vxore, and see there the severall causes of divorces, and how far any of them respectiuely doe extend in power and effect, and in Littletons time many divorces were of force, which the Statute of 32. H. 8. cap. 38. take away, and there see that a man may marry the sister of his first wife, since that Statute.

By Na. br. fol. 44. in the writ of prohibition, and Na. br. 129. and Dyer 28. H. 8. 12. agree, if the woman shall haue the goods not spent, and that detinue lyes for them,

If goods be giuen in marriage with a woman, shée shall recouer them in the spirituall Court after diuorce, and there lyeth no prohibition, 16. Hen. 8. fol. 7. is that if the husband before diuorce had, haue giuen or sold without collusion, such goods as were the wiues before marriage, she is without remedy for them being diuorced.

But if he aliened them by collusion, and bring a writ of detinue, for so much of them as the property may bée decerned of, and for the residue, money and such like, shée shall sue in spirituall Court. If a man which is bound to a woman by obligation marry her, and they be diuorced, she hath her action againe, which was suspended ibid by Fitzh and Norwich. But sée the booke of 11. Hen. 7. 4. p Cur. contrary where the diuorce is causa præcontract', and it is so cited, Dyer 4. Mar. fol. 140.

If the woman diuorced were an Inheritrix, &c. and the husband before diuorcement hath done waste, felled her woods, receiued her rents, granted her wards, presented to her Churches, giuen away her goods, none of these things past in possession executed can be reuersed or recalled: But if the Inheritance it selfe were discontinued or charged, or a release made of it, or hir villaines manumitted, shée shall haue remedy for these things by common Law.

If baron and feme Jointpurchasers be disseised, and the baron release, &c. the wife shall haue a moiety if they bee diuorced, although before there were no moieties betwixt them, for the diuorce conuert that into moieties, which sée Brooke title Deraignement and diuorce 32. H. 8. In Sir Edward Cokes 5. Rep. in Olands case it was holden, that if a Lease bée made to baron and feme during the Couerture, and the baron soweth the land, and after there is a diuorce causa præcontract, the baron shall haue the Corne, and not the lessor, for although the baron prosecuted the suit, yet the sentence which dissolues the marriage is the iudgment in Law, and Iudicium redditur in inuitum.

And

And as by diuorce, that which was intire may bee conuerted or diuided into moeties, so by it, inheritance may bee made francktenement. And if baron and feme donees in taile, haue issue and be diuorced, now they haue but francktenement, and the issue shall not inherit, for it is not like here as where lands are giuen to two men, or to a man and his mother, or to a man and his daughter, and to the heires of their bodies, where seuerall heires shall seuerally inherit, for it was neuer lawfull for them to marry, 7. Hen.4.16. Brooke 9. in titulo Taile, see also, 13. Edw. 3. titulo Deraignment, If land be giuen to baron and feme in taile which be diuorced causa præcontract, &c. they shall hold ioyntly for terme of their liues, and the land goe to the Suruiuor. But by the Reporter, if the gift were in franckmarriage, the party which did not cause the diuorce shall haue all: and agreeing to that difference is Perk. Chap. feoffement, Sect. 238. and also agreeing is Sir Edw. Cokes 9. Rep. in Beamonts case.

12. Assisar p. 22. Donees in franckmarriage were diuorced at the womans suit, the baron continued possession till he died, and afterward the woman died, the possession was adiudged to haue remained alwayes to the woman, because shee neuer made any debate for it, so that the man neuer had it by disseisin, and agreeing to that is Plowden Wymbysses case fol. 58. & Dyer 3. M. fol. 126. 19. Assisar. plac. 2. The Donee in franckmarriage wedded infra annos nubiles, sued diuorce by the barons motiue and the wiues agreement, at their full age, and the woman recouered all the land against her quondam husband by assise. And Titulo Assise in Fitzh. pla. 413. 442. is this case, A man of certaine tenements, infeoffed his feoffor, & his wife in tayle, the remainder to the right heires of the baron, they were diuorced, at the suit of her husband, which kept the woman out of the lands, and she brought an Assise, whereby she recouered a moyty of the tenements by iudgement presently. And propter difficultatem it was adiorned for the other moity to the Commonpleas, where shee had

iudgement of that also, because divorce was at the husbands suit. As a woman may have an Assise against her companion divorced, for lands wherein shee claimeth inheritance, or estate for life, so if he have aliened in fee, fee tayle, or for life, the lands which he had in fee simple, fee tayle, or for terme of life, to a stranger, she may as soone as she is divorced, bring a Writ called a cui ante divortium against the Alienee: And this Writ may be in the per, cui, & post. If shee dye before action commenced, or before recovery, her heire may have a Writ called a sur cui ante divortium, and the Aunt and Neece may joyne in it. But for her estate tayle her heire shalbe put to a formidone. But note Reader, that it seemeth both the woman and her heire may enter after the Statute of 32. Hen. 8. and never bring Cui in vita, nor sur cui in vita, &c. for the opinion in Grenlies Case, Sir Edw. Cokes 8. Rep. fol. 73. is, that if the baron alien, and after the wife is divorced causa præcontract. which dissolve the marriage à vinculo matrimonii, the wife during the life of the husband, or after his death, may enter, for the words of the Act are no fine feoffement, &c. during the Coverture betweene them, and although the Statute saith, But that the same wife, &c. that is to be intended of her which was his wife at the time of the alienation, &c.

Note that whereas West. 2. cap. 3. giveth a cui in vita upon recovery by default against the husband, &c. shee shall have a cui ante divortium upon the like recovery by equity & extension of the Statute, and the processe is summons, grand cape, & petit cape. I will here set the bounds and limits of my third booke, not because this sequell and consequence divorce, I meane, whereby the issue had, is bastardized, and the woman restored to her goods and lands, comforteth with the marriage so perfectly begun as I meant it, for this is not the untying of true wedlocke, but rather a dissipation of marriage tainted at the beginning, and in Christian Court adjudged to a nullity, as if it had never beene, the Baron and Feme that I have spoken

spoken of all this while, if they were not married in their infant loue and very first flowing age, yet were they not frostbitten or so blasted either of them when they were young, but they might well haue fructified, neither was either of them a common Law breaker, intangled with promise or præcontract, and as for consanguinity, or affinity, there was no more betwixt them, than is betweene Iack Flecher and his bolt. You may imagine some matter by onely imagination, perhaps more visible than it could haue béene, being true, whereupon a publike sentence of seperation being published a Thoro & mensa, but then there was a monition of chast liuing, and prohibition to both the parties, that neither of them should flee to other marriage so long as both of them were liuing. And the Author of seperation, that is the party suing diuorce, did put in sufficient caution to doe nothing contrary to this prohibition. So that the holy liues of matrimony were not cleane broken, and pulled asunder, but within a yéere or two they were reconciled, voluntarily of their owne accord. And soone after (so I will make it) hauing the Distaffe, Spindle and Shéeres all in mine owne hand, the husbands life was suddenly cut off, or else the wife had béene sole executrix.

THE WOMANS LAWYER.

The fourth Booke.

Pale death equo pulsans pede pauperum tabernas regnumque turres: Death, I say, to whom the Poet did attribute so much power in this his verse, Omnia sub leges mors vocat atra suas, hath called the husband hence, left the house full of mourning, and specially the wife cannot chuse but sorrow and lament. If my foure legged beast should fall into halues, the one halfe starke dead without motion or spirit, and the other halfe standing still vpright, senting, sééing, féeling, gazing; must it not, thinke you, be wonderfully astonished. If an Elephant, in whom (as some doe write) is vnderstanding of his countries spéech, a wonderfull memorie and recenting of things past, a great delight in loue and glorie, besides prudence, equitie, and religion, should haue his head cut off, his body remaining still for all that vegetable and sensitiue, would he not (trow yée) be excéeding sorrowfull for the forgoing such an ornament, I dare be bold to giue a woman as much as Pliny gaue the Elephant:

phant: She hath understanding, and speech, firme memorie, loue naturall, and kindnesse, desire of glorie and reputation, with the accomplishment of many meritorious vertues: But alas, when she hath lost her husband, her head is cut off, her intellectuall part is gone, the verie faculties of her soule are, I will not say cleane taken away, but they are all benummed, dimmed and dazled, so that she cannot thinke or remember when to take rest or refection for her weake body. And though her spirits and naturall moysture being inwardly exhausted, with sorrow and extreme griefe, she be called and inforced to seeke restauration, by such aliments as life is prolonged by, yet is she nothing desirous of life, hauing lost a moytie of her selfe, yea the principall moytie now best prised and esteemed, but neuer best loued: Time must play the Physitian, and I will helpe him a little: Why mourne you so, you that be widowes? Consider how long you haue beene in subiection vnder the predominance of parents, of your husbands, now you be free in libertie, & free proprii iuris at your owne Law, you may see num. cap. 30. That maidens and wiues vowes made vpon their soules to the Lord himselfe of heauen and earth, were all disauowable and infringible, by their parents or husbands, vnlesse they ratified and allowed them, either expresse or by silence, at the day when such vowes came first to their notice and knowledge: But the vow of a widow, or of a woman diuorced, no man had power to disallow of, for her estate was free from controlment. Must a woman needs weepe thus for the losse of her Buckler, Shield, and defence, in the person of him with whom she held daily commutation of all offices proceeding from loue and superlatiue kindnesse. Let her learne to cast her whole loue and deuotion on him, that is better able to loue and defend her than all the men in the world, Him I meane that hath forbidden to afflict widdowes or orphans, with promise to heare their cries, and vindicate their wrongs, by killing them by the sword, and making the wiues widdowes, and

their

their children fatherlesse, of them which breake this Commandement, Exod. cap. 22. Then because a sober carefulnesse and moderate sedulitie, in businesse of profit or disprofit, doth mitigate greatly the sorrowing for such actions, as opinion or fancie makes thus grievous, let her looke to her affaires as cause and need requireth.

Sect. I.

Of Executorship and Administration.

She is not made an Executor, because the office is troublesome, let her take heed she make not her selfe an Executr' de son tort demesne, by her owne wrong, 33. H.6. fol. 31. Action of debt was had against a woman as Executrix to her late husband. She pleaded that her husband made B. and C. his Executors, which taking Administration from the Archbishop, did deliver to this Defendant three robes, which her husband gave her by will, sans ceo, that ever she administred in any other manner. Ashton Justice held this for no good plea, because here was no colour of any Administration, for that is no Administration to use her owne goods. But if one administer (quoth he) about funerall expences and nothing else, hee may in a Writ brought against him, plead the Administration for this onely cause, sans ceo that he administred in any other manner, for here was a kinde of Administration which shall charge the partie no further than the goods administred will reach. But for a woman to take her owne goods to none Administration at all, Concedimus per Curiam. And there it is said, that the Law allowes a woman convenient apparrell, but not excessive, &c.

Anno primo Eliz. In an Action of debt as against an Executor, upon a plea of ne vnques execut' ne vnques Administrater e de execution. A speciall verdit was found, how the Defendant had recovered 10. l. that was due to the Defunct,

Defunct, and made an acquitance for it, taking also into his hands all the goods and chattels, that were the said Wyrials, so was his name, vsing them as his owne, this was holden a sufficient Administration. And saith Iustice Dyer fol. 166. I take for a rule, that occupation and possession of a dead mans goods, giueth sufficient notice of the person which shall bee charged to administer, bee it either ordinary or Executor. 17. Edw. 3. Action of debt was mainteynable against a Deane onely, gardiam spiritualium sede vacante ad cuius manus bona deuenerunt, without naming the Chapter, and issue was taken vpon the deuenerunt, viz. the possession. And such an action may bee against an Executor alone, which hath possession of the goods, 8. Edw. 3. In a Writ of Dower against one Executor alone that held the ward in his only custody, hee was named Custos and not Executor.

And for this reason it is, that though an Executor bringing action must shew how hee is Executor for the most part, yet the like is not needfull in an action against an Executor, for hee may bee an Executor sundry wayes, by Testament, by letter of the Ordinary, or by his voluntary Administration, and taking vnto him possession, vse, and occupation of the goods long, 50. Ed. 4. fo. 72.

And if an Administrator bringeth an action, hee shall say in his Count qui obiit intestatus, and not vt dicitur, but where one declares against an Administrator, it is the vsuall forme to say qui obiit intestatus vt dicitur for the Plaintiffe, there is not intended to know certainly whether the Defendant bee Administrator or not. And see Greysbrooke cs. Plowd. fo. 276. b. & c. that where letters of Administration are pleaded in Law, they need not bee shewed to the Court otherwise in the Count, &c.

And a woman taking more apparell than is conuenient for her degree, without legacy or licence is an Executor de son tort demesne, 33. Hen. 6. yet there is some possession or medling, that the Law tolerateth, and is cullorable, and yet it draweth no burthen with it, as expences

about

about funerals, or if one be made Coadintor, or Supervisor; or if he haue letters ad collegendum, or if he were Executor, by a former will disproued by a latter will.

Likewise if a Feme Couert bee made Executrix, not medling with any goods, &c. refuse to administer when she is sole. In all these cases there is a Cullor of authority, and the party shall plead the especiall matter, sans ceo, that he administred in any other manner.

But he which claimeth by guift, shall plead absque hoc quod vt Executoris. In the principall Case Dyer concludeth, that the Plaintiffe should be without remedy, if he might not haue the action. And if (saith he) a lawfull Executor by his euill administration, viz. Conuersion of goods to his owne vse shall be charged, it must néeds be thought reasonable, that he should be in better case vndischarged, that executeth but by wrong of his owne carriage: Thus farre Dyer. Sometime the husband dyeth in so good time, that it were madnesse in his widow to refuse administration. Know therefore that by the Statute 21. Hen. 8. ca. 5. When the husband dieth intestate, or the Executors named in the Testament doe refuse to proue it the ordinary or persons, which haue authority to take probat of Testaments, shall grant administration to the widow of him which is deceased, or to the next of his kin, or to both, as by his discretion shall bee thought good, taking suerty of him, or them, to whom such commission shall be made, for true administration of the goods, debts, &c.

And where diuers persons claime Administration as next of kin, which are all in equall degrée, or where one claimeth where indeed diuers bee in equality of kindred with him, the ordinary shall haue liberty to grant it to one or more of them which require it. And where one or more, but not all of them which are in equality of degrée, doe make request, the Ordinary may admit the widow, and him or them onely making request, or any one of them at his pleasure, taking nothing, &c. vnlesse the goods doe amount to aboue the value of fiue pounds, the penalty is forfeiture.

forfeiture of so much money as was receiued contrary to this Act to the party grieued, and ten pound to the King and party grieued besides.

But by the ancient custome of the Realme: If any man dyed intestate, the Ordinary might dispose of his goods in pious vses, he might seise, preserue, giue or grant them, yet was he not chargeable in any action prosecute, by creditors of the intestate, because forsooth hee was a Judge spirituall, and not subiect to temporall suit, for things committed to him vpon confidence.

But Westm. 2. ca. 19. an. 13. E. 1. is: Cum post morte alienus decedentis intestat' & obligati aliquibus in debito, & the goods come to the Ordinaries hands, it is ordeined that hee answer to action as an Executor shall doe, quatenus bona defunct sufficiunt. Then againe, because still the Ordinary might neither meddle nor be meddled with, for things in action as debts, &c. 31. Edw. 3. cap. 11. ordeineth, that in Case of intestate the Ordinary shall depute the most trusty and neerest friends of the dead to Administer, and that they shall haue action of debt, or answer in action of debt, and bee accomptable to Ordinaries, &c. as Executors. I will wade no further here in the office of Executor or Administrator, except it bee onely to shew vnto you, how next of kin in the Statute of 21. H. 8. hath beene taken.

A sonne of Charles Duke of Suffolke, by a second venter, hauing certaine goods by his fathers Will, dyed intestate, and without wife or issue, his mother who was daughter to the Lord Willoughby tooke Administration, which was afterward reuoked after great argument in the spirituall Court, as well by common Lawyers, as Ciuilians, in the behalfes of the said mother Dutchesse of Suffolke, and Lady Francis wife to the Marquis Dorset, sister of the halfe bloud to Henry the Intestate, which sued to reuerse the Administration, and obteined it her selfe, though shee were but sister de demy sanke, for the mother is not next of kin to her alone sonne in this matter, but

must

must descend and not ascend, either by one Law or the other, and children be de sanguine patris & matris, sed pater & mater non sunt de sanguine puerorum. Contrary it is of brethren and sisters, 5. Edw. 6. 47 in Brooke titulo Administraton. There is also this Case, William Rawlins Clericus died intestate, administration was committed to Sir Humphrey Browne, who had married Rawlins his sister, William Shelton, and Iohn Shelton, sonnes to the Lady Browne by her first husband, reversed the administration and obteined it for themselves.

But see in Sir Edward Cokes 3. Rep. in Ratcliffs ca. fol. 40. it is said that the booke of 5. Edw. 6. haue beene often times resolued to bee no Law, and that the goods of the sonne or daughter ought to be granted to the father or mother as the next of bloud, and there is Littleton cited who saith, that although the sonnes lands goe to the vncle, yet the father is next of bloud.

SECT. II.

A reasonable part of the goods.

IF there bee a will proued, the widow must take such goods as were bequeathed her by deliuery from the Executors, but whether here were a will or none in some places, she shall haue a third part of all her late husbands goods. For this there is an ordinary writ to the Sheriffe, where she cannot haue a third part of that which remaines after funerals discharged, and legacies payd and performed, to summon the Executors to appeare and make answer why she should not haue, as the custome of the Court is, that women ought to haue rationabilem partem de bonis & catallis virorum. The like writ is for children, whether they be sonnes, or daughters, or both. And this writ speaketh of a custome in the County, that children which are not heires nor promoted in the fathers life time, shall

haue

haue their reasonable part, 3. Edw. 3. A Writ of debt was brought by a man & Alice his wife against the Executors of his wiues father, & declaration was vpon custome of the Shire, that children not aduanced should haue their reasonable part of their fathers goods, the Executors said, that Alice was married by her father in his life time, iudgement si action, &c. It is no answer said one, to say that she was married by her father, except you say also by, or with her fathers goods, and to her conueniable aduancement, and here the husband at time of the marriage, or after had neuer any land. The Executors said still shee was conueniently married by her fathers procurement, &c. And in the end the Baron and Feme offered to auerre, not married by the father, on which point the issue was ioyned, Fitzh. Dett. 156.

40. Edw. 3. In a rationabili parte bonorum, brought by a daughter counting on the custome of the Towne, that euery son and daughter should haue a reasonable part, the defendant pleaded a reuersion discended to her, which she might sell for her aduancement in marriage, iudgement si action, &c. Mowbray said, the Lords in Parliament would not agree that this action is maintenable by any common custome or Law of the Realme. Doctor and St. fol. 132. a. by the custome of some Country, the children (the debts and legacies payd) shall haue a reasonable part of the goods of the dead. 39. Edw. 3. fol. 9. 10. One brought a Writ of Detinue for certaine goods, shewing the custome of Sussex: That where the father dyed intestate, his heire should haue a reasonable part of his Chattels, and vpon this custome hee demanded goods come to the Defendants hands; It was argued whether the custome were good or no. Morris, such a custome hath beene allowed in Eyre 21. Hen. 6. fol. 1. & 2. In fine casus a woman brought a Writ of detinew against her husbands Executors for a moity of his goods, as for her reasonable part by custome, and the Defendant was compelled to answer.

7. Edw. 4. fol. 20. & 21. In a rationabili parte bonorum,

rum, iudgement was asked of the declaration, because the custome was, that where the Baron dyed sans issue, the wife should haue a moity of his goods, after debts and funerals discharged, but if there were issue, shee should haue but a third part, and here the Plaintiffe had a demanded moity without alleaging that the baron died sans issue, &c.

The Plea was amended by permittance of the Iustices, for Danby said, the widow had as good title to the goods as to lands at the common Law. But Catesby spied another fault in the Count, viz. Continuance of the custome not alleaged.

18. Hen. 6. fo. 4. in a rationabili parte bonorum one Executor appearing, confessed the action, and the others made default, whereupon the Plaintiffe recouered presently by equity of the Statute 9. Edw. 3. cap. 3. by which the Executor comming first must answer. Like, or the same learning is in the former Booke 7. Ed. 4. where Choke said, that alwayes if ne vnques executor, ne vnques administrat cõe executor be a good plea (vt hic) the Executor first appearing must answer.

I see that many times in stead of this writ de rationabili parte bonorum, a writ of debt sometimes, and many times of detinue hath serued, and you may finde further 52. and 56. titulo Detinue in Fitzh. And the great variance is in this, that the action is founded on a custome sometime of the Towne, sometime of the County, and sometime of the Realme, for indeed many haue holden that it is generall like an action of the Case against an Hostler, or an action de igne custodiendo. So teacheth Glanuil, and so Fitzh. who relieth vpon magna Charta. cap. 18. which prescribing how the Kings debts shall be leuied of his goods that is dead, willeth the surplussage to remaine for the Executors ad testamentum defuncti pimplend. saluis vxori & pueris eius partibus rationabilibus, which being of a reasonable part may be restrained to places where custome yeeldeth it, for ought that I perceiue Bracton in this passage, is like a peece of Romane ancient coyne that time hath rusted and defaced.

If

If a man (saith he) make a Testament, he ought to remember his Lord of whom hee holdeth his land with the best thing he hath, and the Church with the next: If the wife dye before the goodman, the Church must have likewise the second best beast of all the flocke heard or drove, but hee saith, this is of grace and permission of the husband, and though a man bee not bound to give any thing to the Church nomine sepulturæ, yet if he doe it is a laudable gift, and Dominus papa will not be against it. A woman that is at her owne commandement may make a Will, and dispose the fruits and corne growing on her Dower lands, whether they be severed from the soile, or not severed, quod olim non potuit sed nunc de gratia potest. She that is sub potestate viri, can make no Will without her husbands ratification, though by custome sometimes women doe make Wills of that which might have fallen to their reasonable part, &c. or of things given them, ad ornatum sicut de robis & iocalibus.

A man may make a Will of all his things moueable, excepting so much as he oweth, for debts are before legacies, and the King before all Creditors. It is lawfull for the Viscount or Kings Bayliffe, shewing his letters Patents out of the Exchequor, to attach all the goods and chattels of him which is dead found within his lay fee to the value of the debt, &c. and to imbreviat them, by view of lawfull men, so that nothing bee amoued till the debt bee payd, and the remainder of all such chattels shall bee to the Executors debitum, vero defuncti quod debetur. Iudeis non vsurabit quamdiu hæres infra ætatem extiterit, neither shall the King when a Jewes debt commeth to him take any more than the principall: neither shall a womans Dower be chargeable with her husbands debt. Dos debet esse libera, and when a man dieth intestate, the execution of his goods belongeth to the Church and his friends deducting first out of them his cleere debts, amongst which must bee reckoned his servants wages, certaine and incertaine, if incertaine they shall be taxed by the nearest

friends,

friends, & the charges of his buriall, & funerall expences taken out of the stocke, that which remaineth must be diuided into three parts, whereof one shall goe to the wife, the second to the children, and the Testator hath absolute power to dispose of the third. If there be no children, vna medietas defuncto, alia vxori reseruatur: If there be no wife, vna medietas defuncto, alia liberis tribuitur: And where there is neither wife nor children, tunc id totum remanebit defuncto: The heire is bound to pay his Predecessors debts, so farre forth as the inheritance fallen to him will extend and further as his owne grace and good liking leads him. Ea quæ dicta sunt locum habent & tenent, all this is Law, saith Iohn Bracton, except custome sway otherwise as in Cities, Boroughes and Townes. London he saith hath a custome, that when certaine Dowry is appointed to a woman, either in money or other chattels or houses, shee shall demand no ouerplus of her husbands goods, except it be the increment which he giueth by his voluntary bequest. And the reason why shee shall haue not plus quam dotem constitutam, is because ipsa prededucet dotem suam ante omnes debitores. His conclusion is that Citizens wiues and children shall haue no more than is bequeathed to them, but be exempted from the generall custome: vix enim inueniretur aliquis Ciuis qui in vita magnum questum facerit, si in morte sua cogeretur inuitus bona sua relinquere pueris indoctis & luxuriosis & vxoribus malemeritis, &c. I am sorry that Bracton seemeth to conceiue no better hope of Citizens wifes, but it may be he was deceiued not onely in his opinion of Borough women, but of Law also, for he makes his diuision of a mans goods into thirds or seconds, shutting it cleane out of Cities and Townes Corporate, to bee generall which Mowbray ere while told you, the Lords would not confesse to be Law, 40. Edw. 3. And many arguments may bee made to the contrary; for indeed it might most properly fit and be conuenient for Citizens, whose estate consisteth very often rather in moueable goods than in lands, and seeing the custome serueth not for heires that haue their fathers inheritance, widowes may most reasonably be barred from it that haue ioyntures, or reasonable part of Inheritance, which are not the widowes of Citizens, for the most part. But let vs end this matter with Sir Thomas Smith, De republica Anglor. lib. 3. cap. 6. Though our Law may seeme somewhat rigorous towards wiues, yet for the most part, they can handle their husbands so well, and doucely, spetially when they bee sicke, that where the Law giues them nothing, their husbands at their death of their good will giue them all, and few there be that be not either made sole, or chiefe Executors of the husbands last Will and Testament, hauing for the most part the gouernment of the children and their portions, except it bee in London, where a peculiar order is taken by the City, much after the fashion of the Law ciuill.

SECT. III.

Of Quarentine.

ALL this while the widow remaines still in the house where her husband dwelt, for as Britton saith, en bone Christien, though perhaps not in excellent French, ne affiert mye que feemes soient botes hors ouesq; le cors de lour barons. Therefore Magna Charta cap. 7. giueth a widow quarentine or forty dayes abode in the capitall messuage of her husband after his decease, except the house be a Castle. If shee must leaue it because it is a Castle, there must presently a competent habitation bee prouided for her, in which she may honestly dwell till Dower be assigned her, and in the meane season shee shall bee allowed reasonable estouers in the common, &c. The Writ that goeth out to the Sheriffe, or Kings Bailiffe, vpon eiectment is a commission commanding speedy Iustice, and therefore

therefore proces is to be awarded upon it against the party offending to appeare within a day or two, not tarrying for the County day, and the proceeding is as in a commission Oyer and Terminer.

Sée 6. Edw. 6. fol. 76. in Dyer, A Writ of Dower was brought, and the Tenant pleaded in abatement of the Writ, that since the darren continuance the Demandant had entred into part, &c. Shewing incertaine which and this was holden a good Plea, and the demand being of francktenement, the demandants entry hath abated the whole Writ, yet 45. Edw. 3. in a scire facias to haue execution of Dower, such an entry pleaded was not good; The Demandant to maintaine her Writ said, that her husband dyed seised in fée, and that hee and shee the same Demandant, cohabitabunt super eodem manerio vt vir & vxor vsque ad diem obitus sui, with protestation, that it descended to the Defendant which entred, and that shée continued possession cohabiting with him, and shee held the same at the pleasure and will of the heire, & non aliter: This, saith Dyer, is holden no good pleading for the quarentine, but shee should haue shewed the death of her husband certaine, and the time of the forty dayes continuing, therefore the opinion of the Court made her waiue her plea, and trauers the entry, nota pro lege: If a woman marry within the forty dayes, shee loseth her quarentine Dower. Brooke ty. Dower 101. 1. M. But if otherwise she be ousted by the heire within the forty dayes, shee shall haue a Writ de quarentena habenda no na br. 161. b.

Sect. IV.

Assignement of Dower.

Now to assignement of Dower, it is true that when it appeares certaine what it is that a woman shall haue in Dower, shee may enter presently when her husband is dead, and tarry for none Assignement, per Littleton, yet Perkins saith, if a man dye seised of iij. s. rent charge in fee, though here the third part bee certaine enough, his widdow shall not distraine for xij. d. before Assignement. Nay further, if shee recover this Dower by action, yet shee shall not distraine for it before execution: But if the Lord of a Manor doe marry with a woman tenant by iij. s. rent and dye, here shee shall haue xij. d. Dower by way of reteiner without any Assignement. And in case where rent is recouered in Dower, the Viscount may deliuer seisen by grasse, by a bough, by a clod of land, or by the distresse of beasts, taken vpon the land, though the day of payment be not yet come. But the party cannot charge any those beasts, 40. Ed. 3. fo. 22.

SECT. V.

who may assigne Dower.

SOmetime Dower is assignable by the husbands heire, as if a man seised of two acres of land in one County, make a feoffement of one acre with warranty and dye, the heire may indow the widdow with parcell of the acre remaining in allowance and full satisfaction of the whole Dower, & bene, for if in a writ of Dower brought by her against the feoffee of her husband, hee vouch the heire, &c. shee shall recouer conditionally against the voucher. And if the heire make a Lease for life of part of such lands as are to him descended, and indow his mother of the parcell remaining in allowance of all, &c. it is good, yet in this case in a Writ of Dower against the Lessee, if hee vouch his Lessor, the recouery shall not be against the vouchee, because he is not bound to warranty as the heire of his father. But if he had beene generally vouched, the heire, and had generally entred into warranty, iudgement perhaps should bee conditionally against him. Sometimes the

the husbands one feoffee, or vendee shall assigne Dower for the rest. And if a woman accept Dower from one of her husbands feoffees, in parcell of his land, in allowance of her Dower of the rest, it seemeth this shall binde her against the other feoffees, yet some haue doubted thereof, because the other feoffees, say they, cannot plead this in an action of Dower against them, neither is there meanes to bring into Court him which made assignement, being a stranger. If diuers Joyntenants bee of certaine lands assignement of Dower, by one of them shall bee good against them all. But if one Joyntenant of land assigne rent in allowance of Dower, his fellowes shal not be distrained for this rent, for there could bee none inforcement to assigne Dower after this manner. Likewise if the Desseisor assigne a rent charge out of the land, this shall not bind the desseisee, causa qua supra.

Assignement of Dower may be by one which is a Disseisor Abator, or Intrudor, &c. if this assignement be without fraud in the woman indowed, and sans tort to any other person, it is good, though the Assignor be a tortious Possessor, but if there bee any such couine, or tort, the assignement is voidable, for the most part by entry. 44. Ed. 3. fol. 46. A woman that had title of Dower, with intent of defeating the Tenants warranty made a stranger to enter, and against him she recouered Dower, it was holden in an Assize, which shee brought afterwards, that her recouery would not serue her, but her estate was gained by deseisin, because of the couine.

Assignement of Dower by him which hath Francktenement is good, and if the wife hath not right of Dower of that which is so assigned by the Tenant of the Francktenement, yet that shall stand vntill it bee defeated. And if tenant per elegit, statute staple, or statute merchant assigne Dower, it is not good. And Assignement of Dower by gardian in soccage seemes not to be good, saith Perkins, for a Writ of Dower lyeth not against such a gardian, see 29. Assis. p. 68. But Assignement by gardian in Chiualry is good till it be defeated; and it shall neuer be defeated, if the womans title of Dower be iust.

SECT. VI.

Assignement to her selfe, or de la pluis beale.

If a man seised of forty acres of land, 20. by Chiualry, and 20. by soccage die, &c. and his wife being gardian in soccage, bring her Writ of Dower in the Kings or some others Court, against the Lord which is gardian in Chiualry, he may plead this matter, and pray to haue it adiudged, that the woman indow her selfe of the fairest in her owne possession, and if she cannot deny the case, it shall be iudged for the Lord, to retaine quietly the lands which hee hath during the nonage of the Infant. And after this iudgement the woman may indow her selfe in presence of her neighbours, by limits and bounds de la pluis beale part of the soccage lands, to haue & to hold to her selfe for terme of her life. This manner of indowment is neuer before iudgement bee giuen for it, either in the Kings or some other Court, and it is to saue the state of gardian in Chiualry. Perkins giueth this matter, which Litleton leaueth thus raw, a turne or two more. And so doth Keble 14. Hen. 7. 26. If, say they, the land which the woman hath by her gardianship, bee not the whole valew of her iust Dower for the smalnesse of it, or because it is charged with some rent, she may shew the matter in her replication: And if the Lord cannot deny it, or doe trauers it, and it is found against him, then shall the woman haue so much of the lands holden in Chiualry, as together with that shee hath in possession already, may make vp iust a third part of her husbands inheritance. If the inheritance were all of soccage tenure, the widdow being gardian cannot indow her selfe de la pluis beale, but shee shall be allowed a third part in her accompt for so long time, as shee is

Guardian,

Gardian, for if she bring her Writ of Dower in this case against the heire he cannot plead her gardinship, and that she may indow her selfe, See 45. Edw. 3. fol. 6. If such a Feme gardian bring a Writ of Dower against one whom her husband infeofed with warranty, hee shall not pray that she indow her selfe, for he may vouch the heire which Gardine in Chivalry cannot doe. It is no good plea for Gardine in Chivalry to say the Demandant was gardian in soccage, &c. but hee must shew that she is gardian in soccage iour del brief purchase, and this is good till shee have shewed by replication the land devested from her possession.

If a widdow gardian in facto, of some lands that were her husbands, and holden in Chivalry, purchase her Writ of Dower against another Gardian in Chivalry, hee shall not plead the speciall matter, and plead vt supra, for the wardship is here to the widdowes owne use and profit.

SECT. VII.

Assignement of Dower by the King. Statutum prerogatiue ca. 4 fact. 17. Ed. 2.

THe Statute is that after the deathes of husbands which held of the King in Capite, the King shall assigne Dower, yea although the heire be of full age, Vidue si voluerunt. And such widdowes before assignation of Dower, whether the heire bee of full age or under, shall sweare not to marry without the Kings licence: If they doe marry sans licence, the King shall take into his hands as a distresse all the Lands and Tenements holden of him in Dower, so that the woman shall take no profit of it, till shee or her husband have satisfied the Kings will by fine, which was wont to be tempore regis Henrici patris regis. Ed. 2. saith the Statute, at full yeerely value of the whole Dower, nisi vberiorem gratiam habuerint mulieres. And women which bee themselues Tenants in Capite of inheritance, what age soeuer they be of, shall sweare likewise not to marry without the Kings licence. Si fecerint, terræ capiantur eodem modo in manus Regis, &c. This Statute is proued to bee but confirmation of the common Law, 24. H. 3. Prerogatiue 27. in Fitzherbert, and by ma. Char c.7. nul a vidua distringatur ad se maritandum dummodo voluerit viuere sine marito: Ita tamen quod securitatem faciat, quod se non maritabit sine assensu nostro, si de nobis tenuerit vel sine assensu domini sui si de alio tenuerit. Fitzb. in natu. br 263. shewes the manner of indowment by the King: The widdow must come into Chancery, and make oath not to marry sans licence, whereupon the King may make the Assignement in the Chancery, and direct his Writ to the Escheator, certifying him that hee hath assigned a third part of such lands, with a third part of the liberty of Court view of franckpledge, &c. commanding him to make liuery of the same to haue in Dower, or the woman may after she hath sworne, haue a writ reciting her oath, and commanding the Escheator to make assignement. But the most vsuall course is vt antea.

And the King though hee hath committed custody of lands to another person, may assigne Dower to the widdow in Chancery notwithstanding, and shee shall haue a Writ to the Escheator, yea and the King may grant a Writ to the Escheator, commanding him to take surety of the widdow not to marry sans licence, and then to assigne her Dower, as præcipimus tibi, accepto sacramento, &c. assignari & liberari facias, &c.

If the Tenant which is dead held by Chiualry of some Bishopricke or such like which is in the Kings hands by vacancie, the widdow must demand her Dower in Chancery, and she shall haue a Writ for her Assignement to the Escheator, but in this case shee sweares not to marry sans licence. So is it also when Dower is demanded of lands, holden of a common person in Chiualry, where the heire is in the Kings ward per nonage.

And

And the King may assigne Dower in Chancery rendring rent to him, because the lands assigned doe exceed a iust third part of the Tenements, whereof Dower is assignable. If the widdow be so weake or impotent that shee cannot travell to the Chancery to take her oath, and demand Dower, she may sue a speciall Writ to some person, both to take her oath, and to receiue Atturney, whom she will constitute to sue in her stead. If livery bee made to the heire being of full age with a reservation of Dower, to be assigned to the King, and then the widdow commeth into the Chancery for Dower as shee must doe, there shall goe a speciall Writ to the Escheator, to warne the heire that he be in Chancery at a certaine day, and the widdow shall bee appointed the same day to receive her Assignement. But if the Writ of Livery directed to the Escheator bee generall, without clause of *salua dota per nos assignanda*, the widdow must now sue for her Dower by Writ of Dower against the heire. If the King when he makes livery reserves Assignement of Dower to himselfe in his Writ to the Escheator, now whether the widdow come and demand dower in Chancery, or demand no dower, yet the reversion is in the heire after assignement, for after the death of Tenant in Dower the heire shall not sue any new livery. Because the first writ commands all the lands to be delivered, and so the Escheator doth deliver all, nothing being reserved to the King, but onely Assignement of Dower. If after this Assignement it be surmised by the heire, or other body, that the land which the woman hath, is of far greater value than it was made by the extent, &c. if the excesse be found and returned, a *Scire facias* shall goe forth to cause the woman to come and shew cause why she should not take a new Indowment.

If she appeare and cannot gainesay the matter, or if she were warned and make default, it seemeth in both cases, she shall be endowed a new. So that parcell of the lands which she hath, shall be taken from her, or the King may, if hee will, make assignment altogether new, by a new

Writ

Writ to the Viscount. If the widow after she is sworne and indowed, doe marrie sans licence, the King sends to the Escheator to seise those lands, which she holdeth in Dower, by a Writ reciting the oath, the indowment and marriage with this in it, Nos contemptum huiusmodi nolentes transire impunitũ, necnon indemnitati nostræ volentes prospicere, tibi præcipimus (si ita est) tunc omnia terras & tenement̃ quæ tenet in Dote, &c. capias in man' nostr̃, Ita quod de exitibus inde prouenientibus nobis respondeas ad scaccarium nostrum quousque nobis de Forisfactura ad nos inde pertinen' satisfactur̃ fuerit. Thus far Fitzherbert.

Stamford argueth, whether Fitzherbert deliuer the Law rightly or no, in this that he saith, the King may assigne Dower in Chancerie, though hee haue committed ouer the wardship of land to some other body: for many writs are in the yeare bookes brought against the Committee in such a case. And in some bookes the woman recouers Dower, the King neuer being made priuie: As titulo aid del roy 23. Fitzh. is the case 4. H. 7. fol. 1 Action of Dower was against the Kings Committee during the heires nonage, the Defendant shewed how it was found by office, that the husbands father tenant to the King, died seised hauing issue, the husband which entred sans office, and died, leauing his heire vnder age, all which matter was found by office: whereupon the King seised, committed the land to the Defendant, &c. Iudgement si actione [illegible]

And the widow was adiudged dowable. Bryan, who at the first was in minde to procœd no further without aid of the King, when hee had considered the Statute de Bigamis, cap. 3. awarded presently that the woman should recouer Dower. The Statute is, Vbi custodes hereditatis maritorum suor̃ custodias habent ex dono vel concessione regis, siue custodes rerum petitarum teneant, siue heredes dictorum tenementorum vocentur ad warrantiam si excipiant quod sine rege respondere non possunt, non ideo supersedeatur, quin in loquela p̃dicta prout iustus fuerit procedatur. Stamford noteth some bookes wherein is found, that

that heires in custodie of Committees vouched to Warrantie, haue come in and had aid of the King, directly contrarie to this third Chapter de Bigamis. But whether the Kings grant in those cases were Durante minoritate, or Durante bene placito, it appeares not in the bookes; and that makes a great difference.

Likewise if the Writ of Dower be against the Committee of a Committee: And if Wardship be committed to the widdow without exception or foreprize of Dower, she is concluded to claime any Dower during the Wardship. In Stamfords opinion the new Nat. Brev. and the case supra 4. H. 7. doe not agree. Howbeit for my part I finde not the repugnancie; for as the King may assigne Dower to his widdowes, though the heire be of full age, Vidua si voluerit, so Fitzherbert saith hee may assigne Dower if he will, though he haue committed the land, &c. And this doth not denie, but rather affirme that in some case the Committee may assigne Dower: If the Committee (as Stamford himselfe confesseth) assigne Dower to one that is not dowable, or if his assignation exceed iust measure, the King may reforme it. And if a woman endowed by the Kings Committee will marrie sans licence, because she stands vnsworne, for in the Common place is no swearing in this point, her lands are neuer a whit lesse subiect to seizure for the contempt, therefore in the end he concludeth, that where a Ward is committed ouer, the woman hath election, whether shee will sue to the King in Chancerie, or at Common Law against the Committee, vnlesse it be where the grant of a Ward is but Durante bene placito, for in that case of necessitie the suit must be to the King. See Sir Edw. Cokes Institutes, fol. 38. the reason why a Writ of Dower is maintenable against the Committee of the King.

Stamford thwarteth Fitzherbert also in that that hee saith, a widdow must demand Dower against the heire, which hath Liuerie without clause of Salua dote per nos assignand'; for when Liuerie is before Assignement of Dower,

Dower, there is commonly a saving in the Writs of Liverie, if so be the woman were found to be wife, &c. by the office. And if she be not found by the Inquisition, then there is a leaving out of Salua Dote, &c. in suing of generall Liverie. Indeed if she were not found to be the Kings Tenants wife in the office, the heire may safely sue Liverie without any such saying: But Stamford agrees with Onslow Plowdē 32. in the case of Mynes, that for Assignation of Dower, if the King have not expressely relinquished it, though the Liverie be sans clause of salua Dote, &c. yet this makes no such waiving of the prerogative, but that the King may assigne Dower to a widdow, that by an office is found to have beene wife to the Kings Tenant at the time of his death, for without so much it seemes she can neither demand it in Chancerie of the King, nor of the Committee, nor of the heire in the Common place, quere vide fol. 109. Prerogative of not assigning. The King hath a prerogative aswell of not assigning, as of assigning Dower. As if the husbands Feoffee in a writ of Dower against him call to Warrantie the heire in the wardship of the King, &c. the woman shall recover against the Tenant, and no recoverie shall be as yet against the heire: But neither any common person, nor yet the Kings Committee of wardship, shall have this prerogative: But for the King himselfe, if in the case Judgement to recover in value be given for the Tenant, he must stay for execution till the Kings hands be amoved, &c.

If a woman be endowed by her husbands Feoffee, of such lands as the husband did not die seised of, whereof also for this reason the King can have no wardship. Stamfords opinion is, that she cannot marrie sans licence.

For by 26. Assisarum Pl. 57. it appeareth that where a woman was endowed, by Gardian in Chivalrie, who was afterward attainted of treason, and his Seigniorie forfeited to the King, she must hold now of the King, and not of the heire which was in reversion of the land: Hee accords with Fitzherbert, that the Statute of Prerogative

is

is understood onely of lands holden in capite, and therefore she must demand Dower of lands holden of a Bishopricke, or of Tenant in capite, when the temporalities, or the heire are in Custodia regis, she must be indowed in Chancery, but she may marrie when she list, and shall take no oath to the contrarie: Also if a widdow will relinquish her Dower of lands holden in capite, she may marrie sans licence. And see Dyer 3. M. 123. b. affirmeth, that the wife of Tenant paravaile shall not be sworne as widdow of the King in the Chancery, when her Dower is assigned to her. The reason per Stamford is the copulative connexion of Et si se maritaverit, to the former words of the Statute of demanding Dower, and swearing not to marrie: The words si viduæ voluerint, he takes to imply no more but election of refusall, or taking of Dower, and that is manifest by the last clause of the Statute.

But by Fitzherberts writ, which hee sets downe for forme of seisure, when a widdow is married sans licence, it appeares that the King may grant to another the marriage of his widdow or widdowes, and for marriage before agreement with such a Grantee the King may seize, and composition with such a Grantee by Baron or Feme before or after marriage, is as good as if it were with the King himselfe. But now by the Statute 32. H. 8. cap. 46. This composition is given to the Master of the Wards and Liveries, with three of the Councell of that Court, who have also authoritie to tax according to the Statute of Prerogative, a reasonable fine for marriage sans licence.

How much it ought to be is plaine by the Statute, as also what lands are subiect to the Statute, as also what lands are subiect to seisure aswell of the husbands lands as of the wives. If that were reason, saith Fitzherbert, a womans inheritance might be seised too, Et semble a moy, the King cannot grant marriage of his widdowes as he may of his wards; for a widdow may remaine sole without penaltie, or paying for it, by Mag. Chart. cap. 7.

But

But Stamford includeth, that a widdow endowed of lands holden in capite by the Kings Committee, or husbands heire, though vnsworne is not freed from marriage sans licence, for she is presently as soone as she is endowed, tenant to the King, and not to the heire which is in reuersion, yet only the heire is he, which shall haue action of waste against her; but if trespasse bee done vpon the ground, she may haue a writ out of Chancerie, supposing entrie vpon the Kings possession. And Auowrie to bee made by the King resteth onely vpon her, as holdeth Wood, 1. H. 7. fol. 17. and 4. H. 7. 1.

Now note that Endowment in Chancerie is of such strength, that be it by wrong or by right, it cannot be auoyded by plea without suit in Chancerie: And if it bee too little, the woman must stand in her owne harmes, that hath once attempted it in Chancerie, bee shee within age, or of full age, as appeares, 18. Ed. 3. fol. 29.

If any office bee trauersed, because the land is holden not of the King, but of some other Lord, who therefore hath an Ouster le maine vna cum exitibus, yet Dower which is already assigned remaineth vndefeated, till another suit be made in Chancerie to auoid it.

Yet in this case, because Admeasurement, is no preiudice to the King of whom the land is not holden, the Lord that tendreth trauerse, may haue a Writ of Admeasurement at ẏ Common Law. And the heire may haue Admeasurement of Dower assigned by his Ancestor: But an Abator cannot haue Admeasurement, neither can Gardian in fait haue Admeasurement vpon assignment by Gardian indroit, nor if the heire were at full age at his Ancestors death, and died, his heire being within age can the Gardian haue Admeasurement, but where a woman is endowed in Chancerie, and afterward the heire, or some other for the King surmiseth excesse of value, it may bee admeasured beginning with Scire facias, as Fitzherbert hath taught supra, and fol. 249. a. If the husband had land in diuers Counties, by reason whereof diuers writs of

diem

diem clausit extremum were awarded after his death into euerie of those Counties, the widdow cannot be endowed till such time as all the writs be returned into Chancery. If after she is once endowed in Chancerie, her Dower be recouered from her by any title, she hath no remedie but to remoue the record of this recouerie into Chancerie, and then vpon the first record which sheweth that she was endowed, and vpon this other of recouerie she shall haue Scire facias, reciting both the records against him which is tenant of the two parts, to reseise them into the Kings hands, and so to bee newly endowed, but not to recouer any dammages, though dammages were recouered against her, Lib. 43. Assisar. Pl. 32. for by the latter part of the Statute Prerogatiue, cap. 4. It seemeth the King hath lost his prerogatiue, and that he is bound by, West 1. cap. 22. Note that woman Joynt purchaser with her husband is not within this Law to fine for her marriage, when she becomes a widdow (say I) therefore well fare a Joynture.

SECT. VIII.

Suit for Dower at the Common Law.

Thus we haue seene how, and when a widdow must sue for Dower in the Chancerie, viz. when either her husband died the Kings tenant in capite, or by knights seruice, his heire vnder age, or otherwise tenant to some other, whose lands are in the Kings hands by vacancie, or nonage of the heire. But if the husband, which held in Socage, or by knights seruice, not of the King, did giue or alien any manner of way his lands, or were disseised of them, or died seised of them. The widdow, if by simple demand she cannot obtaine her Dower to bee assigned her, may haue a writ of Dower Vnde nihil habet at the Common Law against him which is tenant of the Franke-

tenement,

tenement by the old Nat. breuium this writ is maintainable against him which hath possession of the land, by what manner soeuer, or against the Gardian in Chiualrie; in this or like forme, Rex Vicecomiti, &c. command A. to render to B. which was the wife of C. her reasonable Dower, quæ ad eam contingit de libero tenemento, quod fuit prædict C. sometime her late husband in D. vnde nihil habet, & vnde queritur quod A. ei deforciat, &c. & nisi fecerit & B. fecerit te securum de clamore prosequendo, &c. summoneas A. vt sit apud Westm ostensurus. If the Dower were ad ostium Ecclesiæ, or ex assensu patris, or otherwise there is mention made of it in the writ. In London there may be a writ from the King to the Maior and Sheriffes in these words, Quod Iusticietis A. quod iuste & sine delatione, & secundum consuetudinem ciuitatis nostræ London redd' B. quæ fuit vxor C. rationabilem dotem, &c. Et Iusticietis D. quod iuste, &c. Whereby appeares that a widdow in London may haue a writ of Dower against seuerall tenents by seuerall Iusticies, as well as at the Common Law seuerall Precipes against seuerall tenants all in one writ, the Processe in the Common Place, is summons, Grand cape & pettie cape, in the Common Place this writ of Dower, vnde nihil habet, must be returned into the Kings Court, Et per grand reason, saith Britton cap. 10.4. For if two or more women should striue, euerie of them affirming her selfe to be the lawfull wife of him which is dead, not minding to be buried with him, as is the corse in India, but to get a third of his lands: This must be tried by Certificate from the Bishop, vnto whom if any but the King should write for the deciding of debate, it might fall out to be all in vaine, because none hath power but the King to compell the Bishop to make Certificate. In the next Chapter Britton sheweth, that if the Tenant vouch to warranty one which appeareth according to summons, the Plea shall proceed betwixt the Plaintiffe, & the Warrantor, or Vouchee, the Tenant keeping seisen till the Warrantie be determined.

Then

Then if the Garrantie cannot be denied, nor the womans right disproued, if that which she demandeth were certainly assigned to her for Dower from her husband, shee shall recouer against the Tenant, Et le tenant le value.

But if the demand bee of no other than reasonable Dowery the woman shall recouer in value against the Warrantor, and the Tenant shall hold his land in peace: If so be this Warrantor be vnder age, yet the Law fauoureth widdowes so much, that the plaint shal not attend his full age. Therefore if the Tenant shew forth any Charter, Déed, or speciall cause, whereby the Court may perceiue that the Infant is bound to Warrantie by the Ancestors act, he shall answer presently, what age soeuer he be of. And though the Infant in ward be aliened by his Gardian or Gardians from hand to hand, this shall not preiudice the Voucher, for alwayes he shall vouch to warrantie the Heire and not the Gardian, who is bound to present his ward so vouched in Court without difference, whether it be one or many parceners. Thus saith Britton, and 48. Ed. 3. fol. 5. agréeth, that he which voucheth an heire vnder age, must vouch him in ward de vn ciel. If he be a ward, it is said there also, that hee which voucheth an heire at full age, must shew a Déed, quære. But when the lands are in the Gardians owne possession to his owne profit and vse, the writ of Dower must bee brought against the Gardian, and not against the Infant. 46. Ed. 3. fol. 19. Where Mowbray saith, where an Infant is vouched in ward of the King, the woman shall recouer Dower maintenant. 3. H. 6. fol. 17. It was agréed per curiam, that in Action of Dower, if the tenant vouch the heire in the Kings ward within the same Countie where the writ is brought, the Demandant shall not recouer before the warrantie be determined: but the Law is contra, if the Voucher had prayed summons in another Countie, for then the Demandant should recouer maintenant, yet by the Register fol. 7. if in a writ of Dower the tenant vouch in Durham, the Demandant shall abide

S triall

triall of the warrantie, and not recouer presently. But by Fitzherbert for a rule in titulo, Voucher, if the tenant vouch in a forraine Countie, shee shall recouer maintenant, and neuer attend triall of the warrantie, but when Voucher is in mesme le countie. If the heire vouched to warrantie, after hee hath appeared and counterpleaded the warrantie, or before appearance, being lawfully summoned do make default, the Defendant shall haue execution against him maintenant, if hee haue lands within the Countie, Brooke Dower 5. And also Dower the 65. when the heire is vouched in the same Countie, the woman shall recouer against the heire. Dyer 3. Eliz. 202. In Dower the tenant vouch the heire in the same Countie, who comes as one that hath nothing by descent in fee, and renders Dower, the tenant auers, that he hath assets by descent, quære if he should not say in fee, for by Weston and Browne, if the lands be in taile, it doth not saue the tenants lands. And the opinion of the Court was, that the Demandant shall haue Judgement presently against the heire if he hath lands, &c. and if not against the tenant, and that before the issue of the assets tried.

1 Ed. 3. fol. 24. In a writ of Dower against Tenant for life, if he vouch his Lessor, which is heire to the husband, the woman shall recouer against the Tenant, and he ouer against the Vouchee. But when the heire is vouched by Charter of his Ancestor, the Demandant shall recouer against the Vouchee, and the Tenant shall hold in peace: Yet in a Writ of Dower against Lessee for life of the Barons demise, if the heire bee vouched to Warrantie (though here the reuersion which is the cause of the Warrantie were made by the Baron) the Demandant shall recouer against the Tenant, and he against the heire. If the tenant vouch in a writ of Dower, and the Vouchee counterplead the Warrantie, the woman shall recouer maintenant, though in other actions it bee otherwise. 46. Ed. 3. fol. 25. and 49. Ed. 3. fol. 23. In a Writ of Dower the Tenant vouched himselfe, to saue the estate tails.

taile. 2. H. 4. fol. 18. in Dower the Tenant vouched the heire, Processe went on to sequatur sub suo periculo sicut alias, the Vouchee came not, it was awarded the Demandant should recover against the Vouchee, if hee had lands in the same Countie. If not, that shee shall recover against the Tenant, and hee over in value. But first it was examined if the Vouchee were heire to the Baron.

21. Ed. 3. fol. 30. In Dower the tenant voucheth the Barons heire in ward of the demandant per cause de nurture, shewing the Ancestors Deed, he was compelled to plead in barre, because now the woman might be endowed De la plus beale, for Gardeine pur nurture, hath alwayes intendment to Soccage tenure. Vide Brooke Dower 42.

5. Ed. 3. The fathers wife was endowed, the Grandmother brought a writ of Dower against her, she vouched the heire in reversion, the Demandant recovered against the tenant, and shee against the heire a third part of two parts remaining, but not in value. See Brooke Dower 79. If the Grandmother die, the mother may enter into the first dower, and the heire into the second.

SECT. IX.

Plees in a writ of Dower.

ADmitting there were no Voucher, let us run over other matters usually pleaded. 14. H. 4. 33. in Dower was demanded a third part of two mils & of other lands, ŷ tenant asked Judgement of the plaintiffe: for they were during the whole time of coverture, but the site of two mills, viz. tofts. 38. Ed. 3. fol. 13. In a writ of dower against one as Gardian of land, and heire of K. de R. the defendant answered that the Infants father was I. de R. Judgement del briefe, and if the writ were good, hee was ready to render dower: You cannot, said Knyvet, plead to the writ & render dower both at one day, so the demandant praying Iudgement, seisen was awarded her. And because she auerred that the defendant was not touts temps prist, to render dower, an Inquest of dammages was awarded, and that execution should cease till the Inquest were past.

13. Ed. 4. fol. 7. In action of dower the tenant pleaded touts temps prist de render Dower, & uncore est. The demandant said that I. S. her husband died seised, and that such a day and yeere she required the tenant to indow her at Dale, which refused, &c. he replyed that at the same day he offered to goe with her to the lands, and to assigne her dower, but she refused, sans ceo, that he refused: The Court held the Issue well taken by this speciall pleading. But if hee had said generally and barely hee refused not, some thought it had not beene sufficient, insomuch as it denies not the request.

Bryan said the demandant here might not haue seuerall Iudgements of one thing, for note, shee was to recouer dower vpon the first plea, but all the other Iustices were of opinion cleere, that shee should haue Iudgement of Dower maintenant, and 18. Ed. 3. In action of Dower Iudgement was to recouer dower with an inquest for dammages. As in a Quare impedit the Plaintiffe may haue one writ to the Bishop, and another to the Sheriffe to enquire of dammages.

Likewise 14. H. 8. fol. 25. in a plea of dower vpon confession the demandant recouered Iudgement, and after Iudgement auerring that her husband died seised, shee prayed a writ to enquire of dammages, & habuit: for if the demandant in dower will recouer dammages, shee must euer surmize that her husband died seised, though the Tenant confesse the Action, or plead but onely to the Writ, and in the end of her Demise shee may maintaine the Writ, for sur plee & briefe, the dying seised appeares not, without surmise, &c. 22. H. 6. fol. 44.

SECT.

SECT. X.

Deteiner of Evidence.

By Perkins, none may deteine Dower for deteining of evidence but only the heire to whom the evidence belongeth, and the heire, when he pleads, must shew what the evidence is, &c. And they must concerne the lands discended, unto him whereof Dower is demanded; for hee may not deteine Dower of land which the Charters concerne not, or for Charters concerning his purchased lands, or those whereof he hath no seisin. Aliter, if they concerne some reversion descended; But if the heire come in vouched to warranty by the Barons feofee, hee cannot plead this Deteiner of Evidence, because in verity the land is another mans to whom most rightly the Charters belong. But one copercener may have this plea after partition against her mother or other Demandant in Dower, though the evidence concerne the other parceners and her all alike; see 41. Titulo Dower in Brooke, If a widdow that is with child deteine evidence against her husbands daughter and heire, or other heire collaterall, it shall bee no sufficient plea to delay Dower. 1. Perkins 70. & 71.

18. Hen. 8. fol. 1. The heire said, the Demandant deteined a bagge ensealed with the evidence, concerning the land, which if hee would deliver hee was ready to render Dower, bone plee per Curiam.

33. Hen. 6. fol. 51. The Tenant pleaded for part of the land, whereof Dower was demanded non tenure, for another part detinue of Charters, for another part Joyntenancie which his father, for a fourth part demanded view: but it might not be granted, because he tooke notice to himselfe of that part by pleading to the rest. And the Plaintiffe to his plea of survivor pleaded his release made to the father her husband in his life time, Issint seisi que Dowre, &c. The plea of Evidence detained as Litleton

cleton said, went to the whole action, quod fuit negatum, vide Brooke ry. Dower 4 but he was forced to shew what evidence he deteineth, viz. a speciall Charter.

41. Ed. 3. The Tenant pleaded a withholding of Evidence certaine, concerning his inheritance, and shewes what: Et que il ad estre toutes temps prist, &c. the woman made title to two deeds, by gift to her husband and her selfe: and for the other Evidence, shee said whereas the Defendant claimed as brother and heire to her husband, shee kept it to the use of her child: si oue sq̄ soit infeint q̄ terra h ur si dien luy done nostre, and issue was taken, whether she were inf int die obitus mariti, not whether shee were infeint per son baron die obitus. And that booke of 41. Edw. 3. is cited for law, in Sir Edw. Cokes 7. Rep. fol. 9 that a woman may deteine Charters for the heire in ventre sa mere. And 22. Hen. 6. fol. 16. It was agreed that deteiner of Evidence is no plea in an Action of Dower, unlesse it concerne Inheritance discended. Et sic videtur ibidem, saith Brooke, that if it concerne inheritance, though it be not the very land, whereof Dower is demanded, the plea is good. 9 Edw. 4. to plea of Charters deteined, the Demandant answered veies cy le fait & pria dower: the Court reading and perceiving it to bee the deed, &c. gave judgement for Dower.

14 Hen. 6. fol. 4 The Tenant pleaded detinue of a chest with two fines and other Charters: p Martin Justice, if the Chest were open he ought to declare every deed, specially by it selfe, and so it is likewise in action of detinue, for a Chest open with evidence, quod curia concessit.

2. Hen. 7. fol 6. Is set downe, the reason why the certainty of evidence deteined must bee showne, viz. That the Jury may be more able to make their verdict, and the Court to iudge to whom they appertaine: for if they belong to the Defendants purchase, he is put to a Writ of detinue.

And 6. Eliz. Dyer 230. see, a man seised of foure acres soccage land, and of one deed or Charter concerning those lands,

lands, by his last will in writing devised three of his acres to his youngest sonne in fee, the fourth acre to his wife for life, the remainder to a stranger in fee, he dies, his wife got the deed, entred into her acre, and the sonne into the three acres devised to him, the woman brings a Writ of Dower, for a third of these three acres. The sonne pleads detinue of the Charter, which if she would deliver, he is and alwayes had beene ready to render Dower: shee shewed the whole cause by way of replication, & upon that the other side demurred. It seemeth (saith Dyer) that this plea serveth for none, save only the Barons heire, and for no land, but that which is descended: And not for the heire himselfe if he come in by voucher, or as Tenant by receipt in default of Tenant for life: Where hee is no more but tenant per admittance, for such a one cannot say, that he hath beene toutes temps prist a render Dower si &c. Neither can gardian in chivalry have this plea, for he cannot have a writ of detinue of the heires evidence: And this plea is a bar for no lands but those which the Charters deteined do concerne. 22.H.6. Where Newton saith, the reason of this barre is, because the evidence being seene and looked into, may yeeld matter to barre the Demandant of her Dower, for such lands therefore as the Charters doe not touch, Dower shall be granted of them, this plea notwithstanding. Also certainty must ever bee alleaged in this case, if the evidence bee not in some bag, box, or chest, sealed or locked up. And note, the Defendant supra was not named heire by the demandant, neither had he inabled himselfe to this plea as heire, therefore the Court might take it indifferently: As in a quare impedit, if the incumbent bee named Clericus, the Court takes him for a Disturber if hee inable not himselfe as incumbent, or person impersonee. Another fault was found in this Tenants conclusion of his plea, because hee said uncore prist a render Dower, but in very deed hee relied not againe on the condition if the Demandant would deliver the Charter according to the ancient booke of entries.

And at the last iudgement was giuen pro dote.

See Sir Edw. Cokes 9. Rep. in Anna Beddingfelds case 1. That the Charters ought to concerne the land whereof Dower is demanded, and not other lands descended to the heire. 2. He that pleads that plea ought to shew the certainty whereof a certaine issue may be ioyned, or that they are in a chest or box sealed, which import sufficient certainty, whereof certaine issue may be taken, and in both cases action of detinue may be brought by the heire. 3. No stranger although that he bee Tenant of the land, and hath the euidences conueyed vnto him, may plead in a Writ of Dower deteiner of Charters, but that plea is only in priuity for the heire of the husband. Also the heire shall be in the degree of a stranger in fiue cases. First, if the heire hath the land by purchase. Secondly, if the heire hath deliuered the Charters to the wife. Thirdly, so the heire be not immediate vouchee, namely, by the Tenant in the Writ of Dower, but by his vouchee. Fourthly, if the heire comes in as vouchee, hauing no lands in the County where the land is demanded. Fifthly, if he comes in as Tenant by receit. And Gardian in Chiualry may not plead deteinement of Charters, for hee may not conclude his plea if the Demandant will deliuer to him the Charters, &c. for the Charters which concerne the heritage of the heire shall not be deliuered to the Gardian as it is adiudged in 10. Edw. 3. 49.

SECT. XI.

Deteining of the heire.

AS the heire only may deteine Dower for deteining of euidence, so the Gardian in Chiualry onely may deteine Dower for deteining the heire, and that he may plead and conclude q̄ il ad en touts temps prist, for the ward belongeth to him.

It

If a widow eloigne the infant or heire of her husband, though some other body haue him by her deliuery, yet the Gardian in Chiualry may detaine Dower, except shee can redeliuer him to the Gardian in as good plight, as hee was at the time of the eloignment, that is, unmarried if he were eloigned unmarried. But a woman nourishing her owne Infant, the sonne or heire which her husband left her, if a stranger clayming as Gardian take him from her, the right Lord shall not detaine dower for this cause. But if a woman take and remoue the heire from the place where hee was nourished at time of the Barons death; Now if a stranger wrongfully take him from her, the true and right Gardian may detaine dower. And this matter is pleadable by Gardian in Chiualrie, though hee come into Court, by reason that the heire is bouched to be in his ward; for by right the custodie of the Infant can appertaine to none but to him, unlesse it be by his grant or agreement. Certaintie is required in pleading of this detainer, aswell as in the other, viz. that she which demandeth dower hath eloigned or detained J. S. by name, son, or daughter W. &c. 22. H. 6. fol. 16. 2. H. 7. fol. 6.

SECT. XII.

Possession in the Demandant.

39. Ed. 3. 17. Dower was demanded, a third part of a carue of land; the tenant said the demandant her selfe was seised of a third part of it already: Iudgement de briefe per Knyuet it was no good plea, without shewing who assigned it, or that she recouered it. For if shee were in by disseisen, shee must haue dower of the other two parts remaining: neuerthelesse by which the tenant was chased to answer for the two parts. 7. of H. 6. 33. & 34. In action of dower against two, one said he had assigned rent, out of the land six shillings and eight pence annuall

annuall to the demandant for terme of her life, which she accepted, &c. The other pleaded touts temps prist, &c. The assignment was holden a good plea, &c. the demandant said she never agreed. Newton, per Strange, she was to recover a moytie maintenant, though the other plea were not yet tried: for this was a confession of one, and pleader in bar of the other.

2. H.4. fol.7. A Lady sued in Chancerie to be endowed of divers Mannors which were her husbands, where the heire was in gard of the King, as was found by the Diem clausit extremum there returned, and because it appeared that King Richard had committed wardship of the lands and body of the heire till full age of the said heire to her by patent without forprise, or mention of dower, shee was ousted of dower per agard de toutes les Iustices, till full age of the heire, simile, 11. of H.4. in case of the Lady Arrundell. Fitzherbert saith likewise, If a woman take a lease for yeares of land, whereof she is dowable, she shall not sue for Dower during these yeares, Nat. br. 149. e. Bracton propoundeth to be considered what shall be done when the widdow brings her Writ of Dower, vnde nihil habet, and yet it is so that she hath part of her Dower already: If (saith he) it be proued, or she cannot deny it, cadit breue, and she shall not recover the residue, but by Writ de recto de dote: Therefore let her accept no part of her Dower, before she purchase her Writ, and let it containe all the Deforcers, be they in one Countie, or in many.

When they are so put together, if now she accept any thing of her Dower without Judgement, the acceptation of part shall be no exception against her, for she may confesse satisfaction for that part: If peraduenture shee haue already taken part of her Dower from some one person before the obtaining or purchase of her Writ, let his name and the summons for him be in the Writ notwithstanding, and then if it be obiected she hath accepted part, shee may acknowledge that hee hath satisfied her for his

part,

part, and whether before or after suit is not greatly to be stood upon. But if he of whom she received part be not named in the Writ, she cannot against the obiection of acceptance reply, that the land which she accepted is not in the same Towne, but in another. For vnde nihil habet in the Writ non debet referri ad villas sed ad dotem. It is nothing worth therefore, to say she hath nothing in tali villa, if she hath any thing nomine dotis, wheresoever it be it is not then materiall. And when a woman replyeth nihil habet, her defence shall not be per legem that is wager of Law, but per patriam. Likewise, if a woman plead that she hath nothing nomine dotis but by some other title, as ratione custodiæ & huiusmodi, Inquisition may be in the Countie where it is supposed shee receiued Dower, to finde whether shee haue any thing in Dower of the tenements which were her husbands, and if shee had, and now hath not, to enquire what is become of it, this was a Norff. case of Holda the late wife of W. in Trinitie Terme, 4. H. 4. as Bracton in his fourth Booke 13. Chapter and fol. 312. relates vnto me.

SECT. XIII.

Ne vnques seisi que Dower, &c.

There are other pleas that goe to the action and verie right of Dower, as Ne vnques seisi que Dower, &c. id est, The husband had neuer any seisin or state of Inheritance, whereof the wife can claime Dower, see 45. E. 3. fol. 13. The tenant in Dower leased her whole estate to the heire, rendring rent for terme of her life, the heire died, and this was adiudged a seisin, whereof the heires wife might demand Dower, though the first tenant in Dower were still aliue; for the lease was a Surrender, and if a stranger had entred immediately after the heires death, his heire must haue had a Mordancester: Ergo, said one,

one, the wife dowable. Yet marke this case ibid. a man seised, &c. in fee simple dies, his sonne entreth and he dies, the sons sonne enters and endowes his Aylesse: she dies, a stranger abateth. In this case it is cleere, the sons wife shall have no Dower of the portion assigned to the Aylesse: though the sonnes sonne may have a Mordancester per Kirton, Finch, and Mowbray: But betwixt this case and the other, they say, is great oddes; for here the Grandmother endowed, was in from her husband, and the sonnes possession and estate howsoever, to his heire in whom the fee rested it were not destroyed, but hee might bring a Mordancester, yet to his wife it was cleane adnihilate, whereas in the first case, the Fee and Francktenement not a woit impeached by the life of her which surrendred, were perfectly conioyned in the Baron to whom the Surrender was made. And if a reversion be granted to I. S. of certaine lands per fait in pais, in which lands I. T. and his wife have estate for life, which doe atturne and afterward surrender, there is no doubt but I S. his wife, if hee die, shall have Dower, though it bee indeed defeasible after death of T. K. if his wife survive and will undoe the Surrender: whereas in our first case the Surrender is no way avoydable, but the heires wife shall pay rent according to her portion per Finch, ibid. 14. Ed. 4. fol. 6. Tenant by the courtesie granted his estate to him in reversion, rendring rent with clause of re-entrie for non payment, the Grantee married, the rent was arreare, tenant per le curtesie re-entred, hee in the reversion died, his wife was barred of Dower, for the Surrender might well bee upon condition.

2. H. 4. fol. 22. In action of Dower it was pleaded, that the Demandants husband had nothing in the land, but by Disseisin done to the tenant, Iudgement si action, &c. The woman shewed how her husbands father, having two sonnes, leased his land to the eldest sonne, and to his wife for terme of their lives, and that shee her selfe married

ried

ried with the youngest sonne, the eldest died, and his wife married with the tenant: the father died, the reversion descended to the second sonne, being her husband, the tenants wife died, and he kept possession, the Demandants husband did put him out, he re-entred, she prayed seisin, &c. Brooke thinketh she ought to haue trauersed the Disseisin. And if the Baron had not entred after the death of the eldest sonnes wife, she should not haue béene endowed: yet saith he, quære if without entrie there had not béene a seising in Law, and whether the Francktenement which the tenant had once in right of his wife be determined in puncto by her death.

11. H. 4. 73. In action of Dower the Tenant saith, That N. gaue the land to the Baron and his first wife for terme of their liues, the remainder in taile to the tenant, remainder in Fée to the right heires of the Baron, his first wife died, he married this demandant and then hée died, and the tenant entred, &c. he demands Judgement if of this estate she shall haue Dower.

This amounted plaine to ne vnques seisi que Dower la puit, but per Hanke & Thirn, that plea might not serue, by reason of the Fée simple in remainder, which might ingender doubtfulnesse a layes gentes. But where a lease was made to Baron for life, the reuersion to the Lessor, or remainder to a stranger, there in action of Dower ne vnques seisi, &c. is good, for no manner of Inheritance was in the husband.

11. H. 4. 83. Dower was demanded of twentie pounds rent, respondetur, the Baron had nothing, but ioyntly with J. M. who is yet aliue, Iudgement si Dower, &c. (and he was not compelled to shew whether he pleaded as Tertenant, or as Pernor of the rent) the Demandant replyed, that J. N. had released all his right in the rent to her husband. But because she shewed not the Déed of release, shee pleaded by aduisement of the Court seisie que Dower la puit: Quære of the generall Issue, against the speciall matter.

11. H. 4.

11. H. 4. 88. A woman shall haue Dower of rent purchased by her husband in fee, though hee die before day of payment: And if it be pleaded against her Ne vnques seisi que Dower, &c. she shall not shew the speciall matter, but say seisi que Dower la puit, and shew the matter in euidence.

22. H. 6. 42. per Newton. In action of Dower the tenant plead Joynt estate to the Baron, and J. N. in plein vy, whose estate he hath, the demandant shall not say seisi que dower, &c. vnlesse shee shew how, or trauerse that J. N. tooke nothing by the Feofment.

39. H. 6. fol. 9. Against Dower the Tenant pleaded that J. S. seised in Fee, infeoffed him, and hee leased to the Baron, to hold at will, which estate hee continued all his life time, sans ceo, that he was seised of any such estate que Dower la puit, the Judges ordered that for the long continuance of the possession, and dought des lais gens, all should be entred.

10. H. 6. 17. It is not a good plea against Dower to say the Baron had nothing, but for terme of his life: for this amounts to the generall Issue Ne vnques seisi que Dower la puit: But to say the Baron had nothing, but Joyntenement with A. in fee, and that A. suruiued, &c. This by the Fee simple confessed makes a good plea.

14. H. 6. 5, & 6. In action of Dower the tenant said he was seised, till by the Baron disseised, vpon whom he reentred, Judgement, &c. the Demandant said, that before this tenant had any thing in the land, W. being seised in Fee, infeoffed her husband issint seisi, &c. and she prayed to be endowed, per Martin, the replication is not good, for this might be before the Disseisin, and before couerture too, and if so, then the Baron Ne vnques seisi que Dower la puit. That yee may yet perceiue further how cunning a point it is to take or relinquish this plea rightly, marke well the case, 30. H. 8. Dyer, fol. 41. In a Writ of Dower the issue was Ne vnques seisi que Dower la puit: It was giuen in euidence to the Inquest on the Demandants

dants behalfe, that a feofment was made to the Baron in fee, & ẏ deed of feofment was shewed to the Court, it was answered that long time before the feofment, the Baron was seised to him and his first wife in speciall taile, and how afterward hee discontinued that, and takes backe an estate in fee simple to himselfe by the feofment aforesaid, of which estate hee died seised so that the heire in speciall taile was remitted, and the second wife being now Demandant, not dowable.

Mountague would haue demurred and dismissed the Jury, but the Justices were cleare in opinion that the Jury ought to find for the Demandant, because their charge was only vpon the issue, viz. whether the Baron had euer seisin of such estate, that the wife might haue dower. And they were not to regard the Remitter, but onely to looke to the generall issue giuen them in charge. But if the speciall matter had beene pleaded, the Demandant must needs haue beene barred; for if he which makes a feoffement, with condition to reenter for the condition broken, and then in a Writ of dower brought by the feoffees wife, hee will plead ne vnques seisie que dower, it shall be found against him, Knightly therefore would haue the speciall matter found by the Jury, and a verdict at large, but the Justices would not consent.

Yet tempore Edw. 1. there was a case, that the Baron discontinued his wiues inheritance, and died, his wife recouered against the discontinue, and he died, the discontinues wife brought a Writ of Dower against the woman Recouerer, and she pleaded the generall issue ne vnques seisi que dower la puit. All this matter was found by speciall verdict, and iudgement giuen vpon the issue, thus foolishly ioyned, that the Demandant should recouer Dower, which shee should neuer haue done, had the plea beene good: See and marke well this case: and 21. Edw. 4. fol. 60. and the case 28. Ass. pl. 4.

SECT

Sect. XIV.

Recouerie against the husband.

14.H.4. 33. IN action of Dower the Tenant pleaded a recouery in Assise against the husband, iudgement si action, &c. the Demandant said her husband was seised, &c. and married her, and infeofed the Tenant, and afterward disseised him, against whom the Tenant recouered in Assise, the Baron died, she prayed to bee indowed. The Tenant said he was seised, till by the Baron disseised, against whom hee recouered by Assise sans ceo, that the Baron was seised before the disseisin, que dower la puit, the Demandant said, seised before the disseisen, que dower la puit.

Likewise 47.Edw.3.13. the Baron makes a feofment, and ousteth the feofee, the feofee recouers in assize, the baron dieth now in a writ of Dower, if the feoffee plead recouery in assize, the widdow cannot falsifie the recouery, but she may plead that long time before it, &c. her husband was seised que dower la puit, and the Defendant contra.

12.H.4. 20.21. The Tenant said he brought a Formedone against the husband, which Writ hanging, he shewed to the husband a deed of intailment, whereupon presently he rendred the land in pais to the Tenant, which entred and now auerreth the entaile; Iudgement si action, Thirn said the Statute was si vir reddat aduersario suo de pleno Iusticiarii adiudicent mulieri dotem, but he and the whole Court agreed, that rendring in pais doth not defeat meane estates of them which were neither parties nor priuy to the rendring, and therefore they awarded the woman should recouer Dower. Hanke said, fee simple might not be rendered without liuery and seisin, and where there is Lord and Tenant, the Tenant may not surrender to his Lord: Of falsifying of recoueries I haue spoken already.

Note, If land bee recouered in value against the husband,

band, because of warranty made by his Ancestors, the widdow shall have Dower of those lands notwithstanding: for if the Baron had aliened the land before voucher, it should not have beene recovered in value: Consequently, therefore the womans title is more ancient than the vouchers, which beginneth but the day of vouching. By Fitzh in his Abridgement Dower 129. And his natura brev. 150. d.

SECT. XV.

Ne vnques accouple, &c.

SOmetime the unlawfulnesse of marriage is pleaded in barre of Dower. As 39. Edw. 3. 15. the Tenant pleaded the Demandant was first married to A, and hee living she married B. of whose dowment she claimeth, A. being still alive, this was holden no good pleading, and therefore he added & issint nient accouple in loyall matrimony. The entry was only ne vnques accouple, &c. and a Writ awarded to the Bishop to certifie, but for all such pleas deduced at length by old Writers, as stand upon the invalidity of marriage, I will referre widdowes to that which is gone before of marriage and divorce. The pleas also of under 9. yeeres of age of attainder, of non tenure, ioyntenure, or severall tenure, I will not tarry on them. 39. Ed. 1. fol. 4. A woman brought Dower against two by severall precipes, and one of them prayed ayd of the other as parceners, so that it appeareth that severall tenancie is a good plea in action of Dower, Contra in Assise, Brooke 99.

SECT. XVI.

Plea that the Baron is yet aliue.

The Writ de dote vnde nihil habet affords another exception against Dower, because it saith quondam viri sui, for though the fundamentall cause of dower be matrimony quoad le title, yet as to the possession a woman cannot claime it till matrimony be dissolued, therefore by Fitzherbert, if the Baron take habit of religion, the wife shall not be endowed, till the husband be dead re vera, yet by Britton it is issuable, whether the Baron be entred into religion or no, and that issue shall be tried by the Ordinary, and iudged according to his certificat. But when the deforcer will barre Dower by plea that the husband is yet aliue, if the widdow reply he is dead, the proofe regularly belongs to the Plaintiffe. But if the Defendant say the husband is in plein vy & ceo & est prist auerrer, he must proue his auerment, and sometime both parties shall be heard to make their profe, which if it be alike strong on either side, the Demandant may haue iudgement of seisin, finding surety, such as the Court shall award, to restore, if her husband hereafter bee brought into Court, the land with the issues and profits thereof, in the interim receiued. But if the matter be doubtfull, and the woman cannot finde such surety, the seisen shall remaine where it is, and the plea in suspence to be renewed presummons as occasion shall serue. Britton fo. 25.

SECT. XVII.

Iudgement.

Iudgement in a Writ of Dower is framed according to the substance of the title, and circumstance of the pleading.

pleading. It is touched aboue when or how a woman shall recouer dammages by surmise, that the husband dyed seised.

20. Hen. 3. The Statute of Merton cap. 1. ordeineth concerning widdowes, quæ post mortem virorum expelluntur de dotibus suis & dotes suas vel quarentenam habere non possunt sine placito. That whosoeuer shall deforce them of Dower or quarentine in any tenements, whereof their husbands dyed seised, if they bee conuicted de iniusto deforciamento, they shall render dammages to the widdowes, so much as the Dower should haue béene worth to them from the time of the husbands death, till the day where the widdowes recouer seisen of Dower per Iudicium Curiæ. And the Deforcers shall bee in misericordia Regis neuer awhit the lesse.

It is plaine now that the Baron dying seised, if the wife be deforced she shall recouer dammages, which are sometime comprised in the iudgement of seisin, and sometime awarded after iudgement vpon auerment or surmise vt supra. But for all this Statute of Merton de iniusto deforciamento, a widdow shall not in all cases recouer dammages by this dying seised; for if the Tenant plead toutstemps prist, &c. and it be confessed or found to haue béene so, there is now no fault in him. per Cheyn & Hill. 11. Hen. 4. fol. 40. 41. for euery heire hath right to all the parts of his Ancestors inheritance, till the widdow will be indowed.

The case they say obiected, viz. that in a Writ of Cosinage touts temps prist, will not excuse the Tenant of dammages, is no thing like: for the Occupiour there hath not iust title, &c. Doctor and Student tels vs fol. 82. & 83. that though the husband dieth seised, if his widdow doth not demand Dower, she shall recouer no dammages, for it is a good plea in a Writ of Dower when the Tenants appeare the first day, to say touts temps prist a pæl-der Dower, if it be demanded, and that plea shall excuse him of dammages, but if he had made refusall, he shall bée

 chargeable

chargeable as well for dammages before the request as after. But in Sir Edward Cokes 4. Rep. 30. b. in Shawes Case, a woman recouered Dower by plaint in a Court Baron, and shee recouered dammages from the death of her husband because he died seised, and it doth not appeare that there was any request and refusall. I dare not say that it is Idem ius, whether the heire or his feoffee plead his plea; though I cannot finde any president of dammages giuen vpon it being true, but often sur plea de touts temps prist, the iudgement ended thus, nihil de materia quia venit primo edis, vide 12. Ed. 4. fol. 7. I doe referre the Reader for his better instruction touching this matter, where hee shall finde variety of store, Sir Edward Cokes Comment. vpon Litleton fol. 32. b. The second Chapter of Merton giues power to all widdowes to make wils, as well of Corne growing vpon their dowry lands, as vpon their inheritance, saluis seruitiis dominorum de feodis, quæ de dotibus & aliis tenementis suis debentur. Britton seemeth to be taken with a Chancery spirit, vpon sight of this Statute cap. 103. fol. 250. where he saith, that in euery iudgement of seisin awarded of reasonable Dower, there ought to be a forprise or exception de blees cressaunts & femes fauches, I will subioyne Bracton as an Adiutor, perhaps more orthodox, Dower, saith he, lib. 2. cap. 40. shall be assigned by the heire, if he be of full age, or by the Lord in the heires name, if he be vnderage; And this within forty dayes after the husbands death, for otherwise occurrit tempus & sequantur damna, nisi rationabilis causa excuset. This assignation must be made of the land, as it was by the husband, tilled or vntilled, with the fruits growing vpon it, allowing nothing to the heire or Executor for manuring, husbanding, or culture of it, for of old time it was obserued, that in what case or plight a woman had receiued her Dower, whether it were tilled or vntilled, shee must restore in like plight to the heire, &c. she might not make her Will of any corne growing, or fruit not separated, from the francktenement. Sed

nota

noua superueniente gratia sicut patet de prouisionibus apud Merton: A woman may now ordeine her Testament of corne or fruit growing on her dowry, or seuered growing, all is one. If the husband alien all his lands, and the Tenants need not yeeld dower to the widdow as soone as shee demandeth it, if there bee iust cause of calling to warranty, one or more, successiuely till the heire bee vouched; And all that time the Tenants are not charged with dammages or costs. But when the heire entreth into warranty, if he doe not presently yeeld Dower, but stand out obstinately, hee shall pay dammages, as much as dower might haue beene worth to the woman from the time of the husbands death, to the day wherein shee hath iudgement, and the heire shall be amercered. In like manner is it, if a widdow without any assignation enter into her Dower that was certainly nominated to her ad ostium Ecclesiæ, and which shee findeth empty at her husbands death, if she be eiected, or put to suit and delayes, she shall recouer dammages: So shall shee if shee be eiected the tenement assigned for quarentine during the forty dayes, or before dower assigned after the forty dayes. So likewise is it if shee haue no place at all assigned to dwell in, vbi reclinet caput suum, &c. Thus Bracton: and thus long wee haue beene in the Writ de dote nihil vnde habet, which though it bee aptliest brought in the common place for the reason aboue declared, yet it may bee sued in the County before the Sheriffe per Iusticies, as saith Fitzherbert in his na.bre. 148. But then it seemes it must bee remoued by recordari facias, if the Tenant plead ne vnque accouple, &c. so the booke of Entries 223, 224. for in the base Court that issue cannot be tryed.

SECT. XVIII.

The Writ de recto de dote.

There is another Writ called the Writ of right of Dower, not because the former Writ hath any tortiousnesse in it, or claimeth upon wrong title, but because this second Writ hath fewest ambages in pleading, and the forme of it is upon pure right. *Britton* saith, there are cases wherein a woman is driuen to a Writ of right of dower pleadable in Court.

One is where a woman hath lost seisin of her dower, as if shee were disseised, and after long peacable seisin of the desseisor shee reentred with force, if the desseisor recouer against her by assise, she hath no remedy, but onely by Writ *de recto de dote*, counting of her owne seisin: Another is where a woman demands lands or tenements which were her husbands, as part of her dower, when shee is seised of a surplus or greater part already: And the third is when shee demands something as appertenant to her dower. *Fitzherbert* seemes not to allow *Bractons* relation of *vnde nihil habet* in the other Writ, for hee saith, where a woman that hath recouered part of her dower of one Tenant already, demands the remnant against the same Tenant in the same Towne, because the words *vnde nihil habet* will not serue, this Writ *de recto de dote* is vsed of necessity, and is directed to the heires Gardian, if he be in ward, or to the heire himselfe, or to a deforcour: And some say, that a woman losing her dower by default in a *præcipe quod reddat*, she shall recouer by this Writ *de recto de dote*, by the opinion of some. But it seemes shee may haue a *quod ei deforceat* by equity, the Statute *W. 2. cap. 4.* Whereas before shee had no remedy but by this Writ, or by action of deceipt, if shee were not summoned. *Fitzherbert* holdeth also, if a woman lose her dower by assise or other action tryed, shee may

may haue an attainte, but not this Writ de recto, for the land was assigned her once to hold in dower, and by that title shee had possession, so that that title est execute, and so shee ought to sue an action of her owne possession if shee bee deforced, and not demand dower againe. quære.

The forme is: Præcipimus tibi vt plenum rectum teneas B. quæ fuit vxor: C. de tertia parte decem acrarum cum pertinentiis in D. quam clamat tenere de te in dote p liberum seruitium tertiæ partis vnius denarii per annum, &c. And this Writ may bee of the moity of land, according to the custome, &c. or of the profits of an office. Fitzherbert sets downe one for example; Rex Andreæ salutem, we command you that you yeeld vnto B. which was wife of R. her full right and third part of the profits issuing of the Custody of Westm. Abbay goale, with a third part of three Acres arrable, of one rood of meadow, of bread, meat, and bottles of ale weekly, &c. which shee claimeth as belonging to the francktenement, which shee holds of you in dower, &c. by free seruice, and bearing a third part of cost and charge towards the keeping the goale and gate of the Abbey aforesaid, &c. whereof you your selfe deforce her: hereby appeareth plaine that a woman deforced from any thing appendant, or appertenant to dower assigned her, may haue remedy by Writ de recto de dote. The old na.bre. notes that of a Bailiwicke, or any such office in fee, which a woman may execute her selfe, or make substitute or deputy of it, she shall haue dower, but not of Stewardship or Marshalship of England.

And of a common of beasts without number a woman is not dowable, 9.H.7.4. & Park. Sect. 341. And of an vse before the Statute of 27.Hen.8. of vses shee was not dowable, as it is said in Vernons ca. Sir Edward Cokes 4. Rep. fol. 1. And of an annuity shall bee no dower, but of prediall tithes dower shalbe, as appeares by the Countesse of Oxfords Case, cited in Harpurs Case in Sir Edw. Cokes 11. Rep. fo. 256.

The paroll or plea is sometimes remoued in this

Action; As if the Writ be to the husbands heire, which heire being himselfe Tenant of the Land will not doe right: the Demandant may haue out a *pone* to remoue the matter straightway from the heires Court into the Common place, but a tolt to remoue it first into the County, for the originall is, *nisi feceris vicecomes faciet*, and from thence it may bee remoued by the Plaintiffe to the Common place by a *pone* without any cause mentioned in the Writ. But the Tenant in a *droit patent* cannot remoue the Plea out of the County without shewing case in the *pone*; yet as well in a Writ *de recto de dote* as in a Writ of *droit patent* the tenant may remoue the plea, shewing cause, and that immediatly out of the Lords Court, into the Common place by *recordare*: and so out of the heires Court, *quære*.

If a man sell all his land and dye, so that the heire hath nothing by discent, now this Writ must be directed to the feofee, of whom the widdow when shee is indowed must hold, as of her Lord by fealty. But if before the Statute of *quia Emptores terrarum*, &c. if the husband has infeofed a stranger of part of his Lands to hold of the husband, &c. a Writ of right of Dower must haue beene to the heire, in whose Court the matter was to bee pursued, by reason of the remaining Seignory.

So is it if at this day the Baron giue part of his Manor to hold in tayle: But if a man giue away all his land to bee holden of him in tayle, and dye, now the Writ *de recto de dote* must bee against the donee directed to the Sheriffe retournable in the Common place, for the heire hauing only a Signiory in grosse can keepe no Court. And in the Writ shall bee inserted *quia B. capitalis dominus feodi remisit nobis curiam suam.*

If the Baron hauing leased all his lands for terme of life die, &c. And though there be not in Chancerie, or any where else, any matter wherby to proue the Lords remission of the Court: yet if the Lord haue not any demesnes whereupon to hold a Court, he can haue none action against

gainst the Demandant for the false supposall, or surmise: nor let nor hinder the proceedings in Common place.

But if he had a Court to hold plea in, and did not remit his Court to the King, he may haue prohibition to the Iustices, commanding them not to proceed any further. But saith Nat. Breu. quære of that matter. And see Plowd. fol. 74. a. where the Lord hath a Court, and he will remit his Court, his Certificate must bee to the King in his Chancerie, and thereupon a Writ of right shall be returnable in the Court of Common Pleas.

In the Common Place, when the plea is remoued thither, your processe is Grand cape, and Petit cape: In the Lords, or heires Court is vsed first a precept in nature of summons, and of a Grand cape, and Petit cape. And note that in this writ if the parties appeare, they neuer proceed to grand Assise, or triall by battaile (from which the Demandant is exempted) and so consequently here is neuer per Bracton any Essoine de malo lecti. But the tenant may vouch his warrant, if he haue any. And after the woman hath made her narration or demand pursuing her writ, the tenant may in barre, say that shee rendred the land to him of her owne accord: Or if she said he disseised her of her Dower: he may plead her Relege, saith Bracton, Et poterit veritas per patriam declarari.

SECT. XIX.

What things shall be assigned in Dower, &c.

WHen Iudgement is giuen in curia regis against the tenant, either vpon his default at the Grand cape returned, or vpon confession, or issue tried, the chiefe substance of the entrie is no more but consideratum est vt recuperet seisinam de tertia parte, and then either presently, or afterward, at the petition of the demandant, there is awarded a writ, De habere facias seisinam de tertia parte,

to

to the Sheriffe, who must make returne, how he hath executed the Kings commandement. But I finde by Dyer, 11. Eliz. fol. 278. that an Alias habere fac' shall not be awarded after the Sheriffe hath executed the Formedon; the case was that the Sheriffe upon the Habere fac', &c. profer seisin by meanes of a third part, and the Demandant refuse, yet by Harpur and Dyer her entrie was afterwards lawfull, for the certaintie appeared, and they that an Alias habere fac' by no president shal be granted, and as images of this course must be the proceedings in all base Courts which hold of Dower.

So that it is now more than sufficiently perceived, that the third part of everie mans inheritance is assignable for Dower, by the husbands heire, or the heires Gardian, or by the Feoffee or Feoffees of the husband, or heire, or by some other tenant, or tenants, or by the Chancellor, Escheator, or Viscount. But it ought to appeare yet more fully, how these three parts shall be assigned, and wherein See Dyer, 2. Eliz. 187. In Dower against eight, two confesse the action, and the rest plead in barre, six had iudgement for a third part of two in eight divided, and afterward upon verdict against the six, iudgement was of six parts in eight divided.

Parcell of any thing, whereof a woman may rightly claime Dower, is assignable, &c. But other lands than those whereof she is by title dowable, or not assignable.

Acceptance of a greater or lesse part than the third, in name of Dower of all the frankteniement, which the Baron had, bindeth a woman. But assignment of all the land which the Baron had is not good. But I referre you to Sir Edw. Cokes Commentarie upon Littleton, fol. 346. how Assignment is to be made, and what Assignment is good, where it is said eight things are observable to a perfect Assignment of Dower.

The heire is not bound to assigne any widdow Dower in his capitall Messuage, or in any part thereof. But Assignment of such house in allowance of all other lands, or of of other lands whereof she is dowable, for the house is good when it is accepted, And Assignment of a chamber in the husbands dwelling house, when other lands are not, whereof to make assignation is good, being accepted. But a woman is not bound to accept this kinde of Dower, except she list: A rent may be assigned her out of the house, and this shall be good sans fait. Likewise it is of Common, of Estouers, of Pasture assigned in allowance of lands, or other things whereof a woman is dowable. And lands in Wales may be assigned for a whole Dower: and thereby a woman may be excluded from her Dower in England. If upon Judgement of Dower, and before execution, the tenant assigne a rent per paroll, issuing out of the land, whereof the Judgement was given, and the woman accepts it in stead of Dower, this is a good barre in a Scire facias, and it is distrainable of common right; but if the Assignment had beene by paroll of other lanes, than of such as wherein the woman might have claimed Dower, it would not have barred execution, because it was not pursuant to the first Judgement, Dyer, 1. Mar. fol. 91. It is said in Sir Edw. Cokes 4. Rep. fol. 1. in Vernons case, that at the Common Law no collaterall satisfaction or recompence made to a woman in satisfaction of her Dower, was any barre of her Dower, for no title of Francktenement or inheritance may be barred by any collaterall satisfaction.

When the Writ of execution comes to the Sheriffe, he shall deliver seisin by mets and bounds, but this rule cannot stretch to things not boundable. Therefore if Dower be demanded or recovered of three shillings rent, assignation of one shilling is sufficient; And when dower of a Baylihwike or mill is demanded, a third part of the profit, &c. shall be assigned, and it is a good Indowment without certaintie. Et el molera toll free, & serra contributarie. And so dower of a villeine, either the third dayes worke, or every third weeke, or moneth. And so of the profit of the third part of Stallage, of the third part of the

the profits of a Faire, and so of the third part of the profit of a Parke, and of a Doue-house, and so of the third part of a Piscarie, viz. Per tertium piscem, vel iactum tertium retis, &c.

Sect. XX.

New Indowment.

If that which a woman holdeth in dower be lawfully against her will, and without her fault deuested and euicted, &c. she shall be new indowed of the other lands, whereof the state which her husband had remaines still vndefeated, for example: The Baron seised of three Acres dies, the widdow is indowed of one Acre, which he gained by disseisin, if she be ousted she shall be indowed of the other two Acres. Tenant in taile of three Acres, discontinueth in fee, the Discontinuee marrieth, and dieth, his wife recouereth dower against his heire; the issue in taile brings a Formedon against the widdow, she voucheth the heire, he enters into Warrantie, loseth, and the demandant hath execution, though the estate which the heire hath in the other two Acres remaining be defeasible, yet the woman shall be newly indowed of them, till they be defeated: yea, though the Discontinuee his heire haue aliened, the widdow shall bee newly indowed notwithstanding. Againe, a man seised of two Acres in fee, within one Countie, takes a wife, enfeoffeth a stranger of one Acre with Warrantie, and dying hauing issue a sonne which entreth into the other Acre, the wife brings a writ of Dower against the Feoffee, which voucheth the heire, and the heire loseth by default, so that the Demandant hath Judgement conditionall, and execution against him, to recouer of the land which he hath by discent within the same Countie where the Writ was brought. If now the Vouchee be restored by a Writ of deceipt to the land which

which the woman recouered, shee shall haue Scire facias against the Feoffee that was tenant in her first Writ, to be newly endowed of the other Acre. And if he haue thereof infeoffed a stranger, yet this stranger shall be bound by the first Iudgement in dower that was conditionall.

If a woman that is dowable take a second husband, and be endowed by his assent per metes & bounds, if now the Baron discontinue in fee, and die, the wife may haue a Cui in vita: and Perkins leaues it not cleane out of doubt, whether she may not be new endowed of such other possessions, as were her husbands during couerture, because the endowment was not by Writ.

This new endowment is when the euiction is loyall, & maugre le test del feme; for when it is otherwise, she must recouer the land againe by such meanes as she may, from him which recouered it.

50. Ed. 3. fol. 7. Ioane, late wife of L. W. brought her Writ of dower against T. H. demanding the third part of a Mannor. It was pleaded, Que el ne poet nens demander, for anno 12. huius regis, a fine was leuied of the said Mannor betwixt I. and E. and the tenant sued Scire facias out of the fine against the now demandant, which came and pleaded to parcell that shee held it in Dower, of indowment from her husband, by assignment of W. C. & pria aide de lui. &c. for another part, she claimed for terme of her life, by lease from W. C. of whom likewise shee prayed aid, and had it granted. C. came in by processe, and ioyning in aid, pleaded a Feoffment made to himselfe in fee, by L. the baron, sonne and heire to I. W. whereunto the tenant pleaded Riens passa per le fait, and the processe continued against the Iury till a day certaine, at which day C. made default, and this demandant maintained the issue which was found against the now demandant, viz. that Riens passa per le fait, and execution awarded for the plaintiffe in the Scire fac. Iudgement si incounter cest recouerie a quel el fuit party, el poet nens demander, and the demandant demurred.

Per

Her pretence was, that by the recouerie she was remitted to her action paramont, because the recouerie affirmes her husbands possession. But the better opinion was, that when her Dower once lawfully assigned was recouered against her, she had here no remedy, but by errour or attaint, for a writ of right shee might not haue: But if in the Scire facias shee had alleaged to that part which she claimed in Dower, that she held it in Dower of the Assignment of W. C. Prist dattender, a que le court voile a garder, she had saued her estate by protestation, and the reuersion might haue beene iudged to him which had right, whereas pleading as she did, some thought shee had forfeited her Dower, but that was denyed by Tresiliam. Belknap, who said, that when one is in per tort, as if the Disseisee or his heires enter vpon him which is in by discent, or if a widdow enter vpon a discontinuee of her husband, and then vpon issue taken sur seisin, or disseisin, it is found for the plaintiffe, the tenant is remitted to his Action paramont, Briefe d'entrie in the one case, and in the other a Cui in vita. But if a recouerie bee against a Tenant that hath rightfull possession, the remedie must be by errours, attaint, or writ of right. And therefore in the last cases, if the tenants had pleaded a release, or other matter, which might extinct the right: if it had passed against them, their remedy must haue beene by writ of right, per Clopton, quære.

Wich. said, if a recouerie be had against the Baron vpon a delatory plea, as non tenure misnosmer of the town, or such like, a woman may falsifie such a recouerie in a writ of Dower: It seemes to be otherwise, saith Brooke, if a recouerie be had in that manner against the woman her selfe who is endowed.

SECT.

SECT. XXI.

Admeasurement of Dower.

ADmeasurement is in a kinde a recoverie against a woman, not of her whole Dower, but of part of it; for if the heire whilest hee is under age, or the Gardian whilest the heire is in ward, doe indow a widdow of more land than she ought to hold in Dower, the heire when hee commeth to full age, may have a writ *De admensuratione dotis* against her, and the *Surplus* or excesse shall be restored to the heire: but there is in this case onely an amputation without any novell assignment. If the heire being under age assigne Dower to largely, before his Lord and Gardian enter into the land, or seise his Ward, the Gardian may have a writ of *Admeasurement* by *West. 2. cap. 7.* And if the Gardian pursue the writ faintly against the woman indowed, the heire may have a writ of *Admeasurement* by the same Statute, *Custodi de caetero concedatur breve de admensuratione dotis, nec per sectam custodis si fictae & per collusionem sequatur versus mulierem tenentem in dotem, praecludatur haeres cum ad aetatem pervenerit ad dotem admensurandam, &c.*

If the plea be in the Countie, the Plaintiffe may remove it without cause, and the Defendant may remove it with cause shewed in the writ, as in a *Replevin*. And when the writ is removed by *Pone* into the Common place, the processe is summons, attachment and distresse, &c. according to the Statute. Then the Sheriffe cannot make admeasurement, but he shall extend the land particularly, and returning the Extent into the Common place, the Justices shall admeasure Dower. Note if the Gardian assigne Dower excessive, and then grant over his estate, his assigne shall never have a writ of *admeasurement*. Likewise if the heire under age assigne Dower, which his Gardian may admeasure when he hath entred, &c. but the

the Action is not grantable, for the Gardian assigned or grantee shall not admeasure: But an heire may have the admeasuring of Dower assigned in his Ancestors time. And if a woman be indowed in Chancery per le Roy, &c. the heire may have a Writ of Admeasurement, if a woman after shee is indowed make any improvement of the land, so that it becomes of farre greater value than it was of at the time of the Assignement, there lieth no admeasuring upon this improvement. And Bracton saith, Non erit estimanda melioratio mulieris quā fecit in dote sua post assignationem, tempus enim assignationis dotis erit spectandum. But if this improvement bee by casualty in some myne of coale or lead, which had beene formerly found and occupied in the husbands time, the matter is somewhat doubtfull. But see Sir Edward Cokes 5. Rep. fol. 12. a. in Saunders cap. q̃ sc. That if the myne appeared at the time of the ad assignement admeasurement lieth.

As for new mynes, a widdow may not make or dig any that is waste, thus farre Fitzherbert. Briton cap. 112. and Bracton lib. 4. cap. 17. shew with what circumstance admeasurement shalbe made by the vicount surserement de probes homes præsentes & per bone & legale extent. They say, that the amputation is not onely of excesse and superfluity by this Writ of admeasurement, but also of that which ought not to bee assigned, admensuratio debet esse, tam de indebito, quam de superfluo.

And therefore if a Castell or head of a Barrony were assigned in Dower by the Gardian without any necessity: the heire may have this Writ: for enter hee cannot, say they. They shew also what plea a woman may have against admeasurement, viz. that the Plaintiffe himselfe made the assignation, or confirmed or allowed it being of full age, &c.

SECT.

SECT. XXII.

The charge of Dower.

ADmitting the Dower assigned to be both for quality and quantity iust, there is yet to be declared with what immunity a woman shall hold her Dower. First Bracton saith, Si peculia mariti sufficiant ad solutionem tenentur, sed vxori dos sua deonerabitur. Et heres defendere dotem & warrantizare eam mulieri debet & pro ea sequi comitatus hundreda & curia dominorum, vt viduatæ domui suæ intendat & nutritioni suorum (si qui fuerint) puerorum. If the husbands goods bee not sufficient for payment of his debts, the heire must discharge Dower of the burden, &c. for he is the widdowes warrant of her Dower, and ought to follow for her, County Court, Court leet, and hundred, &c. That shee may see to her house, and nurture of her children.

Fitzherbert in his Writ of Admeasurement, first affirmes, that a woman shall not be distreined in her Dower, in her Inheritance, or in the ioynt purchased lands to her or her husband, for her husbands debts. The Writ which he sets downe for remedy, saith almost as much, Rex Vicicounti, &c. cum secundum legem & consuetudinem regni angliæ, mulieres in terris & tenementis quæ tenent in dotem de dono virorum, vel quæ sunt de ipsarum hæreditate, vel quæ sibi quesiuerint, pro debitis virorum distringi non debent, &c.

And in some Writs is this Clause, Dum tamen hæredes vel Executores testamenti ipsius, &c. ad debita illa reddenda nobis sufficiant. But it seemes reasonable, saith Fitzherbert, that a woman shall not bee distreined in her Inheritance for the Kings debts, neither in her Dower or Joynt purchased lands which her husband, if her title commenced before her husband became debtor, and there is a Writ in the register importing no lesse, yea hee affords it to be good reason that lands purchased by Baron and Feme, after the Baron is entred in debt to the King should be discharged in the widdowes hands. But let widdowes agrée with the King as well as they can, the heire is lyable to the debts of his Ancestor before the widdow: The heire likewise dischargeth her of suit and seruice, and is so farre forth her warrant, that by Britton, if shee be impleaded and vouch any other to warranty, she forfeiteth her Dower pur sa malice, and though her husbands feofée be not called her warrant: yet if she be indowed by him shee must hold of him. And regularly Tenant in Dower must be Attendant to her husbands heire, or to the heires Gardian, or to the Gardenis Executor, or to him in the reuercion, according to the rate of rent whereby they hold ouer: if Tenent by fealty and xij. d. rent bée disseised and dye, his wife being indowed by the disseisor, shall be an attendant to the same dissessor of iiij. d. annuall. And now if the heire will bring a Writ of entry in lo quibus against the woman thus indowed, shee may shew her speciall matter, and that shée is ready to attend to whom the Court will award: which shall award, that she retaine her Dower still, and bee attendant to the heire, quære, saith Parkins if the heire haue any other remedy, for hee cannot enter vpon the Tenant in Dower. D.st. 82. a. saith, That a Feme tenant in Dower leaueth the reuersion in him against whom shee demands her Dower, although he be a disseisor, and doth not reduce the reuersion by her recouery to him which hath right, as other Tenants for life doe. And as it is said in Sir Edward Cokes 8. Rep. 35. in Paynes ca. if she recouer against Tenant for life, shee leaueth the reuersion in him. But by nat. br. fol. 265. a. if the King assigne Dower in Chancery as Gardian, the reuersion reposeth in the heire, for which he shall sue liuery. If after iudgement the heire grant his reuersion, and the woman atturne, she shall be Attendant to the grantée. If Lord Meane & Tenant be, the Tenant holding by iij. d. rent, and the Meane by 20. d. If the Tenant marry, and the Meane release to him all his right in the tenancy,

tenancy, the Tenant dieth, the wife must bee endowed, according to her husbands best possessions, and therefore shall bee Attendant to the heire by a penny, and not the third part of twenty pence. If hee which holdeth by fealty and xij. d. hauing a wife, sell the tenancie to his Lord, and the estate is executed, the Tenants wife shall be indowed sans attendancie, for the Seignory extinct is not reuiuable: If Lord Measne and Tenant be, the Tenant holdeth by xij. d. which dieth, & his wife is endowed, shee shall bee attendant to the heire by iiij. d. now if the Lord release all his right in the tenancy to the heire, the meanalty is extinct, and the attendance gone, for it was but in respect of the charge which the heire was at to his next Lord.

But where there is Lord and Tenant by fealty and xij. d. rent, if the Tenant make a gift in tayle of the land to hold of him and his heires by xx. s. rent &c. if the donee dye without issue, his wife endowed, shall be attendant to the donor by v. s. and viij. d. although the Lord release to the donor, for his attendance is not in respect of the charge ouer, but by a speciall reseruation.

If there be Seignor Meane and Tenant by fealty and iij. s. rent, the Meanes wife after he be forejudged in a Writ of meane, and dead, shall be endowed without attendance. If Tenant by fealty and xij. d. make a gift in taile of the land, reseruing xij. d. rent, &c. and the donee hauing a wife and issue by her, discontinueth in fee, and dieth, now though the wife recouer Dower, and haue execution of it against the discontinuee, yet she shall not be attendant to him, for hee is not chargeable as the Baron was, because the Dowers auowry resteth of necessity upon the issue, to whom: for all that the widdow shall not bee attendant, till hee haue recontinued the estate tayle, quære tamen, saith Perkins. If the Tenant whilst hee liued held of his Lord by fealty, and a nag of forty shillings price, the Tenants widdow when shee is endowed shall bee attendant by xiij. s. iiij. d. But if the tenure were by fealty, and a nag without expresse value, shee shall bée Attendant by a nag every third yéere. Perkins fo.84.Pe.

Sect. XXIII.

Of the cui in vita.

I Haue béene long in Dower, and I feare mee some women had rather neuer be endowed that is, they had rather die with their husbands, or soone after them, than bée bound to learne this Catechisme, yet I must come to it once againe.

But first let vs sée how lands whereunto a woman may haue right by ancient indowment, or by discent, or gift in franckmarriage, or by some other acquisition, before or during Couerture in fee, fée tayle, for life, or for yéeres, may bee reduced, if the husband haue aliened them, for if the possession continued alwayes in the husband till his death, then by his death the widdow is made sole Tenant of them, so little néeding either assignation, or other circumstance, that without new entry, claime or challenge, shee may haue action of her owne possession against any other that shall enter.

If the husband aliened intirely any lease for yéeres of his wiues, it is gone irreuocable, and if hee make no sale, and the wife dyes, hee shall haue the lease, except shee bee ioyntly possest with another, and the seruing ioyntenant shall haue. Commentar. vpon Fitzherbert. 185. If he aliened part of the estate, as for ten yéeres next ensuing, where the terme was for twenty, the widdow may enter when ten yéeres expired. But sée in that Case, that if the husband rested a rent, and dyes, the Executors of the husband shall haue the rent, for it was not incident to the reuersion, yet the wife shall haue the residue of the terme, Sir Edw. Cokes Commentar. vpon Fitzherbert fol. 57. b. if he aliened for the ten last yéeres shee may continue possession,

session; till those ten yeeres be commenced. If the husband devise away by his last Testament, a terme for yeeres, which he hath by right of his wife, I suppose the devise is void as well as if it were made of some higher estate, as it appeares by Perkins chap. Devises. and Plowd. 419. in Bracebridges case. And the Law is all one in all respects, where the Baron and Feme are possessed of lease for yeares by intierties (that if the estate be made to them during their coverture, or by moyties that is to them joyntly before marriage) or where the Baron is possessed of a lease iure vxoris. See Dame Hales case, Plowd. 260. And if the Baron possest of a lease for yeares in the right of his wife, charge the land with a rent, and die, the rent is gone, Plowd. 418. in Bracebridges case, for shee is remitted. And if Feme Gardian in Soccage be, and her Baron alienateth it and die, the wife may enter. And see Dyer, 8. Eliz. 251. the same is of Coppy-holds per render, to the use of a Feme for yeares, & the wife die, the estate rests in the husband without a custome be to the contrary. If an husband be possest of a terme for yeares in the right of his wife, and Iudgement is had against him, and the terme is extended, and the husband dieth, it shall be good against the wife, as appeares by Sir Edw. Cokes 8. Rep. 96. in Mannings case. And see the 9. case of 50. E. 3. lib. Ass. note Sir Edw. Cokes Rep. in Fulwoods case, and Plowd. 261. in Dame Hales case, where a lease made to Baron and Feme is extended for the debt of the King after the wives death.

If a man possest of a terme, deviseth it to one for his life, the remainder to a woman for her life, who takes an husband, the husband may release that to the particular tenant, although it be but a possibilitie, Sir Edw. Cokes 10. Rep. 47. Lampetts case. And if a woman hath a lease for yeares as Executrix, and takes an husband, hee may sell it per tot. curiam, præter Fitzherbert, Dyer 28. H. 8. 7. A woman hath a terme as Executrix, the husband submits to arbitrement, upon which a moytie is awarded to the

 the

the pretendor of the title, the wife is bound thereby, but because the defendant in detinue brought by the wife for the Indenture of lease, plead non detinet, and not the speciall matter, Judgement was against him, Dyer, 2. Eliz. 183. & 21. H. 7. 6. agrees.

If the husband discontinue the Francktenement of his wife, the apt instrument whereby to recouer it, when she is a widdow is a Cui in vita: Which, though it be not so necessarie and needfull, perhaps, since the Statute of 32. which disableth husbands to discontinue as it was before, yet I perceiue not by what reason the use of it is forbidden, euen in those cases where the entrie is congeable, for the vertue of the Writ is not decayed by lawfulnesse of the entrie, neither doth free libertie to take possession, prohibit the resort to Justice and action at Law, when perhaps a woman cannot, or dares not enter.

By Common Law therefore if the Baron alien in fee, the heritage of his wife or her Francktenement, by Feoffment or by Demise, for terme of life, or in taile, she may haue remedy after his decease by this Writ. Of which the generall forme is, Præcipe A. quod reddat B. quæ fuit vxor C. vnum messuagium cum pertinentiis, quod clamat, esse ius, & hereditat' suam. Et in quod A. non habet ingressum, nisi per C. quondam virum, &c qui illud ei demisit, & cui in vita contradicere non potuit. This writ may be in the per cui and post, and some varietie it hath according to title of the Demandant, as Quam clamat ve ius hæreditatem, or Vt ius & maritagium, or Vt ius ex dono I. qui ipsam B. & C. virum suum feofavit, & in quo, &c. or Quam clamat tenere sibi, & hæredibus de corpore suo, & de corpore C. quondam viri sui exeuntibus ex demissione I. or Quam clamat esse dotem suam ex dono E. primi viri vel secundi, &c.

If Baron and Feme lose the wiues lands by default, shee may haue this Writ when shee is a widdow. But if the wiues lands be recouered in a Cessavit, per default of Baron and Feme, upon a Cesser during espousals, she shall

shall neuer haue a Cui in vita, 4. Ed. 2.

If Baron and Feme, and a third person, being Joyntenants in Fee, the Baron alien the intiertie, and die, his widdow shall haue a Cui in vita of a moytie, during the life of the third person; for it seemes the alienation was a seuerance of Joynture, saith Fitzherbert. But hee sends vs to 26. Ed. 3. in his Abridgement, titulo Cui in vita. By which booke the wife in this case cannot haue a Cui in vita for any part, so long as the third person suruiueth, because they two may ioyne in a Writ of right, and if hee die, she may haue a Cui in vita of all: Vide Librum.

Of lands which a man and woman purchase ioyntly before couerture, the Cui in vita shall be but of a moytie: but of lands purchased ioyntly during couerture, the Cui in vita is of the intiertie, and being brought of a moytie, the Writ is not good, 39. H. 6. 45. for in the one case they are seised by moyties, in the other by intireties.

A woman by excepting lands, which she and her late husband tooke in exchange, or by excepting rent reserued out of it, shall be barred in a Cui in vita, or any other action, Fitzherbert, and 16. Ed. 4. 8. Idem ius, if shee accept parcell of her owne land in Dower: but 17. Assisarum pl. 3. Brooke 24. Cui in vita. If the assignment of this Dower be sans fait, it is no barre or conclusion, but a Remitter; otherwise if it be by Deed or Record. If a man giue lands to a woman to marrie with him, and after espousals he alieneth the same land and dieth, she may haue a Cui in vita. And note, that the gift or demise alleaged in a Cui in vita is trauersable. Thus much Fitzherbert.

48. Ed. 3. 8. In a Cui in vita, claiming to hold sibi & hæredibus de corpore, without shewing of whose donation, the tenant pleaded to the Writ, and it was abated. But in a Quod ei deforceat, the Demandant needs not shew by whose gift she claimeth.

49. Ed. 3. fol. 29. The Writ was, Quam clamat tenere sibi & hæredibus de corpore ex dono W. N. The tenant said, she neuer had any thing of the gift of W. N. per Bel-

knap, the answer was not good, for were the gift from one or other, if the husband aliened, she might haue the action, and the Writ may be Quam clamat vt ius & hæreditatem: though she purchased the lands, & adiornatur. The latter point is affirmed, 7. H. 4. fol 5 & per Littleton accorded: but for the first, vide 50. Ed. 3. fol. 6. In a Cui in vita quam clamat tenere ex dimissione per termino vitæ I. N. it was omitted vpon argument: a good answer per Curiam, for where one maketh title it ought to be true.

And there finde sur release made to Baron and Feme, and to the heires of the baron by I. N. was holden no demise, for it must be supposed the baron and feme were in possession tempore finis: And Persy said it had béene adiudged, if a woman claimed in her Writ ad terminum vitæ, if it were found she had estate taile, the Writ should abate.

So likewise if a woman claime by lease for terme of life per A. and it was found that A. made no lease: shée had now no estate, and consequently hath none action. Likewise (said Kirton) if in Assize of nouell disseisin, the plaintiffe make his title by feoffment of A. and is found that A. infeoffed him not, but B. did, hée shall bée barred in the Assize, for where a man maketh his title vpon a point which is found against him, it cannot be intended that he hath a better title, and there he shall not haue aduantage of any other.

39. H. 6. fol. 38. In a Cui in vita quod clamat esse ius suum ex dono I. which infeoffed the Demandant and her late husband, with declaration, that they were seised as of Franktenement, and lye les explees, as tenants for life, &c. Prisot said, That in cases speciall this Writ ought to make mention of whose gift, lease, or demise, the Demandant claimeth, as, Ad terminum vitæ ex dono I. S. or, Sibi & hæredibus ex dono I. S. But in demand of Fée simple it is enough to say, Quam clamat vt ius & hæreditatem, without shewing by whose gift or feoffment.

7. H. 7. fol. 2. If this Writ be against baron and feme

for

for lands holden in the wiues right, it must bee in quod vxor ingressa est per I. N. & non quod vir & vxor ingressi sunt per I. N.

SECT. XXIV.

west 2. Case 3.

2. Ed. 4. fol. 13. If a man be seised in right of his wife, and recouerie is had against them by default, the woman after his death, may haue a Cui in vita, but not a Quod ei deforceat, per Moyle Iustice: It seemes that at Common Law, this writ of Cui in vita was onely granted vpon actuall discontinuance by the baron: for West 2. case 3. is, Quando vir amiserit per defaltum tenementum quod fuit ius vxoris suæ, durum fuit quod vxor post mortem viri non habuerit, aliud recuperare, quam per breue de recto propter quod Dominus Rex statuit, vt mulier post mortem viri habeat recuperare per breue de ingressu cui ipsa in vita, &c. But in this case, if the tenant can proue that hee had right on his side when hee recouered: Mulier nihil capit per breuem. Note also by the way, that this heat wels. Si vir se absentaverit, & noluerit ius vxoris suæ defendere vel si in vita vxoris reddere voluerit, si vxor ante Iudiciū venerit parata petenti respondere, & ius suum defendere, admittatur vxor. Now note further for recoueries If Iudgement of forejudger be giuen against Baron and Feme, this is not void as soone as the Baron is dead, but voydable by error, for the woman cannot haue a Cui in vita, 9. Ed. 4. fol. 2.

A recouerie by sufferance is plaine alienation; and therefore vpon such a recouerie, as soone as the husband is dead, the woman may haue a Cui in vita by the Common Law, 4. Ed. 3. Brooke, Cui in vita, 18.

If a recouerie be had by default in a Writ of waste, the wife cannot haue a Cui in vita: either because the recoueris uerte is not meerely by default, or else because the Writ of waste hath no demand of land, quære if shee shall haue a Quod ei deforceat, 9. Ed. 4. 16. If Baron and Feme be impleaded, by one which hath good title, and the Baron confesse the action, the woman hath no remedie. Yet the Statute is that vpon rendring by the Baron, the wife may be receiued, &c. But if Baron and Feme be receiued vpon default of tenant for life, where the reuersion is in the wife, the Baron cannot confesse the action, for hée must be receiued, Ad ius vxoris defendendum, 7. Ed. 4. 17.

SECT. XXV.

The Sur cui in vita.

If shee which hath cause to bring a Cui in vita, of Fée simple lands, die before shee hath sued, &c. her heire shall haue a Sur cui in vita. But if the wiues lands, which the husband aliened, were in state of Fée taile, and the wife neuer sued, her heire must sue a Formedon in discender, and not a Sur cui in vita: for though both these Writs bée the children of the ancient Common Law, and were before West. 2. Yea, and this latter Writ was maintainable for lands giuen to the mother in francke marriage, or to the heires of her body (which at the first was Fée simple) yet when West. 2. made estates taile, it did also expressely set downe a Writ, whereby the heire should recouer such estates. The Sur cui in vita, for it is no more but Præcipe quod reddat, &c. quod clamat esse ius & hæreditaté suam, in quod non habuit ingressum nisi per E. and so in the Cui, or in the Post. And the Aunt and Néece may ioyne in it vpon alienation made by the husband of their common Ancestor, or vpon recouerie had against him and her. If a second husband alien his wiues Fée simple lands, and shee dieth, the issue by her first husband may sue a Sur cui in vita presently, the second husband still liuing, if hée were

neuer

never intituled to be Tenant by the Curtesie. But if he were intituled by the Curtesie, the Action is stayed, so long as he liveth: And this Writ lyeth of a V: Mi. 21. Edw. 3.

144 Edw. 3. 4 & 5. A man seised in right of his wife discontinued, and after divers alienations, hee repurchased the lands to himselfe, his wife died, the heire brought a sur cui in vita against him: præcipe W. B. quod reddat, &c. cui contradicere non potuit: exception against the writ, because it was not by another name, but it was disalowed, and the writ awarded good. If the Baron alien his wives fee simple with warranty, and leaving assetts to discend in fee, he and his wife dye, and the heire alieneth the assetts and dieth, his heire shall be barred in a sur cui in vita: But if an heire intaile, alien the assetts and dye, his issue shall not be barred.

Sect. XXIV.

The quod ei deforciat.

The quod ei deforciat, though it be not meerly a womans Writ, yet perhaps it comes not more aptly into consideration any where than in this place, after the cui in vita.

If Tenant in taile, or Tenant in Dower, or Tenant per Courtesie, or Tenant for terme of life, lose their land by default in any præcipe quod reddat brought against them, they have no remedy, if they were summoned according to Law, but by this Writ which is given in expresse forme by West. 2. cap. 4. And see the Comment. upon Fitzherbert the Writ lyeth against the recoverer and his heires, in which case the particular Tenant was without remedy at the Common law, for a writ of right hee could not have. The Statute having first appointed how a woman shall recover Dower, where the husband lost his land by by default, viz. by writ of Dower (in which the Tenant must not plead the iudgement alone, but he must also prove her right) sheweth also how actions run together. When a woman already indowed, or Tenant by the curtesie, or in franckmarriage, or by other in taile, or for life, demand the estate which they thruise ues lost by default, in which cases when it is come to that, that the Tenant must prove his right, the Demandants, which cannot answer without them in the reversion, may vouch them sic sicut tenentes in priori breue. And so the Tenant erit loco actoris, and if the Action were a Writ of right, they may proceed to the grand assise or battaile. And further, Cum mulier ius non habens impetierit breue de dote super custodem, & custos per fauorem mulieris dotem reddiderit vel defaltam fecerit, vel placitum ita fictè per collusionem defenderit, vt dos fuerit mulieri adiudicata: prouisum est quod cum ad ætatem venerit hæres habeat actionem petendi seisinam antecessoris sui, &c. ita tamen vt salua sit mulieri exceptio quod ius habeat in dote, quod si ostenderit recedat quieta & sit hæres in misericordia & grauiter amercietur secundũ discretionem Iustic'. Then to the quod ei deforciat. Si hæres vel alius, de dote sua implacitaverit mulierem, & si dotem suam per defaultam amisserit, fiat ei tale breue: præcipe A. quod iuste reddat B. qui fuit vxor C. vnum messuagium cum pertinentiis in N. quod clamat esse rationabilem dotem, vel de rationabili dote sua & quod idem A. iniuste ei deforciat. So is Fitzherbert, but by the old nabre. it must not be called an iniust forcing. Ps. car le poll. iniuste non habetur in Statuto, which is true, ad istud breue habeat tenens exceptionem ad ostendendum quod mulier ius non habeat in dote quod si ostendat, recedat quietus, &c. Last of all because vntill this time the Law gaue no remedy vpon losse by default, but only a writ of right, which serued not for them, that could not speake de mero iure, viz. Tenants for life, in free marriage, or in taile; The Statute to auoid that preiudice, giues them likewise their seuerall writs of quod ei deforciat, framed according to to their title, either, quam clamat ad termium vitæ, vel vt ius & maritagium, vel sibi & hæredibus de corpore. Tenant by the curtesie, likewise though it be not expressed by the Statute, may haue a quod ei deforciat, quam clamat tenere per legem Angliæ, which is by equity, saith Fitzherbert, If any Tenant of those particular estates, lost by default, by reason of non summons, he may haue a quod ei deforceat, or a writ of deceipt, at his pleasure. If a man lose by default in a writ of waste sued against him: hee shall not haue a quod ei deforciat, because the waste must be found by verdict: nouell na. bre.

Yet 2. Hen. 4. fol. 2. Hanc. said, if a writ, to enquire of waste, were awarded, the Defendant which lost the land might haue a quod ei deforciat, videtur lex esse contra, saith Brooke, for it was there agreed by all the Court, that attaint lyeth in an Action of waste: and the party may challenge the Jury: yea, the booke at large is that the Viscount may quash the pannell, though it be of his own making so, that this kinde of recouery is by verdict, and not by default. Note, that 21. Hen. 6. Challenge is denied, but by Newton and Vaston Justices, Markham and Portington, Serieants, attaint lieth. But see Sir Edw. Cokes Comment. vpon Fitzherbert fol. 355. that is resolued, that if the Tenant in a Writ of waste in the tenet lose by default, a quod ei deforceat lieth, as well as in assise, and it is no reason to say that attaint lyeth against the Jury, for so it doth in assise, yet it is there said, that attaint doth not lye after a Writ of inquirie of waste, for it is but an inquest of office. But there it is said, that if the iudgement be a nihil dicit, there a quod ei deforceat lyeth not, for that is after appearance, and is not a iudgement per defaultam.

And note there, that if Tenant for life make default after default, and he in the reuersion is receiued and plead to issue, and it is found by verdict for the Demandant, the default and the verdict are causes of the iudgement, and yet the Tenant shall haue a quod ei deforceat, & vide Dod. fol.

fol. 556. more est quod ei deforceat. 33. Hen. 6. 46. Littleton saith, that Tenant for life, or in taile, may haue a quod ei deforciat, as well vpon disseisen done to them, as vpon recouery against them by default, for before West. 2. there was a quod ei deforceat at Common. And all is one, whether it be brought vpon a disseisen, or a recouery, for neither Writ, nor Declaration make any mention of any recouery, and the Tenant may chose whether hee will plead the recouery or other matter in barre, which if he doe, the Demandant cannot vouch, acsi esset tenens: Neither is nul tiel recouery a good plea prima facie, saue only for the Demandant, when the Tenant pleads a recouery by default.

2. Edw. 4. fol. 11. Littleton stands to his old opinion, that there was a quod ei deforciat at the Common law, and hee would haue it maintainable still by one that hath cause to bring a formedone, or an assize, or writ of entry, sur disseisin; But the Court seemes to wonder at his sayings, and also at the first, when Billing comes, and demands oier del record: for the Tenant in a quod ei deforceat, the Court askes him quæ intendes per ceo: so that with questions of admiration they seeme plainly to reiect both opinions, that there is any quod ei deforciat at the Common law, giuen otherwise than vpon recouery by default, and then the Tenant may plead nul tiel record; for neither the writ nor the declaration makes any mention of the recouery: But Littleton comes once more, 10. Edw. 4. fol. 2. and said, that once he brought a quod ei deforciat for his mother, of lands which shee claimed to hold in Dower, the Tenant said, there was no record to proue, that the lands were lost by default. And Littleton challenged the plea, because it might be the recouery was in a Court Baron by default in a Writ of right, in which case a quod ei deforceat lyeth: and therein is no record, yet it is a record by default: the Tenant said, there was neither record nor recouery where any losing by default appeared, and this was holden a good plea, per les Iustices. And Littleton relinquished his suit. 44.

44. Edw. 3. fol. 42. A quod ei deforciat was brought against the heire of one which recouered in an assize, hee prayed the plea might stay for his non age, and vouched to warranty W. N. &c. the voucher was allowed but not his age: because he might not haue had it in his first Action: So that it appeares, this writ lyes vpon recovery in assize, and the Tenant may vouch: But by Thorpe, if it had beene the party himselfe which recouered, he could not haue vouched; Et mirum saith Brooke, that vpon a recouery in assize, which is by iury and not by default, this writ should be. And if yee looke this booke at large, yee shall finde againe, that this writ and the proceeding in it, is meerly by the Statute vpon a recouery by default, therefore a quod ei deforciat lieth, and that vpon a recouery by default in a quod ei deforciat. As 13. Edw. 1. a woman recouered in a Writ of Dower, by default against Tenant for life of rent, and afterward the Tenant, which lost by default, brought a quod ei deforciat against the woman, and she lost by default, and then sued a quod ei deforciat, &c. This is the highest Writ which these particular tenants can haue of their owne possession, as it were their writ of right, and it lieth against him which is Tenant, though he be not party to the recouery, as against the feofee of him which recouered. But it lyeth seldome or neuer for a stranger to the recouery. Yet 41. Edw. 3. fol. 30. the Baron and Feme ioyned in a quod ei deforciat of lands lost by the Feme before marriage, & bene. And by Belknap it lyeth vpon a recouery in a sciri facias, and it lyeth without shewing the record.

The Tenant in this Writ, whether it be he which recouered, or his alienee, shall not haue view. 41. Ed. 3. 8.

If a man lose by default in a writ of right brought in a Court Baron, he may remoue the record, and haue a quod ei deforciat, in the Common place, and quære saith Fitzherbert, if he neuer remoue the record, if he then may not sue his quod ei deforciat in which Court hee will, either the common place, or the Court Baron. He agreeth if a

woman

woman lose by default, and then marrie, she and her husband may haue this Writ: but if Tenant in taile lose by default and dye, his heire must sue a Formedon: for that is his Writ of right.

If lands be giuen to Baron and Feme in especiall taile, the remainder to the Baron in generall taile, and the wife die sans issue, now if the Baron lose by default, in a Præcipe quod reddat, his writ of Quod ei deforceat must be Quod clamat tenere sibi & hæredibus de corpore suo, for so soone as the wife died, the state apres possibility drowned in the remainder, 50. Ed. 3. fol. 4. If in a Scire facias brought in Chancerie by an heire of full age, to auoyd indowment assigned in Chancerie, whilest he was ward, he recouer by default, the woman may haue a Quod ei deforceat in Commune Banco. So likewise if a man recouer land by default in Scire facias, out of some record in the Kings Bench, the Tenant which lost by default may sue a Quod ei deforceat in the Common Place. If two coparceners tenants in taile, lose by default, they may ioyne in a Quod ei deforceat, yet the default of one is not the default of the other. 46. Ed. 3. in Fitzherbert, Nat. Breu. Brooke hath it also. A Quod ei deforceat brought by two men, heires in taile, of Gauill kinde, Quam clamat sibi tenere & hæredibus de corporibus exeuntibus was awarded good, though they could haue none issue of their two bodies. 46. Ed. 3. 21. If tenant for life, or in taile appeare in a Præcipe quod reddat, and afterward depart in despite of the Court, he shall lose the land, but yet he may recouer by Quod ei deforceat, for the recouerie is by default, for that he doth not appeare when he is demanded. But if tenant for life, or in taile, after the mise ioyned in writ of right, depart in despite of the Court, they shall lose the land, and not haue a Quod ei deforceat, for the Iudgement is finall. If Baron and Feme seised in droit le feme for her life lose by default, in a Præcipe quod reddat, they may haue a Quod ei deforceat, by Fitzherbert, which is denied in the old Nat. Breu. 155.

A

If tenant for life lose by a default in a Cessauit, he shall haue a Quod ei deforceat. by this Statute of West. 2. If he in reuersion vpon default of tenant for life pray to bee receiued, plead, and lose by action tried: yet the tenant for life may haue a Quod ei deforceat, for the Judgement must be against him by his default. If in a Præcipe quod reddat, the Tenant vouch, and the Vouchee will not appeare, so that the Tenant loseth by default of the Vouchee. Fitzherbert makes it a question, whether hee may haue a Quod ei deforceat, or no, because the Judgement is not giuen vpon the tenants owne default. But cleere it is, if the Vouchee appeare, enter into Warrantie, and lose by default, that now the Tenant shall not haue a Quod ei deforceat, but Judgement to recouer in value against the Vouchee. If Baron and Feme, tenants for life in the wiues right, lose by default, and the Baron dye, a Quod ei deforceat lieth not, but a Cui in vita, as vpon a Demise made by the baron: In a Quod ei deforceat the Demandant must count, that he was seised, &c. in his Demesne as of Francktenement, or in his Demesne as of Fee taile, laying the Esplees in himselfe, but he needs not shew of whose gift, lease, or demise, though he claime for life, or she claimes in Dower, or sibi & hæredibus de corpore. And the Defendant must deny the Demandants right, &c. and shew how he recouered in a Formedon, or in some other Action: concluding that he is ready to maintaine his right and title aforesaid, &c. vnde petit iudicium. Then the Demandant must either trauerse it, or shew matter in barre: but he shall not make defence, and then plead in barre, as he shall doe in a Formedon. Fitzh.

10. Ed. 4. fol. 2. Dictum fuit, and the tenant may plead a release of all the Demandants right in a Quod ei deforceat. But the old Nat. Breu. obserueth, that if the Demandant vouch one that entreth into Warrantie, hee which recouered shall not plead the Vouchees release made after recouerie. In a Quod ei deforceat the Tenant may vouch, and so may the Demandant. 50. Ed. 3. 25. But if the

the Demandant vouch, his Vouchee cannot vouch over. 10. H. 7. 39. The old Nat. Brev. acknowledgeth, that in a Scire facias there lies no voucher: yet if a man recover by default in a Scire facias, out of a fine, against Tenant in taile, which bringeth a Quod ei deforceat: if the Recoverer maintaine the title of his first Writ, the Tenant in taile may vouch. The Law seemes to be otherwise: see Plow. 112. & 206. & 14. H. 7. 18.

The questions arose upon the Demandants vouching, 10. H. 7. fol. 10. The first, whether he must shew cause of the Warrantie, or no. The second, whether hee may vouch one that hath nothing in the reversion. The third, whether he shall recover in value. Frowicke answered; The Voucher is by Statute, and hee needs not shew any cause, for the Statute of W. 2. cap. 3. saith, Concedatur ei quod vocet ad warrant' ac si esset tenens in priori breue: in which case he should shew no Deed: Second, hee shall not vouch any stranger; for the Statute is, Ideo concedatur eis quod vocentur ad warrantum quia non possunt sine his ad quos spectat reversio respondere. Third, the Statute giving voucher, meanes that he shall have the effect of his vouching, id est, to recover in value. And if a Statute give action for a thing, whereof the action did not lye at Common Law, the partie shall have iudgement; processe and execution incident or belonging to that action, and a reversion is a cause of voucher, and of recoverie in value. Frowicke said further: That though he which leased cannot disclaime, yet his Grantee may, and award his charge, and if voucher here should be no more, but an aid prayer, the Grantee might not disclaime; for if Tenant for life pray in aid of him in reversion, hee shall not disclaime. And Tenant by the courtesie cannot vouch, for he shall never recover in value.

SECT.

SECT. XXVII.

Admonition for women to take heed of him in the reuersion.

THe rest of this fourth booke shall consist most in warnings to widdowes and women tenants in particular estates, that they doe nothing preiudiciall to their warrant. It is true for the most part, Ex quibus rebus maxima vtilitas, ex iisdem summa pernicies: Water washeth and drowneth, fire reasteth and it burneth, the Sunne ripeneth, and it scortcheth and seareth. They that can help can hurt. The reuersioner of a widdowes estate, of whom she shall haue aid to defend her, shall take her estate from her in many cases, if she offend him in his reuersion.

SECT. XXVIII.

Of waste.

EUen by the antique Law of England, if Bracton say truth, fol. 316. The Gardian in Chiualrie, committing waste, did lose the wardship, was auerred, Et damna restaurabat. But if Tenant in Dower committed waste, there was no forfeiture of her land, or parcell of it, but he in reuersion might stop and let her, from doing waste, and such hinderance was no Disseisen. Also he might haue, if need required, a Non permittas to the Sheriffe, commanding him not to suffer waste, vendiction or exile in lands, tenements, houses, woods, garden, &c. and he might haue attachment against the widdowes, or a Pone per vadios & saluos plegios, to make her come, &c. shew why shee committed waste. If the waste in a wood were found by Inquisition, the paine was no more, but that from thenceforth shee should take no manner of Estouers, either to build, burne, or inclose, but it must be per visum forestariorum hæredis. And Bracton sets forth the Writ for placing and appointing of the Forrestor, or by the heire ad prædict' boscum custodiendum. But now by the Stat. of Gloc. cap. 5. A writ of waste lyeth against Tenant in the courtesie, or for life, or for yeares, or in Dower, and the partie attainted in waste shall lose the thing wasted, and make gree to trebble value of so much as the value shall be taxed at. This Statute made 6. Ed. 1. ordaineth also that the Gardian which loseth his wardship for committing waste shall render dammages, if losse of wardship be not equiualent to the harme. Peraduenture Bracton wrote after the Statute. for in one part of his Booke Ed. 1. is named H. 3. But it is said Sir Edw. Cokes 3. Rep. fol. 40. a. that Glanuile wrote temps H. 2. Bracton, temps H. 3. Britton, temps Ed. 1. and in Sir Edw. Cokes 8. Rep. in John Webs case, fol. 46. b. he saith, that Bracton wrote in fine del Roy H. 3. and Fleta wrote in temps E. 1. But note a woman shall not answer for waste done before her time: yea, if land bee leased to Baron and Feme, for terme of their liues, and they commit waste: if the Baron die, now the widdow is not punishable for this waste: For that which the Baron did during couerture, was only his act and offence, dead and determined with his person. Concessum per curiam, 2. H. 4. and Br. 59. in his Writ of waste. Yet if the lease had beene made to a Feme sole, who takes a husband which commits waste, otherwise it is by 9. H. 6. 52. women need no further warning to take heed of waste, they are of themselues so hauing.

SECT. XXIX.

The Writ of Entrie in casu prouiso.

But let euerie good woman take heed, how she maketh any gift or alienation of such lands as she holdeth in Dower.

Dower. For Glocest. cap. 7. is, if a woman sell, or giue away in fee, or for life, the tenement which shee holdeth in Dower; the heire, or he which is in reuersion, may maintenant haue his recouerie by Writ of Entrie, and this is termed a writ of Entrie in Casu prouiso. There is no doubt but Fee in this Statute signifieth both Fee simple and Fee taile. And he which hath Fee simple, Fee taile, or Estate for life in the reuersion, may haue this Writ against the Alienee, or against him which is tenant of the Francktenement. And this during the life of the tenant in Dower which alienced, for when she is dead, it lieth not per tiel Nat. Breu. The Statute expresseth not the writ, but the forme is, Præcipe A. quod reddat B. vnum tenementum quod clamat, in quod non habet ingressum nisi per C. quæ fuit vxo D. qui illud ei demisit & illud tenuit in dotem de dono prædicti D. quondum viri sui cuius hæres, &c. & quod post demisionem per istud C. præfat' A. contra formam Statuti Glocest. &c. ad præfatum B. reuerti debet per formam eiusdem Statuti. And it may be in the Per, Cui, or Post. If a woman recouer Dower against the heire, and then alien in Fee, the recouerie must be mentioned by the heire in his writ of Entrie in Casu prouiso. In like manner as it must be in a writ of Entrie ad Communem Legem vpon an alienation by tenant in Dower, and though this alienation be but in taile, or for life, yet the forme of the writ varieth not: If he which hath the reuersion in Fee grant it to another, and the Tenant in Dower after Atturnment, alieneth in Fee, the Grantee of the reuersion shall haue Writ specifying the grant. Likewise if the heire grant his reuersion with Atturnment, and the Grantee grants it ouer with Atturnment, the third Grantee may haue a writ specifying that the woman held of the first, second, and third, ex assignatione, &c. The Aunt and Neece hauing the reuersion by discent, may ioyne in this writ, and the processe is summons, grand and petit cape.

SECT. XXX.

The writ of Entrie in Casu consimili.

THis Writ is in nature like the other, and it lyeth when Tenant by the courtesie, or Tenant for his owne life, or another mans, alieneth in fee, or in taile, or for terme of life, he in the reversion which hath it for life, or in taile, or in fee, may have this Writ of Entrie in Casu consimili, during the life of him which aliened, and this is formed and granted upon West. 2, cap. 24. which willeth, That as often as there is a Writ found in Chancerie for one case, and another case falling sub eodem iure, and requiring like remedy, there is none in the registrie of the Chancerie, for that the Clerks of the Chancerie shall concord in framing a writ Vel atterminent quærentes in proximo Parliamento, & scribantur vsus in quibus concordare non possunt, &c. & referant eos ad proximum Parliamentum, & fiat breve de consensu Iurisperitorum: ne contingat de cætero quod curia Domini Regis deficiat conquerentibus in Iustitia perquirenda.

The Writ is, Reverti debet per formam statuti in consimili casu provisi. And it supposeth alwayes alienation in feodo, although the Tenant leased or demised it, but for terme of another mans life, or in taile: And so the writ of in Casu proviso: And that of Entrie ad Communem Legem: This writ may be in the per, cui, and post: And without title made in the writ, if it so be that the Demandant himselfe made the particular estate of him which aliened: But if the father or other Ancestor make a lease for terme of life and die, and then the Tenant for life alieneth in fee, now the heire in reversion shall have a writ comprising his title in it selfe. And if this writ be brought upon alienation made by Baron and Feme, the writ supposeth that the wife aliened with her husband, but yet shee may have a Cui in vita after her husbands death, the alienation

nation

nation not letting it: If Tenant for life grant his estate to another, and the grantee alieneth in fee, the Writ shall be in quod non habet ingressum nisi per C. cui D. qui illud tenuit ad vitam ex demissione B. demisit ad eundem tenementum &c. If a man make a lease for life, and dye, and his heire grant the reversion to B. and the Tenant attournes; If now the lessee grant his estate to another, which alieneth in fee to A. B. shall have a Writ comprehending the assignation and grant of all the estates.

If lands bee given to two men, and to the heires of one of them, and he which hath the fee simple dies, and then the Tenant for life alieneth in fee, now the heire of him in remainder may have this Writ, for it lyeth as well for him as for Tenant in reversion.

If any Abbot or Prior make a lease for life, the lessee alien, the Prior dye, &c the successor may have this Writ; Also tenant in taile may have it, if hee make a lease for life, and his lessee alien in fee. And it seemes if Tenant in taile make a lease for life of the lessee, and dye, the issue in taile may chose to bring a Formdon, or Writ of Entrie in Consimili casu against the alienee, whilst the lessee for life is yet living, for the alienee, which is Tenant in the Action, cannot plead in Abatement of the Writ, that the Demandant hath title to a Formedone: But if Tenant in taile make a lease for terme of his owne life, which is no discontinuance, if now the lessee alien in fee, and the lessor dye, his heire cannot have a Writ de consimili casu; but he is driven to his Formedone, for in this case, he hath no title to other Actions by colour of any demise. But in the former case he had title, by reason of the discontinuance made for life, to claime by right of the new reversion discended; so that hee had a double title, the reversion reserved sur le leas and the title in taile, consequently election of Action: Quaere.

P. 17. Ed. 3. A lease made for life, the remainder to another in fee, the lessee aliened in fee, and a writ de consimili casu brought by him in the remainder, and it abated, for the Court said, that hee in remainder, was not possessed in fait, till the remainder did fall after the death of the lessee.

Saith Fitzherbert, the Law is not so taken at this day, but that hee in remainder hath the remainder vested in him, as well as hath hee in the reversion, for hee may haue an action of waste, and enter for alienation of his tenement as well as hee in the reversion may: Ergo hee hath his remainder in fait, and mee seemeth, this Judgement was not well giuen, saith Fitzherbert. And Hill 18 E.2. it was held by Herle Justice, that the Writ lieth well enough for him in remainder. And Tri. 31. E. 1. the heire in taile maintained a writ of entry in Consimili casu vpon alienation made by tenant le curtesie.

Sect. XXXI.

The Writ of Entrie ad communem legem.

THe Writ of Entry at Common law, is giuen in Case where Tenant in Dower, or per curtesie, or for life doth alien in fee, or in taile, or for life, &c. now if the Tenant which aliened doe dye, hee in the reuersion must take this Writ of Entry ad communem legem, which is very like the former Writs, and may be in the per, cui, & post; If a woman recouer Dower, alien, and dye, the Writ of Entry ad communem legem, must make mention of the recouery; And if Tenant by the curtesie alien in fee, and dye, he in the reuersion if he be heire in fee simple, may sue this Writ, or his Assise of Mortdancester, giuen by the Statute of Glocester. ca. 3. If Tenant for life alien in fee, and dye, the Writs for him in reuersion are in diuers formes, for if hee haue the reuersion by discent, the Writ is in quod idem A. non habet ingressum nisi per C. cui D. pater vel antecessor, of the Demandant cuius hæres, &c. demised, &c. But when the Demandant himselfe

himselfe made the lease to him which aliened, then the Writ is or may be Præcipe quod reddat, &c. omitting these words, quod clamat vt ius & hæreditatem; and note, if Tenant for life alien in fee, and dye, hee in reuersion may chuse whether he will haue this writ, or an ad terminum qui præterit. If Tenant for life grant his estate, and hee in reuersion grant his reuersion with Atturnement, if now the Tenant which atturned alien in fee, the grantee of the reuersion shall haue a Writ, mentioning the grant and assignation, &c.

SECT. XXXII.

More of forfeitures, and how a particular Tenant may forfeit his estate without alienation.

NOte. If Tenant for life, lease the land to J. S. for terme of life of J. S. which dyeth, the first leasee still liuing, hee shall not haue the land againe, because hee leased more than was in him, and therefore, hee in the reuersion shall haue it: But if two be seised for life, the inheritance in fee to one of them, and ioyne in a lease for life, and the leasee dyeth, they shall bee ioynt tenants againe. y Littleton 13. E. 4. fol. 4. Because hee which had the fee was priuy to the lease, and so the other gained no new reuersion.

It is yet further to be understood, both that he in reuersion may enter upon alienations made by particular Tenants, vt supra, to his disinheritance, without suing the aboue mentioned Writs: And also that there are sundry other forfeitures to the Reuersioner besides expresse alienations, which I would haue widdowes to take heed of.

6. Edw. 3. fol. 17. In Action of waste by an Infant against Tenant by his fathers demise, he pleades, that the father

father confirmed his estate to have and to hold to him and his heires in fee, by his deed shewed to the Court, Judgement si, &c. It was said for verity, that if the claime were found false, the heire might enter. Page 64. in Fitzh.

And if a reversion bee granted by fine, and the conuse brings a quid iuris clamat against the Tenant for life, which pleadeth that shee hath estate in taile, by deuise in Testament from the Commissors, if it bee found by verdict that shee hath but estate for life, that estate is forfeited, Quod vide Plowd. fol. 212. in Saunders in Fremans Case, where the entry for the conusee is consideratum est, pro seisina & reddit præd' cum partium versus &c. occasionæ & clam' & placit prædict' forisfact' habend' (si voluerit) persequatur ac etiam quod finis præd' si voluerit ingrossetur. Plesingtons Case 6. R. 2. was this. A man made a lease for yeeres, and granted further by Indenture, if he aliened the reversion, or dyed within the terme, that the leassee should haue franchetenement, and livery was made, the fee simple was granted by fine &c. and in a quid iuris clamat, the leassee claimed franchetenement, iudgement was giuen that the cognisee might enter for a forfeiture, and that the fine should be engrossed, (si voluerit) See 3. & 4. Eliz. Dier. 209. in a like case the iudgement was, not quod quærens recuperet seisinam, but quod prosequatur pro seisina si voluerit, & finis ingrossetur &c.

SECT. XXXIII.

The Statute of 11. H. 7. cap 20.

THE Common Law restrictiue of it selfe, and helped something by the Statute of Glocester, was sufficient, a great while, to bridle women from making alienations for any land that they held in Dower or Joynture, as arguments of their owne good deserts and testimonies of their husbands loue; But time, which made the

the art of fencing more fine than it was at the first, when Combattants fought all at head and shoulders, and it was greater shame to strike vnder the girdle than it is now, made law also more subtile than in the beginning it was, when lands went altogether, or for the most part by liuery of seisin.

And women witty of themselues, instructed by crafty men, grew cunning at the last, that they could alien lands, holden for life, or in taile, to whom they listed in fee. And hee which suffereth disinheritance should not easily helpe himselfe by Writ of Entry, either *ad communem legem* or *in casu prouiso*: for remedy whereof was made this seuere statute in effect as followeth. 11.H.7.

If any woman, which hath had or hereafter shall haue any estate in Dower, or for life, or in taile, ioyntly with her husband, or only to her selfe, or to her vse in any Manors, Lands, Tenements, or other Hereditaments of the inheritance, or purchase of her husband, or giuen to the husband and wife in taile, or for terme of life by any Ancestors of the husband, or by any other person seised to the vse of the husband, or of his Ancestors, and haue, or shall hereafter being sole, or with any other after taken to husband, discontinued, or discontinue, aliened, released or confirmed, alien, release, or confirme, with warranty, or by couin, suffered, or suffer any recouery of the same, against them, or any of them, or any other seised to their vse, or to the vse of either of them, after the forme aforesaid, that all such recoueries, discontinuances, alienations, releases, confirmations, and warranties, so had, and made, and from henceforth to be had, and made, be vtterly void, &c. And that it shall be lawfull to euery person and persons, to whom the interest, title, or inheritance, after the decease of the said woman, of the said manors, lands, or tenements, or other hereditaments being discontinued, aliened, or suffered to be recouered, after the first day of December next comming in the forme aforesaid should appertaine, to enter into all and euery of the Pre-

missés,

misses, and peaceably to possesse and enioy the same, in such manner and forme, as he or they should haue done, if no such discontinuance, warranty, or recouery had beene had or made: And if any of the said husbands and women, or any other seised, or that shall be seised to the use of them of the estate afore specified, after the said first of December, doe make or cause to be made, or suffer any such discontinuance, alienations, warranties, or recoueries, in forme aforesaid, that then it shall be lawfull to the person or persons, to whom the said manors, lands, and tenements should or ought to belong, after the decease of the woman, to enter into the same, and to possesse, and enioy them, according to such title, and interest, as they should haue had in the same, if the woman had beene dead, no discontinuance, warranty, nor recoueries, had as against the said husband, during his life, if the discontinuance, alienation, warranties, and recoueries, be hereafter had by or against the same husband and woman, during Couerture and espousals betwixt them; Prouided, that the said women, after the decease of their said husbands, may reenter and enioy, &c. according to their first estate; And ouer this it is enacted, that if the woman, at the time of such discontinuance, alienation, recouery, warranty, &c. be sole, that then shee shall bee barred and excluded of her title and interest in the same from thenceforth, and the person or persons, to whom the title, interest and possession of the same should belong, after the womans decease, shall immediately after the discontinuance, alienation, warranty, and recouery, enter, possesse, and enioy, the same Manors, Lands, &c. according to his or their title; Prouided that this Act extend not to auoid any recouery, discontinuance, or warranty, after the forme aforesaid, heretofore had, made, or suffered, but only where the husband and wife, or either of them, now being aliue, or any other to their use, now haue title and Interest to the said Manors, &c. or take the issues and profits to their use; Prouided also, that this Act extend not to any recouery

uery or discontinuance, where the heire next inheritable to the woman, or he, or they, that next after her death, should haue estate of inheritance, &c. be assenting or agreeing to the recoueries, where the same assent and agreement is of record or inrowled. Prouided also, that it shall bee lawfull to euery woman being sole, or married after the death of her first husband, to giue, sell, discontinue, &c. for terme of her life only, after the course of the common Law.

SECT. XXXIV.

The Exposition.

BEfore this Statute, if Tenant in Dower had aliened in fee with warranty, and dyed, the warranty discending vpon him in reuersion, had barred him; for against collaterall warranty of Tenant in Dower, or for life, the Statute of Glocester cap. 3. determined nothing. Litleton fol. 164. He addeth, that if the heire were vnder age, both at time of alienation, and also when the warranty discended, hee should bee at no preiudice by this collaterall warranty: But if he were vnder age at time of the alienation, and came afterward to full age, during the womans life, and neuer entered, then perchance hee should be barred; This was Law when Litleton wrote, and had continued so aboue two hundred yeeres, and during the raigne of nine Kings after the making of Glocester cap. 3. which Statute Dyer comparing with the later, he reputes the last cruell against women; for by this Act of 11. Hen. 7. all alienations, recoueries, releases, and warranties of Tenant in Dower, or Joynture of the husbands lands are of no strength. And where Glocester alloweth Tenant by the curtesie to alien with warranty and assets: this from women is cleane taken away, this, he saith, is vn case fort dure. That if a woman Joyntresse in in taile, whose warranty is lineall to her heires, doe alien, and leave assets, yet the heire may enter; Therefore hee is of the minde that this Statute being rigorous of it selfe, ought to receive a streit and litterall interpretation, fol. 148. But Stamford, Browne, & Brook, expounded these words, (given by the Ancestors) to bee intendible of all manner of assurances, for money or otherwise: There are two Cases in Plowden that moued great Arguments upon this Statute; The first is betwixt Wimbishe and Falbois, a man enfeoffed divers persons to the use of himselfe and his wife in speciall taile, before the Statute of 27. Hen. 8. of uses, and after the Statute the husband died, a stranger recovered in a formedone, per ment deduc, the first day, by covin, and upon false title, he to whom the title appertained, after the womans death entred, and the entry was adiudged lawfull, though hee could not have Iudgement for a default in the pleading, and that was want of certainty in his replication, and not shewing how he was heire, or the party to whom the entry was given by the Statute.

The greatest matter upon the Statute obiected to inforce a proofe, that the widdow, which suffered the recovery, was not bound by this Act, was, that she held not ioyntly with her husband, any lands or tenements, but only shee was seised of an use in taile. (for they tooke it cleare on all parts, that the case came into consideration, as if the Act of 27. had not beene made) and that seemes to bee directly within the letter of the Lawes; But Montague chiefe Iustice, shewing how greatly the marriage of women, and their advancement by it, is respected in Law, as appeareth by the Writ of causa matrimonii prolocuti, and the cui ante divortium taken by equity of West. 2. cap. 3. and also by that, that where donees in frankemarriage are divorced; the woman shall have all the lands: affirmeth it to bee reason against such women thus favored, and who abuse such favors as the Law bestowes upon them, and will be of Covin and Falsity, to impaire their

deceased

deceased husbands inheritance, and disinherit their heires, to construe this Law for their correction, for the Law-makers of the statute were bent extremely against them, though it be penall in some sort of it selfe. And so it was agreed, that if the widdow were not within the words, yet shee was within the intent and meaning of this Statute.

The other case was this betwixt Eitton and Stud. Baron and Feme levied a fine of lands of the wives inheritance, taking backe an estate in taile the remainder to the right heires of the wife, the question was whether the woman after her husbands death, might alien without danger of this Statute, adiudged that she might, because shee was cleare without the intent and meaning of the Act: For whatsoever the words import, the matter that this Statute aimed was, and is, to restraine women which have Joyntures, proceeding originally from their husbands, or the husbands Ancestors, that they should doe nothing preiudiciall to the heires. But in this case there came no Joynture from the husband, but contrariwise, the wife had made a Joynture to her husband, and after his decease, to bridle the woman to doe what shee listed with her owne inheritance, were against all reason, and as farre from any affinitie with 11. H. 7. as it should be, when a woman seised in Fee simple gives lands to the father of him whom she intends to marrie, to the intent that he regrant this land to his sonne and her after marriage, with a remainder in taile, &c. to restraine her, when after marriage regranting, and death of the husband, she should levie a fine to other uses, or suffer a recoverie, which case though it be cleane out of the Statute, yet it is within the words, for the Joynture was made by the Barons Ancestor, though not originally, &c. And so note those two cases of Plowd. one is taken to be within the intent, though out of the letter, and the other though within the letter, yet out of the intent, and yet both constructions most reasonable and iust.

And see Sir George Brownes case, Sir Edw. Cokes 3. Rep.

Rep. that a lease made by a woman tenant in taile of the gift of her husband, &c. make a lease for three liues that is not warranted by the Statute of 32. H.8 and although the lease be without clause of Warrantie, yet it is within the Statute of 11. H. 7. for those words in the act (with warrantie) refer to releases and confirmations which makes no discontinuance without warrantie, for the intent of the Act is, to prohibit not onely euerie barre, but euerie manner of discontinuance, which puts the heire to his reall action. And in that case it was resolued, that if the issue in taile had before the womans forfeiture granted his remainder onely in that case, hee by the expresse letter of the Act shall enter vpon the discontinuance of the woman, for his act doth not binde his estate. But when the issue in taile leuie a fine with proclamation, in the life of the woman tenant in taile, &c. that shall binde the taile, and therefore there the Conusee shall enter, for hee which hath the immediate title, interest, or inheritance, at the time of the forfeiture, shall enter by that Statute. And it was said by Anderson, Chiefe Justice of the Common Pleas, that where it was inuented for to make euasions out of the Statute, that if such a woman tenant in taile accepts a fine sur conusans de droit come ceo, &c. and by grant and renders the land for a thousand yeares, that is an alienation within the intention of the Act, although the words of the Act are discontinuance, alienation, &c. and of that opinion was Wray Chiefe Justice, and Dyer, and all the Court of Common Pleas was of the same opinion, 18. Eliz.

And in Sir Edw. Cokes 3. Rep. Lincolne College case. It was resolued, that if the heire in taile conuey the lands to others, and the woman tenant in taile release, or make confirmation with warrantie which is not but to perfect and corroborate the estate which the heire in taile hath made, such a warrantie is not restrained by the said Act, for that which the woman hath done, is for the benefit of the heire, and not for his preiudice, and by his assent. And

the

she and the heire might have joyned a fine, and so barre the estate taile, notwithstanding the Statute of 11. H. 7. therefore such Acts by the woman shall not be void, to grant the heire, or any else, any advantage by the Statute of 11. H. 7. And note the opinion of Sir Edw. Coke in the said case of Lincolne College, that the sonne borne after, shall by this Statute out the daughter, who entred for forfeiture, and shewes other opinions concurring, yet in Dyer 21. Eliz. 362. the heire in such a case is said to be in by purchase.

And note, Reader, that it hath beene adjudged, that although the Deed of conveyance, and assurance of the womans Joynture or estate, doth expresse her marriage portion, as well as her marriage, to be the cause and consideration of such Joynture or estate, yet if the estate proceeds from the husband or his Ancestors, she is within the said Statute of 11. H. 7. and see Villers and Beaumonts case, 4. Mar. 146. But enquire if the portion money appeare to be the full price of the land, if that differ not the case.

See Sir Edw. Cokes Comment upon Littleton, 365. These cases put a man seised in Fee, levie a fine to the use of himselfe for life, and after to the use of his wife, and of the heires males of her body by him begotten, and had issue male, and after he and his wife levied a fine, and suffered a common recoverie; the husband and the wife dies, and the issue male entred by the Statute of 11. H. 7. and the entrie was holden lawfull, and yet this case is out of the letter of the Statute, for she neither levied the fine, &c. being sole, or with any other save her husband, who made the Joynture, Sed qui hæret in littera, hæret in cortice; and therefore this case being within the mischiefe of the Statute is within the remedy. But note, Reader, that this case was denyed for Law by the Recorder of London, in his argument in the case hereunder specified, betweene Copland and Pyat. Another case in Sir Edw. Cokes Commentaries upon Littleton, which agree with Eiston and Studs case in Plowd. is; A man seised of land iure vxoris and they two leuie a fine, and the Conusee grant and render the land to the husband and wife in speciall taile, the remainder to the right heires of the wife, they haue issue, the husband dieth, the wife taketh another husband, and they two leuie a fine in Fee; the issue entreth, this is within the letter of the Statute, and yet is out of the meaning, because the state of the land moued from the wife, so as it was the purchase of the husband in letter, and not in meaning. But where the woman is tenant for life by the gift, or conueyance of any other, her alienation with Warrantie shall binde the heire at this day.

The case of Copland and Pyat adiudged Hillar. 7. Car. in Banco Regis, in effect was thus. I. S. his sonne was to marrie to the daughter of I. N. And the Deed declareth that I. N. for the consideration of foure hundred pounds paid by I. S. and of a marriage, &c. and for the preferment of the bloud of I. N. couenants to stand seised to the vse of the sonne of I. S. and his daughter whom the sonne of I. S. should marrie, entaile the remainder to another daughter of I. N. the remainder to the heires of I. N. the husband dieth hauing issue, and the wife alieneth by fine. And it was resolued, that it was not within the Statute of 11. H. 7. notwithstanding the foure hundred pounds paid by the husbands father, for the land first moued from the wiues father, and the preferment of the bloud of I. N. shewed the intent that the husbands heires should not be preferred, but the wiues. And the Bishop of Exceters case was in that case cited, which was that in consideration of kinred to the woman, and seruice done by the man, the Bishop gaue the land to them in taile, the remainder to the heires of the Bishop, it was said to be adiudged, that the woman Donee after her husbands death, had no estate within the said Statute of 11. H. 7. but that she might sell it without danger of the Statute.

SECT.

SECT. XXXV.

what Actions concerning chattells doe suruiue a widdow.

I Hold it good wisdome for a widdow, and for all persons, to haue greatest care of matters of greatest moment, and not to contemne the lesser: Now that we haue done with matters of Francktenement, we will see a little, in what Actions concerning Chattels reall, or personall duties a widdow may be Plaintiffe, or Defendant, to make an end of reckonings begun before, or whilst she was a wife. If Feme couert deliuer Deed to J. S. she may haue Action of Detinue for the Deed after her husbands decease, for though the deliuerie were voyd betwixt J. S. and the Baron, yet it is good betwixt J. S. and the wife, if the Baron dye, 3. H. 6. 50.

If a lease be made to Baron and Feme for yeares, and the Baron die, the wife shall haue the terme, and if the Lessor out her, she may haue Action of couenant, 47. Ed. 3. 12.

If a man be bound to Baron and Feme in Statute Merchant, the Baron alone may make defeasance, and by some opinion the Audita querela must bee against him alone: but if he doe not release, &c. the Statute suruiueth to the wife, and she may sue execution, & executors nemy. And, per Finch, the Law is all one of an Obligation and a Statute. Likewise in a plea of land, if Baron and Feme recouer the land with dammages, and the Baron die, his wife shall sue for dammages, and not his Executors.

So likewise by Belknap, If an Obligation be made to Alice the wife of Robert, this is a good Obligation, and Alice and Robert may ioyne in an action vpon it, and if Robert die before he haue released, for he may alone release it, Alice alone shall haue the Action, 48. Ed. 3. 12.

simile 7. H. 6. fo. 2. See the Commentaries of Sir Coke vpon Littleton, fol. 350. It is said that Chattels reals of a mixt nature, namely, part y in possession, and partly in action, happening during couerture, if the wife haue her husband, she shall haue them by the Common Law, as if the husband be seised of a rent charge, rent seruice, or Secke, iure vxoris, the rent incurreth during couerture, if the husband dye the wife shall haue the arrerages, and so of an Aduowson of the Church during couerture, & sic de similibus. And in those cases the husbands shall gaine them by suruiuership: but for arrerages, or auoydance of the Church before marriage, the husband could haue no help by suruiuership, and so of releases. But now by the Statute of 32. H. 8. cap. 37. By suruiuership the husband shall haue the arrerages as well incurred before the marriage as after.

If an Estray happen within the Mannor of the wife, if the husband dye before seisure, the wife shall haue it, for that the propertie was not in the wife before seisure.

But as to personall goods there is a diuersitie betwéene a propertie and a bare possession, for if personall goods be deliuered to a woman, or if she finde goods, or if goods come to her hands, as Executrix to a Bayliffe, and taketh an husband, this bare possession is not giuen to the husband, but the Action of Detinue must be brought against the husband and the wife.

If Baron and Feme make a lease for yeares, and the Baron die, the wife may bring an Action of waste, 22. H. 6. 24.

If an Obligation be made to Baron and Feme, and the Baron die, the widdow may haue the Obligation. 4. H. 6. 5. Quære, for the booke is not so cleare, as Brooke makes it, the woman was Obligée with her husband, and sued as Executrix.

Generally where title, or cause of Action, is giuen to a woman before marriage, or during marriage, and the husband releaseth not, &c. the Action suruiueth when hée

dies.

dye. But there may be a release in land as well as in fact implied, as well as expressed. And therefore the case is 8. Ed. 2. Br. Dett. 156. and cite Plowd. 184. in Woodward and Darcy his Case, If a man be bound to a woman, and to another, and the Obligor marry the woman, all the obligation is extinct although the wife over-live her husband, or although shee dyes, living the other obligee, for either of the obligees hath power to release, and that intermarriage is a release. And gifts in Law of the chattels of the wife as well reall as personall are outlawry or attainder of the husband. If a man marry with a woman executrix, and then release to Creditors, all manner of Actions generaly, this extendeth to his proper accords, and to those which his wife hath, either in her owne right, or as executrix. Baron and feme 80. in Brooke. See Brooke couenant 6. Action of couenant was brought against Baron and Feme, lessees of a Manor for terme of life, rendring 20. li. per annum, and they were bound to the Plaintiffe, that hee should haue such surety for his rent as his Councell deuised; the Counsellers deuised the Assurance, and the Defendants refused to make it, it was ruled for Law, that if the Baron died, nothing should bind his widdow, saue onely the lease and reseruation, if shee agreed to the lease post mortem viri: And shee shall bee charged with payment of the rent, or double it, or pay fine nomine pœnæ, or hold it subiect to reentry, according as the lease was made: But a collaterall couenant, as that the lessor shall distraine in other lands for his rent, or a couenant, to charge the lessees persons in twenty pound for non payment, &c. such like agreements binde not the widdow, when the Baron is dead, and the Writ abated.

Note, that widdow is a good Addition, to bee put to the Defendants name in any originall Writ of Action personall, appeale or inditement, wherein exigent lieth, &c. According to the Statute, 1. Hen. 5. cap. 5. And 14. Edw. 4. fol. 7. Starkey demanded of the Iustices in the Chequer chamber, if an Action were brought against a woman that was neither maid, wife, nor widdow, what addition should be given her, some say she should be called single woman: and there it is doubted, whether seruant bee a good addition, or not; for it was no addition by the Common Law, as some said.

Wee are past the greatest, and most difficult part of Law, peculiarly belonging to a widdow, and come now to consider, whether she shall marrie againe, or no. If Iohn Boccace de Certaldo, in his Booke De duris mulieribus, may be beleeued, When the sister of couetous King Pigmaleon, and widdow of Sycheus, Hercules his Priest, had built the Wals, Temple, Market, Towne house, and priuate dwellings of Carthage, giuing lawes and rules of life to the inhabitants, amongst the rest that were filled with loue of her great vertues and singular beautie, the King of Malaca was one, he grew so vehement in his desires, that he threatned the Citizens of Carthage with warres, and vtter subuersion of their new Citie, vnlesse he might haue the Foundresse of it to be his wife: They knowing how highly their Queen would remaine displeased by any direct sollicitation to a second marriage, & not knowing how otherwise to saue themselues, determined to win her assent without asking. The chiefe of them went therefore to Dido, and told her how the King of Malaca required Masters and Instructers of humanitie to be sent him out of Carthage, from whom he and his people might learne to doe off their naturall barbarousnesse and inciuilitie, and further, how hee had menaced fire, sword, and extreme dissolution, vnlesse his request were accomplished: But they knew not (they said) whom to send, or who would be willing to goe, and leaue his owne habitation, to dwell with a King of such sauage nature, and wilde behauiour, as was this King of Malaca. Dido, when she heard them, answered, that she was ashamed there should be found in any Carthaginian, such sloth and cowardly feare, affirming plainly, that men were not borne onely for themselues, and whosoeuer he were that

would

would not adventure losse, perill, yea, and death, though it were certaine, for safegard of his Countrey, hee was (shee said) unworthy to dwell in Carthage, or that either he or his posteritie should ever be received to any honour or reputation amongst them. The Carthaginians thought they had obtained their desire, and uncovered their counsell to the Queene, telling her plainly the Kings demand. Dido not knowing how to reply against her owne redargutions, replenished with sorrow and anxietie, was enforced to yeeld her assent to wedlocke, and craved a day, before which she said she would goe unto her husband; but before th[e] terme was expired, she caused a great fire to be made in the most eminent place of the Citie, and there in view and concourse of all other people, after many ceremonies and offering of sacrifice, as it were to appease the ghost of Sicheus, she suddenly with a knife strake her selfe [to] the heart, and told her subjects that now she went to her husband, her Sicheus, her deare Sicheus, on whose name still invocating, she sunke to the ground, having chosen rather to shed her dearest lifes bloud (as she said) than to violate the vowes of chaste widdowhood. Boccace mine Author here may have some colour of reason, to extoll the resolution of Dido, but not to condemne so bitterly (as he doth) all women that marrie a second husband. Some of them are destitute of friends, their parents, brethren, and kindred dwell farre off, sutors come everie day, who can resist them? Another widdow hath lands, rents, store of goods, some suits at Law, and no body that she can trust, in help to governe that which shee hath, or to inherit it when she is gone. Another is tolled to marrie by mightie perswasions of her dearest friends and kindred. Another hath fervent youth on her side; and let Indians leape into the dead mans fire, if they will, she hath learned that it is better to marrie than to burne.

SECT.

SECT. XXXVI.

A Caueat to marrie so, that it be not uncertaine who shall be father to the next childe.

I For my part, that am like neuer to be feared, vnlesse some widdow be moued with compassion towards mee, will not speake villanie of Bigamie, or Octogamie, let euerie woman marrie when shee seeth her time, but festinare lente, as I wis speed perhaps will be best, and let her examine well whether the pannier be emptie, or no. If (saith Sir Thomas Smith, in his Treatise De Repub. Angliæ, fol. 104.) I marrie the widdow of one lately dead, which at the time of her husbands death was with childe, and the childe is borne after marriage solemnized with me, this childe shall be mine heire and lawfull sonne, so precisely doe we take the letter, Pater est quem nuptiæ demonstrant. Littleton saith, 18. E. 4. fol. 30. If a man marrie a woman which is grossment enseint by another, and within foure dayes after marriage she is deliuered, this childe shall be his that hath newly married the woman, and inherit his land, for it is no bastard. It seemeth hee would haue it vnderstood of a woman enseint by hap-hazard, and in such cases it is reason, that hee which takes the Dame should haue the Fole. So is it also when a woman elopes with a stranger in aduowterie, and hath a child, her husband Iohn at Noke being betweene the foure seas, must father the childe, and it shall be his heire, if he die; for the Law will not bring into triall directly, who begat the childe, 44 Edw. 3. fol. 10. and 7. Hen. 4. fol. 10. But though issue may not be taken, whether a woman were enseint by her husband, at the time of his death, leauing out the question by whom, as appeareth by the former Bookes, and 1. H. 6. fol. 3. Then if it may be found by Enquest, that a woman was with childe at her husbands death, the Law which permits not to enquire by whom,

affirmes

affirmes it to be the husbands, and that husbands which might lawfully beget it. I thinke surely, Sir Thomas Smith mistooke the Law: for by Thorpe and Willowby, 21. E. 2. fol. 29. If a man dye seised of land in Fee simple, and the wife which is priuement enseint with a sonne, marrie againe, and after is deliuered, this sonne shall bee adiudged sonne and heire to the first Baron and not to the second: Though Iustice Bere there were of opinion, that the Infant might chuse his father: It were better reason perhaps, that the second husband might chuse whether hee should be his sonne, or no, and by allowance make him his heire.

Sir Ed. Coke in his Comment vpon Littleton, fol. 8 a. saith, If a man hath a wife, and dieth within a verie short time after, the wife marrieth againe, and within nine moneths hath a childe, so as it may be the childe of the one or the other, some haue said in this case the childe may chuse his father, Quia in hoc casu filiatio non potest probari, and so is the Booke to be intended: For auoyding of which question, and other inconueniences, this was the Law before the Conquest, Sit omnis vidua sine marito 12. mensibus, & si maritaverit perdat dotem. But if women had all béene of such sobrietie, as many are, many of these questions had never risen, and I must confesse it is great petulancie in any widdow, that slippeth to second wedlocke, whilst she yet nourisheth in her wombe, the pledge of vnion and loue, betwixt her and her late husband: I thanke God, I cannot say that I haue knowen in my lifetime any widdow so wanton. In old time women vsed now and then to faine themselues left with childe, and to bring forth borrowed brats, to depriue the Deceaseds right heire of his inheritance, sometimes of their owne mischieuous malice and deceitfulnesse, and sometime by consent and combining with the Lords of whom the lands were holden. Bracton in his second Booke, cap. 32. hath a large discourse, De partu supposito: and there is a Writ to the Sheriffe, to call before him, and the Keeper of Pleas

of

of the Crowne, the woman that pretendeth to be enseint, to haue her examined, by tractation and search of good and lawfull women, per vbera & per ventrem, whether she be pregnant or no, and if the matter be found doubtfull, to commit her to a Castle, and warie custodie, without accesse of any suspected woman, Quousque de partu suo constare possit. But this is a peece of learning so obsolete and worne out, that I thinke since I was borne, and a long time before, there neuer was any such Writ put in vre. I conclude therefore, that our widdowes now adayes are honester than they were in Henry the thirds time, in the fifth yeare of whose reigne, Mariell widdow of William Constable de Mauton in Comitat. Norff. practised this cousenage: widdowes of this age are nothing so deceitfull, though deceiued sometimes by bad husbands.

(*.*)

THE

THE WOMANS LAWYER.

The fifth BOOKE.

THe widdow married againe to her owne great liking, though not with applause of most friends and acquaintance. But alas what would they haue her to haue done, she was faire, young, rich, gracious in her carriage, and so well became her mourning apparrell, that when shee went to Church on Sundayes, the casements opened of their owne accord on both sides the streets, that bachelours and widdowers might behold her, Hic trahebatur & ille, & erat cunctis amor vnus habendi. Her man at home kissed her pantables, and serued diligently; Her late husbands Physitian, came and visited her often; The Lawyer to whom shee went for councell, tooke opportunity to aduise for himselfe. If shee went to any feast, there was euer one guest, sometimes two or three, the more for her sake; If she were at home, suitors ouertooke one another, and sometimes the first commer would answer the next, that she was not within; All day she was troubled with answering petitions. And at night when she would go to rest, her maid Marion was become a Mistris of requests and humble supplications. This kinde of life the widdow liked not: I aske againe what she should haue done; he to whom shee gaue a deniall would not take it; if shee denied him twise, hee said two negations made an affirmation; and hee challenged promise: therefore to set mens harts and her owne at rest, shee chose amongst them, one not of the long robe, not a man macerate and dryed vp with study, but a galiant gilded lad; that might well be worthy of her, had hee béene as thrifty as kind hearted, or halfe so wise, as hardy and aduenturous; This youth within lesse than a yeere, had set the Nuncios which his predecessor kept in prison at liberty round about the Countrey, the bags were all empty, the plate was all at pawne, all to kéep the square bones in their amble, and to relieue Companions; One of which notwithstanding, that had cost him many a pound, for none other quarrell, but vous mentes challenged him one day into the field, which was appointed, and there my new married man was slaine; Now his wife will bring her Appeale.

SECT. I.

Appeale of the husbands death.

By Bracton li. 3. cap. 29. A woman can haue an Appeale, but only in two cases; per quod alicui lex debeat apparens adiudicari. As in case where iniury and force is committed against her person by rauishment, or when her husband is killed inter Brachia sua: This forme of appeale therefore is, A. late wife of B. appeales C. that whereas B. her husband was at such a place, such an houre, such a day, and such a yéere, C. came with force, nequiter & in felonia contra pacem regis, and killed him betwixt her armes, and that he did this against the Kings peace,

peace, and felloniously, shee will proue and maintaine as the Court shall thinke good; Againe, the same A. appeales E. of this, that at the same place, the same yeere, day and hower, E. came with C. felloniously, and against the Kings peace, and held B. till C. killed him, &c. If hee which is appealed, de facto, were taken vpon the fact; with his knife or sword all bloudy, and this verified by Testimony of good and lawfull men; non erit vlterius inquirendum. Thus Bracton.

Now let vs see how shee shall be vnderstood, there is no doubt, but a woman may haue other Appeales, besides these two, of rape, or death of her husband.

11.Hen.4.fol.93. An Appeale of Robbery was brought by a woman, the defendant said, the Appealant was his niefe, iudgement, si el serra respondue, and to the robbery, non culpable. So that hee pleaded to the fellonie, and the niefty admitted a good plea. And a woman may haue an appeale of mayhem. 13.Hen.7.14. Hussey saith, it was demanded of him for a doubtfull question, where parish Clarke fell out with another man, and threw the Church doore keyes at him with such force, that they flang out at the Chamber window, and put out a womans eye, whether it were mayhem or no? And for the euill intent of the Clarke, it was deemed mayhem; but consideration ought to be had in assessing dammages. But true it is a woman shall not haue appeale of any mans death, saue only of her husbands, therefore if a man bee killed that hath neither wife, nor sonne, but his next heire is either daughter, sister or female Cosin, albeit he hath many other kinred, Cosins, or Vncles, the proximity of a female heire, takes away the Appeals quite and cleane; for of her Ancestors death, if he had no wife, the Appeale belongs ouer to the heire, who here cannot haue it, because it is a female; for Mag. Char. doth directly deny it. Cap. 34. Nullus capietur aut imprisonetur, propter apellum feminæ de morte alterius quam viri sui. And vpon such an Appeale brought by an heire female, the Defendants cannot

cannot bee arraigned at the Kings suit, because the Appeale was neuer good. Neither shall the Defendants recouer dammages, because (as Shard maketh the reason) hee may bee arraigned and condemned otherwise ad Sectam regis, for any thing yet done to the Contrary. 27. Ass. p. 25.

A daughter or sister, &c. can haue none Appeales of a fathers or brothers death, no more can a mother haue Appeale of the death of her sonne. If a woman haue issue a sonne, which is murdred, and there is no heire to him on the fathers side, by Billing chiefe Iustice, Needham, and Choke, none vncle nor other kinsman which must conuey as heire by the mother, can haue the Appeale, because the Statute, before remembred, excludeth her, from whom they must deriue: Brian, Littleton, Neale, and the chiefe Baron are contra. For, said they, the Vncle on the father side may haue Appeale of the Nephewes death, which the father from whom the Vncle must conueigh, cannot haue any more than the mother. But Billing tels them, the Cases are nothing like, for a father may haue an Appeale of his Ancestors death; but so cannot another in any case; the bridge therefore being once broken, id est, the meane of conueyance stopped and disabled, the Appeale is altogether, and for euer taken away. 17. Edw. 4. fol. 1. And so is it adiudged likewise 20. Hen. 6. fol. 43. where there was grandfather, mother and sonne, the mother died, the grandfather was murthered, the sonne might not haue Appeale, because hee conueyed by a woman, scilicet, by his mother, and there it was stood to, that an Appeale shall neuer discend, but hee to whom it first falleth, shall haue it, and if he dye, the Action dieth. It is a good case well argued in the booke at large. See the booke of 11. Hen. 4. 12. It appeares that in Appeale of Rape by the husband ne vnques accouple, &c. nest plea for the husband in Act or possession shall haue that where the marriage is not void, and yet that plea is good in Appeale by the wife of the death of her husband, for there shee shall

shall not revenge his death to whom she was not lawfully married, and see 50. E.3.15. Britton agrees with Bracton qui null fee, puisseare appeller de felonie, de mort forsque de mort son baron, tue deins lan & le iour enter ses bras. And it is true, that by the ancient Law neither woman or other person might haue appeale of death, vnlesse the appellant were present, or did see the dead man, at the time when hee was slaine. But the Law is changed by Gloc. cap. 9. which willeth that no Writ henceforth shall goe out of Chancery, for the death of man, to enquire whether a man killed another, by misaduenture, or in his owne defence, or otherwise feloniously, but he shall remaine in prison, till the comming of Iustices errants, or gaile deliuery, and before them, put himselfe to the country, for triall of good and euill. And if it be found by the country, that, what he did, was in his owne defence, or by misaduenture, the Iustices shall doe the King to wit, and the King doe the party grace, si luy pleist. Also it is prouided, that no Appeale shall be abated si legierment come auaunt ad rem; but if the Appealour shew the deed, the yeere, the day, and hower, le temps le Roy, the Towne where, and the weapon wherewith the slaughter was committed, the appeale shall stand good, and none appeale shall bee abated for want of fresh suit, if it bee persued within a yeere and a day after the fait committed. Before this Statute the Appellour alwayes counted of his proper view, now it needs not. The woman that shall bring this appeale, must be wife to the party slaine, de facto & de iure, for ient accouple in loyall matrimony is a good plea, in barre of her appeale, as before is said: But this plea is not so peremptory, but that after the Bishop hath certified loyalment accouple, &c. the Defendant may afterward plead non culpable and this in fauorem vitæ, but he cannot plead on to the fellony immediately vpon the first plea. Therefore here is requisite two trials, as it seemeth 50. E.3.f.15. Idem 27. Assis. p.2.

Furthermore it is requisite, that she be sole and vnmarried,

married that made this Appeale, for if she marrie againe her Appeale is gone, though the new married husband be dead within the yeare and day after his death that was slaine. Yea, and not onely a widdow which hath an Appeale, hanging abateth her Appeale, and loseth it for ever, by new marriage, but also if after Judgement and before execution, she take an husband, she loseth execution of the Judgement, 11. H. 4. fol. 48 By Brian and Hussey, 21 E. 4. fol. 72, 72. If a woman pursue her Appeale till the Defendant be outlawed, and then marrie, she may sue execution. And so did Skreene hold the Law to be in the Booke, 11. H. 4. But Gascoigne Chiefe Justice denyes it. And 1. or 2. Mariæ, Brooke Appeale 100 the Justices of the Kings Bench did all agree, that a widdow loseth her Appeale, by taking of a second husband. Et idem videtur, (saith Brooke) de executione; for the reason wherefore this Action is given to a widdow, is not as Glanuell makes it, Quia vna caro est vir & vxor. For then the Baron might have an Appeale De morte vxoris, which is never granted, but her heire shall have it. And if the wife kill the husband, his heire shall have the Appeale. And I heare, saith Stanford, Plees del Coron. fol. 59. it hath been adiudged, If she King pardon the woman all manner of treasons, the heires Appeale is gone. But the true reason why a woman hath the Appeale De morte viri, is because by his death, shee is thought lesse able to live and maintaine her-selfe; so said the Judges in Queene Maries dayes, and that therefore when she taketh another husband, cessante causa, cessat effectus, and her Appeale is gone, like as a widdowes Quarentine is determined, when she is once remarried. But where a woman continueth sole, she and none other shall have this Action, either in her life or after, though she dye within the yeare, and before Appeale commenced, 20. H. 6. 42.

It is not requisite that the Appellant here be dowable of his possessions which is slaine, for though a woman elope from her husband, and never be reconciled, yet shee may

may have Appeale of his death, per Inglibie, 50. E. 3. 15. Sir Edw. Cokes Comment upon Littleton, fol. 37. saith, That if the Baron be attainted of treason, &c. his wife shall not be indowed, and yet if any doe kill him, the wife shall have an Appeale. So likewise agrees the Booke of 35. H. 6. 58. where, in an Appeale de morte viri the Defendant said, the Baron was indited, arraigned, found culpable, and judgement to be hanged &c. and to the felonie nient culpable: It was agreed, that there is no such corruption betwixt a man and his wife, by Attainder, as is the corruption of bloud betwixt a man and his heire, for the heire of a man attainted shall not have an Appeale, and she is his wife notwithstanding the Attainder, but the other is not heire. And per Markham, If an Appeale bee not good, the Defendant shall not bee arraigned at the Kings suit, when the Plaintiffe is at non suit: Also in this case it was delivered, that the Marshall of the Kings Bench, the Viscount, or such Officer, that is commanded to execute a man condemned, is a Felon, if hee execute him in other manner than he is commanded, as if he cuts off his head where the judgement was he should be hanged. But if he doe execution according to the judgement, then he may justifie in an Appeale, and needs not plead non culpable: Yet in Appeale against a Judge, for adjudging a man to death, he cannot justifie, but must needs plead non culpable, and give the matter in evidence, Simile 27. assi. p. 41. where, in Appeale de morte viri, the Defendant pleaded utlagary de felonie. Judgement si, &c. Shard said it was no more lawfull to kill an Outlaw, than to kill another man, and therefore the Defendant pleaded non culpable. Ludd said, that one was excused of the death of the Baron of Woodhall by the Outlawrie, &c.

It appeares now what wife, and of what husbands death she may have an Appeale. Stanford in his third Booke, cap. 15. notes, that in ancient time there were certaine presumptions so vehement, that they were a condemnation of the partie without other triall, they bee not so at this day, but everie man shall haue his triall, how great soeuer the presumption were. But the vehemencie of presumption may oust battaile. For 6. H. 3. The Coroner and others testified, that the Defendant was taken cum cultello sanguinolento, &c. ideo consideratum est, quod se non defendat per duellum.

SECT. II.

How a woman shall sue this Appeale.

IT séemes that all Appeales ought to be sued in proper person, and not by Atturney, as Appeale of Mayhem must be in proper person, 21. E. 4. 72, & 73. A woman which was grossment enseint, sued this Appeale, and the Defendant was attainted, the womans appearance was recorded for the whole terme, and yet by the better opinion, she might not pray execution, by her Councell, but ought to come in proper person; therefore one of the Iudges did ride to Islington to her, to sée if she were aliue, and desired execution, which she required, and the Defendant had iudgement. An Appeale is called but a suit of reuenge, and therefore is not much fauoured, Dyer 5. M. 152. If one of the Defendants in an Appeale makes default, the Court cannot procéed, but otherwise in an Inditement, as it is there said. This by Common Law; If any Liege subiect be slaine by another subiect in any forreine Realme, the wife of him which was slaine, may haue an Appeale in England, before the Constable and Marshall, &c. And this is by Statute, 1. Hen. 4. cap. 14. Stanford, fol. 65. Feme auer' appeale de mort viri tue in escore per commen Ley comme semble, 13. H. 4. Brooke 153. By the said Statute it is also ordained, that none Appeales from henceforth bee pursued in Parliament. Likewise I finde by Statute, viz. 15. R. 3. cap. 3. That of the death of a man, and of Mayhem done in great ships,

being

being and houering in the streame of great riuers, onely beneath the bridges of the same, nigh to the sea, and in none other places of the same riuers, the Admirall shall haue conusance, &c. sauing to the King all manner of forfeitures, &c.

SECT. III.

The Statute 3. H. 7. cap. 1.

But for the ordinarie course of suing of Appeales, 3. H. 7. cap. 1. layeth the best foundation: This Statute reciteth the Law of the land to be, that if any man bee slaine in the day, and the Felon not taken, the Township shall bee amerced. If any man bee wounded, and in perill of death, the offender should be arrested, and put in suretie, till knowledge be had, whether hee which is hurt will liue or no. And where any man is found dead, the Coroner vpon view of the body, should enquire who were the murderers, their abettors, consenters and who were present at the murder committed, whether man or woman, and he ought to inroll, and certifie their names. The vse had beene also (as saith the Statute) that within a day and yeare after any death or murder, the felony should not bee determined at the Kings suit, and that for sauing of the parties suit, or else the partie was agreed with, by which it is the more chargeable, and thereby murders were increast: and also, he that will sue in Appeale, must sue in proper person. The constitution of this Law therefore is, that euerie Coroner henceforth doe his office, and that if any man be slaine or murdered, the slayers, murderers, their abettors, maintainers, and comforters should bee indicted, arraigned, &c. at the Kings suit, within the yeare after the felony or murder done, without tarrying a yeare and a day for any Appeale. And if any, either principall or accessarie thus arraigned, bee acquited at the Kings suit with'n the yeare and day, the Justices before whom he is acquite, shall not suffer him to goe at large, but either remit him againe to prison, or let him to baile, till the yeare and day be past: And the wife or next heire of the partie slaine, may take their Appeale within the yeare and day, after the felony or murder done, (if the benefit of Clergie be not yet had) with all aduantages that acquitall or Attainder at the Kings suit notwithstanding. Furthermore, the wife or heire of the person slaine or murdered, may commence their Appeale in proper person, any time within a yeare after the felonie done, before the Sheriffes and Coroners, &c. or before the King in his Bench, or Justices of Gaole deliuerie: And the Appellant in any Appeales of murder, of death of man, where battaile by the course of Common Law lieth not, may make Atturney, and appeare by the same in the said Appeales, after they bee commenced to the end of the suit, and execution of the same. And if the murderer doe escape vntaken, the Township, &c. shall be amerced, and the Coroners shall deliuer their inquisition afore the Justices of the next Gaole deliuerie, which Justices shall proceed against the murderer, if they bee in Gaole, or else the said Justices shall put the Inquisition before the King in his Bench. The Statute also giueth the Coroner thirteene shillings and foure pence, for taking inquisition super v sum corporis.

By this Statute and the other of Gloc. cap. 9. a woman perceiues that within a yeare and a day, she commeth timely enough with her Appeale. Stanford notes, that (though the Law haue beene taken otherwise) if hee which is robbed make fresh suit, albeit he commence not his Appeale, two or three yeares after the robberie, yet his Appeale is good: for if the partie robbed haue his endeuour to take the Felon, he may commence his Appeale at any time, at the Justices discretion. For Gloc. if it be rightly vnderstood, seemeth to speake only of Appeales de mort. And where it saith, Deins l'an & iour apres le fait,

this

this (le fait) is understood the felony, whereupon Appeale must commence. Therefore if a man bee strucken and wounded on one day, and dye within the yeare another day, the Appeale must be begun within a yeare and a day after the wound given: And if a yeare after a murder committed, one become accessarie, there lyeth an Appeale against this accessarie, as it seemeth within the yeare and day after he became a Felon. And the Appellant is not confined to a yeare and a day next after the murder committed, Stamford fol. 63. a.

But in Heydons case Sir Edw. Cokes 4. Rep. fol. 42. Wray Chiefe Justice said, that the common experience of the Kings Bench was, and so was the Law without question, that the yeare for the bringing of the Appeale, shall be accounted from the death, and not from the stroke, against Stamfords opinion. And the rest of the Judges there said, that there is no felony untill the death. And in the 7. Rep. fol. 20. it is said, If the Appeale be delivered to the Sheriffe within the yeare, and before its returne, or that the Sheriffe hath done nothing, and the King dieth, and the yeare ends before the returne, in that case the Plaintiffe shall have a Certiorare to the Sheriffe, returnable in the Kings Bench, and upon that the Plaintiffe shall have Reattachment, &c. and that for necessitie, &c. otherwise she should lose her Writ lawfully purchased.

SECT. IV.

within what Countie an Appeale must be brought.

Regularly this Appeale ought to be brought into the Countie, where the homicide or murder was committed. But admitting that a man be wounded in one Countie, and goes into another and there dye, where shall the appeale commence, by Common Law: Tauloccorone.

In Fitzherbert 59. it appeares, that it was commenced in the Countie where the wound was given: but both Counties ioyned in triall, as well where the wound was, as the death. And in the same title Placito 60. in such case the Appellant commenced in the Countie where the partie died; and triall by ambideux Counties. By these bookes it should seeme, that at Common Law the Appellant might chuse his Countie, but now the Statute, 2, & 3. H. 6. is plaine, which ordaineth, whereas Iurors in one Countie could not take knowledge of things done in another by the Common Law. That in cases, vt supra, an Inditement found by Iurors of the Countie where the death happeneth, whether before the Coroner, supra visum corporis or before Iustices of Peace, or other Iustices or Commissioners, which have authoritie to enquire of such offences, shall be as good, as if the stroke, wound, or poysoning had beene in the same Countie, where the partie shall die, &c. And the Iustices of Gaole deliuerie, or of Oyer and Terminer, in the same Countie where such Inditement shall be taken, And the Iustices of the Kings Bench (after the Inditement remoued before them) may procéed as if the stroke, or poysoning, and the death had béene all in one Countie. And the partie to whom Appeale is giuen, may commence, take, and pursue in the same Countie, where the partie feloniously stricken or poysoned shall dye, against the principals, or accessaries, in whatsoeuer place or Countie the same accessaries shall be guiltie. And the Iustices before whom the Appeale shall be commenced, sued, and taken, within the yeare and day after the slaughter committed, shall procéed against all such accessaries in the Countie where the Appeale shall be so taken in like manner and forme, as if the offence of such accessarie had béene done and committed in the same Countie, where such Appeale shall be taken, as well by triall of twelue men of the same Countie wherein such Appeale is so sued, vpon plea of not guiltie, or otherwise. And further it is ordained, that where murder, or

any

any manner of felony shall be committed in one County, and another person or more shall become accessary, or accessories in another County; an Indictment found or taken by Iustices of Peace, or other Iustices or Commissioners, to enquire of fellonies, in the County where such offence of accessories is committed or done, shall bee as good, as if the principall offence had béene committed and done in the same County, wherein the Indictment of accessary is found. The Statute appointed further, how the Custos rotulorum, or Keeper of the Records, of the principals attainder, or aquitall shall certifie, &c.

Before this Statute, if one man had committed murder in one County, and another had béene accessary in another County, there was no remedy against this Accessary by the Common Law, Stanford fol. 63. yet Kinuet said, 43. E. 3. fol. 18. If a man were slaine in one part of the Towne, and another man received the Manqueller in another part of the Towne, which is in another County, Appeale might bee sued against them both in the County where the killing was committed, and that so it had béene adiudged.

Sect. V.

Before whom appeale shall be sued.

By the afore recited Statute it appeares before whom appeale must be sued: but Stanford sets it out yet more largly, Libro 2. cap. 14. The party entitled to an appeale, is at election to take it by Writ or by Bill. If he take it by Bill, he must sue al procheuie County maintenant, as soone as the fellony is committed, and by Britton fol. 5. the Plaintiffe must finde two sufficient pledges, lyable to the Viscounts distresse, to pursue his appeale, according to the Law of the land, and the Coroner shall enter the appeale, and the name of the pledges. Then it it shall bee commanded to a Bayley or seriaunt du pais, wherein the fellony was done, that hee have the bodies of the appellees at the next County, to make answer, &c. If the Serieant testifie at the next County, that hee cannot finde them, it shall be awarded, that the principals which are appealed d[e]l fait, be solemnly demanded to come to the Kings peace and due triall of the fellony, whereof they be appealed, and so they shalbe called from County to County, untill they appeare, or untill they bee outlawed. So saith Britton, and with him accordeth 22. Assis. 97. 98. which seemes a marvellous matter to Stanford, viz. that any Viscount or Coroner should award processe of outlawry in such a case. Because, Magna Charta. 17. (written long time before either Britton, or the booke of Assizes) is, that no Viscount, Constable, Escheator, Coroner, or other the Kings Officers may hold any pleas of the Crowne. Therefore many doe hold opinion, that when appeale is commenced, before the Sheriffe or Coroner, although they may award processe till exigent, yet the exigent it selfe they cannot award, neither if hee appeare, can they put him which is appealed to answer, but onely commit him to prison, because of the Statute. And when appeale is commenced before the Viscount or Coroner, it may be removed into the Kings Bench by a Certiorari, out of either the Chancery or Kings Bench, and this Certiorari shall be directed to the Viscount and Coroners, as appeares by the Register fol. 76. So that by the register, and by Westm. cap. 10. which willeth that Coroners shall attach and represent the pleas of the Crowne, and that the Viscount shall have Counterroules with them, as well of appeales, as of enquest of Attachment, or of other things which belonge to that office, &c. as also by the Booke, 4. Hen. 6. fol. 15. (where a Certiorari directed to the Viscount onely, for remove of an Appeale was holden void) and so it is evident, that an appeale is of record as well before the Viscount as before the Coroner, and so did the makers of the Law 3. Hen. 7. cap. 1. take it, as is to bee seene by the Letter.

Also

Also appeale by Bill may be begun before Iustices of Goale deliuery, but then the appellee must be in prison in the same Goale, &c. at time of the appeale so taken against him, or at the least one of the Appellees must bee in prison, &c. else the appeale ought not to be taken, and if it be it is not good, 13.H.4.fo.12. 9.H.4.fo.2.

But an Approuer may appeale them which be at large by the Statute de Appellatis. Note that, when appeale is commenced before Iustices of Goale deliuery, against diuers, whereof one only is prisoner before them, the appeale must be remoued, into the Kings Bench, and from thence processe shall goe against such as are at large. And if Iustices of Goale deliuery haue power to receiue appeales by Bill, the Iustices of the Kings Bench may doe it much more, for as Scot said 17.E.13.fol.13.they are the chiefe Coroners of the land.

If a man be in prison for fellony in the Kings Bench, or before Iustices of Goale deliuery, and afterward hee is let to Baile, appeale by Bill may bee against him notwithstanding: for hee is prisoner still when hee goeth by bailement. 21.Hen.7.fo.33. 32.Hen.7.f.4. & titulo Maineprise in Fitzherbert, for there Shard said, that they which tooke him to baile were his Gardenis, and should bee charged vpon his escape. And some said, that they might bee hanged for him. 33. E. 3. maineprise. But pla. 13. in the same title Fitzherbert saith, semble que non, for the entry is [illegible] manuceperunt. And by the booke of 33. Edw. 3. aforesaid, the entry is traditur in ballium. And where a prisoner is deliuered vnto two in baile, they may imprison him if they will, per Wilby. 26. E. 3. And 21. Hen. 7. supra. he which is let to Baile shall finde surety to answer all men.

But a man cannot haue appeale against him which goeth at large by maineprise, 9.E.4. fol.1. & 29.Hen.6.37. for he is not in ward. There is some difference betweene baile and maineprise, but learne how it stands, and whether appeale may bee commenced before Iustices of the

Peace:

Peace or no, quære, for theire Commission is to heare and determine fellonies. Also, quære, if a man be stroken in France, and dieth in England; Whether appeale lieth thereof (if the parties were not in the Kings service in France,) before the Constable and Marshall, &c. by the Statute of 1.H.4. ca.14.

SECT. VI.

Of Appeale by writ.

How an appeale shall bee begun by Writ, Stamford saith no more thereof, but onely chescun sceit comment a ceo purchaser: And as his knowledge made him presume that other men were not ignorant of it, so my ignorance makes me presume, that many doe not know it. Bracton li.3.cap.30. saith, that sometime it happeneth by negligence of the Viscount and Coroner, that the appeales must be attached by the Kings Writ in hac forma: Rex vicecomiti, &c. si A. fecerit te securum de clamore suo prosequendo, tunc attachiari facias B. per corpus suum, qd' sit coram Iusticiariis nostris ad primam assisam, cum in partes illas venerint: responsurus eidem A. de morte L. mariti, &c. vnde eum appellat, &c.

He sets downe likewise the Writ for remouing of appeales begun, and already attached: to fetch them into the Kings Bench with a pone per vadium saluos plegios, for the Defendant to be there ad respondendum prædict' le plaintiffe de prædicto Appello. But if this Writ bee granted at the instance of the Defendant, then it is with a summoneas per bonos summonitores; to the Appellant ad sequendum appellum, &c. and those words per vadium & plegios are omitted. After much like matter not vnworthy to be obserued, he comes to the Writ when appeale is begun before the King in his Bench immediately; Rex vicecomiti, &c. salutem. si A. fecerit te securum de de clamore suo prosequendo, pone per vadium & saluos plegios. B. & C. qd' sint coram &c. tali die ad respondendum eidem A. de morte. D' patris vel alterius antecessoris, vnde eos appellat. And at the day, he saith, they which are attached may essoine themselues, vnlesse they be appealed for death of man, or for a more hainous crime. West. 2. cap. 13. is against the appellee, non iaceat de cætero appellatori in appello de morte hominis essoinum, in quacunque curia appellum fuerit terminandum; Now whether Bractons forme of the Originall pone per vadium & saluos plegios, be good or no, when any appeale of murder commeth in the Kings Bench, learne, for the booke of Entries is præceptum fuit vicecomiti quod si A. fecerit eum securum de clamore suo prosequendo: attachiaret B. per corpus, &c.

SECT. VII.

Diuers appeales for one felony is but in few Cases.

By the ancient Law one might haue diuers appeales, against the principall, one; and against the accessory, another, as appeares by the old Writers. And 28. E. 3. fol. 90. But since that time the Law hath beene changed, so that vnlesse in a few speciall cases a man can haue but one appeale, which must comprehend both principals and accessaries. And therefore 9. Hen. 4. fol. 12. in appeale against two, whereof the one was present, and the other appeared not, the Plaintiffe declared against them both, and the Law which compelleth to declare at one time against all the appeales, compelleth to make but one appeale. The case was, 47. E. 3. that a woman brought an appeale against one as principall, which was attainted and hanged at her suit, and then shee brought an appeale against two others of the same fellony, against one, as principall,

principall, and against another, as accessary, and awarded que el prendrariens p lon breif.

And so should it haue béene if the first appealée had béene acquit, or if the appellant had béene at non-suit after appearance. 47. E. 3. fo. 18. and sée more of this matter Stamford li. 2. cap. 15.

SECT. VIII.

The Declaration in Appeale.

THe Count or Declaration in Appeale of murder, according to the ancient forme was thus. A. appellat. B. de morte. C. fratris sui, &c. quod cum ipse A. & C. essent in pace Dei & Domini regis apud S. &c. venit idem B. cum talib. &c. & nequiter & in felonia, in assultu premeditato, contra pacem domini regis fecit idem B. prædict' fratri suo & vnam plagam mortalem in capite cum quodam gladio, vel quouis alio genere, armorum multorum, &c. vt obierit infra triduum de plaga illa. Et quod hoc fecit nequiter & in felonia, & contra pacem Domini regis, offert se dirationare versus eum per corpus suum, sicut ille qui præsens fuit & hoc vidit, sicut curia Domini regis considerauerit, Et si de eo male contigerit per corpus fratris sui, vel alterius parentis, &c. Et sic plures possunt appellare vnum de vno & eodem facto, si loqui possunt, de visus sui testimonio. So that Bracton sheweth, if one of the appellants had died, or made default, the other might take the appeale, and bee admitted ad dirationandum. But if the Appealée had defended himselfe against one, or béene aquit by iudgement; hee was fréed from them all. The reason why no man was admitted to bring appeale de morte, vnlesse hee could speake of his owne eye witnesse, was (saith Stanford) the reasonablenesse, which séemed to bee in it, that a man should not combate for the truth, when the Accuser was not able to verifie it, but by relation from others. And therefore

therefore in a Writ of right, untill West.1. cap 40. had changed the Law, the Demandants Champian in his oath, did euer affirme, that he or his father, had seene the seisin of his Lord or Master, so that his owne sight, or his fathers, caused him to combat. And as it seemes battaile did not lye in any appeale de morte in Bractons time, except the wound were giuen with some sword, dagger, or such like, as he cals arma moluta. Also his forme speaketh nothing of the length, breadth or deepnesse of the wound, as the Declarations doe at this day; I will leaue Stamfords president, and take one or two out of the booke of Entries. There fol. 43. Katherin Iohnson, late wife of Robert Iohnson, comes in person and doth instantly appeale, Iohn Bishop late of Harling in the County Norff. Yeoman, and W. F. late of the same Towne and County, Yeoman, and R. W. late of H. in the same County, Yeoman, of the death of the aforesaid Robert Iohnson late her husband. videlicet, of that, that whereas the said Robert Iohnson was in Gods peace and the Kings, at Harling aforesaid, upon Munday next before the Feast of Saint Mathew the Apostle, in the second yeere of our late King H. 7. about two of the clocke after noone, of the same day, Iohn Bishop, and W. F. there came felloniously, and as Felons of our Lord the King that now is, of their premeditate assault, against our Lord the Kings peace, Crowne and dignity, in the day, yeere, houre, place, and County aforesaid, and the aforesaid Iohn Bishop with a sharp pointed weapon called a dagger of twelue price, which hee had and held there in his right hand, did feloniously strike the aforesaid Robert Iohnson upon his breast, and into the hart, giuing to the same Robert Iohnson then and there, a mortall wound foure inches deepe, of the which mortall wound, the said Robert Iohnson, did forthwith then dye, at Harling aforesaid. And so the aforesaid Iohn Bishop, did then feloniously kill and murder the aforesaid Robert Iohnson, at Harling aforesaid. And W. F. the same munday, in the same yeere, at the same towne of of Harling, was present, feloniously procuring, consenting and keeping the same Iohn Bishop, to doe the felony and murder, in forme aforesaid done and committed. And after the felony and murder aforesaid committed by the aforenamed Iohn Bishop, the same W. F. and R. W. the same Munday in the same second yeere of our Lord the King, at Harling in the County aforesaid, did feloniously receiue the said Iohn Bishop, harboure, comfort, and maintaine him, knowing that he the said Iohn, had done the felony and murder in forme aforesaid, and as soone as the same felons had committed the said murder and felony, they fled, and the said Katherin did fresly follow them from Towne to Towne, into foure of the next Townes, &c. And if the Felons will deny the felony abouesaid, in forme aforesaid alleaged against them, Katherin the Appellant, is ready to proue it against them, as the Court shall thinke meet.

Againe fol. 51. is another Declaration. Thus, Elizabeth, &c. in person doth instantly appeale the aforesaid Iohn Clerke of this: That whereas the aforesaid Iohn Browne was in peace of God and our Lord the King that now is, at W. in the City of N. in a certaine place called Carrow, the twelft day of January, &c. about ten of the clocke aforenoone; There came the aforesaid Iohn Clerke which now appeareth, and the aforesaid William Clerke which appeareth not, and whom the aforesaid Elizabeth would likewise appeale, of the death of her said husband, if he were present; And they two did feloniously, and as felons, of our Lord the King that now is, in the day, yeere, houre, and City aforesaid, giue to the aforesaid Iohn Browne a certaine drinke, which they, the said Iohn Clerke and William Clerke, had mixed and compounded with powders, and intoxicatiue spices, viz. Ratsbane, and others, and they did feloniously incite and prouoke the said Iohn Browne, to drinke vp the said drinke so intoxicate, which said Iohn Browne hauing good trust & confidence in them, and being vtterly ignorant of the intoxication

cation aforesaid, did then and there, and at their perswasion, drinke vp the said drinke, and therewith was then and there, by the said John and William feloniously poisoned: And afterward the said John Browne at Billingford in the County of Norff. the 20. day of January next ensuing in the same yeere, being so poisoned of the same poison, died, and so the aforesaid John Clerke and William Clerke, feloniously, and as felons of the King, at Billingford aforesaid, in the County aforesaid, the 20. of January, the aforesaid John Browne did kill and murder, &c. And if John Clerke, which now appeareth, denyeth the felony aforesaid of death and murder layed against him, the aforesaid Elizabeth is ready to proue it against him, as the Court shall thinke good.

It might bee collected out of these presidents without any more helpe, that a woman may maintaine her appeale, without expressing any arma moluta, as the fashion was: Bracton saith, the Appellant needs not set downe the houre wherein the party was slaine, but the Statute of Gloc. makes it materiall, yet Stanford acknowledgeth, that the Declaration which was at Common Law, without the houre may be vsed at this day, because Gloc. is but affirmatiue and prohibits nothing. But the place where, &c. must needs be set downe certainly in the count, for so commandeth the Statute, therefore in Appeale against diuers men, naming them to bee of sundry places and Townes, if it be said afterward, at the place aforesaid, this is not good, there are diuers other formes of Declarations in this Appeale: As 44 E. 3. fol. 33. in Appeale against three as principals, the Appellant declared that one of them, such a day, and houre, wounded her husband to the braine, whereof hee died, and at the same houre another, with a dagger stroke him to the hart, so that if hee had not died at the first wound, he must haue died of the second, and the third wounded him in another place, &c. counting seuerally against them, that euery one gaue him a mortall stroke, according to the fact. For so willeth the Statute

que

que il counta le fact, and this fact must bee declared as it was done, or as the Law doth expound it to bee done; Therefore if two bee present at the death of a man, and one of them striketh never a stroke, but onely commandeth the other to kill, &c. in the appeale, declaration must be, that they both did wound him mortally, 11. E. 4. fol. 71. And there it is said, that where the Count goeth, that they all did stricke, &c. the stricking is not traversable. So is it in Appeale of Rape, where one doth the Rape, and the other being present doth abet him, for there the Count shall goe that both ravished her, for so the Law saith. In the same booke 21. E. 4. in appeale de mort against two, whereof but one appeared; the Plaintiffe declared against him which appeared, and would have counted against them which made default, that they likewise wounded, &c. and the Justices bade him speake, but only of him which appeared. Gascoigne was of contrary opinion 9. Hen. 4. fo. 2. and with Gascoigne agrée very many presidents. But sée Waits Case Sir Edward Cokes 4. Rep. fol. 47. there ought to bee but one Appeale against all the principles and accessaries, except where there bee accessaries after the Appeale brought, for there they may bee another appeale brought against them, for that they could not bee named in the first Writ, and if an Appeale bee brought against diverse, and all but one make default, yet the Plaintiffe ought to count against all, saith that booke.

Sect. VIIII.

Defence in Appeale.

The Defence in Appeale, is that the Defendant came and defended all felonies, awaits, assaults, forethinkings, and all that is against the Kings peace, Crowne, and dignity, and pleaded non culpable. Et ponit se super patriam de bono & malo. This is the generall plea, &c.

Sect.

SECT. X.

Pleas to the Writ.

AGainst the Writ to abate that, may be pleaded false Latine, or want of forme; And note that none may have more writs of Appeale than one of one fellony hanging at once. 7. Hen. 7. fol. 6. Yet where there are two such Writs hanging, they must not be abated, but by notifying to the Court, that they bee both pursued by the Plaintiffe, and that must appeare by some act of his. As that he hath appeared and declared upon them both. For though one Writ were delivered to the Viscount of Record to serve it, this might be as well the Act of a stranger as of the Plaintiffe, and therefore no conclusion towards him, but that he may say, it was not at his suit.

So where an Appeale is commenced in the County by bill, removed to a Court of Record, and there hanging, if now the Plaintiffe pursue another appeale of the same felony by writ, the appeale by writ abateth: But where the Appeale by briefe is purchased, before the Appeale by bill removed out of the County, there the Court ought to send, for the Appeale in the County without abating the Appeale which is commenced by Writ, for the Appeale by Writ is more worth than that Appeale commenced in the County, which is not but a plaint, untill it be removed in an Appeale against two; one may plead that his companion named with him in the Writ died at such a place before the Writ purchased; or that there was no such person in rerum natura, when the Writ was purchased, as is named with him, for there is no body else to plead these pleas, but only he which appeareth: But he cannot plead, that the partie named with him in the Writ is entred into religion, or is a married woman, &c. for there is another party to plead so, but in the other cases there is none. And in these cases of appeales against more than one, an appeale abated towards one is abated towards all. In appeale where misnomer of the Plantiffe is pleaded, if it be confessed, the Plaintiffe shall be examined whether it were by covin or no. The case is 9. Hen. 5. fol. 1. A woman sued appeale by name of Cicely, W. whereas her name was Iohan, and after the defendants imparlance she came and said, her name was Iohan, shee was examined, and it was found to be done sans covin. p q̃el ala sans faire fine, quere si el avera nouell appeale p. nosme. Iohan Brooke Appeale 38.

It seemeth in appeales the Defendant may have 1, 2, 3, or 4. or more pleas to the Writ, as well as hee which is Tenant in an Assise may; But then hee must take good heed, that one be not Contrary to another. Bracton, Et in omnibus appellis maioribus vel minoribus non potest appellans variare vel appellum suum in aliquo mutare, adiicere tamen potest interdum, vt si prius non dixerit, quibus armis, &c. potest nominare arma, scilicet gladium vel bisacutum, Et potest, qui actionem ciuiliter intentauerit mutare eam, & agere criminaliter & sic accrescere & appellum augere, sed non contra. In the booke of Entryes fol. 47. the Defendants came in proper person, & defenderunt vim & iniuriam, quando &c. omnem felloniam & quicquid, &c. and they said that in the said County of W. there were two Townes called M. one old M. and another new M. absque hoc, that in the County, there was any Towne, Villadge, Hamlet, or place, knowne and named by the name of M. only, without addition, & hoc parati sunt verificare, vnde petunt iudicium de breue illo & petunt inde allocationem & quoad feloniam prædictam seperatim dicunt quod ipsi in nullo sunt inde culpabiles, & inde de bono & malo ponunt se super patriam. It was found non habebatur aliqua villa, &c. named M. tantum. Ideo consideratum, vt nihil capiat per bre. and that the Defendants eant inde sine die, and the Plaintiffe capiatur. 9. H. 7. Ro. 33.

SECT.

SECT. XI.

Pleas in Barre of the Action.

IN Barre of the Action may bee pleaded, that the woman which bringeth the Appeale, &c. hath taken another husband, or that shee was neuer accoupled in loyall matrimony, to him of whose death shee brings the Appeale: And if it bee brought by the heire, it is a good plea in Barre, to say, the wife of him which is dead, is yet aliue, and the Action giuen to her.

In the booke of Entries fol. 50. Prædicta Alicia dicit quod tempore mortis prædicti Thomæ eadem Alicia fuit vxor prædicti Thomæ, in quo casu, eidem Aliciæ, & non prædicto Nicholao, de iure pertinet habere, & prosequi appellum, &c. Et vlterius eadem defendens dicit, quod prædictus Nicholaus appellum prædictum versus eandem Aliciam inter Alios per couinam ea intentione, ad eam de prosecutione appellinus de morte, prædicti Thomæ excludendam impetrauit, que oia & singula, &c. & petit inde allocationem &c. & quoad felonia, non culpabilis. Et inde, de bono & malo ponit se super patriam. 30. H. 6.

Also it is a good plea in Barre to say, that the Plaintiffe hath succeased her time, in that shee hath not brought her Appeale within the yeere and day after his death, which is supposed slaine; or to say, that he of whose death the Appeale is brought, is yet aliue at such a place, and to bring him in the Court, that hee may bee viewed and knowne; see thereof 43. Assis. pa. 26. in Appeale de morte viri, the Defendant pleaded le Baron in vie, &c. and the Plaintiffe contra; day was giuen to bring in their proofes, which, when they came, were found, one both sides defectiue; The Defendant therefore, for his safest way pleaded non culpabilis videtur ergo, that the first issue if it had beene found against him, should haue beene peremptory, and that hee may waiue it before triall, in fauorem vitæ.

And note, that if a man plead not guilty, and puts himselfe upon the Jury in an Inditement of felony, and hee may confesse the fact before verdict and pray a coroner, otherwise in an Appeale as it was holden 11. Hen.7.5.

8. Hen.4.fol.18. In Appeale de morte viri, and at the day the Baron was brought into Court examined and knowne: and the woman for her false Appeale was committed to prison, till she payd a fine. The generall barres against all Appeales, of which some may bee objected against the Plaintiffe here, are these; That the Plaintiffe is attainted of felony or treason, or a Monke, or a Priest, a mayhemed body (by some other than by the Plaintiffe) or of non sane memorie, or deafe and dumb, or a lazar, or a naturall foole. Attainder by outlawry, if it be erronious, is a barre no longer than untill it bee reversed; It is a good plea in barre also; that heretofore the Plaintiffe brought an Appeale of the same felony, in which shee was at nonsuit after Declaration, or withdrew her selfe from her Action: Or that heretofore shee sued Appeale of the same fellony against another person, which was acquited or condemned at her suit. Or the Plaintiffes release may bee pleaded in barre, if it were made to the Defendant himselfe; for release made to another will not serve, though it were made to one, joyned with the Defendant in the Appeale. Corone in Fitzherbert 9 . and 2. Rich.3.9. agrees. And so if the Plaintiffe withdraw her selfe, as against one of the Defendants, her Appeale shall stand good against the other. And note where the Defendant pleads in barre any of these pleas, yet in favour of life the Law permits him to plead over to the fellony, and his pleading shall not therefore be counted double, except in the case of release, in which indeed he may not plead to the felony, for not guilty is contrary to accepting of release, which implieth guilt. So also if a woman bring Appeale of robery, and the Defendant pleads villenage in the Plaintiffe, hee shall not conclude over to the felony rien culpable, for that were an infranchisment.

But

But perchance when the villenage is found against the Defendant, hee may then take his plea of rien culpable as well, as hee shall haue when hee plead any other pleas, for if he plead them without concluding to the fellony, hee may after his barre is found against him plead rien culpable notwithstanding. quod vide 28. E. 3. fol. 91. 22. E. 3. fol. 38. 18. E. 3. fol. 32. except only in pleas of release, as is said, which implieth alwayes a confession of felony. 9. Hen. 4. fol. 2. in Appeale de morte viri, the Defendants pleaded the wives release, made since the darraine, continuance of all accords, reall and personall, and shee demurred, the best opinion was, that reall actions are of things reall and durable, as lands, rents, &c. and personall actions are of dammages and such like, yet p Hulls, personall is as well the punishment of the person as dammages, and the punishment here is death, which is released & le barre is good.

But Littleton teacheth vs contrary in his booke, for hee saith, that Appeales of robery, rape or death, or any Appeale wherein the iudgement is of death, are more high than personall Actions, and therefore they are not barred by release, vnlesse it be of all manner of Actions, or of all Appeales.

See Sir Edward Coke in his Commentaries vpon Littleton fol. 287. b. in any Appeale wherein iudgement is of death, a release of all Actions reall and personall is no barre, for that release extendeth but to common or civill actions, and not to criminall, but if a release of actions personals is good in an Appeale of mayhem for every Action wherein dammages are onely recovered, is in Law taken for personall, fol. 288. a. And in Sir Edw. Cokes 4. Rep. in Hudsons Case it is said, although the Appeale of mayhem runneth feloniously, luy mayma, yet he shall recover but dammages, and therefore recovery in trespasse is a good barre therein.

SECT. XII.

Auterfoits acquit.

ALthough it be now no plea in Appeale of death, for the Defendant to say, that he was heretofore acquite of the same felonie; yet because Stanfords handling of it containeth good learning, and it may still serue in appeale of rape: And likewise in Inditements of death, for hee that was acquite in appeale may haue it: I will not omit it. By Common Law therefore, in all Appeales or Inditements of felony, for the Defendant to say, that hee was Auterfoits arraigne de mesme le felonie, before such Justices, and acquited (vouching the record) is a good plea; and he néeds not to haue the record in Court, because this plea is not delatorie, but in barre, Coron. in Fitzherbert, 2 2.

This plea the Common Law disalloweth not, because it alloweth, that a man should not put his life in ieopardy twice for one and the same offence. The acquitall then must be of the verie same offence, or else this plea is to no purpose: Therefore if two men be indited of felony, as principals, and afterward by another Inditement, it is found that one of them did the felonie, and the other did feloniously receiue him, after the felony committed; hée that is secondarily indicted and arraigned as accessarie, shall not be discharged, by pleading arraignment, and acquitall vpon the first Inditement; for the offence is not supposed the same and one, but committed at diuers dayes, 27. Ass. p. 10. And this for accessaries after the felony: But when felony is done by force of commanding, and procurement of another, he that shall be arraigned as accessarie, may plead that he was acquit, &c. though it were as principall, and the offences were at diuers dayes; for, Vulnus, preceptum, & factum, sunt quasi vnum factum. Yet Stanford noteth the antient Law to haue béene taken

taken otherwise. See 8. E. 2. is, Potest quiuis acquietari pro morte alicuius per patriam; & hoc non obstante ex indictamento, vel secta alicuius de auxilio, abetto, vel procuramento, potest suspendi pro morte eiusdem. And note that hee that was indicted and arraigned of the death of Iohn at Stile, may plead that hée was heretofore indicted and acquite of the death of Iohn at Noke, auerring that Iohn at Stile and Iohn at Noke were one person. Et serra discharge. Fitzherbert Corone, 189.

So likewise if a man were slaine two yeares since, and one which was indicted and acquit of his death, is againe indicted of the same mans death, supposing that he killed him this present yeare; he shall plead the first acquittall, and bee discharged notwithstanding the variance; for a man can be slaine but once, and the Court in this case shall charge the Inquest with the time of his death, which is supposed slaine, and whether it were the same person supposed to be slaine, by the last Indictment. So likewise if a man be indicted, and acquit in one Countie, and afterward indicted of the same death in another Countie, the acquitall at first shall discharge, &c. But in robberie it seemeth otherwise: for one and the same man may be robbed by one other man sundrie times; and therefore acquittance of a robberie done at one day, is no discharge of a robberie done at another day. Now if a man be indicted of robberie in one Countie, he shall not plead that he was indicted and acquit, of the same robberie, in another Countie, 4. H. 7. fol. 5. But it is said there, that in appeale of robberie it is a good plea; because the Plaintiffe is to recouer his goods againe by the Common Law; not so in Indictments, in the booke at large the Defendants plea is, that hee was indicted of taking the same goods, &c. which Fisher said must be taken beneficially for the King, that the same goods were stollen twice. Fairefax said the Countrie might not ioyne in triall of the auerment del mesme le felonie, when one Countie had acquitted him. Frowicke said, That by the same reason, whereby by he might be found culpable in one Countie, of felonie done in another, by the same reason acquitall in one should discharge him in another.

See Corone in Fitzherbert, 220 41. ass. p. 9. A man indited in the Kings Bench of rape and robberie, pleaded acquitall at the Countie of Cornwall, at the Assises, and it was adiudged good. Stauford bids vs enquire where the Kings Bench was at the taking of the Inditement, and whether any other Inditement in Cornwall, of that matter, were remoued into the Kings Bench, because the Booke saith, one indited in banke le Roy, &c.

Yee must know, that if there were not sufficient matter of felony in the Inditement or Appeale, vpon which the acquitall was had, autersoits acquite is no plea, to stay a man indicted of new from new arraignment, for it fals out vpon the matter, that the parties life was neuer in ieopardie.

And so is it if a man be acquite in an erroneous Appeale, which acquitall is reuersed by errour; hee may bee arraigned at the Kings suit vpon Inditement; for by the reuersall he is become as neuer acquited. But before reuersall autersoits acquite is good plea, and if the errour were onely in the processe, it is not materiall, for appearance salues those defects: And it seemeth also, that hee which was once acquited in appeale, shall not answer any more to the Appellant, though the acquitall be reuersed by errour howsoeuer, for so the Court might be deliuered in infinitum, and the Defendants neuer be deliuered.

But if one bring an Appeale, which hath no cause or title to it, as perhaps one which is neither wife nor heire, &c. and the Defendant takes none aduantage of it, but pleads rien culpable, and is acquited, this will not serue to barre the right heire or wife in their appeale, or the King vpon arraigning him vpon Inditement, or vpon the new Appeale, if the wife or heire be at non suit therein.

And if one be arraigned vpon Inditement at the Kings suit and acquited, whereas by order of Common Law, the

the King should haue stayed, till the Appeale hanging had béene determined. Yet this is no errour, for the plea of auterfoits acquite shall serue the Defendant in Appeale well enough. And Auterfoits acquite in Appeale is no plea against the King, in an Indictment of the same felony; if the acquitall were by battaile and not by Inquest, 12. E. 2. Corone in Fitzherbert, 275. For battaile lieth not against the King, and therefore that triall against another shall not binde. Quære, saith Stamford, for Bracton is contra. Si à pluribus appellatus, sic de vno facto & vna plaga, & versus vnum se defenderit recedet quietus versus omnes alios appellantes, & etiam de secta regis, quia per hoc purgat innocentiam suam, &c. Before the Statute 3. H. 7. cap. 1. Whereby Auterfoits acquite is become no plea in appeale of death, if a man were indicted of another mans death, the Justices would not arraigne him, (as appeares by recitall of the Statute) till the yeare and day were past. And in Corone Fitzherbert, 44. Yée may sée that in 22. E. 4. the Justices of England aduised, all men of Law to obserue this order and course thorowout the Realme; yet before this time it appeares, 7. H. 4. fol. 10. & 21. H. 6. fol. 32. That where there was no appeale hanging, if suggestion had béene made to the Justices, that the euidence was manifest and apparant against the party indicted, they would arraigne and try him vpon the Indictment, although it were within the yeare. Likewise if the Appellant were vnder age, the Justices did vse to arraigne and try him that was indicted in meane time. For otherwise the partie indicted might cause by Couin, that the Appeale should be brought by an Infant vnder age, as perhaps thrée yeares old, and so perish the Kings suit for euer. But all this séemeth now to be remedied by the Statute, in Appeales which are of death; but other Appeales are left as they were before. The Common Law therefore vnchanged is, that if a man be indicted of robberie, whereof there is an Appeale hanging, and the Appeale is procéeded so farre, that the Justices may perceiue the

the felonie is all one, they ought to surcease triall upon the Indictment, as it is 1. 31. H. 6. fol. 3. For note that in Appeale of robberie when it is by Writ, the robberie cannot be certainly knowen before Declaration. Otherwise it is, if it be commenced by bill, or that the Appeale be of death of a man any.

SECT. XIII.

Auterfoits attainted.

This is a sore saying, which some men have to plead for themselves, viz. that they are already condemned to be hanged, and aske Judgement, whether during the Attainder, they should answer to the felony whereof they are condemned, or to any other: And this plea serveth, where the partie condemned hath already forfeited as much as he can forfeit, so that it is to no purpose to travell him any further. But in some speciall cases, when there is some end of it, a man already condemned may bee arraigned againe. As if a man attaint of felony, were guiltie of treason also, at the time of the felony committed, hee may now bee put to answer the treason: because thereby the King shall have the Escheat of his land, of whomsoever it were holden, 1. H. 6. 5. Otherwise it is if the treason were committed after the felony; or at the least, if it were after the attainder had of felony, for then the title vested in the Seigniors, before the Kings title, might not be devested by matter accruing ex post facto. And if divers men have divers Appeales of robberie against one, to the end that everie man may have againe his goods, whereof he was robbed, by making fresh suit, he shall bee attaint at everie one of their suits. But note (saith Stamford) in cases where the Defendant will discharge himselfe of answering, by attainder of any other felony, than that whereof he is arraigned; it may be replyed

plyed either for the King or the partie, that since the Attainder the King hath pardoned him the said Felonie and Attainder, whereby he is now restored to the Law, and ought to answer to all other felonies, though they were perpetrated before the felony whereof he saith he was attainted. Titulo Coronæ in Fitzherbert, 227. 10. H. 4. &c.

But to the felonie whereof a man is attainted hee shall answer no more after he hath his pardon of it. Thus far Stamford. See Brooke, Titulo Coronæ, 11. Quære, Whether a man attainted of felony, and pardoned, shall answer at the Kings suit, to other felonies before committed, and whereof he was not indicted at the time of the Attainder, per aliquos videtur quod ita, as well as at the suit of the partie in Appeale; yet some held otherwise, 10. H. 4. That a man can die but once at the suit of the King, and he that is pardoned is as a new man, all former Judgements, as against the King, being determined: Quære de Appeales, Car il est fore dure de maintainer Appeale in le case. For all Appeales were determined once by the Judgement upon Inditment.

Note that it was resolved in Wrotes case, Sir Edw. Cokes 4. Rep. fol. 45. That Auterfoits convict of manslaughter upon an Inditement of murder, and Clergie allowed is a good plea in an Appeale of murder, and that although the conviction was had hanging the Appeale. But it was also there resolved, that if the Inditement upon which the conviction was had were insufficient, the offender may, notwithstanding that conviction, bee indited or appealed againe, for that his life in judgement of Law was never in ieopardie: and so it was resolved also in Vauxes case in the same Report.

SECT.

SECT. XIV.

Clergie.

If the Defendant in Appeale craue his Clergie, and the Plaintiffe say that he is Bigamus; if he be so certified it is peremptorie, and he shall be hanged without pleading Ouster to the felony. See 11. H. 4. fol. 10. That Clergie is allowed in Appeale de morte viri. In the Booke of Entries, wherein scil. fol. 5. is the Kings writ to certifie, whether the partie appealed were Bigamus as C. which appealed him of the death of A. her husband alleaged: But at this day Bigamus shall haue his Clergie, by the Statute of 1. Edw. 6.

SECT. XV.

The Kings pardon.

If a woman which bringeth an Appeale de morte viri, let fall her suit, the Kings suit is not preiudiced thereby, and if the wife release all Appeales, and afterward by verdict in Appeale brought by her, the release is found, the entrie is, De appello prædict' quoad sectam prædictæ Aliciæ sit quietus, & quod ipse eat inde sine die, &c. Sed quoad sectā Dom. Regis in hac parte instante allocutus est qualiter se velit acquietare, & dicit quod in nullo est inde culpabilis, &c. See the Booke of Entries, fol. 47. b. So likewise in Appeale De morte patris, or De morte viri, the Kings pardon cannot take away execution, 13. H. 4. But it is a good plead against the King, when an Appeale is once determined. And if the Appeale be determined not by act of the Appellant, but by act of Law, the Kings pardon shall not be allowed without the Appellants priuitie. At if the Plaintiffe pursue her appeale till the Defendant

fendant be outlawed, by this Outlawrie the appeale is ended: and now if the King pardon the felonie, &c. this pardon shall not bée allowed without Scire facias against the partie, at whose suit the Felon was outlawed. And at the day of Scire facias returned, the partie may appeare, and pray execution, which is grantable, the pardon notwithstanding. But if the Sheriffe returne, that hée warned her to appeare, and she make default, the pardon shall be allowed without more adoe. And this Scire facias, vpon pardon granted, may be required against the Appellant, though the Appellée neuer desire it, and though hée shew no release or other matter in discharge of the Appeale. For he shall come timely enough with that, when the other appeares vpon the Scire facias. Also the Scire facias is grantable, though the Charter of pardon haue not the clause. Ita quod stet rectus in curia.

Vide Fitzherbert. p. 17. titulo Charter, 11. R. 2, In appeale against Principall and Accessarie, the Principall was pursued till Outlawry, and Exigent went out against the Accessarie, and at the day of the returne, the Plaintiffe was at non suit in his Appeale, and then came the Principall with his Charter of pardon, and prayed it might be allowed, because the Plaintiffe was at non suit. Gascoyne made answer, That the non suit could not help him, for the Appeale had run his full course, and was determined as towards him, by the Outlawrie.

Sect. XVI.

Dammages in Appeale.

Now to draw towards an end of this matter, though a woman cannot be put to triall by battaile in appeale, any more than the King may in his suits, yet shée prosecutes appeales, not altogether without danger, as yée may perceiue by the entrie made in the Booke of Entries,

tries fol. 49.b. and by the Case 8. Hen. 4. fol. 18. likewise 41. Assis. pl. 8. In appeale de morte viri in the Kings Bench, the Plaintiffe was at non suit after appearance, wherefore it was awarded, that shee should bee taken to pay a fine, and she came and paid it, the Appellee was afterward discharged, and inquiry made of dammages and abbettours, and two abbettours being found, dammages were taxed to a hundred pounds, and the appellant was not worth aboue a hundred shillings, yet it was awarded, that the Defendant should recouer his dammages taxed at a 100. li. against the woman, and that hee should sue against the abettours if hee would, but no Capias against the woman, because she had fined before.

It is by the Common Law, saith Iustice Stanford, that dammages in Appeales of felony are alwayes for the defendant, when hee is acquit, for common reason wils, when a man is put to undergoe a triall, whereby his lands, goods, life and reputation are all put in hazard, without desert or matter of good foundation, by only the malicious accusation, of his aduersary, and he is found by due acquitall of Law, a loyall true man, that he haue amends against his false Accuser, and (if the Accuser be himselfe insufficient) against them, which procured and abated the Plaintiffe to pursue the Appeale, but for so much as dammages were not recouerable against Procurers and Abbettors, but by originall Writ of conspiracie, which was no such speedy redresse or satisfaction, as the great mischieffousnesse of the offence required, a Statute was made for a more quicke remedy.

SECT. XVII.

West. 2. ca. 12.

As followeth. Because many men of pure malice and purpose to grieue others, procure false appeales, to to bee brought of homicide and other felonies by Appellants, which are nothing worth, and therefore can neither answer the King for their falsety, nor yeeld dammages to them whom they Appeale. It is prouided, that if any man be appealed of felony, and acquite himselfe in due manner in the Kings Court, at suit of either the King, or of the Appellour, the Iustices before whom such Appeale shall be heard and determined, shall punish the Appellour by one yeeres imprisonment; and neuerthelesse such Appellours shall render dammages to the Appeales, according to the Iustices discretion, hauing regard to the arrest and imprisonment, which the Appeale hath sustained, and to the Infamy, which by the imprisonment or otherwise, the Appellees haue incurred. And neuerthelesse they shall bee grieuously fined towards the King. And if peraduenture such Appellours haue not wherewith to make amends for the dammage aforesaid, it shall bee inquired, by whose abatement the Appeale was malitiously thus formed, if he which is appealed doe so require that. And if it bee found by the Inquisition, that any man were an Abbettour by malice, he shall be distrained by a Iudiciall Writ at the Appellees suit, to come before the Iustices; And if he be in due manner conuicted of abbetting by malice, he shall be punished by imprisonment, and restitution of dammages, *sicut de Appellatore superius dictum est.* And from henceforth in appeale of death of a man, there shall lye no essoine for the Appellour, in what Court soeuer the Appeale shall bee determined. The Statute is against Appeales by malice, &c. therefore if the Defendant were indicted of felony, before the Appeale sued (though he be acquit afterward,) he shall recouer no dammages, for it is to bee intended, that the inditement induced the appeale, and not malice; Otherwise it is, if hee were not indicted till after the appeale commenced, or if there be a variance betwixt the appeales and inditment, as the acquitall of him vpon the one, is no acquitall of him vpon the other, as if he be indited as a principall, and appeales

peales as an accessary, vel contra But if the variance be in things of no substance, so that the acquitall in the one bee an acquitall in the other, there shall be no dammages. And though the word malice by the letter of the Statute doth seeme to reach onely to the Appellours and Procurours, yet it is to bee understood by the bookes, that it reacheth as well to the Appellant as to them. And the word felony in the Statute stretcheth to felonies, so made after this Statute, and ancient felonies made so before the Statute. Acquited in due manner is as well where the Defendant is acquit by battaile, as if it were by the Country, and he is intended acquit by battaile, when the Appellant acknowledgeth in the field his appeale to bee false (which is a kinde of vanquishment) for if the Appellant bee slaine in the field, the dammages are gone; Now there is as well an acquitall in Law, as an acquitall in fait. Therefore if two be appealed, one as principall, and the other as accessary: the accessary shall recouer dammages, upon acquitall of the principall (if the enquest, which tried the principall, were charged with the accessary,) though they gaue no verdict of the accessary, for the accessary in such case may haue by the Common Law his Writ of conspiracy, as appeares 33. Hen. 6. fol. 2. But if the principall bee acquited, the accessary neuer appearing, but hanging still in processe, he shall neither recouer dammages by this Statute, nor haue a Writ of Conspiracy by Common Law, till he come and be acquited by verdict, as appeares 41. Assis. p. 24. vn bone case. If the Defendant barre the Plaintiffe in appeale, hee shall not recouer dammages, except the barre did acquit him of the felony; Therefore if his plea were bastardy in the Plaintiffe, or that he hath an elder brother, or ne vnques accouple in legall matrimonie, and such like pleas, although these pleas may discharge the appeale as well against the King, as against the party, yet notwithstanding any such plea in barre, he may be afterward indited, and attaint of the felony, and therefore hee is not to recouer dammages, for those pleas try not

not his innocencie any more, than pleas which are onely in abatement of the Writ. So is it likewise, if the Plaintiffe bee barred upon a demurrer in Law, and so, where it is found by verdict a killing *se defendendo*, or by misadventure, for this is none acquitall of the felony, in so much as the Defendant can never be cleered thereof without purchasing his pardon: So is it also, when the Defendant upon arraignement takes him to his Clergy, and the Court takes an enquest of office, whereby hee is found *riens culpable*: this is none acquitall, whereby hee may recover dammages; for claime of Clergy, is rather by implication, confession of felony than otherwise: But hee that will waive his Clergy, and put himselfe in inquest, if he be acquit hee shall recover dammages: So if the Appellee have both the Kings pardon, and the Appellants release, and yet he will waive them, and plead *riens culpable*, hee shall recover dammages, if the Country acquit him, yet hee hath done a matter of record, which by implication acknowledgeth the felony, *quære*: for if the pardon were by Parliament *sans question*, hee might not waive it. See thereof 11. Hen. 4. fol. 40. He is not acquited *debito modo*, that is, acquited erroniously, without dew processe, As 9. Hen. 5. fol. 2. the Defendant came in by exigent, upon which the Viscount had returned *ceperi corpus*, whereas he should have returned *exigi feci* and the Defendant appearing upon the exigent, without taking advantage of the processe, pleaded *riens culpable*, to the appeale, and so was found; but yet he could not get judgement to recover dammages, for the cause aforesaid *quære*. for 19. E. 3. *Titulo Corone* in Fitzherbert 444. is contra. that errour in the processe is not materiall, so long as there is no errour in the Writ of appeale, Declaration or pleading; for the Defendant is arraigned upon the originall, and not upon the meane processe.

The Statute speakes thus, *vel ad sectam domini Regis, vel appellatoris*. The Kings suit here is understood in appeale, when after arraignement of the Defendant, the Appellant having declared, is at non suit, for if the Defendant bee acquit at the Kings suit upon an Inditement of the same felony, he shall recover no dammages.

And the manner of recovering dammages, when acquitall is at the Kings suit, differeth somewhat from recovery upon suit of the party, &c. for in the first case hee which is acquited, shall recover no dammages, till he have sued, scire fac. to bring the Plaintiffe into Court, which by non suit was become out of Court. But in the other case hee shall recover dammages without other processe. Titulo Dammages in Fitzherbert 7. 7. Where the Case was, that the Appellant tooke a husband after non suit, and yet scire facias was awarded against the woman onely. The Statute is further, that the Justices before whom, &c. shall punish the Appellour, &c. this cannot bee understood by Justices of Nisi prius, though by the Statute 14. Hen. 6. cap. 1. they have power to give Judgement in treason and felony tried before them, and that as well where the Defendant is acquited, as where hee is attainted; But yet within this Statute they are not, because the plea of the whole appeale is not heard before them, nor any more, save only the triall, as you may see, 10. E. 4. fol. 14. The Statute is further, that the dammages shall bee considered, having respect to the imprisonment, &c. Therefore if appeale bee against divers men, and they all are acquited, dammages shall be taxed to them severally, because perhaps one is more dammified than another, for one may be appealed as principall, and another as accessary, and one may bee a Gentleman, and another none, 8. Hen. 5. fol. 1. and 40. E. 3 titulo Dammages in Fitzherbert p. 77. But note that this recovery of dammages is not for every one, for if an appeale bee against a Monke, or Feme covert, without the joyning the Soveraigne or husband, as it must bee, (except the Soveraigne with his Monke, or the Baron with his wife committed the felony) the Monke or Feme covert shall recover no dammages, though they bee acquit. Titulo Corone in Fitzherbert 276.

276. 22.E.3. The principall Case was an appeale against a Monke, and the Justices said it was all one for Law, if it had beene a Feme covert. quære. for if an appeale bee against Baron and Feme, which are acquited, dammages shall bee taxed, and recovery severally, viz. The Baron sole shall recover for his owne imprisonment, and the Baron and Feme joyntly for the imprisonment of the wife. The Statute is moreover, versus Dominum regem graviter redimantur. This fining to the King is never, but where the Defendant is to have dammages also, for otherwise the Plaintiffe shall not fine, but only bee amerced, as 9.Hen.5. fol.1. the appeale abated for misnosmer, and the Plaintiffe was but only amerced. vide 41. Assis. Corone 219. the appellant was at non suit after Declaration, and the Court presently awarded processe against the Appellant, to come and make fine, agreeing that if the party were afterward acquit, at the Kings suit, so that hee recovered dammages against the Appellant, yet shee should not pay a new fine. Put the case therefore, that at the Kings suit the Defendant had beene found culpable of the felony, what remedy there might be, for the Plaintiffe to recover his fine againe, which hee payd before none, as it seemeth, for it seemes the Plaintiffe which is at non suit in the appeale, shall pay a fine by the Common Law, and this was the cause why they awarded it to bee payd maintenant. Then for enquiry of Abbettours, &c. Cum appellatores non habeant vnde prædicta damna restituere, inquiratur per quorum abettum. These words imply, that if dammages be not by Law recoverable against the Appellours, there shall be none enquiry of Abbettours. And where the Statute is, that if the Appellants are not able to restore dammages, it is intendible all the dammages, for if the Appellant bee sufficient to render part, but not all the dammages, enquiry shall be of the Abbettors, and they shall be charged. 8.E.4.fol.3.& 8.Hen.5.& 219.titulo Corone in Fitzherbert. The Statute is, si appellatus hoc petat. Of office only therefore, and without request, as

as it should seeme, the Court cannot enquire of Abbettors. And 48. Assis. 22. titulo Corone. where they had enquired of Abbettors, at the desire of one Defendant, and they found none, and afterwards another of the Defendants, being acquited, prayed enquiry likewise, it might not bee obtained, because it appeared by the first verdict, that there were none Abbettors, there remained therefore no more to be enquired of, but what dammages were susteined. This Stamford affirmes to bee in appearance against Law, for saith hee, it is against the words of the Statute, and against reason, for what reason is it, that a man should bee bound by an enquest, whereunto he is not privy, and against which hee can have no remedy, because it was but an enquest of office, for albeit that commonly the enquiry of Abbettors, is by the same enquest that acquited the Defendant, yet their enquiry in this point is but of office, for if they finde Abbettors, these Abbettors when they come may traverse all that is found in this point; As if it be found, that the Appellant is not sufficient, and A. and B. were Abbettors, A. and B. may come and say by protestation, not knowing the felony for plea, that the Appellant is sufficient, or that they never abetted. 8. E. 4. fol. 3. and the words, Si legitimo modo conuictus fuerit de huiusmodi abbetto per maliciam, prove also that answer is allowed, to that which is found by the enquest. And note that it is a good answer for the Abbettor to shew matter, wherefore the Defendant ought not to have dammages, or to shew that hee was acquited, not lawfully, but erroniously. But the Abbettors shall not take exception, against the Inquisition, for that it is not found at what day, yeere, or place they abetted, for the Abettment simply found satisfieth the Statute, which willeth, vt inquiratur per quorum abettum. And when that it is once found, the Defendant may supply that which wanteth, adding to the inquisition, the yeere, day and place. Titulo Corone in Fitzherbert 45. 22. E. 4. By the words, per breue de iudicio ad sectam appellati distringantur ad

veniendum

veniendum coram Iusticiariis, &c. And the processe should seeme to bee distresse infinite. But Titulo Corone, 102. the Court awarded first a Venire facias, & then Distresse, which course hath little authoritie for it, for all the other Bookes giue a Distringas for the first Processe, which is alwayes sued out by him which is acquited. And for his better speed, he may pursue this if he will, though the Appellant bee not in Court. As if the Appellant bee at non suit, and the Defendant arraigned at the Kings suit is acquited, his dammages taxed, and his Abbettors found, now he may haue Processe against the Abettors maintenant, though the Judgement of dammages bee suspended till Scire facias be sued, and returned against the Appellant: and note if the Defendant which is acquited in an Appeale, be non suit in his Processe against the Abettors, this is not peremptorie, but he may commence processe againe of new, if he will, Corone, 186. And 3. E. 2. titulo Action sur le Statute, 28. An originall Writ brought for Abetment and Declaration against the Abettors, for greater dammages than were assessed in the Appeale is awarded good. For of dammages taxed in Appeale, there lyeth no attaint, because the Enquest, as to the dammages, is but of office, and the Defendant cannot compell the Justices to encrease dammages, therefore it is reason that he aid himselfe by Action. So saith Stamford.

SECT. XVIII.

Of the old Law.

I Haue waded further into this vindicatiue Action than I thought to haue done, and yet not touched what the Princes warrant of a mans life may auaile him, against the instant appeale of a widdow. I know one or two that are thought to be buckled against Appellants, by a lease of their owne liues from the King; but how true it is, or how concording with Law, I know not: Howsoever it be, I aduise a widdow, that is full of spléene for the slaughter of her husband, to read ouer mine instructions here, to allay choller, and then if composition be offered, not to refuse it. For first I doe you to wéet, that appeales du mort are but slipperie Actions. Be iudged by the case, 33. H. 8. Dyer fol. 50. Warnford of the Temple was sued in an appeale of murder: the Writ was, Ad respondendum A. B. alias dict' A. B. fratri & hæredi, to him that was murdered, and the Defendant was discharged, because the Plaintiffe was not named brother and heire in the substance of the Writ, but onely in the Alias dicto, for it ought to haue beene, Ad respondendum A. B fratri & hæredi, alias dicto, &c. This was the chiefe cause why the Defendant was discharged. Then, I say, it is a more Christian thing to take fiue hundred pounds of a mankiller, for a release, leauing him to agree with the King for his necke, as good cheape as he can, than to séeke bloud and death (though of one which hath deserued it) in anger, malice, and reuengefulnesse. Last of all I affirme, that it agréeth with the eldest custome, and ancientest English Lawes. For that which learned M. Lamberd in one place speaketh but as coniecturall, is (me thinketh) true without all peraduenture. Id est, that this forme of procéeding against an homicide giuen to the dead mans heire, or widdow, is a reuengefull Action first giuen to appease such quarrels and capitall enmities of families and kindreds, as the Northerne men yet vse and call Feawds, which heretofore (but a long time since) were generall, and ouerspread the Realme. So that an Appeale du mort, is but an image of deadly Feawd. The inducements to thinke so are these. The action of Appeale is preferred before the Kings action: the offer of triall by the Appellant, by Bracton is, per corpus, &c. & si de eo male contigerit per corpus fratris, &c. And the ancient vse was, when the Appellée condemned went to execution, that all they which were of bloud to him that was murdred, should

draw-

draw the man-slayer to the gallowes, by a long rope, or cord, to shew loue to their kinsman, and desire of reuenge, per Bromley in Plowdens Commentarie, 306. And 11. H. 4. fol. 12. When Tirwit had affirmed, that by the ancient Law in Appeales de mort, the dead mans kindred and his wife should draw the Felon to execution. Gascoigne added, Hoc fuit in diebus nostris. By these dayes Appeales de mort shewed, by their outward face and phisnomie, from whence they sprung. But by the old Lawes of King Inas, King Edmund, and the rest, yee shall plainly perceiue, that Feawd was their mother, and that money was the quencher of the quarrell, verie often, if not alwayes. See therefore in M. Lamberds Booke, De priscis legibus, the Law 7?. of Inas: If a bond man kill an English man, his Lord shall deliuer him into the hands of the Lord or kinsman of him which is slaine, or redeeme him at sixtie shillings: If the Lord will not pay the money, he shall at the least emancipate his bondman, and the kinsman of the murderer so emancipate, may vndertake for him, to pay the price of him which is dead. If hee haue no kinsman that will doe so much for him, Metuat sibi malum ab aduersariis, Let him be at the hazard of his enemies. And I haue read an old Law which I cannot finde againe, Parentibus occisi fiat emendatio, vel guerra eorum portetur. But in the same booke, De priscis Legibus, yee may finde that King Edmund, which reigned an hundred yeares and more before the Conquest, by the aduice of Odo of Canterburie, and the Archbishop Wolstan of Yorke, with many other of the Clergie and Laytie, made Lawes, amongst which one hath this Preface; Etenim nos omnes harum taedet pugnarum quotidianarum: and therefore we ordaine as followeth.

SECT. XIX.

King Edmunds Law.

If any man hereafter doe kill another man, hee alone shall take upon him, and sustaine the deadly enmitie of the dead mans kindred, unlesse he can by the helpe of his friends pay the whole price and estimation of his head, whom he hath killed, (what condition soever he were of) and that within the space of twelue moneths: If his kindred forsake him, and refuse to pay any thing for him, hee alone shall beare the quarrell, and his kinsmen shall not be reputed as enemies: But if they giue him sustenance, or haue any peace and societie with him, he that doth so shall forfeit all that he hath to the King, and bee taken also as an enemie to the blood: But otherwise, if any man to reuenge his kinsmans death, pursue and kill any one, but only the first murderer, he shall lose all that he hath to the King, and be deemed an enemie to the King, and to all that loue him. This Statute abridges Feawes, excepteth the Felons kindred, forbidding to kill in Witherrain, and for money it seemes the Feawd was stripped.

SECT. XX.

Of Rapes.

Chuse now whether yee will imagine, that the widdow hath agreed with him which was her husbands bane, or that she hath pursued him to death: She remaineth from henceforth a widdow, giuing her selfe to almes and deeds of charitie, and of this good minde are many of our widdowes, which purpose constantly to liue out the residue of their dayes in a deuout remembrance of their deare

deare husbands departed, to whom perhaps they made vowes neuer to marrie againe after their deaths. But to what purpose is it for women to make vowes, when men haue so many millions of wayes to make them break them? And when sweet words, faire promises, tempting, flattering, swearing, lying will not serue to beguile the poore soule: then with rough handling, violence, and plaine strength of armes, they are, or haue beene heretofore, rather made prisoners to lusts theeues, than wiues and companions to faithfull honest louers: So drunken are men with their owne lusts, and the poyson of Ouids false precept,

Vim licet appellant, vis est ea grata puellis.

That if the rampier of Lawes were not betwixt women and their harmes, I verily thinke none of them, being aboue twelue yeares of age, and vnder an hundred, being either faire or rich, should be able to escape rauishing.

This is therefore a matter concerning maids, wiues, widdowes, and women of all degrees and conditions, if either they be, or possesse any thing worth the hauing, and because the ignorance of Law may here turne a mollifying heart to harme, I were to blame, if I left my Schollers without warning to take heed.

SECT. XXI.

Rauishment is in two sorts.

THere are two kindes of Rape, of which though the one be called by the common people, and by the Law it selfe, Rauishment; yet in my conceit it borroweth the name from rapere, but vnproperly, for it is no more but Species stupri, a hideous hatefull kinde of whoredome in him which committeth it, when a woman is enforced violently to sustaine the furie of brutish concupiscence: but she is left where she is found, as in her owne house or bed,

bed, as Lucrece was, and not hurried away, as Helen by Paris, or as the Sabine women were by the Romans, for that is both by nature of the word, and definition of the matter: The second and right rauishment, Cum quis honestæ famæ fœminam, siue virgo, siue vidua, siue sanctimonialis, sit inuitis illis in quorum est potestate, abducit. Neque refert, an quis (volente vel nolente rapta) id faciat, nam vis quæ Parentibus vel Curatoribus fit, maxime spectat. It seemeth the first kinde of rape deserued allwayes death by Gods Lawes, vnlesse the woman rauished were vnbetrothed, so that the rauisher might marrie her, as you may read Deuteronomy, chap. 22. vers. 23. and by the Ciuill Law. Raptores, in the second kinde, subjiciebantur pœnæ mortis rapta si fuerit ingenua. How hainous they bee both, and haue a long time beene, by the Lawes of England, yee shall now perceiue.

SECT. XXII.

The old Law of libidinous Rape.

BRacton in the eight and twentieth Chapter of his third Booke sheweth, that by the antique Law of King Adelstan, Hee that meeting a virgin sole, or with company, did but touch her vnhonestly, was guiltie of breaking the Kings Edict, Et emendabit secundum iudicium comitat. If against her will hee threw her on the ground, hee lost the Kings fauour; if he discouered her, and cast himselfe vpon her, he lost all his possessions; if he lay with her, he suffered iudgement of life and member: yea, if he were an horse-man, his horse lost his taile and maine, (as Stamford citeth it to be, lib. 2.) But the words are, Equus suus ad dedecus suum decoriabatur de superiore labro, & cauda quæ proprius natibus abscindere debent; item canis si secum habeat, &c. eodem modo dedecorabitur. His Hawke likewise lost her beake, tallons, and

and straine. And the virgin had in recompence all his land & money by the Kings warrant. This was in King Adelstanes dayes, at least an hundred and twentie yeares before the Conquest, when *corruptores virginitatis & castitatis* were hanged, and their fautors also. But in Bractons time it seemeth, that these kinde of ravishers were otherwise punished, they lost their eyes and were gelt. Shee that brought an Appeale was to complaine her selfe presently to the next neighbour, or to the chiefe men of the Hundred, or to the Coroner, or Viscount, shewing her garments bloudy and torne, and in the first Countie to enter her Appeale, and pursue it, at comming of the Kings Justices. Before whom, unlesse the offender aid himselfe by exception, that the Appellant was still a virgin, (which was tried by inspection of women) and if she were found a virgin, the Appellant was imprisoned for her slander, or that he held her before time as his Concubine, or that she consented to his imbracements, or some other like plea, he lost his eyes and stones, for they *calorem stupri induxerunt*. Except the woman before judgement given, demanded him for her husband, for that was onely in the womans election, and not in the mans, because of the inconvenience which otherwise might have happened, if some hardy strong Leacher had ravished a Dame noble, or of great birth, he should either goe away unpunished, or else by meanes of one pollution, perpetually desire her, to the disgrace of her whole stocke. Thus farre Bracton. And in the Booke, *De priscis legibus*, it is set downe for a Law made by King William the Conquerour; *Interdico ne quis occidatur vel suspendatur pro aliqua culpa, sed eruantur oculi, & abscindantur testiculi, vel pedes vel manus, ita ut truncus vivus remaneat, in signum proditionis vel nequitiæ.* I command that from thenceforth no man bee hanged, or put to death for any transgression, but let the offenders eyes be pulled out, or his stones, feet, or hands cut away, that the trunke or mutilate body still left alive, may remaine as a testimony of

his

his prodition and lewdnesse. Now if this mangling Law of King William were still in force in Bractons time against ravishers, was it Mag. Chart. cap. 29. Or what was it that made the Law so meeke in Edward the first his time, that the first Statute against Rape, speaketh of it so mildly, as if it had beene at Common Law a verie small trespasse.

SECT. XXIII.

West. 1. cap. 14. anno 3. E. 1.

THe King commands, that no man ravish or take by force any damseil within age, either with her consent or without. Nor any dame or damsell (of full age) or other mans wife, against her will. If any doe, the King will doe iustice and common right, at his or her suit, that shall sue within 40. dayes, if none commence suit within 40. dayes, the King shall haue the suit, they which are culpable shall bee imprisoned two yeeres, and bee ransomed at the Kings pleasure. And if they haue not to satisfie the ransome, they shall suffer a longer imprisonment, as the trespasse shall require, a man may well suspect that there was something, which had allayed the rigour of former Law, before this Statute was made. It may bee the importation of Clergy men urging satisfaction according to Moises Law, if the woman ravished were unmarried, and otherwise the bashfulnesse of those which are betrothed and espoused, kept in the truculent Law of King William. Howsoeuer it were, this Statute of West. 1. (in my poore opinion) being rather affirmatiue than otherwise, runneth not in favour of ravishers, to abrogate their old punishment, but inflicteth a greater punishment upon them, than that which had lately beene put in practice. Or it may bee very well that the common right, which King Edward promised here to doe for them that

that would pursue within forty dayes, was according to the severity, which Bracton speaketh of.

SECT. XXIV.

west. 2. cap. 35.

The mitigation of the old Law, one way or other, in a few yeeres brought forth so many enormities, That at the next Parliament, which King Edw. held ten yeeres after, it was ordeined as followeth.

It is ordeined, that if any man ravish any woman espoused, or damsell, or other woman, which consenteth not afore, nor after, that hee shall haue iudgement of life and member. And whosoever ravisheth any woman by force, though she consent afterward, shall haue iudgement as afore is said, if he be attainted at the Kings suit. And if any women bee carried away with the goods of their husband, the King shall haue the suit, for goods so carried away. This Chapter conteineth also the ordinance against Elopement, and another for Nunnes, qui monachialem a domo suo abducat, licet monachialis consentiat, puniatur per prisonam trium annorum, &c. & satisfaciat domui, a qua abducta fuerit & nihilominus redimatur ad voluntatem regis.

SECT. XXV.

6. Richard. 2. cap. 6.

A Man would haue thought, that this Statute should haue repressed for ever, all violence towards the persons of women, but quantos motos scies, reclamante ratione, Priape: In the first yeere of King Richards reigne, and about the 16th. of his age, this villany of rape was

so

so encreased, and women so little offended with the injury, or so ashamed to confesse the outrage, that a new Law was made to punish women, which consented to their ravishors, vt sequitur. Against ravishers of Ladies and daughters of Noble men, and other women in every part of the Realme, now a dayes more violently offending, and oftener than was wont; It is ordained, that wheresoever, and whensoever such Ladies, daughters, or other women bee ravished, and after rape doe consent to such ravishers, that as well the ravishers, as they which be ravished, bee from henceforth disabled, to have or challenge Heritage, Dower or Jointfeoffement after the death of their husbands, and ancestors. And that incontinently the next of the blood of those ravishers, or of them that bee so ravished, to whom such Heritage, Dower or Jointfeoffement ought to revert, remaine, or fall, after the death of the ravisher, or of her that is so ravished, shall have title incontinently after the rape, to enter upon the ravisher, or her that is ravished, and their Assignes and lands, tenements, in the same heritage, Dower, or Jointfeoffement, and the same to hold in State of Heritage.

And that the husbands of such women, if they have husbands, or if they have no husband living, the father or other next of the bloud, have from henceforth the suit to pursue against the Offenders and Ravishers in this behalfe, and to have them thereof convict of life and member, though the woman after such rape doe consent to the ravisher. And the Defendant in this Case shall not bee received to wage battaile, but that the truth of the matter shall bee tried by the Country. Saving allwayes to the King and other Lords of the Realme, their escheats of the Ravishers, if they be convict.

This is a shrewd Statute. Till this time he that had ravished a woman might hope for a clemencie, at the least at her hands, because he had ventured his life for her sake, but what shall lusty leachers now doe: the more a woman is worthy to bee won, because shee hath or shall have wherewith

wherewith to keepe a man, the more danger it is to medle with her. She that perhaps might haue beene perswaded, (had this Statute not beene) to forgiue a matter of greater astonishment, then dammage, dares not now be mercifull, lest shee bee cruell to her selfe. Therefore now men looke on faire Gentlewomen, heires, and widdowes, as the catt looketh at a fish in the water, she would faine be dealing, but is loth to go wetshod.

And now comes in the second rape by abduction, wherein auarice is as great an agent as carnality, and something wiser in auoiding of danger, now men turned themselues for loues sake into Centaures first, and tooke on them the shape of Buls afterward.

SECT. XXVI.

31. *Hen. 6. cap. 9.*

THerefore in the 31. yeere of Hen. 6. was a Statute made, beginning with complaint, that in all parts of the Realme, diuers people of power, moued by insatiable couetousnesse, against all right and gentlenesse, had found new inuentions, to the danger, trouble, and euill intreatings of Ladies, Gentlewomen, and other women sole, hauing substance of land, tenements, or moueable goods, perceiuing their great innocency and simplicity, willing to take them by force, or otherwise come to them, seeming to be their great friends, promising them their faithfull loues, and so by great dissimulation, they caught them into their possession, conueying them into places where the Offenders were of power, not suffering them once gotten into their gouernance, to goe at liberty, till they had bound them by Obligation or Statute merchant, and enforced them to marry against their owne liking, otherwise they would leuy the said summe in the said Obligation or Statutes, to preuent danger of forfeiture of the same.

same Obligation or Statute, or further perill to their persons. The purueyance of this Statute, is but a Grant of a Writ, whereby to call before the Chancellor, or before the Iustices of Assises in the County, or before some other noble persons, assigned by the Chancellor of England, the persons offending, to make void the Obligation or Statute, if there be cause, with a severe penalty of 200. li to bee forfeited by the Sheriffe, if hee did not execute the same Writ duly, according to the tenure thereof. This Statute was too meeke and gentle, something like him that made it. H.6.

SECT. XXVII.

3.H.7.c.2.

BUt 3.Hen 7.cap.2. beginning with a better complaint against takers for lucre, of maids, widdowes, or wives hauing substance of lands or goods, or being heires apparant, which takers sometimes married them, and sometime deflowred them, to the breach of Gods Law, and the Kings, the disparagement of such women, and vtter heauinesse and discomfort of their friends, ordaineth, that whosoeuer taketh against her will vnlawfully, any maid, widdow, or wife, shall together with the procurers, abbetters and receiuers of any such women (knowing her to bee so taken against her will,) bee felons, and euery of them beene reputed and iudged as felons principall. But this extendeth not to taking, where a woman is claimed as a ward or bondwoman. And Mr. Lambard noteth, that anno 3. & 4. Phil.& Mar. this Statute was construed to make no felony, vnlesse the woman married were either taken or deflowred.

SECT.

SECT. XXVIII.

4. & 5. *Phi. & Mar. cap.* 8.

THerefore to supply what hitherto was wanting against takers, and also intisers, ravishing by allurements and flatterers, 4. & 5. Phil. & Mar. cap. 8. saith, that for want of sufficient Law, it remained still a familiar and common mischiefe in the Realme; That maidens and women children of Noble men, Gentlemen, and others, which were heires apparant, or had lands in great substance left by their Ancestors or friends, by flattery, trifling gifts, or faire promises of light persons, and also by subtility of such as bought and sold them for reward, were many times allured to contract matrimony with unthrifty persons, and thereupon oftentimes with sleight or force were taken from their parents, friends or kinsfolke, to the high displeasure of God, the disparagement of the children, and perpetuall condolence of their friends; Therefore it is ordained, that it shall not bee lawfull to convey any maid or woman child, unmarried, or under the age of sixteene yeeres, out of the possession, and against the will of her father, or of such person, to whom by his will or otherwise in his life time, he shall have appointed the keeping, education and governance of her, except such taking, as shall bee without fraud by the Master or Mistris, or Gardian in Socage, or in Chivalry, of or to such maid or woman child. And if any person that is above the age of fourteene yeeres, shall convey, or cause to bee conveyed, any such maid being within the age of sixteene yeeres, out of the possession, and against the will of the father or mother, or any other person which then shall have by lawfull meanes, the order, keeping, education, or governance of her, the offender duly attainted or convicted (other than such, of whom shee shall hold by knights service,) shall suffer two yeeres imprisonment, without baile or mainprise, or pay such fine, as shall bee assessed by the Queenes Councell in the Starchamber.

And if any shall take away, and deflowre any such maid, or woman child, or shall against the will of her father, or he not knowing (if the father be in life) or without the assent or knowledge of the mother hauing custody and gouernance of the child, the father being dead, by letters, messages or otherwise, contract matrimony with any such maid, (except it bee by the consent of the person or persons, by interest of wardship intituled to haue the mariage) he shall suffer (being lawfully conuicted) fiue yeeres imprisonment, without baile or maineprise, and pay such fine as shall bee assessed in the Starrechamber, &c. the one moity of all which fines shall bee to the Queene and her successors, and the other to the grieued.

And the Councell in Starrechamber, by Bill of complaint or information, and Iustices of assise by inquisition or inditement, (in which processe shall be awarded, as inditements of trespasse at the Common law) haue authority to heare and determine the offences.

Moreouer, if any woman child, or maiden, being aboue the age of twelue yeeres, and vnder sixteene, doe at any time consent to such person as shall make contract of matrimony contrary to the forme of this Statute, the next of kin to whom the inheritance should come after her death, shall from time of such assent haue and enioy all such lands, tenements, and hereditaments, as shee had in possession, reuersion, or remainder, at the time of assent, during the life of such person, so contracting matrimony, and after her decease so contracting, &c. then the said lands shall descend, reuert remaine, and come to such person or persons, (other than to him that shall so contract matrimony) as they should haue done, in case this Statute had neuer beene made. But this Act extendeth not to diminish any liberty, custome, or authority, in London or like corporations, as touching Orphanes, their lands, goods, or chattels.

Se

See Ratcliffs Case in Sir Edward Cokes 3. Rep. fol. 38. upon this Statute of 4. and 5. of Phil. and Mar. In an Eiectione firme upon speciall pleading, a speciall verdict was thus in effect, that William Wilcokes married the daughter and heire apparant of Iohn Edols and Alice his wife, and hath issue by her, Iohn, Elizabeth, and Martha, William Wilcokes afterwards by his will in wrighting appoints the order, custody, education, and governement of his said three children, to their said grandfather and grandmother, during the grandfather and grandmothers lives, and then dyes, the widdow of Wilcokes marrieth Raphe Radcliffe, Iohn Edols dyes, and his widdow being Tenant in fee simple of the lands in question holden in soccage by her will, deviseth them to her grandchild Iohn Wilcokes in taile, the remainder to Elizabeth and Martha, and the heires of their two bodies equally to bee divided, the remainder in fee to her said daughter and heire apparant, the mother of these three devisees, and dieth, Iohn Wilcoke dieth without issue, his sister Elizabeth married one Andrewes, and he, his wife, and her sister Martha enter the lands, and were seised accordingly, and Martha abiding with Raph Ratcliffe, and his wife being above fourteene, and under sixteene yeeres of age, with Raph Ratcliffe his consent, and of her owne accord departs eight miles off from them, where six houres after shee was married to Edward Ratcliffe, who enters and made the Plaintiffe his lease: And (the issue being whether Elizabeth Ratcliffe the wife of Raph Ratcliffe had the custody of Martha the wife of Edward Ratcliffe the lessor at the time of their contract and marriage,) all the Judges and Court of Kings Bench resolved that Elizabeth had the governance of her daughter Martha at the time of her contract and marriage within the intent and meaning of the Statute.

It was resolved in that case, that those words father & mother within the second branch of the Statute shall bee expounded father or mother after the death of the father.

 And

And it was resolued in that Case, that there bee two manners of custodies or wardships, the one by the Common Law, the other by the Statute: And that also at the Common Law there are foure manners of Gardians, namely, Gardian in Chiualry, Gardian in Socage, Gardian in nature, and Gardian for nurture, and now the Statute makes a new Gardian, namely by assignation; but the mother in that case cannot be Gardian for nurture, because her daughter was past 14. yeeres of age. But shee had the custody of her within the prouision of the Act iure naturæ, and the assent of Raph Ratcliffe the mothers husband was not materiall, for the custody of a child is an inseparable incident to the parent, and marriage may not transferre that to a husband. And that was resolued, that although the issue was whether Elizabeth had the custody of Martha at the time of the contract, and that did appeare, that shee departed from her mothers house six houres before the contract, yet in iudgement of Law her mother had the custody of her at the time of the contract. And that was resolued, that in that Case Edward Ratcliffe, and Martha his wife, had good title to the land against Andrewes and his wife, for the one daughter, as that Case is, shall not take benefit of forfeiture of the other, for the statute giues the forfeiture to the next of kin, to whom the inheritance should descend or come after her decease, during the life of such person that so shall contract matrimony, so, that first hee ought to be of the bloud, and secondly, to whom the inheritance should descend or come, &c. and although the wife of Andrewes bee of the bloud, yet in that Case by the death of Martha, the land if shee hath issue, shall descend to her issue, and if shee hath not issue, that shall reuert to her mother, &c. but iudgement was against the Plaintiffe, for that the issue was found against him.

These are the Lawes, whereby rapes and rauishments of women are repressed, which if they bee well looked vnto, will proue that there is now no cause, why lying

lying Laonicus Chalcondilus should be beleeved, who wri-ting of Englishmen, affirmeth that we haue no care what becomes of our wiues and children; That in our pere-grinations and trauels wee interchenge and vse one the others wiues mutually: That we count it no reproch by whom soeuer our wiues or daughters bee got with child; That (with vs) if a man come to his friends house, hee must lye with his wife the first thing that he doth, vt deinde benigne hospitio accipiatur. And though some of the last recited Lawes were vnmade, when Chalcondilus did write, aboue one hundred yeeres since, yet there were then Lawes enough to proue him a deepe lyer; and had hee beene in England, to haue trussed him vp two perhaps for lechery, had his learning steaded him no better than his honesty; this is no lesse cause, why I should be thus bitter against Chalcondilus a dead man, for that it may seeme he wrote by hearesay, nullo odio gentis: and in other mat-ters hee reporteth honourably of vs. But it is strange that a man writing, not a great while since, but euen the other day, not at Athens, neither at Rome, or Reams, where they vse to belie vs head and foot, but here at Lon-don should be bold to write and put in print matter to this effect, That beggers and the poorest sort of our women, we doe vse to punish and to whip them, when they are taken for leachers and dishonest liuers. But Gentlewomen and Ladies of honour and worship, they are neuer puni-shed for incontinency, but rather for their amorous wan-tonnesse, and lubricity the more esteemed and magnified. This fellow deserueth plainly better to bee hanged, than to bee beleeued. For neither is it true that any woman with vs can better her reputation by dissolute life and manners; Neither can any woman learne a more deuil-lish lesson, than so to be perswaded. And seeing the Lawes themselues declare what detestation they haue of bruitish concupiscence, by punishing consent, with losse of inheri-tance; I would I could perswad all women to eschew, not only these gulfes, but also the ecclesiasticall Censires, (which I meddle not with) together with the infamy, which they purchase sometime with outward lasciviousnesse, from the report of them, which iudge a carelesse liberty in behauiour, an infallible argument of sensuality, whereby some men haue béene imboldened to offer force, because they thought it was expected.

SECT. XXIX.

Appeale of rape.

NOw let vs consider a little how these Lawes ought to bee put in practice, if any virgin, widdow, or single woman be rauished, shee her selfe may sue an Appeale of rape, prosecute the felon to death, and the Kings pardon (as it séemeth) cannot helpe him. If a Feme couert be rauished, shee cannot haue an Appeale without her husband, as appeares 8 Hen. 4. fol. 21. But if a Feme couert be rauished, and consent to the rauisher, the husband alone may haue an Appeale, and this by the Statute 6. Rich. 2. cap. 6. The husband that this Statute speaketh of, which may sue the Appeale, must be a lawfull husband in right and possession, for ne vnques accouple in loyall matrimony is a good plea against him. 11. Hen. 4. fol. 13. So doth Iustice Stanford affirme the booke to proue without question: and that the Law is so too, where Appeale is brought by Baron and Feme. Brooke abridging the case, 11. Hen. 4. séemeth to incline to the contrary opinion. The case at length is thus, Thomas Hausegle sueth Appeale de rauishment sa feme against Thomas V. and others according to the Statute. 6. Rich. 2. rehearsing in his Declaration the order of the Statute, and that they had rauished her against the forme of the said Statute. The Appellées said, the Plaintiffe had another Writ hanging, returnable the same tearme, of the same rape, and because the Writ was not serued, he had obtained a

sicut

sicut alias, Ergo, this Writ of the same nature should abate; Hall said, he might pursue which Writ he would. And by their writ a Præcipe quod reddat, or an Assise for the like cause shall abate, for of one land a man cannot have two recoveries. But in this case it may bee, there were two rapes at severall times, &c. and also the first Writ was not entred in the roll, nor the sicut alias in the Record, then the Declaration was challenged as insufficient, because it was felonice rapuit, and not carnaliter cognovit: but to that it was answered, that felonious rape implied carnall knowledge, for rape without such knowledge is but trespasse; Another exception to the Declaration was, that two had ravished as principall, &c. which, Rolfe said, could not be, therefore the Plaintiffe ought to have declared against one as principall, and against the other as accessary, or else to have brought severall Appeales, whereunto was answered, that if two or twenty goe and come together, to commit any felony, as robbery or murder, though one of them onely commit the Act, yet all the rest are principals. A third exception against the Declaration was, that the Plaintiffe had not shewed how his wife assented after the ravishment, and the Appeale was given by West. 2. to the Baron and Feme, and not to the Baron alone by the Statute of Rich. 1. But this exception also was disallowed, because the Count had recited the whole purveyance of the Act, and the ravishment was contra formam &c. Last of all, the Appellées pleaded, that long time before the espousals, betwixt the Appellour & the woman supposed to be ravished, one of the Appellées had affianced the same woman, after which affiance the Appellour married her, at a certaine Church against her will, (after which marriage, whereunto she never agreed) she came of her owne accord to the Defendant who had now married her, so that the Appellour and she were never coupled in loyall matrimony. This manner of pleading was said to be a confession both of the first marriage and of the ravishment, which the Councell would haue taken by protestation. But Gascoigne told them, they might not haue protestation, to proue them guiltie of felony. Therefore the Defendant pleaded generally, Ne vnques accouple. &c. which the Plaintiffe accepted of his owne accord, and a Writ was awarded to the Bishop. But all mens opinions seemed to be, that this was no good plea, because the Statute is, that the husband shall haue the Appeale, though they agréed that when the Action is by Common Law, as an Appeale De morte viri, ne vnques accouple, is a good plea, for no woman shall reuenge her husbands death by Appeale, vnlesse shée were wife as well in right as in possession.

The Statute of Richard giueth the Appeale, where the woman rauished hath no husband, to her father or next of blood, &c. which is vnderstood vt supra, where the woman consenteth to the rauisher, for otherwise the woman her selfe must pursue the Appeale, vpon Westm. 2. cap. 34. For the father cannot haue by the Common Law, either Appeale of rape of his daughter, or of death, either of son or Daughter: But it séemeth that by this Statute, if a woman be next heire to her which is rauished, and consenteth, she may haue an Appeale of rape against the rauisher, as well as any procheuie heire male may. And learne, If a woman which is rauished dye, and her husband takes another wife, whether hée may now haue an Appeale or no. It is said, that if a Lord rauish his Nief, she cannot haue an Appeale of rape against him; but the King may punish it by way of Inditement.

SECT. XXX.

Within what time Appeales of Rape must be commenced.

By Bracton, Si virgo sit corrupta & oppressa contra pacem Domini Regis, she ought to goe straight way, Dum

Dum idem factum recens est, and with Hue and Cry complaine to the good men of the next towne, shewing her wrong, her garments torne, & sanguine tinctas, and then shee ought to goe to the chiefe Constable, to the Coroner, and to the Viscount, and at the next Countie to enter her Appeale, and have it enrolled in the Coroners roll: and then day was to bee given her, till the comming of the Kings Justices, before whom she was againe to re-intreat her Appeale, and if she varied from the Coroners roll, she lost her suit. Brutton tieth the commencement of this Appeale to fortie dayes after the fact, agreeing with West. 1. cap. 13. But by this Statute (saith Stanford) rape was but trespasse, insomuch therefore, as it is since made felony by another Statute, and no time limitted, within which the suit shall be begun, it seemeth a woman is at choyse to bring it when shee listeth, so that shee exceed not time reasonable.

SECT. XXXI.

Within what Countie Appeale of Rape shall be brought.

APpeale of rape must be brought within the Countie, where the ravishment was committed, and if a man take a woman against her will in one Countie, and leading or carrying her into another Countie he there ravisheth her, the Appeale must bee where the ravishment was committed: and though the Declaration be, of taking in another Countie, yet the triall shall be onely where the Writ was brought, Titulo visne, in Fitzherbert 28. And it seemeth, that to speake of the taking in another Countie, in a Declaration of Rape, is but surplussage and more than needeth; for it abates not the Count if it be left out. But perhaps such a leaving out in Action of trespasse, would abate the Writ, because the Plaintiffe is to reco-

ver

uer dammages; for the taking in another Countie, and they of the Countie where the Writ is brought, cannot assesse dammages for the taking: But in this Appeale there is nothing to be recouered, but onely that the offender suffer death for his offence.

SECT. XXXII.

The Declaration in Appeale of Rape.

47. E. 3. fol. 14. IS a good forme of Declaration in this Appeale, where in a Writ of Appeale of rape, the plaintiffe counted, how she was in Gods peace and the Kings, such a day, such a yeare, and in such a place, and the Defendant came feloniously, and as a Felon against the Kings Crowne and dignitie, then and there did rauish her, and carnally know her, and that shee did pursue him from Towne to Towne, and from Countie to Countie, till he was taken at her suit; and that A. and B. were at the same time and place in force and aid of the same Felon, &c. And if the Defendant will this deny, she is ready to proue it, as the Court shall award, that a woman ought.

But know that the seuerall Statutes haue made two seuerall formes of Appeales of rape, one vpon the Statute of West. 2. and in that there needs no mention of any Statute. But in the other which is vpon the Statute of Richard, the vse is alwayes to recite the Statute in the Declaration, and that the words, Contra formam statuti, implyeth sufficiently, that the woman hath consented to the rauisher.

SECT.

SECT. XXXIII.

Pleas to the writ.

PLeas to the Writ may be many, as false Latine, or want of forme, or that the Plaintiffe hath another Writ hanging, of the same felony, as is shewed you before in the other Appeale. And 5. H. 6. fol. 1. Exception was taken against the Writ in Appeale of rape, because it was ad respondendum the Plaintiffe secundum formam statuti, &c. Whereas it ought to haue béene, Vnde eum appellat secundum formam statuti. Whereunto it was answered, that the Statute of 6. R. 2. giueth not the Appeale, for that is by the Common Law, but he must answer according to the Statute, which outeth battaile; for the Statute saith, Ad duellum vadiandum non recipiatur & issint le briefe bone.

Another exception was taken against the Writ, because it was not, felonice rapuit, but the Defendant durst not stand vpon it, but pleaded ouer, rien culpable.; for rapuit implyeth felony. But in euerie Appeale of rape, if the Writ want the word rapuit, it shall abate, though it haue words amounting to as much as carnaliter cognovit, or any such like, 9. E. 4. fol. 26.

SECT. XXXIV.

Pleas to the Action.

THough it bee true, that where one shall bee charged with rape in Appeale or otherwise, it must be by the word rapuit, and not carnaliter cognouit onely, yet by Bracton it is a good plea in Appeale of rape to say, Non abstulit ei pucellagium suum, quia adhuch virgo est, & veritas probabitur per aspectum corporis, & per quatuor legales

gales feminas iuratas de veritate dicenda, quære. Stamford saith it is a good plea for the Defendant, though hee lay with the woman, yet hee did not carnally know her, for the force of the Declaration resteth in that. And by Briton. fol. 45. If at the time of rape supposed, the woman conceiue childe, there is no rape; for none can conceiue without consent. Also by Bracton, it is a good plea, to say that before the rape supposed, he kept the Plaintiffe, and vsed her as his Concubine. But by the same Bracton, it was no plea to say she was another mans Concubine, or Harlot, Quia licet meretrix fuerit antea, certè tunc tempo-ris non fuit, cum nequitiæ eius reclamando consentire noluit.

And note, if she which is rauished, assent for feare of death at the time of the rauishment, it is a rape against her will, notwithstanding such consent; for assent must be voluntarie, per curiam, 5. E. 4. Crompton, 44.

SECT. XXXV.

A question what is meant by rauishment with force, in West. 2. cap. 34.

STamford leaueth it doubtfull, and to be learned what the difference is betwixt rauishment with force, and without force. M. Lambard thinketh the word to be but declaratorie, signifying all rauishment to bee forcible. And it is true, that no woman is rauished in this sort only by parroll, or influence of Rhetoricke. But in mine opinion, the Statute must needs intend two kinde of rauishments, because it maketh one more odious than the other, and propoundeth death ineuitable to him which rauisheth with force, though the woman forgiue him, and consent to him. A more detestable villany, I thinke, therefore was meant in this parase, of him which being himselfe ouercome with concupiscence, ouercommeth a woman hand

hand to hand, by length of breath, and strength of his owne sinewes. You shall understand therefore, that about those dayes there was an Appeale of force in use, as it were against the ravishers yeomen of the stirrup, viz. against him or them which were holders, and assisters to the principall carnall oppressour, as appeareth about the end of the 28. Chapter of Bracton, Lib. 3. Eadem A. appellat C. quod eadem die eodem anno, &c. quo prædict' B. & eadem hora dum idem B. abstulit pucellagium suum fuit idem C. in fortia, ita quod tenuit eandem A. dum idem B. abstulit pucellagium suum, vel concubuit cum ea, postquam, &c. Such fellowes were termed appellati de fortia, and they which take such Coadiutors, might verie well be called ravishers with force and aid, of all other most hatefull, in iudgement of all indifferent honest women.

SECT. XXXVI.

De muliere abducta cum bonis, &c.

This Statute toucheth also the most covetous ravishment, that is, when a mans wife and his goods are ravished together: so much against womans minde, that she is loth to leave either money or plate behinde her, and because some men used in those dayes, to let their goods goe, lest otherwise they might perhaps call their wives home againe, the suit is given to the King, if the husband neglect it, 44. Assi. p. 12. A man brought a Writ of trespasse against a Knight and his Lady, and two others in Banke le Roy, for taking away the Plaintiffes wife, and his goods, and they all came by Capias in custodie of the Viscount, and the Plaintiffe counted of ravishment of his wife, and his goods carried away, &c. a protection was shewed forth for the Knight and his wife, and allowed, and Iudgement was demanded of the Writ, because the Plaintiffe and his wife were divorced. Iustice Knivet said,

said, that though the woman were dead, the husband might haue the Action of rauishment notwithstanding, and so is it if they were diuorced. For he was not to recouer his wife by the Action, nor any thing else, saue dammages for the trespasse. Then it was said, the diuorce was causa frigiditatis; Kniuet said, the weather might wax warmer with him, Il poet recouerer son nature, & ouerer come home, & reauer sa feme; and therefore answered to the Writ. Then Iudgement was asked againe of the Writ, because it was against a man and his wife, and one woman cannot rauish another, sed non allocatur; for a woman may be assenting or aiding to any rauishment, therefore the Defendants pleaded non culpable. The verie same, or verie like case is againe, 23.E.3. 23. Sée 21.H.7.fol.13. The opinion of Fineux, that it is lawfull for a man to travell with another mans wife to London, at her request, and to carrie her behinde him, when shee will ride to sue a diuorce, or a reuersment of Outlawrie, or for a warrant of the peace, against her goodman. Yaxley was of contrarie opinion. And where the partie which taketh another mans wife, cum bonis, &c. is indited at the Kings suit of trespasse onely, the Inditement is, Quod vi & armis, Mariam vxorem cuiusdam A.B. apud S. rapuit, & eam cum bonis & cattallis, viz. &c. ipsius A. B. cepit & abduxit, & ea eidem A. B. adhuc iniuste detinet, contra pacem, &c. & contra formam statuti, &c.

So likewise at the husbands suit the Writ is, Attachias B. quod sit coram nobis, &c. ad respondendum prefato A. quare vi & armis vxorem prefati A. apud N. rapuit, & eam cum bonis & cattallis, &c. ad graue dampnum, & contra formam statuti, &c. as appeares by Fitzherbert. So that you sée the difference betwixt rapuit in Trespasse, and in Appeale, or Inditement of felony. Presidents whereof are in M. Lambards Booke, and M. Cromptons.

SECT.

SECT. XXXVII.

The case of Elizabeth Venor.

NOw that women may learne to stand upon their owne guard partly, and not trust altogether to defence, or courtesie of Lawes, which are not more rigorously penned, than sometime put in execution against them, let them marke this case. Lands were given in taile to William Veror, and to Elizabeth his wife, and to the heires of their two bodies, the remainder to the said Elizabeth and the heires of her body, the remainder to Robert Babbington in taile, the remainder to the right heire of T. S. father of Elizabeth. William Venor dyed without issue, and Elizabeth being sole seized, was afterward ravished by Iohn Worth, which after that hee had married her, was indited of rape, and tooke Sanctuarie at Westminster, Elizabeth his wife being there with him, was advised to disassent, and to part from him to save her inheritance, which she refused to doe, and was afterward brought before the Councell in the Star-Chamber; being there demanded if she assented or not, and shee answered, that Iohn Worth was her husband, and she would not forsake him, whereupon the issue of Robert Babbington, (Robert being dead) entred upon her land by the Statute of 6. R. 2. which willeth (saith Brooke) if any woman assent to the ravisher, that he to whom the land should descend, revert, remaine, or escheat may enter. And though it were confessed, that there was another person, more neere in bloud to Elizabeth than was this issue of Robert Babbington, yet because he was next in remainder, his entrie was lawfull. But Elizabeth did oust him, and hee brought an Assise. Then to prove the assent, it was given in evidence that she had married him, assenting to him as well in Sanctuarie, as before the Councell. And for Elizabeth, it was alleaged, that the espousals and all the assentings

tings were by dures and force, and for feare of the rauisher, which might not be called assenting, for none consenteth but frankly, voluntarily, and sans feare, Quod videtur Lex ibidem. But in the end, because shee might haue disagréed before the Councell, and did not, her assent was holden voluntarie, and the Assise passed for the Plaintiffe. And it was agréed for Law, that if title of entrie into lands be giuen to a daughter by force of this Statute, and she entreth: that she shall retaine and enioy them, notwithstanding the birth of any sonne Posthumus comming afterward, though he be more néere, or worthy of bloud. And so it is generally where the entrie is giuen by Statute: but if by Common Law, a discent bée cast vpon a daughter which entreth, shee must giue place to a sonne borne afterward. It was remembred in this case, that in former time a woman being rauished, after she had continued seuen yéeres with the rauisher, and had borne him a childe, escaped from him, and sued in Parliament in the time of H. 6. against him, till he was attainted. And being demanded how she could now say, that she neuer assented, hauing conceiued, &c. shee answered, that her flesh consented to him, but her soule and conscience did euer abhorre him, 5. E. 4. fol. 58.

SECT. XXXVIII.

The Statute 18. *Eliz. cap.* 7.

I Am at the end of my voyage; but before I take shore I will shew you how our late most excellent Lawgiuer, renowned Quéene Elizabeth, (whose vigilant care hath allwayes béene, that all her people might liue vnder her in peace, and without oppression) hath giuen strength and perfection to the former functions of other Princes, to make them a firme bulwarke against all manner of iniurers that possibly might oppresse women; and

I

I can but maruell, that when so damnable a crime as rape, had giuen so often to the whole Realme, such cause of bitter complaint; and men in sundry ages, had beaten their braines so carefully in finding out remedy against it: how it was possible, so long space together, to leaue such a priuilege to him that could read the blessed Psalme of Miserere, &c. that though hee had rauished the fairest Lady in the Land, hee might almost goe away without touch of breast for it. Therefore the eighteenth of Queene Elizabeth, for repressing of felonious rapes, and rauishments of women, and of felonious Burglaries, it was enacted that they which were found guiltie by verdict, or by confession, or outlawed of or for such felonious Rapes or Burglarie, they should suffer death, and forfeit as in cases of Felony had beene vsed by the Lawes of the Realme, without allowance of priuilege, or benefit of Clergie. Further, that they which were in other cases to haue benefit of Clergie, should immediately after burning in the hand, according to the Statute in that case prouided, be forthwith enlarged by the Justices, and not be deliuered to the Ordinarie. But yet that the Justices, before whom the Clergie shall be allowed, may detaine such persons in prison for correction, as long as they shall think conuenient, so it be not aboue a yeere: Then because in the fourteenth yeere of her Maiesties reigne (as you may perceiue in Dier, fol. 304. in the case of a Scot which had rauished a girle, being not past seuen yeeres old, the Justices were in doubt whether rape could be of a childe of such tender yeeres, not yet nine yeeres old, and therefore they went not to iudgement of the Scot, though by euidence of diuers Matrons he seemed guiltie, this Statute ordaineth, that if any person, vnlawfully and carnally, know and abuse any woman childe vnder age of ten yeeres, euerie such vnlawfull and carnall knowledge shall be felonie, and the offender being duly conuicted shall suffer as a Felon, without allowance of Clergie. And as M. Lambard and M. Crompton doe both of them note, it is not materiall whether she consent or no, for the Law adiudgeth her unable to consent, at so tender age. The last proviso of this Statute is, that they which are admitted to their Clergie shall answer to all other manner of felonies, whereof they haue not formerly béene acquited, conuicted, attainted, or pardoned, as they should haue done, if as Clerkes conuicted they had béene deliuered to the Ordinarie, and made their purgation.

Sect. XXXIX.

The Statute 39. Eliz. cap. 9.

Lastly, because this exemption of Clergie was leuelled onely against Burglaries, and felonious rapes by violence, and of the antique Faulkoners fashion, leauing unto couetous rauishers by abduction, and I might say by insinuation, the benefit of their Booke, by reason whereof diuers maids, widdowes, and wiues, had of verie late dayes, béene first carried away, and then defiled, married, &c. It was enacted at the first Parliament, begun Ann. 39. of the late Quéene Elizabeth, That whosoeuer shall be conuicted, or attainted, of or for any offence made felony by the Act aboue specified, 3. H. 7. or which being indited, or arraigned, of or for any such offence, shall stand mute, or make no direct answer, or shall challenge peremptorily aboue the number of twelue, shall in euerie such case suffer death, without benefit of Clergie, prouided that nothing in this Act contained, shall extend to take Clergie from any person or persons, which bée not either principals, or procurors, or accessaries, before the offence committed.

SECT.

SECT. XL.

The Conclusion.

THus haue I sailed betwixt the capes of Magna Charta, and Quadragesima of Queene Elizabeth, collected the statutes principally belonging to women, conioyning customes, cases, opinions, sayings, arguments, iudgements, and points of learning of like sort and subiect, dispersed in our Law bookes: now comming to take hauen, God grant I may fall in at port Grace, and good acceptance of all that shall read what I haue gathered, they which are lesse learned than my selfe in this studie (which I accompt to be those, that haue but newly taken acquaintance of Littleton) may spend some time here, not without some fruit and profit. They that are better learned than I, (into which company some may crowd, that perhaps might bee challenged of intrusion) will giue mee no thankes for my paines. Rather I must thanke them if they vouchsafe to read them without open scorne and bitter censuring; but they to whom my trauels are chiefly addressed are women, so many as beare the title of honest women, how good and vertuous soeuer they be, I see not how they can scape the taint of ingratitude, if they giue not a reasonable fauour and applause to my good intention and labour, whereby things behouefull for them to know are laid plaine together, and in some orderly connexion, which heretofore were smothered, or scattered in corners of an vncouth language, cleane abstruded from their sex. Which concealement, because it seemed to me neither iust, nor conscionable, I haue framed this worke, admonishing them not to take it for so strong and substantiall a peece as London bridge is, whereon you may boldly set vp great buildings; but I will say to you, as Littleton said in his Tenures to his sonne: There bée some things in these Bookes which are not Law, yet euen those may enable you the better to vnderstand the reasons and arguments of Law, and to conferre and enquire what the Law is, amongst the sage Masters thereof.

FINIS.

For Product Safety Concerns and Information please contact our EU representative GPSR@taylorandfrancis.com Taylor & Francis Verlag GmbH, Kaufingerstraße 24, 80331 München, Germany

Batch number: 10730804

Printed by Printforce, the Netherlands